Educating CITIZENS

Educating CITIZENS

International Perspectives on Civic Values and School Choice

Patrick J. Wolf
Stephen Macedo
editors

with
David J. Ferrero *and*
Charles Venegoni

BROOKINGS INSTITUTION PRESS
Washington, D.C.

ABOUT BROOKINGS

The Brookings Institution is a private nonprofit organization devoted to research, education, and publication on important issues of domestic and foreign policy. Its principal purpose is to bring knowledge to bear on current and emerging policy problems. The Institution maintains a position of neutrality on issues of public policy. Interpretations or conclusions in Brookings publications should be understood to be solely those of the authors.

Copyright © 2004
THE BROOKINGS INSTITUTION
1775 Massachusetts Avenue, N.W., Washington, D.C. 20036
www.brookings.edu

Library of Congress Cataloging-in-Publication data

Educating citizens : international perspectives on civic values and school choice /
Patrick J. Wolf and Stephen Macedo, editors; with David J. Ferrero
and Charles Venegoni.
    p. cm.
Includes bibliographical references and index.
ISBN 0-8157-9516-5 (cloth : alk. paper)
ISBN 0-8157-9517-3 (pbk. : alk. paper)
    1. School choice—Case studies. 2. Civics—Study and teaching—Case studies.
3. Private schools—Finance—Case studies. I. Wolf, Patrick J. II. Macedo,
Stephen, 1957– . III. Title.
    LC47.E38 2004
    379.1'11—dc22   2004011977

9 8 7 6 5 4 3 2 1

The paper used in this publication meets minimum requirements of the
American National Standard for Information Sciences—Permanence of Paper
for Printed Library Materials: ANSI Z39.48-1992.

Typeset in Adobe Garamond

Composition by Betsy Kulamer
Washington, D.C.

Printed by R. R. Donnelley
Harrisonburg, Virginia

To our fathers

RICHARD DELANO WOLF, 1933–2001

CELESTINO D. MACEDO, 1926–2001

ROBERT ANTHONY FERRERO, 1941–

CHARLES D. VENEGONI, 1924–1975

Contents

Preface

Opponents of greater choice in K–12 education worry that choice will increase the power of religious and ideological extremists, promoting social fragmentation, greater inequality in education, and further erosion of shared civic values. Choice proponents who take these civic concerns seriously (by no means all choice proponents) sometimes seek to allay those doubts and anxieties by summoning up the long experience of other nations with publicly funded school choice.

Why should Americans fear public funding of school choice if most—in fact, nearly all—advanced democracies have embraced this policy with no ill consequences? choice proponents ask. Indeed, the argument goes, peace and harmony in schooling and political society are promoted in Canada, England, the Netherlands, and elsewhere by enlightened, liberal policies of public subsidy for a wide array of nonpublic and religious schools among which parents are allowed to choose. Indeed, in the ultra-generous, ultra-enlightened, and ultra-liberal Netherlands, the national constitution ensures the right to public funding of groups of parents who claim that their religious values or educational philosophy is not represented among existing subsidized schools. If public funding of parental choice in education works so well in so many other advanced constitutional democracies, why should Americans worry?

We were, in short, collectively intrigued and provoked by this "no need to worry" argument about school choice. It's an apparently powerful argument, but how were we to unpack and assess it?

We decided to look at a range of nations and ask how much choice each permits in K–12 education (or the equivalent). Equally important, we wanted to know what civic values are taken seriously and how education policy and regulations promote those values. We will admit to being suspicious of the "no need to worry" argument: three of us are at least somewhat sympathetic to proposals for greater school choice, but we all regard public educational goals and policy frameworks as important. We came together, after all, as part of the National Working Commission on Choice in K–12 Education, and, as the title of our recently issued report declares, *School Choice: Doing It the Right Way Makes a Difference* (Brookings, 2003).

We convened a conference in London, chaired by Macedo, entitled "Regulating School Choice to Promote Civic Values: What Can the U.S. Learn from the Experience of Other Nations?" This gathering included leading experts on school choice in various advanced democratic, Western countries. We selected places representing a range of policy options and different kinds and degrees of choice, places that appeared to offer lessons that we could learn from. (We also decided not to focus on countries, such as New Zealand and Chile, that have been widely discussed in American policy and academic circles.)

What we found was that civic values do matter to nations that embrace choice in education and that those values infuse their policy frameworks and shape their regulatory structures, including curriculum requirements, inspection regimes, and national testing. Greater parental choice is only part of the story; the other equally important part is that all funded schools are highly regulated, far more so than the unfunded private schools in the United States. That is one main lesson of this book.

The idea for this volume grew out of our work on the aforementioned commission. Within that larger group, we were charged with reporting on the civic dimensions of school choice. We are grateful to our colleagues on the commission for helping to fertilize the intellectual soil in which the seeds that developed into this book sprouted. We owe special thanks to Paul T. Hill, chair of the commission, for his intellectual guidance and willingness to support our desire to break out in mid-course and pursue what might have been construed as a digression.

The research presented in this volume would not have been possible without a generous grant from the Annie E. Casey Foundation. We are very grateful for the foundation's support, and we wish to acknowledge in particular the assistance of Bruno Manno, senior associate for education at the foundation, who attended the conference and made valuable contributions to our discussions. We thank the Bill and Melinda Gates Foundation for its support of the commission. We also are indebted to the Brown Center for Education Policy at the Brookings Institution, in particular to its director, Tom Loveless, and administrator, Paul DiPerna, for providing administrative support for the project. Paul DiPerna also joined us in London and contributed in many substantial ways to our thinking.

While we happily register the generosity of these important institutions— Gates, Casey, and Brookings—along with the contributions of our fellow participants on the commission, we also affirm that all claims presented in this book are those of their author or authors alone and do not necessarily reflect the views of any of these institutions, their officers, or staff.

Will Cavendish, counselor on education, Prime Minister Blair's Forward Strategy Unit, provided a spirited and stimulating keynote address for our London conference. Professor Moshe Cohen-Eliya, a professor of constitutional law at Ramat-Gan Law School in Haifa, Israel, joined us at the conference and offered important insights on the Israeli educational experience and many other matters.

The conference was hosted by the Institute for U.S. Studies at the University of London. We gratefully acknowledge the assistance of Gary McDowell, the institute's director at that time, and of Lucy Rainbow, its administrator, who provided a setting that was convivial and inspiring. Valerie Kanka, of Princeton's University Center for Human Values, provided valuable logistical support.

Stewart Wood, of the Council of Economic Advisors, Her Majesty's Treasury, provided important advice during the planning stages of this volume, as did chapter authors Charles L. Glenn, Sjoerd Karsten, and John F. Witte. Elizabeth Quilligan of the Georgetown Public Policy Institute contributed valuable research assistance. Susan McWilliams, a graduate student in politics at Princeton University, made important contributions to editing and clarifying a number of the essays.

Our debt to the Brookings Institution Press is significant. Director Robert L. Faherty and acquisitions editor Christopher Kelaher provided extremely useful advice and managed to nurse this project through the many phases of a demanding publication schedule. Eileen Hughes was a superbly acute and speedy editor; we appreciate her patience. Susan Woollen provided expert graphics and production support.

While many have helped bring this effort to fruition, any remaining flaws are the responsibility of the editors and authors.

Educating
CITIZENS

1

Introduction: School Choice, Civic Values, and Problems of Policy Comparison

STEPHEN MACEDO AND PATRICK J. WOLF

Our mandate for contributors to this volume was, at least apparently, simple. The United States is in the midst of historic experiments with publicly funding school choice in K–12 education. Other nations have long experience with the funding and regulation of nonpublic schools (as we would call them), including religious schools. What, we wanted to know, can U.S. policymakers, public officials, and citizens learn from those experiences? In particular, we wanted to know how other countries have regulated or structured public funding of educational choice with an eye not just toward improving test scores and the like, but also toward instilling civic values in students—for example, tolerance, civic cohesion, and democratic values such as integration across lines of class, religion, and race.

Do other countries take seriously the sorts of civic anxieties that are widely voiced by opponents of school choice in the United States? What is their experience with vouchers or other forms of publicly subsidized educational choice? Is publicly funding parental choice a source of civic conflict? Do public funds flow to separatist or just plain weird schools? How do other countries strike a balance between parental choice, educational pluralism, and school competition on the one hand and the public's concern with common citizenship, tolerance, and the integration of social, ethnic, and religious groups on the other?

In posing these questions we did not expect contributors to produce simple policy "lessons" as if they were cases of French wine or boxes of Belgian chocolate to be packaged for export to the United States. Nevertheless, like untold other students of public policy, we wished this time to heed the admonitions of our colleagues who study education from a comparative perspective and learn from the experience of other democracies abroad.

We were far from disappointed in what we learned from our international colleagues, and we hope readers agree. It cannot be said, however, that their response to our mandate was in any respect "simple": the long experience of other nations with publicly financed school choice does not yield simple or unambiguous lessons for makers of American education policy.

Every nation surveyed in this volume permits or encourages the public funding of nonpublic educational options, though the degree and kind of educational pluralism vary a great deal. The Dutch and Belgians go so far as to regard public funding of choice in education as a fundamental constitutional right. The Dutch educational system is founded on the principal of educational pluralism and, as a few American scholars (such as Charles L. Glenn) have for years pointed out, in the Netherlands at least, this principle seems to promote peace and satisfaction.

Nowhere among the countries we surveyed did we find dire consequences of publicly funding choice. That is not to say that all is well. All nations struggle with educational problems, and some of them are quite familiar to Americans. Everywhere, it seems, segregation by class and race in schools, because it is a consequence of residential segregation, is difficult to overcome. And nearly everywhere there is, to one degree or another, a growing concern with schools that are, or might be, run by illiberal religious minorities. All of the nations whose educational policies we discuss take a wide range of civic concerns seriously when they decide how to fund and regulate nonpublic schools.

Indeed, these countries have decided to fund nonpublic schools partly because of civic concerns. As several of our authors note, nonstate schools are generally viewed in these countries as proxies for the state in performing many important civic functions. Such a vision of broadly shared responsibility for civic education is not entirely alien to the United States. For example, Abraham Lincoln, in one of his earliest published speeches, said of respect for the laws: "[L]et it be taught in schools, in seminaries, and in colleges; let it be written in primers, spelling books, and in almanacs; let it be preached from the pulpit, proclaimed in legislative halls, and enforced in courts of justice."[1] It is one thing to argue, as Lincoln did, that nongovernmental institutions should assist the state in promoting civic values, but quite another to assert that the government should pay for such assistance. In the countries that we review here, it is seen to a great extent not only as defensible but also as oblig-atory for the government to provide resources to private schools to help them produce educated and responsible citizens. With public dollars come a wide variety of government regulations. These include the outcome-focused accountability mechanisms of Alberta, Canada (and to a lesser extent Flemish Belgium), which, because they rely on tests, are relatively unobtrusive with respect to the operation of schools. Then there are the more intrusive inspec-tion systems of Britain, Germany, and France, which focus to a much greater degree on teaching and the educational process itself.

In one important respect the accounts presented here are largely consistent with the claims of scholars such as Charles L. Glenn and Terry M. Moe, who have long asserted that the principal lesson for Americans to take from the international experience with publicly funding school choice is that parental choice is not nearly as frightening a policy as many critics suggest. Glenn in particular has long argued that the fears of school choice opponents in the United States—fears of balkanization or social disintegration and conflict—are exaggerated and at odds with the experience of virtually the entire civi-lized world. From the essays that follow, Glenn's claim would appear to be true enough—but we have not yet gotten to the whole story or even to the most interesting part.

The fact that other advanced democracies embrace publicly funded parental choice without falling prey to civic disintegration is but one side of the coin. More striking still, we believe, are the astonishing systems of regulation, accountability, and control that accompany public funding in other nations. They do not provide public funds to nonpublic schools with just a few strings attached; rather, they include a host of requirements regarding curriculum, testing, teacher qualifications, and admissions. Indeed, from an American point of view, these publicly funded schools of choice hardly seem "private": government-funded schools abroad are regulated and controlled to an extent that makes them quasi-public, essentially part of one public educational sys-tem. In most of the countries we survey here, the distinction between public and private schools is not nearly as important as it is in the United States.

One major difference between attitudes toward the issue of choice over-seas and those in the United States is that we did not hear much in our con-versations, nor do we read much in the chapters below, of the benefits of educational markets and competition among schools. Perhaps other societies simply take the fact of competition among schools for granted. As Charles L. Glenn argues in his commentary, claims about the relative effectiveness of private and public schools—so important in U.S. policy debates—are likely to be less salient where educational choice is a fundamental right.

But it is important to understand the nature of the "right" to educational pluralism as it exists in the Netherlands and elsewhere. That right does not bring with it strong exemptions from generally applicable rules and conditions. In many European countries, the constitutional right to establish a private school coexists side by side with state authority to inspect and close down such schools. Moreover, in some societies the right to school choice is the result of historical struggles between the state and an established church, which gave rise not to a system of competing schools, with frequent entry and exit of providers, but rather to a stable division of educational responsibilities among public and religious corporate entities and pervasive public regulation of all schools. France is most striking in this regard: the only major nonpublic educational option is Catholic schooling, and the proportions of public and Catholic school pupils are kept stable by mutual agreement. The Catholic option thus serves not as an active competitor to the public sector but as a "safety valve," as Denis Meuret puts it.

In the pluralist Netherlands, groups of parents who want their children to attend a school that has a distinctive educational philosophy have a constitutional right to have the government establish and fund such a school if one does not exist nearby or if the ones that do exist are full. This commitment to educational pluralism is qualified by an extensive system of public regulation and curricular mandates, as Charles Venegoni and David Ferrero emphasize in their commentary. Even the bold Dutch experience with school choice does not represent a strong commitment to private competition and market values as such, since parents have no right to form a school simply because it would be "better" or more efficient than available schools. In the Netherlands, when it comes to starting a new school with public funds, the question is not whether you can do it better but whether you want to do it differently. And educational differences are conditioned by common requirements that include uniform teacher training and student testing.

The story that follows is in the main about a certain sort of publicly funded pluralism in education: pluralism justified by value differences but contained by significant regulation and tamed by systems that ensure accountability. This is not a story about wide-open market competition among minimally regulated schools.

Policy Comparisons and the Importance of Context

So far the story may seem simple enough. The United States could, if it wished, import European-style school choice: choice snugly contained with a regulatory framework that makes private choice an instrument of public policy, part of a larger strategy for achieving the public purposes of education. We fully recognize, however, that it may not be so simple. The wide range of educational, social, and political contexts in Western countries makes generalization hazardous.

It is rarely easy to find regulatory options that could simply be transferred to the United States. Some public school systems abroad have features that Americans will find quite surprising; in the United Kingdom, for example, public schools have mandatory Christian prayers. Policymakers in Europe are frequently careful to weigh the conformity of their school choice policies with European Union and international law. This is not to say that there are no lessons to be learned here: our commentators in Part 2 are virtually unanimous in recommending that U.S. policymakers consider outcome-based oversight policies such as that in Alberta for testing the civic knowledge of all students.

We fully recognize that some scholars have examined major school choice programs in other countries and come away with decidedly pessimistic conclusions. Edward Fiske and Helen Ladd have drawn a well-known "cautionary tale" from their study of New Zealand's program of national parental public school choice.[2] They found that New Zealand's choice program did instigate a "flight to quality," as market theory would predict. However, economically disadvantaged families proved to be less fleet of foot than their more advantaged counterparts, resulting in a worrisome concentration of lower-income students in the worst-performing schools.[3] Martin Carnoy and Patrick McEwan similarly cite evidence suggesting that more advantaged students have been the first to exit the public schools under the countrywide education privatization program in Chile.[4]

Those evaluations of the experiences of New Zealand and Chile with sudden, comprehensive, and largely unregulated school choice policies should—and do—give us pause. It is certainly not our aim to recommend such an approach. While the aim of this book is to inform rather than to recommend, we have been impressed by the ways in which the countries we examine here regulate school choice for the sake of promoting the public benefits of choice. In our other work on the National Working Commission on Choice in K–12 Education, we have been concerned with the effects of school choice on "non-choosers," or those who are slow to choose.[5]

Our mission here is to inform and to stimulate creative thinking rather than to proselytize for choice. However, we would urge readers not to reject choice because some countries have enacted what may be regarded as radical and precipitous policies. The U.S. policymaking process is famously slow, incremental, and prone to compromises that often involve government oversight and regulation.[6] School choice policies in Chile, on the other hand, were established in 1980 by edict of the Pinochet government, which came to power in the wake of a military coup in 1973. We do not expect that to happen in the United States.

In fact, the latest incremental extension of publicly financed school choice in the United States could hardly differ more from the New Zealand and Chilean examples. Beginning with the 2004–05 school year, the recently enacted District of Columbia School Choice Incentive Act of 2004 will provide federally funded school vouchers to about 1,700 of the district's 79,000 elementary and secondary school children. Eligibility will be limited to families whose household income is below 185 percent of the poverty line, additional funds will be provided to the D.C. public school system to help improve educational outcomes, and the five-year voucher experiment is to be closely monitored by the U.S. Department of Education, the D.C. Mayor's Office, and a team of independent researchers.[7] When U.S. policymakers enter the waters of a controversial reform such as school choice, they typically wade in slowly and cautiously. We recognize the prudence of such an approach and hope that policymakers find some inspiration in the chapters that follow.

Just as we should not too readily reject school choice because of the experiences of some nations whose school choice regulations are inadequate, so should we not uncritically embrace the choice policies and regulatory frameworks that exist abroad. To put it bluntly, we cannot accept at face value sunny reports about how school choice works in smaller and more homogeneous European societies, which turn out in any case to cringe when, for example, Muslim citizens seek their own share of public funds for schools. The Europeans seem to have found ways to filter out many schools that particular groups of parents might wish to chose; in practice these "pluralist" systems do not really accommodate all forms of diversity to the extent that their principles (or some of them) might suggest. Hence, at the end of his account of the Dutch system, Ben Vermeulen speculates that in the face of deeper cultural conflicts Europeans may come to appreciate some of the virtues of the American system of common schooling. While it certainly is true that taking civic values seriously means that some schools will be filtered out, it is necessary to critically examine particular patterns of exclusion and to investigate the degree to which these can be justified by civic values.

In the United Kingdom, as already noted, public schools tend to have a distinctly Christian ethos. In Belgium, schools offer courses on religions approved by the state, but not on Hinduism or Islam. In practice, these vaunted pluralist societies may take fairness between majorities and minorities less seriously than we do, or at least they seem to interpret the requirements of fairness among majority and minority religions in ways that are unfamiliar to us.

Some will argue that any comparison of the United States and another country with respect to school choice policies is seriously undermined by the greater size and diversity of the United States and by the fact that it is a much more religious country that has distinctive constitutional principles (the "free exercise" and "nonestablishment" clauses of the First Amendment) protecting religious diversity. Cautionary notes such as these should be taken seriously, but they should, as much as other claims, be considered critically.

In many respects the United States is far more homogeneous than it once was, and in some respects it is more homogeneous than European societies. Insofar as a common language is important to establishing a shared public culture in a political society, it is worth noting that the percentage of non-English-speaking people residing in the United States is much lower today than it was in the late nineteenth and early twentieth centuries. Many European countries—not to mention Canada—are far more deeply divided than the United States by language and ethnic and national culture. The United States is indeed far more religious than other advanced democracies, based on surveys of church attendance and self-reported levels of religious commitment, but as Alan Wolfe and others have argued, religion does much to unite Americans.[8] We do not intend these remarks to settle these complicated issues, we mean only to suggest that just as international comparisons can be glib, so too can the assertion that comparisons are impossible due to differences of context.

We will comment in closing that we believe that the American constitutional principles that provide for the separation of church and state are altogether consistent with a regulatory framework that ensures that all funded schools serve the public interest. That public interest includes educational equity and open access to students regardless of religious affiliation, and that in turn requires nondiscrimination in admissions practices as well as freedom from required religious exercises.[9]

U.S. policymakers know too little about how choice works abroad. We believe that Americans can learn from the experience of other nations, but the process of learning will not be easy, and it will require us to think about the differences as well as the similarities in our experiences and those of other societies.

Crafting School Choice to Serve Public Purposes

When policymakers and citizens consider regulating school choice to advance public values, at least three general questions arise:

—Why regulate? For the sake of which values?

—Who should do the regulating?

—How should schools be regulated? This question is multifaceted. What is the most effective regulatory framework? How much regulation is too much? Should particular regulations extend to public schools only, to publicly funded schools, or to all schools? Finally, when should schools be regulated? When they are founded? At regular intervals thereafter? Only when complaints arise?

Why should democratic governments regulate education? That question has been addressed by political philosophers and educators from the beginning of recorded history. Education is not a purely individual good. Political communities have a significant and legitimate interest in ensuring that children are educated effectively. Democratic societies have a special interest in ensuring that children are prepared for the responsibilities of citizenship. Citizens in a democratic society exercise political power over one another, and to do so responsibly, reflectively, and justifiably they need certain capacities, dispositions, and an adequate grasp of political institutions, history, and the world around them. Something like this general civic justification for regulating publicly funded schools appears to be broadly shared by the United States, Canada, and the European countries featured in this volume.

Who should regulate whom when it comes to elementary and secondary education? Here, Americans seem to be at least somewhat divided, whereas Europeans exhibit a stronger consensus. Some supporters of school choice and private schooling in the United States argue that parents are the optimal regulators of their children's education. Stephen Gilles and others have argued that parents have a stronger stake in the nature and quality of their child's education than does the state.[10] Parents also are more intimately informed about and involved in their child's education, according to this view; so as long as parents support core democratic values, the state should leave them the responsibility for overseeing their children's education.

Many other American scholars and citizens support a division of educational authority that gives the political community more scope to regulate the educational institutions that it funds. Many worry that with respect to children's values, parents inevitably have the predominant influence, good or bad; in the latter case, schools can be an appropriate counterweight. Some parents may care deeply about their own children's welfare, but they may not care sufficiently about the extent to which their children's education promotes tolerance and the capacities and knowledge needed for civic engagement. The political community has a greater interest than individual parents in these and other public values, so the state and its officials ought to have the authority and responsibility to regulate education to advance public purposes. This view of who should regulate is almost universally embraced by America's democratic neighbors to the north and across the Atlantic, and evidence suggests that it is predominant—if not undisputed—in the United States as well.[11]

How, finally, should schools be regulated? There are various regulatory options, focusing on curriculum, testing, teacher qualifications, admissions, and other factors. How much regulation is another facet of this question: in many European countries there is, by American standards, a great deal of regulation. And which regulations should be applied to which schools? Should government's authority to regulate be limited to those students who are using public funds to attend private schools, or should all schools, public or private, state or privately funded, fall within the government's regulatory ambit? The European and Canadian experiences appear to be consistent on this point: the government has both the authority and the responsibility to regulate all schools, public or private, though the extent of regulation sometimes varies across and even within school sectors.

When should schools be regulated? Upon establishment? On a regular basis? Only when complaints arise? The Canadian province of Alberta gives schools a great deal of flexibility in their operations, then requires all students to take what appears to be a rigorous examination on civic knowledge. Such an approach is consistent with John Witte's call, in his commentary, for information-based regulatory systems that provide both U.S. parents and taxpayers with useful information about the performance of all schools, whether public or private, yet respect diversity of education. A similar argument is endorsed by Charles L. Glenn: governments should exercise quality control over publicly funded private schooling while still permitting a thousand different educational flowers to bloom.

Obviously, these three general questions cover a great deal of regulatory detail. Readers of the chapters and critical comments that follow will find a range of answers and also some important commonalities and patterns. Our conviction with respect to publicly funded and regulated school choice is that the details matter a great deal. We hope that these essays help to broaden American thinking about the ways in which choice can be part of a public commitment to educational excellence for all.

The Netherlands: Where School Choice Is the Norm

Our chapters begin at the pluralist or choice-dominant end of the educational spectrum and proceed, roughly, toward systems that provide less scope for school choice. We begin with the pluralist Dutch.

As already noted, the freedom of parents to choose among publicly funded private schools is such a central and widely accepted principle in the Netherlands that it enjoys constitutional status. Moreover, what the Dutch constitution protects are not vague principles, but a set of detailed commitments that would surely surprise most Americans: private primary and secondary schools have a constitutional right to funding equal to that of public schools, on the same terms, and they have the right to appoint teachers and to "provide education according to their religious or other beliefs." As Ben Vermeulen explains, these freedoms have been interpreted to mean that groups of individuals having a distinctive religious viewpoint or educational philosophy that is not already represented in the school system may found a new school, one entitled to full government support enabling children aged four to sixteen to attend for free. Pluralism thus appears as the first principle of school policy in the Netherlands, and, indeed, more than two-thirds of Dutch pupils attend private school at public expense.

Nevertheless, as Vermeulen emphasizes, "the autonomy of private schools is not absolute." The constitution itself also charges the state with responsibility for ensuring the quality of all schools. Public authorities lay down curricular requirements and minimum criteria for the quality of teachers in all government-funded schools. Moreover, those who wish to establish a school must provide evidence that the school can attract a considerable number of pupils: from 200 to 300, depending on the locale. Establishing a new school is easier if it represents a denomination or philosophy that is not found at another school, but that is for public authorities to decide. Vermeulen emphasizes that such decisions—of whether a proposed school really represents a distinctive strain of Islam, for example—have proven to be difficult to make and (not surprisingly!) divisive. The system has proven disadvantageous to religious believers "new" to the Netherlands, especially Muslims and Hindus.

The Netherlands's principled commitment to strong pluralism in education appears to coexist with the reality of constraint. Vermeulen reports that according to Dutch law as it now stands, it would be unconstitutional to inhibit the founding of new Islamic schools based on civic concerns about increased ethnic segregation or about the teaching of intolerant or sexist attitudes: in Dutch law, religious and cultural pluralism trump these civic concerns when it comes to publicly funded schooling. And yet, of the nearly 130,000 Muslim pupils who attend primary schools, only 8,000 attend Islamic schools. What explains the small number of Islamic schools in the Netherlands? For one thing, public authorities insist that teachers in all publicly funded schools must be qualified and certified, and there are very few certified Muslim teachers. Nevertheless, in the Netherlands as elsewhere in

Europe, the prospect of a large increase in publicly funded Muslim schools is a source of anxiety. Explicit and implicit restraints, regulations, and controls impose limits on educational pluralism, and there may be more such controls in the future. In spite of the central principle in the Netherlands supporting strong pluralism, in practice there is less educational diversity than one might expect.

What happens in the tolerant Netherlands when educational pluralism runs into Dutch society's general commitment to nondiscrimination, for example, to protecting the rights of homosexual teachers? So far, Vermeulen explains, the courts have permitted schools to discriminate if they can make a credible case that discrimination is mandated by the principles of their denomination and if they apply those principles consistently. Private schools are likewise allowed to reject pupils on the basis of denominational criteria, subject to the same consistency rule. With respect to curriculum and the amount of time spent on various courses, there are detailed national standards and national examinations, enforced by the Education Inspectorate, which operates under the authority of the Ministry of Education and has a very broad mandate. Charles Venegoni and David Ferrero argue in their commentary that core features of this extensive regulatory regime are instructive for U.S. policymakers. However, the Dutch opposition to state paternalism apparently discourages the promulgation of shared civic values, aside from tolerance: there is no separate subject of citizenship education in the Dutch national curriculum.

In spite of its striking commitment to pluralism, therefore, the Dutch system also is characterized by robust regulations regarding who can teach and what will be taught, and those regulations are enforced by national educational authorities. Freedom of education is one thing, Vermeulen argues, and "absolute educational autonomy" is quite another.

Finally, growing anxieties surround schooling in the Netherlands, and these anxieties seem to be encouraging many to reconsider the possible attractions of something more like the American system of common schooling. Vermeulen deems any revolution unlikely; nevertheless, he does allow that some important changes (such as the creation of more magnet schools) may be a consequence of concerns over the increasing number of separate Muslim schools, which also are predominantly "black."

In the end, Vermeulen argues that at the very least the Dutch experience suggests skepticism is in order regarding fears that an extensive system of publicly funded school choice must strike a severe blow to social cohesion and integration. This is not to say that the Dutch system avoids all of the problems faced elsewhere, including in the United States. Vermeulen expects that the rising concern with segregation by race and the (possibly exaggerated) fears of the antidemocratic, anti-Western tendencies of some Muslim schools could lead to a greater emphasis on civics in the national curriculum.

Anne Bert Dijkstra, Jaap Dronkers, and Sjoerd Karsten focus on the policy dimensions of school choice in the Netherlands. Public financing of private schooling has been widespread in the Netherlands for more than 100 years. Even though Dutch society has become much more secular over the past few decades, religious schools remain the predominant form of private schools; their continued popularity appears to derive from their willingness to teach moral values explicitly, a subject public schools are thought to shy away from (as in the United States).

Children in Dutch religious schools also seem to learn more than children in both private nonreligious and public schools. This, the authors argue, may be because private religious schools are, to a greater extent than other types, distinctive educational communities in which pupils and teachers share a common ethos. It also appears that the educational performance of all schools is enhanced in areas where they coexist in a "balance of power" and no single type of school dominates the others.

Studies have identified few significant differences between Dutch public, private nonreligious, and religious schools regarding their influence on children's attitudes and civic values. This may be due to the common curriculum and other public mandates that apply to all types of schools in the Netherlands, as Venegoni and Ferrero suggest. Some evidence suggests that parental choice is leading to greater ethnic segregation within each school sector in the Netherlands. However, Dijkstra and his colleagues point out that where choice of public schools is most widespread, the private school sector is less segregated and elite. In addition, where private schools are most numerous, they tend to be more integrated by race and income.

England and Wales: Broadly Regulated School Choice

Neville Harris describes the legal and policy context of school choice reforms in England and Wales over the past sixty years. Harris's account is consistent with our central theme: in bringing greater parental choice to education, reformers also brought much greater regulation to nonpublic schools. All government-financed schools (including those that are privately run) are heavily regulated in the areas of initial accreditation, hiring, facilities, and curriculum. Surprisingly—especially to Americans—most government-run schools include Christian religious services and religion classes in their educational program, although children may opt out of services at their parents' request.

All British schools, even those purportedly independent of the government, are subject to many state regulations and periodic inspection by education officials. State inspectors determine whether a school's facilities and staff meet government standards for promoting learning and protecting the welfare of students and if its educational ethos is "suitable" for creating good citizens. Independent schools with a strong religious culture are considered suitable as long as their students are "left with the capacity to choose some other way of life later on." Promoting a religious and values-laden identity is considered acceptable, but outright brainwashing is forbidden.

In addition to periodic and on-demand inspection, another core element of regulation in the English system is the national curriculum. Curricular requirements cover a broad swath of subjects, from math to citizenship, and they are more or less mandatory. State-operated and -aided schools are required to follow the national curriculum unless they demonstrate, through performance on exams, that their students are performing well on the topics covered. Independent schools are not required to follow the detailed national curriculum, though some do.

Aside from independent schools, England and Wales have offered schooling options that are comparable to U.S. public charter schools of various types. "Grant-maintained" and "foundation" schools are like American public schools chartered by the U.S. Department of Education instead of the local school district. They are the least constrained of English "public" schools, yet they are more heavily regulated than is a typical U.S. public charter school.

In the 1990s, the Conservative government in Britain experimented with a school voucher–type arrangement called the "assisted places" scheme. Government funds allowed some low- and moderate-income students to attend elite independent schools, provided that the students passed admissions tests. The experiment was justified, as Harris describes, partly by the "perception that many independent schools and faith schools in the private sector are particularly attuned to civic values as well as safeguarding minority religious and cultural identities." The assisted places program was phased out by the Labour government beginning in 1997. Nevertheless, recently the Labour party has publicly acknowledged the civic functions of independent schools in promoting social and religious tolerance, providing educational options to parents, and showing state-operated schools how to improve.

Harris asserts that in Britain, parents' choices among state-run schools are somewhat limited and highly regulated. Although parents are entitled to announce a preference regarding the school that their child attends ("open enrollment"), parental preferences need not determine the actual assignment of a child to a school. The local education authority (LEA) makes the assignments, and LEAs tend to rely heavily on geographical districts (or "catchment areas"), diversity considerations, and the need to fill empty spaces in unpopular schools. This last practice represents a marked deviation from a market model of school choice, where popular schools would be encouraged to expand and unpopular schools would be shuttered. Still, 80 percent of parents report that their first preference for school assignment was honored. Disappointed parents have a right to appeal, a right that nearly 95,000 parents exercised in the 2001–02 academic year. Parents tend to prevail in about one-third of school assignment appeals.

Harris considers the availability of properly regulated school choice in England and Wales, properly regulated, to be a creative vehicle for promoting democratic values. He reminds us that democratic participation is not limited to voting in government elections but also includes decisionmaking and involvement in a number of social contexts. In his conclusion, he argues that "rights of choice can be as much a facet of 'citizenship' as of consumerism, because this form of participation brings an extra degree of attachment to the service or institution in question by virtue of the commitment made by the participant."

Stephen Gorard provides an empirical assessment of the impact of the 1988 school choice reforms on the level of integration in the schools of England and Wales. He concludes, quite encouragingly, that "a considerable increase in choice has not led to balkanization of the school system." Indeed, the reforms reduced segregation by social class and race, more so in densely populated areas where there were many secondary schools and transportation was easily available. Gorard argues that increased choice has the potential to promote integration. Whether it actually does depends on how choice is structured and how segregated schools were before choice policies were enacted.

Twelve years after parents were given substantial say in what schools their children would attend, the schools of England and Wales were slightly more integrated than they were in the years immediately preceding the choice initiative. Reformers' capacity to use school choice to promote integration is severely limited, Gorard points out, by the extent of residential segregation: geography is virtually destiny when it comes to the social stratification of public schools. That is true in the United States as well.[12] Therefore, it should be unsurprising that in the United Kingdom the effects of choice on integration, while positive, were small.

National curriculum requirements in the United Kingdom regarding citizenship are general and thematic. Nevertheless, Gorard observes that—as we will find elsewhere—greater parental choice of schools in England and Wales has tended "to drive schools toward uniformity." No school wants to disappoint parents by failing to provide a standard academic curriculum, and schools tend to adopt the "best practices" associated with the most successful schools. While critics once argued that increased parental choice would produce diverse kinds of schools with homogeneous student bodies, the reality has been the opposite: there are more diverse student bodies in more homogeneous schools.

Recent government reforms have sought to increase the diversity of public schools in England and Wales. Gorard raises concerns about such an approach, arguing that greater diversity in types of schools tends to be associated with greater segregation by socioeconomic characteristics because parents who share the same preference for school type and theme also tend to come from the same social class.

Belgium: Pluralist Policies and Pluralist Schools

Jan De Groof discusses the case of Belgium, with particular attention to the Flemish region of the country. As in the Netherlands, public financing of school choice is quite common in Belgium, where about 70 percent of elementary and secondary students in the Flemish region attend privately run schools at public expense. Belgians view school choice as a way to accommodate diverse religious, language, and cultural groups and thereby to promote social cohesion. As De Groof reports, educational "neutrality" in Belgium implies respect for "the philosophical, ideological, or religious conceptions of parents and students," which is demonstrated by deliberately incorporating them into the government-financed school program.

Belgian citizens (again like the Dutch) have the constitutional right to establish a publicly funded school with a distinctive character and ethos. In Belgium, this right to establish schools and the school choice policies that come in its wake are linked to the constitutional right to "freedom of association." De Groof points out that most of Belgium's private schools have a specific religious affiliation; however, some are based on nonreligious moral or philosophical precepts, such as secular humanism or the Waldorf-Steiner education model. A small number of Belgian private schools are designated "pluralist" schools whose express purpose is to bring together students from a variety of religious, ethnic, and cultural backgrounds and to foster a free exchange of ideas.

Here as elsewhere, there is a strong regime of public accountability. Education officials in Belgium monitor the quality of private schools by examining the performance of students on standardized tests. This emphasis on results-based accountability even extends to the area of special education, where schools are evaluated on the basis of the extent to which their disabled students attain specified developmental goals. However, consistent with the muscular pluralism that motivates school choice policies in Belgium, education inspectors are not allowed to regulate the religious or philosophical elements of schools or schooling.

"O Canada": Choice, Civics, Federalism, and Results-Based Accountability

While some American advocates of vouchers and other forms of publicly funded school choice have cited the Canadian experience as something the United States should emulate, David E. Campbell points out that public policy regarding school choice varies a great deal by province. No Canadian province has anything like a fully developed voucher system, but a number of provinces do use public funds to subsidize religious schools. The very variety of choices does indeed yield some interesting contrasts and at least one important possible lesson (from Alberta) for the United States.

Campbell points out some of the principal ways in which Canadian education policies are shaped by the national experience and by the experiences of the specific provinces that he examines. The original Canadian constitution—the British North America Act of 1867—specified that provinces joining Canada should preserve the religious character of existing schools. But the chief reason for this was to preserve the schools of language minorities in Ontario and Quebec: the French-speaking (and Catholic) minority in Ontario and the English-speaking (and Protestant) minority in Quebec. Canadians generally speak of the civic responsibilities of their school system in terms not unlike those of Americans, except that Canadians generally put more emphasis on multiculturalism and pluralism, especially with regard to language, ethnicity, and religion.

The bulk of Campbell's chapter examines the disparate origins, extent, and nature of public funding of school choice in four Canadian provinces. Newfoundland has recently moved from a system in which all of the province's schools were denominational to a system in which publicly funded denominational schools have been abandoned altogether, largely it seems for reasons of economy. Quebec also recently abandoned its religiously based public school system, in which students had a choice, but only between Catholic and Protestant schools. In Quebec, the motivating factor for instituting a public system was not economy but a civic concern with better preparing students for "engagement in a democracy rich with diversity," as Campbell puts it. Nevertheless, the French schools retain their dual linguistic basis, while otherwise standing uniformly for inclusive and democratic values. The province of Ontario recently abandoned its policy of funding both public schools and a quasi-public Catholic system. It now instead gives a tax credit for parents who pay private school tuition. Like other nations, Canada has not extensively studied the civic effects of different forms of schooling. There are anxieties that the Ontario tax credit could lead to the proliferation of new schools subject to little regulation.

Campbell argues that the United States has the most to learn from the Alberta model. Alberta provides public funds for Catholic schools and private schools, including other religious schools. But Alberta also has put in place a curriculum-based exit exam that promises to ensure the teaching of civics to all students and to provide data for evaluating the civic consequences of different school types. Campbell describes and defends Alberta's essay-based, province-wide exam, arguing that the Alberta model allows for "considerable choice *and* a relatively unobtrusive method—subject to democratic oversight—of evaluating the civic consequences of the choices available."

Germany: "Private" Schools Complete the Public System

The education system in Germany, according to Lutz Reuter, leans heavily on the country's federal form of government in seeking to provide schooling that promotes important public values while responding to community preferences, especially regarding religious education. Many decisions are delegated to local and state governments—as they are in the United States—so that Germany has sixteen rather different education "systems."

Reuter explains that all German states permit parents to choose among schooling options, public and private. While Germany's constitution declares it to be the right of anyone to establish a private school, educational authorities ensure that private schools do not increase social segregation and that they operate as a support, not a replacement, for the public school system. In practice, this means that private schools must demonstrate that their operation is helpful to public schools—for example, by providing a distinct pedagogical approach that is especially appropriate for slow learners. Most states fund most costs of most private schools after the schools have survived a two-year proving period in which they must rely on their own resources. Students who have completed their course of study at a private school must pass examinations designed and supervised by public education authorities before they can graduate and obtain a diploma.

As it is elsewhere in Europe, religion is taught in German public schools. State-run schools offer denominationally specific religion classes as electives, as requested by local religious groups. Students who do not take religion electives are required to take a secular course on ethics and values. In fact, education law in Germany requires the promotion of a number of important values in all schools, including "respect for God" and "religious, political, and social tolerance." One might therefore describe the typical public school in Germany as religious, pluralistic, and tolerant. Social cohesion is threatened most, Reuter argues, by ability tracking within the public school system. Public schools in Germany rely heavily on ability tracking in the upper grades, a practice that often promotes class segregation due to the close association between a student's family background and his or her educational performance (similar effects have been observed in the United States). Most private schools are partially funded by the state, and they are primarily middle-class institutions—not dominated by social elites but with proportionately few poor or immigrant students.

France: School Choice as Modus Vivendi

Denis Meuret's account of school choice in France locates the peculiar (to American eyes) shape of today's controversies around French education policy in the tumultuous, centuries-long rivalry between the Roman Catholic Church and the modern French state. While church and state in France struggle mightily for the minds and (or) souls of French students, Meuret argues that the two sides have one thing in common: both discount the educational interests of families and children in favor of the corporate interests of the nation or the Church. "In France," as Meuret puts it, "individuals have to show that they are worthy of their institutions more than institutions have to show that they serve individuals." With respect to education in particular, both parties utterly dismiss the primacy of parents' or children's rights. Meuret quotes a proponent of state authority: "The idea that education has to meet children's needs, to say nothing of parents' demands, is considered nonsense."

In the wake of these struggles, Catholic schools have obtained an acknowledgement of their distinctive identity as educational institutions ("le respect de leur caractère propre"), together with almost total public financing. The current situation in France is one of equilibrium, according to Meuret: existing schools are financed, and it is very hard but not impossible to create new ones. Private schools are seen as a necessary alternative to the public system: while a minority of French students are enrolled in private religious schools at any one time, many children move into the religious sector temporarily, perhaps when they encounter difficulty in a public school, so a much higher proportion of children have some experience of both school sectors. Catholic schools are a safety valve and a valued alternative, like private schools in Germany, but they also are seen as a sufficient safety valve, and so none of the major political parties clamor for an expansion of choice.

Religious schools are heavily publicly subsidized, but in return, subsidized schools are subject to a range of regulations that seem astonishing from the American perspective. There is one national curriculum and one set of national examinations for all schools. Publicly subsidized schools cannot exclude any student on the grounds of his or her religion, lack of religion, or ethnic origin, and teachers in these schools are recruited among persons who, in brief, pass the same examinations as public school teachers.

In France, as elsewhere, allowing parents and pupils to choose among schools clearly seems to increase their satisfaction with schooling. As Jaap Dronkers points out, some preliminary studies suggest that the public school sector in France is more democratic at the input stage than it is with respect to outcomes. French public schools educate a wider range of students than French private schools, but graduation from a public school depends more heavily on the family background of the student than does graduation from a private school. This "equalizing" tendency of Catholic schools has been observed in the United States as well.[13] Beyond this finding regarding graduation rates, there are no studies of the long-term impact of school type in France. We are unable to compare different schools' impact on students in terms of their social values (tolerance, sense of solidarity, sense of belonging, adherence to democratic values, feelings of responsibility, absence of arrogance, commitment to equity), personal traits (ability to take initiative, imagination), or religious beliefs (do Catholic children who enroll in Catholic schools remain Catholic more often when they grow up?); therefore we cannot compare their impact on social cohesion. There is not a strong tradition of school choice within the public sector in France. While greater choice has been allowed recently, little is known about its effects.

Italy: The Great School Choice Challenge

Luisa Ribolzi describes the case of Italy—the only country discussed in this volume that has less publicly financed school choice than the United States—as "the impossible choice." Still, the Italian case highlights tensions between state and parental authority as well as conflicts between government control and religious freedom that resonate with Americans.

The Italian educational system, Ribolzi recounts, was shaped by the larger political project of building a unified Italian state: education was to play a crucial role in creating a citizenry and a shared sense of national identity from a rather disparate group of regional cultures. In Italy as in Germany, education authorities have permitted private schools to open but the state has retained sole authority to issue diplomas. The motive behind the Italian system, as in centralized public school systems in many countries including the United States, was the desire to promote social equality through standardization of education and to promote community through neighborhood assignment. Unfortunately, Ribolzi argues, the latter goal clearly undermined the former. Furthermore, the insistence on strict value-neutral teaching has resulted in public schools imparting an increasingly thin concept of morality to their students. Foreshadowing points made by Charles L. Glenn in his commentary, Ribolzi views such an educational environment, in which many value-based arguments are ruled out of bounds, as deleterious to the goal of preparing Italian students to be active democratic citizens.

Italy's centralized system of public education succeeded in virtually eliminating illiteracy by the late twentieth century, an important public goal in any advanced democracy. However, Ribolzi argues that the system often has been inflexible and unresponsive to broader social interests, including calls for a greater parental role in decisionmaking regarding education. In her view, the treatment of parents as clients of the state instead of partners in the realm of education has decreased their willingness to serve as active participants in other areas of communal decisionmaking.

Now that the Italian state is established and largely secured from the potentially fragmenting power of regionalism, Ribolzi argues that Italians are wondering whether they might be better served by having more choice in education. Recent legal and administrative changes in Italy have for the first time opened up the possibility that public funds might be used to support private schooling, and more than 100,000 Italians are eligible for modest government subsidies to partially offset the cost of attending nongovernmental schools. It remains to be seen whether this experiment with school choice will take root and grow and whether Italy will join other European states in embracing regulated educational pluralism. In the meantime, Italy remains an exception to the long-standing policies of choice in the other countries featured here. Until very recently, the pursuit of state-sponsored education exclusively through state-run schools equipped Italians with the basic competence to be democratic citizens, but now, Ribolzi fears, the state-dominated system fails to provide Italians with sufficient opportunities to exercise choices to which democratic citizens are entitled.

Private Schooling and Civic Values in Europe:
Reviewing the Evidence

School reform debates in Europe and North America commonly assume that religious schools are equal or superior to public schools with respect to both learning, broadly defined, and the acquisition of civic values. That is, of course, a notable change from the perception fifty years ago, at least in the United States.[14] Jaap Dronkers concludes Part 1 by providing an overview of the empirical evidence about the relative effectiveness of public and religious schools in seven European countries: Flemish Belgium, France, Germany, Hungary, the Netherlands, Scotland, and England. He argues that the European evidence on this question should be especially revealing because "contrary to the situation in the United States and England, parents in a number of European societies have long had the opportunity to make a real choice between comparable schools—mostly between public and religious schools—without paying very high school fees for the latter schools." The heavy subsidies that are provided to both religious and public schools in some European countries should help eliminate some of the "selection bias" that is present when families must pay a significant amount for their children to attend religious schools, as is the case in the United States.

Dronkers provides a brief description of education policies with respect to publicly subsidized and regulated school choice in each of the countries he discusses, including a brief account of the historical events that led to the current state of education policy. He argues that there are clear differences in school success and cognitive achievement in public and religious schools in Belgium, France, Hungary, the Netherlands, and Scotland and that those differences cannot be explained by differences in the social composition of the schools or by obvious social characteristics of pupils, parents, schools, or neighborhoods. The differences in effectiveness are less clear in Germany, although there are some indications of the greater effectiveness of German religious schools.

With respect to the effects of religious and public schools on students' civic values, Dronkers finds very little difference, though there is less evidence on this score. In Flemish Belgium, for example, Dronkers finds that "pupils from Catholic schools have more or less the same attitude toward abortion, euthanasia, and homosexuality as their counterparts in public schools." What differences there are among public and religious schools in Belgium appear to be the result not of the religious dimension in religious schools but rather of the fact that public schools have a higher proportion of students enrolled in the vocational and technical track than do religious schools, which offer a general educational track almost exclusively.

Dronkers also emphasizes just how limited the empirical evidence is on the relative effectiveness of religious and public schools in the European countries that he considers, with the Netherlands as a partial exception. In some instances, he points out, the reason is that the division of public dollars between the religious and public sectors is highly politically sensitive. There is a widespread fear in many countries (as Denis Meuret also observed in France) that empirical studies might upset fragile and politically sensitive policy settlements.

What Have We Learned? Experts Weigh In

Part 2 gathers together a set of critical comments and observations on the chapters in Part 1. Our contributors are experts on education policy and law who represent a variety of points of view about school choice and government regulation.

William A. Galston emphasizes the complexities involved in taking seriously the aim of this volume, which is to consider what the United States has to learn from the experience of other countries. The divergent stances toward choice reflected in the preceding discussion reflect different assessments of the education market and different conceptions about the proper relations between groups and the state or the political community as a whole. In France, republicans remain hostile to groups and deeply suspicious of religious schooling, as is amply demonstrated by the intensity of recent controversies surrounding the wearing of head scarves by Muslim girls. In the Netherlands, on the other hand, freedom of education is a revered right. The continuum tracks not simply attitudes toward pluralism and choice, but also toward the extent of public regulation. These two nations help illustrate the opposite poles of a policy continuum on which the United States falls somewhere in the middle. Galston uses this continuum to illustrate competing tendencies in U.S. education policy, which he illustrates by discussing famous court cases concerning legal restrictions on religious schools.

Does the postion of the United States between these two poles—neither too French nor too Dutch—lead Galston to conclude (like Goldilocks) that the United States is "just right?" Not quite. Galston emphasizes that each nation's educational system seems to reflect its own particular history and public culture. It is not easy to detach institutional arrangements from their context, and so we must proceed with caution. Nevertheless, it may sometimes be possible to discover a nugget of exportable policy gold amid a mass of context-dependent idiosyncrasies. An example, Galston argues, is the Alberta model of civic education discussed by Campbell.

Richard W. Garnett examines these questions with respect to the constitutional guarantee of freedom of religion, as he understands it. He welcomes the U.S. Supreme Court's *Zelman* decision, which permits the public funding of religious schools. While granting the legitimacy of the civic mission of American public education—"to create a well-educated and tolerant citizenry"—he warns against "overblown" concerns that vouchers could lead to social fragmentation and intolerance: "Students whose parents are permitted to choose their schools—public or private, religious or secular—are no less tolerant, respectful, decent, and public-minded than today's government-educated children."

In addition, however, Garnett warns of the "regulation, oversight, and homogenization" that often comes with public funding of private education in the countries examined by our authors. The United States should not replicate heavy-handed regulatory requirements that threaten the "mission and freedom of authentically religious schools" or the distinctiveness and independence of private schools generally. The U.S. Constitution "meaningfully constrains" the ability of government to engage in the "ideological commandeering" of private schools—especially religious schools—through regulations accompanying vouchers.

Most controversially, Garnett argues that parents exercising their publicly funded ability to choose among schools should be considered "speakers," protected by the Constitution's First Amendment speech clauses. In Garnett's view, exercising school choice through vouchers should be understood as creating a "public forum" in which private speakers—school administrators and parents exercising choice—convey important messages to children; it is equivalent to the exercise of political speech and therefore should be almost entirely free of government regulation. Garnett argues that such an understanding sets the U.S. Constitution in four-square opposition to the strongly "statist" approach of the French but also in no small measure puts it in tension with the strong regulatory framework of the supposedly pluralist Dutch. Garnett is not specific about what sorts of regulations fall on which side of the line demarcating permissible and impermissible; he instead calls for public deliberation in light of the general principles he has sketched.

Charles L. Glenn views the European and Canadian experiences with school choice as rich with possibility as well as significant dangers for the United States. He obviously sympathizes with the European tendency to base educational pluralism and publicly funded school choice on parents' "rights of conscience." Glenn also claims that government financing of school choice enables schools, both public and private, to be bolder in the degree to which they feature controversial but important subjects in their educational programs. Governments can require such subjects as sex education or religion to be taught to all students as long as their parents can choose the environment in which instruction occurs. Public schools in the United States are more restricted in what they can teach, Glenn suggests, because parents pressure education officials if their assigned public schools propose to teach potentially uncomfortable topics. His argument here echoes the recent work of Diane Ravitch documenting how value conflicts have resulted in U.S. textbook publishers following the path of least political resistance.[15] The result, according to Ravitch, is educational materials that are both unengaging and uninformative.

Regarding the overall quality of education provided to citizens, Glenn emphasizes that many of the countries featured in this volume require all schools to meet certain educational standards but permit individual schools to choose the methods by which they do so. This approach, mandating outcome but not process, has come to be called "smart regulation" in the public management literature.[16] Even as policymakers strive to be "smart" in regulating school choice, Glenn urges all involved to be reasonable in forming expectations regarding choice. "School choice has not been a disaster in any of our countries," Glenn observes, "nor has it been a magic solution to problems that are deeply embedded in the nature of the educational system." More or less effective school choice is a matter of design. Glenn suggests that Americans can learn much from other countries about which approaches to emulate and which to eschew.

John F. Witte continues the discussion of how Americans ought to regulate school choice, arguing that government oversight of schools should be "humble and devolved." Extremist schools that threaten the U.S. government and democratic values are rare and short-lived, according to Witte: neither the government nor significant numbers of families are likely to support them. Americans therefore ought to design their regulatory system with an eye toward typical, not fringe, schools.

Parents and governments have conflicting values when it comes to schools, Witte argues. Parents with the opportunity to choose their children's schools tend to value diversity in curriculum and pedagogy, so that they can better match their child's particular needs with the school best designed to satisfy them. Taxpayers and government regulators may seek more consistency and a greater focus on basic skills due to their interest in equity and in at least minimal competence. The ideal compromise, according to Witte, is for government to regulate all schools in the United States, public and private, but do so with a focus on student achievement and the proper use of public funds. He is wary of government regulation that would prescribe curriculum or instruct schools on how they must handle religious topics.

Witte expresses concern about recent efforts by the U.S. Department of Education to enforce common standards and accountability requirements on all public schools, warning that U.S. public schools are overregulated while private schools are underregulated. He contrasts this with the situation in most European countries, where, he claims, both public and private schools are overregulated regarding curriculum, teacher qualifications, and admissions. Most important, Witte asserts, "education regulation should primarily be about information." As long as the public and parents know what different schools are doing and how well their students are achieving, the interest of both are well served in a system of school choice.

The concluding essay, by Charles L. Venegoni and David J. Ferrero, strikes a theme that contrasts with some others in this volume. Venegoni and Ferrero warn against viewing parents as consumers of education. They argue that the success of the Dutch experience with school choice is due not to the market but to "a model of professionally organized centralization." Far from inhibiting school choice, they argue, the regulatory system contributes to its vitality.

Venegoni and Ferrero echo a common theme of this volume: regulations should focus on outcomes and rely on a system of standards and assessments that are common to all schools, public and private. However, they argue that a common national curriculum—something that the United States has never developed—would be both desirable and helpful to individual teachers, since "most educators share at some level" a set of common aims regarding the education of children. Generally, they argue that students thrive in schools of choice in the Netherlands because of those schools' commonality, not because of their diversity.

Venegoni and Ferrero argue that extremist schools are a greater threat to U.S. society than John Witte would have us believe. They join Richard Garnett in wondering whether a system of extensive government regulation securely established in law, like that in the Netherlands, can be achieved in the U.S. constitutional context.[17] In the end, Venegoni and Ferrero wonder how best to realize an educational system that attains "that hitherto elusive combination of freedom and cohesion, fairness and excellence."

We join our collaborators in this project in posing that central question. What combination of choice and regulation, legal limits, requirements, tests, and incentives will allow U.S. society to realize all of its important public educational values? Our authors do not agree, and we know that this volume will not settle the controversies surrounding public funding of school choice.

We do hope that readers will think more creatively about the available options after having seen how some other advanced democracies have implemented strong public policies making school choice an integral part of public education.

Notes

1. Abraham Lincoln, "The Perpetuation of Our Political Institutions," address before the Young Men's Lyceum of Springfield, Illinois, January 27, 1838, in Roy P. Basler, ed., *The Collected Works of Abraham Lincoln* (Rutgers University Press, 1953).

2. Edward B. Fiske and Helen F. Ladd, *When Schools Compete: A Cautionary Tale* (Brookings, 2000).

3. But see Stephen Gorard, chapter 5 in this volume, for a critique of Fiske and Ladd's research methodology.

4. Martin Carnoy and Patrick J. McEwan, "Does Privatization Improve Education? The Case of Chile's National Voucher Plan," in David N. Plank and Gary Sykes, eds., *Choosing Choice: School Choice in International Perspective* (New York: Teachers College Press, 2003), pp. 24–44.

5. See National Working Commission on Choice in K–12 Education, *School Choice: Doing It the Right Way Makes a Difference* (Brookings, 2003).

6. Regarding the last point about policy compromises, see Terry M. Moe, "The Politics of Bureaucratic Structure," in John E. Chubb and Paul E. Peterson, eds., *Can the Government Govern?* (Brookings, 1989), pp. 267–329.

7. *The D.C. School Choice Incentive Act of 2003*, H.R. 2673, title III, secs. 301–10.

8. Alan Wolfe, *One Nation After All* (Viking, 1998).

9. See Stephen Macedo, "Constituting Civil Society: School Vouchers, Religious Nonprofit Organizations, and Liberal Public Values," *Chicago Kent Law Review*, vol. 75, no. 2 (2000), 417–51.

10. Stephen G. Gilles, "On Educating Children: A Parentalist Manifesto," *University of Chicago Law Review*, vol. 63 (Summer 1996). For a critique of Gilles's argument, see Stephen Macedo, *Diversity and Distrust: Civic Education in a Multicultural Democracy* (Harvard University Press, 2000), pp. 241–44.

11. See the poll results in Terry M. Moe, *Schools, Vouchers, and the American Public* (Brookings, 2001). Moe finds among other things that Americans generally have positive attitudes toward their own public schools if not the public school system as a whole: only about 25 percent of parents are unhappy with their own children's public schools. Since a majority of Americans are unsatisfied with the education system in America, that figure might be considered surprising—comparable to the phenomenon that voters hate Congress but love their own congressman or congresswoman.

12. The sociologist Douglas Massey developed the index mentioned as a way of measuring residential segregation; see Douglas S. Massey and Nancy A. Denton,

American Apartheid: Segregation and the Making of the Underclass (Harvard University Press, 1993).

13. See James Coleman, Thomas Hoffer, and Sally Kilgore, *High School Achievement* (Basic Books, 1982); and Anthony S. Bryk, Valerie E. Lee, and Peter B. Holland, *Catholic Schools and the Common Good* (Harvard University Press, 1993).

14. See Bryk, Lee, and Holland, *Catholic Schools and the Common Good.*

15. Diane Ravitch, *The Language Police: How Pressure Groups Restrict What Students Learn* (Knopf, 2003).

16. See Malcolm K. Sparrow, *The Regulatory Craft: Controlling Risks, Solving Problems, and Managing Compliance* (Brookings, 2000).

17. But see Macedo, "Constituting Civil Society," for a contrary view.

PART 1

Country
Case Studies

2

Regulating School Choice to Promote Civic Values: Constitutional and Political Issues in the Netherlands

BEN P. VERMEULEN

Freedom of education has always been a main characteristic of the Dutch school system. This freedom has two dimensions. First, groups of individuals are, within certain legal limits, free to establish and operate state-independent primary and secondary schools according to their own religious, philosophical, or pedagogical principles. These schools, when they fulfill the criteria set by law, are fully funded by the state. Second, parents are free to choose the school that they want their children to attend, and when the chosen school is funded by the state, it has to be free for all pupils ages four to sixteen. To this extent, it is confusing to speak of school choice programs in the Netherlands. To do so suggests that there are a few schemes based on school choice for a limited number of pupils, when in fact freedom of school choice is one of the primary principles of the Dutch system as a whole.

Although educational freedom is still cherished and the system is still supported by the majority, the last fifteen years have given rise to some problematic developments. The growing number of fully funded Islamic schools is a cause for concern, as is the fact that freedom of choice has led to "white flight" resulting, at least partially, in a division between "black" and "white" schools.

This chapter describes the structure of the Dutch school system and discusses the aforementioned issues. In particular, it asks whether school choice should be limited—or the freedom of schools restricted—in order to promote civic values. It begins with a sketch of the fundamental norms regulating the Dutch school system. The first of these is article 23 of the Dutch constitution, the legal foundation of the binary structure of public, religiously neutral schools and private, predominantly denominational schools. It also discusses the relevant international norms that limit the legislature's ability to shape the educational system.

The constitutional right to freedom of education for private schools is then examined, in particular with regard to those regulations and conditions of funding that actually restrict or may restrict that right in order to foster civic values, social cohesion, and other public aims. These topics are discussed in light of specific issues facing a multicultural and multiethnic society like the Netherlands. Next, some fundamental debates and questions concerning the Dutch educational system are explored, in particular the tension between, on one hand, freedom of education and parental school choice and, on the other, the demands of equality and citizenship. The chapter concludes with some final observations.

The Dutch School System

Article 23 of the Dutch constitution defines the basic structure of the Dutch educational system and the legal norms that govern it. The legislature implements its provisions, although international norms put certain demands and limits on the legislature.

The Constitution

The Dutch system of primary and secondary schools is to a large extent determined by article 23 of the Constitution, which reads as follows:

1. Education shall be the constant concern of the Government.

2. All persons shall be free to provide education, without prejudice to the authorities' right of supervision and, with regard to forms of education designated by law, their right to examine the competence and moral integrity of the teachers, to be regulated by Act of Parliament.

3. Education provided by public authorities shall be regulated by Act of Parliament, paying due respect to everyone's religion or beliefs.

4. The authorities shall ensure that primary education is provided in a sufficient number of public-authority schools in every municipality. Deviations from this provision may be permitted under rules to be established by Act of Parliament on condition that there is opportunity to receive the said form of education.

5. The standards required of schools financed either in part or in full from public funds shall be regulated by Act of Parliament, with due regard, in the case of private schools, to the freedom to provide education according to religious or other belief.

6. The requirements for primary education shall be such that the quality of private schools fully financed from public funds and of public-authority schools is equally guaranteed. The relevant provisions shall respect in particular the freedom of private schools to choose their teaching aids and to appoint teachers as they see fit.

7. Private primary schools that satisfy the conditions laid down by Act of Parliament shall be financed from public funds according to the same standards as public-authority schools. The conditions under which private secondary education and pre-university education shall receive contributions from public funds shall be laid down by Act of Parliament.

8. The Government shall submit annual reports on the state of education to the States General [Parliament].

It must be stressed that the framers of this provision, which in essence has remained unchanged since 1917, had in mind primary education and parts of secondary education; article 23 therefore primarily concerns schools for pupils up to age sixteen, who are subject to compulsory education. But today many of the principles laid down in article 23 are also applied to other sectors: for instance, there is now equal funding for the entire secondary education sector, as well as for vocational training and higher education. The precise constitutional status of these areas is not entirely clear. Must it be assumed now that they also are covered by the text of the Constitution? Or, as far as these sectors are concerned, must these principles be regarded as customary constitutional law? Or is it entirely up to the legislature to analogously—or not—apply the principles to other sectors?

It is at least clear that not all aspects of article 23 can be applied to institutions of vocational training and higher education, such as, for instance, the freedom to refuse pupils whose parents do not subscribe to the religious views of the school. The laws regulating vocational training and higher education require such institutions to be freely accessible to all students. Furthermore, the public/private distinction that is of vital importance in primary and secondary education is of much less relevance here, because most of these institutions—even though they are run by civil law corporations and often are formally denominational—are in fact religiously neutral and function as public institutions. The issue of regulating school choice to promote civic values is therefore not a primary concern of vocational training and higher education, as it is with primary and secondary schools.

Although the boards of private primary and secondary schools enjoy a broad, constitutionally guaranteed freedom of education, their legal position is not as strong as one might expect. Laws that are adopted by Parliament—acts of Parliament—cannot be declared unconstitutional by the courts. And insofar as legislative and administrative acts of the Minister of Education, the Education Inspectorate, and other officials flow from an act of Parliament, they are not subject to judicial review. Only decrees and measures of the minister or the inspectorate that are not mere technical measures implementing an act of Parliament can be challenged in a civil or administrative court on the basis of their alleged unconstitutionality.

One System, Two Schools

The basic structure of the Dutch education system, as laid down in article 23 of the Constitution, is binary. It consists of two types of schools, public authority schools and private, nonpublic schools, which are to a certain extent opposites, complementing and supplementing each other.[1] Public authority schools are generally governed by an organ of the state, often by the municipal executive. They do not enjoy autonomy in the sense of being free to ground their educational principles in a specific religion or belief, but they are free to choose a specific pedagogical approach, such as Montessori or Dalton. Education provided by these schools is regulated by law: it must be nondenominational, based on the principle of neutrality. Public schools are not allowed to select pupils and teachers on the basis of denominational criteria.

Public authority schools, which are freely accessible to all pupils, have a certain primacy, since the government guarantees that within a short distance from home there is a public school for every pupil who wants to attend one. Otherwise, both subsystems—public authority schools and private schools—have equal status. The public authority schools and private schools are funded according to identical or equivalent criteria.

Private schools are run by corporate bodies under civil law and, although they are in general fully funded by the government, enjoy a constitutionally safeguarded autonomy: freedom of education. This freedom includes three rights:

—*vrijheid van richting*: the right to shape a school according to a religious or philosophical world view and to provide in that school education of a distinctive religious or philosophical character

—*vrijheid van inrichting*: pedagogical and organizational autonomy, which overlaps the first right

—*vrijheid van stichting*: the right to establish a school, implied in the freedom to provide education.

The right to give private, government-funded schools a distinctive religious or philosophical character—*vrijheid van richting*—may be regarded as the core of the freedom of education. It is this aspect of *vrijheid van inrichting* , pedagogical and organizational autonomy, that is guaranteed best. Article 23 declares that when the government issues quality standards (funding conditions for the private schools), this freedom must be respected, especially—but not only—in relation to the choice of teaching materials and the right to appoint teachers.

Vrijheid van inrichting, pedagogical and organizational autonomy, is less well protected when school policies are based on nondenominational considerations. For instance, the school board's discretion in admitting pupils is much broader when it is based on religious criteria than when it is based on secular standards, such as purely pedagogical criteria.

The right to found a private independent school, *vrijheid van stichting*, also is strongly linked to *vrijheid van richting*, the freedom to give such a school a distinctive religious or philosophical character. Established denominations occupy a privileged position in that it is easier for their schools to meet funding criteria than it is for nondenominational private schools and those of smaller denominations.

Guarantees of the educational freedom of private organizations can be regarded as safeguarding pluralism and thereby parental choice, ensuring that parents can send their children to a school based on their preferred religious or pedagogical principles. The parental right of choice *as such* is not guaranteed explicitly in the Consitution's provisions. Nevertheless, in my view this right, being one of the main reasons for respecting the freedom of education of private schools, has the status of an unwritten constitutional principle.

More than two-thirds of all Dutch pupils go to private school. At the primary level, some 32 percent of pupils attend public school, whereas 33 percent go to a Roman Catholic school and 27 percent to a Protestant school. Some 8 percent attend other private schools, often based on a particular pedagogical approach. At the secondary level, 27 percent of pupils go to public school, whereas 28 percent go to a Roman Catholic school, 26 percent to a Protestant school, and some 19 percent to other private schools.[2] It has to be stressed, however, that a majority of Catholic and Protestant schools do not, in fact, have a strongly distinctive religious character anymore and tend to present themselves as "open" and pluralistic.

International Law

The basic structure of the Dutch binary school system is in harmony with international law. It must be emphasized that this consideration is particularly relevant for the Netherlands. Due to the Dutch monistic legal system, self-executing provisions of treaties and of decisions of international organizations—without being implemented by the legislature—may be invoked before domestic courts and may set aside conflicting statutory law, even provisions of the Dutch constitution.

Several human rights treaty provisions containing some version of the principle of equality or of the freedom of education are relevant.[3] Article 26 of the International Covenant on Civil and Political Rights (ICCPR) contains the general principle of equality. The first sentences of article 2, protocol 1, of the European Convention on Human Rights (ECHR)[4] and article 13, section 1, of the International Covenant on Economic, Social, and Cultural Rights (ICESCR)[5] guarantee the right of equal access to primary education. Article 28 of the Convention on the Rights of the Child (CRC) contains similar provisions.[6]

Article 5(e)(v) of the Convention for the Elimination of Racial Discrimination (CERD) demands that states guarantee the right of all citizens to equality in the right to education and training.[7] An instrument that specifically addresses the issue of discriminatory practices in the educational sphere is the Convention against Discrimination in Education (CDE). Article 1, section 1, of this treaty defines discrimination as "any distinction, exclusion, limitation or preference which, being based on race, colour, sex, language, religion, political or other opinion, national or social origin, economic condition or birth, has the purpose or effect of nullifying or impairing equality of treatment in education." According to article 3(b)[8] and article 4(a),[9] states must undertake to ensure that there is no discrimination in the admission of pupils to educational institutions, that primary education is free and compulsory, and that secondary education is generally available and accessible to all.

These provisions nevertheless leave enough room for the existence of denominational schools, which may select students on religious grounds. The right to establish nonstate denominational schools is implicitly guaranteed in article 2, protocol 1, of the ECHR.[10] Article 13(4) of the ICESCR explicitly guarantees the freedom to establish and direct educational institutions, including that of legal persons or entities, while article 2(b) of the CDE explicitly states that the establishment or maintenance, for religious or linguistic reasons, of separate educational systems or institutions should not be regarded as a form of discrimination within the meaning of article 1 of the convention.

Within certain limits, such schools are allowed to select students on the basis of religious affiliation. Article 26 of the ICCPR has no direct "horizontal effect"—that is, it is not as such applicable to the relation between pupils and private schools.[11] Likewise, article 2, protocol 1, of the ECHR (in conjunction with article 14) is not applicable to relations between denominational schools and pupils or parents. This does not imply that denominational schools are free to reject pupils in an arbitrary manner; however, they are free to select pupils if their policy is based on a consistent application of religious criteria.[12] Likewise, it may be assumed that the CRC does not prohibit such a policy; see article 29(2) of the CRC. Article 13(4) of the ICESCR and article 2(b) of the CDE, which explicitly guarantee the freedom to establish and direct such schools, thereby also grant the freedom to select. Finally, the CERD must also be presumed to allow rejection of pupils on religious grounds.[13]

Complementing the freedom to establish and operate a denominational school is the right of parents to choose such a school. This right is formulated in article 2, protocol 1, of the ECHR: "In the exercise of any functions which it assumes in relation to education and to teaching, the State shall respect the right of parents to ensure such education and teaching in conformity with their own religious and philosophical convictions." And according to article 13(3) of the ICESCR and article 5(1)(b) of the CDE, the state has to respect the liberty of parents to choose nonpublic schools to ensure that the religious and moral education of their children conforms with their own convictions. However, as observed above, this parental right does not imply an enforceable claim of parents to have their children admitted to the nonstate denominational school of their choice. Such a school is free not to admit pupils when its admission policy is based on a consistent application of the criteria flowing from its religious or philosophical character (*richting*).

Finally, Directive 2000/43/EC of the Council of Ministers of the European Union (June 29, 2000), which implemented the principle of equal treatment among persons irrespective of racial or ethnic origin, must be mentioned in this regard. [14] Article 2, sections 1 and 2 of this directive—in conjunction with article 3, section 1(g)—forbids direct and indirect discrimination in the field of education.[15] However, the directive does not forbid positive (or affirmative) action (article 5).[16]

Neither the council directive nor other provisions of community law prohibit the existence of denominational schools. Such a prohibition would be incompatible with articles 149 and 150 of the Treaty on the European Community, which protects the sovereignty of the states in the field of education. Also, the council directive does not prohibit differentiation on denominational grounds—for instance, in employing admission policies based on denominational criteria. That kind of differential treatment might be regarded as a form of indirect "discrimination"—in that, for example, an admission policy based on students' Christian orthodoxy may put pupils and parents of Turkish or Moroccan descent, who seldom are Christians, at a disadvantage. Nevertheless, article 2, section 2(b) of Directive 2000/43/EC allows such a selection process when it is "objectively justified by a legitimate aim and the means of achieving that aim are appropriate and necessary." It may be presumed that a consistent admission policy is regarded as an appropriate and necessary means to achieve the legitimate aim of maintaining the denominational foundation of the school.

It must be stressed that although the aforementioned provisions of human rights treaties and community law allow for the existence of separate denominational schools, they probably do not oblige the state to fund such schools.[17] There is no case law that mandates government funding for private schools. It therefore appears that the state is free to choose the Dutch system but is equally free to fund only public schools or to fund private schools only partially. Nevertheless, public funding of private schools that meet general quality standards complements freedom of education and school choice, and to some extent it is a necessary condition for exercising that freedom. Financial support of private schools by the state is crucial to realizing a pluralistic system of education; without such support these schools would be forced to charge considerable tuition fees, with the result that in general they would be available only to the well-to-do.[18] (I refer again to these norms of international and community law whenever they play a particularly relevant role in Dutch debates and court cases.)

The Autonomy of Private Schools and Its Limits

The autonomy of private schools is not absolute. Schools can never be entirely independent of the state because they perform a public task and the state has a responsibility for ensuring the quality of their performance. For that reason, the law lays down certain minimum requirements with regard to the quality of teachers and government supervision of schools. More standards—concerning, for example, the minimum number of pupils required, quality of the curriculum, administrative regulations, and conditions of employment—are applied to public authority schools as well as to private schools that are funded by the government. Those standards, of course, form constraints on the freedom of education.

The Right to Found Private Schools

As discussed, article 23 of the Dutch constitution guarantees the freedom to provide education, which includes the right of individuals and of corporate bodies to found schools (*vrijheid van stichting*). The presupposition underlying article 23 is that the freedom to establish private schools will result in a plurality of schools and thus in some kind of a "market" that gives parents and pupils freedom of choice.

The right to establish schools has practical meaning only when it also comprises a right to government funding. The current funding conditions are rather strict, and in recent years they have been changed to hinder the establishment of new schools. Today, a school board that wants to set up a new school has to show that the school will be attended by a considerable number of pupils. For primary schools, this number varies from 200 to 300 or more, depending on whether they will be set up in the country or in a major city; for secondary schools, the numbers are higher.

Another obstacle is that in general the proof that the new private school will attract the required number of pupils is that the school is linked to a specific religious or ideological philosophy (*richting*). For instance, a Christian school of a specific denomination must produce a credible prediction that in the near future the necessary number of pupils will attend that specific school. In this regard there are at least three complications:

—the religion/philosophy of the school must qualify as a distinct denomination

—if there are free places at other schools of the same denomination in the neighborhood, the number of those places will be subtracted from the predicted enrollment of the proposed school

—the predicted enrollment must be based on extrapolations of the existing situation.

These conditions demand that government officials—and ultimately, the courts—make difficult and potentially controversial decisions. They must determine, for instance, whether a certain Islamic tradition is to be regarded as a denomination, distinct from other Islamic traditions that already are recognized by the government, or whether an Evangelical school is fundamentally different from an orthodox Christian school. This is not an easy task, of course: agents of the state such as officials and judges are not particularly qualified to answer such questions, which are in essence theological. Moreover, such a role is hard to reconcile with the neutrality of the state.

Consequently, the case law in these matters is neither consistent nor well grounded. For instance, in 1992 the Council of State (*Raad van State*) decided that the Evangelical movement did not qualify as a distinct denomination.[19] In 1997[20] and 1998,[21] however, the Council of State reversed its point of view, coming to the conclusion that the movement indeed had to be regarded as a distinct denomination within Protestantism.

The difficulty of this task is enhanced by the current trend toward further religious differentiation caused by the growing number of non-Christian believers in the Netherlands. These days, the administration and the courts have to figure out whether different Islamic or Hindu traditions count as separate denominations. (The Council of State currently accepts the view that within Islam there is at least one liberal and one orthodox denomination.)[22] Further differentiation in the future seems evident: within Protestantism, several different persuasions have been recognized.

Another problem is posed by the legal rules concerning the enrollment prediction that the board of the new school has to produce, which in general is not based on an inquiry into the actual preferences of parents (direct measurement) but on extrapolation from the current sitation (indirect measurement). For instance, if 5 percent of all the pupils in a municipality currently attend Islamic schools, it is presumed that in the future 5 percent of new pupils will be sent to such schools. Only in exceptional circumstances may one also use the results of direct measurement, and the school board has to organize and finance such studies.[23]

It is clear that this system is disadvantageous to religions such as Islam and Hinduism. Court cases in which adherents of such religions demanded that it become easier for them to found schools—for instance, by allowing them more general use of the results of direct measurement or by allowing indrect measurements based on conditions within only a part of the municipality—have until now failed because of the strict wording of the law.[24]

After a debate in Parliament in 1998, the undersecretary of state promised to allow more frequent use of direct measurement. But that did not end the controversy. Both methods currently employed, direct and indirect measurement, are based on the assumption that the choice of a school is motivated exclusively by religion or world view. And both assume that the state is able and entitled to decide whether one religious tradition is "really" different from another. These assumptions are not easily defended. Most parents and pupils today base their choice of school not on religious but on pedagogical considerations ("This is a Montessori school"); on didactical concerns ("This school takes into account the individual abilities of the pupils"); and on practical arguments ("This school is near our home" or "All of our child's friends are going to this school"). Moreover, it is doubtful whether the state is capable of adequately deciding theological questions such as whether one religious persuasion is essentially different from another.

For these reasons, the Education Council (Onderwijsraad)—the main adviser of the Minister of Education—has proposed to return to the former system of "parental declarations," in which it was sufficient that the required number of parents officially state that they would send their children to the new school. In such a system, only quantity counts; the motive—whether religious, pedagogical, or pragmatic—is irrelevant.[25] Successive governments have reacted in a positive vein, but a bill has not yet been passed.[26]

Regardless of whether the system changes, a rise in the number of Islamic schools may be expected. There are now some forty Islamic schools, including two secondary schools, in the Netherlands. Of the 130,000 Muslim pupils who attend primary schools, only 8,000 attend Islamic schools, but every year a few new Islamic schools are set up. Considering demographics alone, a continuing increase in the number of these schools seems obvious.

It has to be stressed that it would be unconstitutional to stop this trend on the grounds that Islamic schools are counterproductive because they tend to be "black" schools or because they recruit their pupils only from ethnic and cultural minority groups. Furthermore, it may be that such schools are instilling in their students values that are not fully in line with the basic principles of Western society, such as individualistic humanism and the separation of church and state. Even if this last allegation was true, as long as these schools fulfill the legal criteria—minimum requirements—they have the constitutional right to funding.

Nevertheless, at the end of 2003 the Liberal Party (one of the parties in the current administration) began a frontal attack on Islamic schools, citing the growing division between "white" and "black" schools. Time and again members of this party have stated that mono-ethnic schools—Islamic schools in particular—impede the integration of immigrant children. In November 2003 a Liberal member of Parliament, Hirsi Ali, introduced a motion asking the government to explore the legal possibility of putting additional conditions on funding for new religious schools, such as requiring that they not be mono-ethnic and that the native tongue of the majority of their pupils be Dutch.[27] The motion was rejected, because such requirements would be applied only to religious schools and not to neutral private and public schools, contravening the equality principle in article 23 of the Constitution.

However, this debate probably will continue for a long time. In December 2003 the Liberal secretary of state, Gerrit Zalm, rephrased the demands of his party, suggesting that all newly founded schools with too many pupils with learning disabilities should not receive government funding. This proposal—although not prima facie unconstitutional—nevertheless is problematic. First there is a practical problem in that it in fact prohibits the founding of (all) new schools in urban areas where mainly ethnic and cultural minority groups—and thus a concentration of pupils with learning disadvantages—live. Another problem is that in consequence, no new Islamic schools can be established—which is, of course, one of the main reasons behind the Zalm proposal. As mentioned, Islamic schools recruit their pupils primarily from immigrant children, who often have learning disadvantages; all of them are "black" schools. Thus an ostensibly neutral criterion in fact amounts to differential treatment of Islamic schools. Such differential treatment is not always prohibited; however, it should be justified by strong arguments. The question therefore is whether a restriction of the freedom to establish a school that primarily affects religious minorities can be justified. Until now, such a justification has not appeared, and the Zalm proposal is not (yet) backed by a parliamentary majority.[28] However, in a policy document of April 2004, the cabinet accepted this proposal and will introduce a bill to implement it. [29]

Recruitment of Personnel

The government has the right to examine the competence and moral integrity of teachers in designated schools. The Primary Education Act and the Secondary Education Act require that to be appointed a teacher, in public as well as private schools, one must have certain degrees and certificates attesting to one's competence and good conduct. The significance of the requirement that all schools employ certified teachers should not be underestimated. For instance, until now the worries concerning anti-integration tendencies in Muslim schools have seemed to be exaggerated. Due to the lack of qualified Muslims, the average teacher at an Islamic school, to put it bluntly, is a white, middle-aged Dutch woman, interested in Islam but surely not a Muslim. When a school board consisting of conservative Muslims tries to impose strict criteria on its personnel, it often escalates into a labor conflict, resulting in the departure of teachers who are unwilling to submit to such criteria.[30]

Personnel at public schools are civil servants. That implies that there must be equal access to the jobs in this sector (articles 1 and 3 of the Constitution), and these schools therefore are not allowed to select on the basis of denominational criteria.[31] These constitutional provisions concern state institutions such as public authority schools and are not directly applicable to private, denominational schools governed by corporate bodies under civil law. Denominational schools can claim their right to freedom of education and the freedom to express in their curriculum their own religious and philosophical views on humankind and society—rights that also imply the freedom to select teachers on the basis of criteria derived from those views. This provision should be interpreted broadly; it also includes the right to appoint school management and other nonteaching staff and the right to dismiss them. In sum, private denominational schools can ask their employees to commit themselves to a particular religious or philosphical mission.

In 1994, the General Equal Treatment Act (*Algemene Wet Gelijke Behandeling*, or AWGB) came into force. This act endeavors to give "more substance" and efficacy to the general, broad principle of equality expressed in article 1 of the Dutch constitution. Whereas article 1 is not directly applicable to private denominational schools, the AWGB is not only applicable to "vertical" relations between government and citizens but also to "horizontal" relations—relations between individuals and private organizations such as denominational schools.

The basic principle underlying the AWGB is that differential treatment on certain grounds—political persuasion, race, sex, religion, and so on—is prohibited in certain areas, such as work, commercial transactions, and education. Article 5, section 1, of the AWGB, for instance, prohibits differential treatment on these grounds in the case of—*inter alia*—offer and termination of a labor contract and appointment and termination of a civil servant; it also prohibits establishing differential terms of employment on these grounds. According to article 5, section 2, the first section of that article does not take away the freedom of a denominational school to set requirements for a position that the school may regard as necessary to realize its religious or philosophical principles. Such requirements may not lead to differential treatment based on the *sole fact* of political persuasion, race, sex, nationality, sexual orientation, or civil status, but the AWGB does permit differential treatment solely on the basis of religious grounds. The AWGB thus creates a statutory framework that tries to strike a balance between equality and freedom.

There is a quasi-judicial Committee for Equal Treatment (Commissie Gelijke Behandeling, or CGB), which can, on written request, examine a case to determine whether there has been differential treatment prohibited by the AWGB and give a legally nonbinding judgment. In applying the AWGB, the courts do not feel themselves to be bound by the judgments of the CGB, but they have tended to regard them as important guidelines.

When the AWGB came into force, many expected it to severely limit the discretionary power of the boards of denominational schools. That has not been the case. A potential *locus classicus*, much debated in Parliament, concerning whether a Christian school may refuse to hire a teacher because of his or her sexual orientation, has until now never been decided by a court. And until now the CGB has dealt with the refusal of a Christian school to appoint a homosexual teacher only once.[32] The CGB, in discussing the question of whether the requirements leading to his exclusion were necessary to realize the principles underlying the school, stressed that it was primarily up to the school board to answer that question; the CGB had to examine only whether the board had decided on reasonable grounds. Nevertheless, the CGB used as a criterion whether there was "an objective bond between the realization of the religious views of the school and the requirements." These requirements had to be based on a consistent policy, necessarily flowing from the denominational principles of the school. It was up to the school board to explain this policy. Because the board had not given the candidate the opportunity to express his views, it had to be presumed that the board's rejection was based solely on the fact of his homosexuality and therefore was incompatible with the AWGB.

In other cases, the CGB has dealt with the question of whether a school board was justified on the basis of article 5(2) to dismiss or refuse personnel who no longer fulfilled the denominational criteria. In general, it concluded that the school board was justified because it consistently applied those criteria and was able to show that they were linked to the religious identity of the school.[33] The consistency criterion is probably derived from the Dutch supreme court decision in the *Maimonides* case, discussed below.

Admission of Pupils

Within certain legal limits, private denominational schools have the right to refuse to admit pupils on the basis of their own standards. When the refusal is grounded on denominational criteria, this right is protected by *vrijheid van richting*, the freedom of education guaranteed by the Constitution. In the famous *Maimonides* case (1988) the Hoge Raad (Supreme Ccourt), the highest civil court, ruled that an orthodox Jewish school could exclude a boy from a liberal Jewish family because its decision was based on the consistent application of school policy and because that policy was directly related to the religious foundation of the school.[34] Due to legal technicalities, the court did not decide the other core issue, which was whether this orthodox Jewish school's application of religion-based criteria linked to ethnicity should be regarded as racial discrimination. In this case, the school regarded even nonbelievers as Jewish when they had a Jewish mother (the mother being Jewish when she is the child of a Jewish mother, regardless of whether she adheres to Judaism).

The General Equal Treatment Act (AWGB) also is relevant. Article 7, section 1, of the AWGB prohibits differential treatment when "offering goods and services," which includes education. Article 7, section 2, contains an exception (similar to that in article 5, section 2) for denominational schools. Just as the AWGB gives denominational schools the freedom to use criteria derived from their religious "mission" to select their teachers, it also allows them to decide which pupils they admit on the basis of such criteria, so long as they do so in a consistent manner. This means that the *Maimonides* case would probably be decided in the same way under the AWGB as it was in 1988. For instance, in a recent case the CGB ruled that a Roman Catholic school could expel female Muslim students because they began wearing head scarves: this school could rely on a strict policy forbidding—on denominational grounds—clothing with non-Christian connotations.[35] However, if a denominational school applies denominational criteria only on a case-by-case basis, it cannot appeal to article 7, section 2, of the AWGB, and often it will be in breach of article 7, section 1.

Private denominational schools also have the authority—guaranteed by the *vrijheid van inrichting*—to apply admission criteria that are not linked to their religious identity. For instance, they can refuse pupils on practical grounds (the school is full); for pedagogical reasons (the schools does not have the specialized teachers that handicapped pupils need); or for reasons of "public order" (students who wear clothing that suggests Nazi sympathies can be refused because of possible conflicts with students from ethnic minorities).[36]

However, this freedom is less well protected than the freedom to select on denominational grounds. In particular, when the selection process leads to refusal on the basis of a criterion that affects mostly religious or ethnic minority pupils, the school board has to show a compelling legitimate interest in applying this criterion. In my opinion, a mistake was made in this respect in a judgment concerning the expulsion from a Catholic school of two Muslim girls who refused to attend swimming lessons because of their religious beliefs. The Court of Appeals in Den Bosch ruled this expulsion lawful based on freedom of education: "The school has referred to their constitutionally guaranteed freedom of education. This freedom comprises in any case the freedom to regard swimming lessons as a necessary part of the curriculum; in this regard the board is also free to teach this in 'mixed' classes, and to appoint male teachers."[37] The Court of Appeals here allowed the school board a margin of discretion that is too wide: the board's decision was not based on a religious view (*vrijheid van richting*)—the decision was not grounded on the Catholic identity of the school—but merely upon its general pedagogical freedom (*vrijheid van inrichting*), which is less well protected than its religious autonomy.

In another case, a court of appeals quite correctly rejected the admissions rule of a school for hotel management that admitted an equal number of male and female students, thereby rejecting proportionally more female than male candidates.[38] The educational philosophy of the school was not based on denominational principles but on the aim to adequately prepare students for management positions within the hotel sector. Requiring an equal male-to-female ratio was not regarded as necessary to fulfill the pedagogical mission of the school.

Potentially far-reaching was a case in 2000 in which the CGB (the Committee for Equal Treatment) ruled that public and private schools that for pedagogical reasons denied a Muslim girl the freedom to follow lessons because she wore a chador—a veil covering the entire face except for the eyes—were in breach of the AWGB in that this policy in fact amounted to discrimination on the ground of religion.[39] According to the CGB, in this case the school board had not proven that this hindered the eductional process significantly. However, in March 2003, the CGB found that such a policy was not discriminatory. Although the committee still maintained that this policy primarily affected Muslim girls, it was justified on pedagogical grounds. The school board had demonstrated sufficiently that the chador hindered the educational process and was not compatible with the requirements of the types of jobs for which the students were educated.[40]

Content and Quality of Education

The autonomy of private schools is restricted by numerous qualitative and quantitative standards relating to the educational process in schools and the results that they are required to produce. The government and the Minister of Education have formulated many funding conditions, especially for primary and secondary education, relating to school type, teacher qualifications, compulsory and optional courses, minimum and maximum number of lessons, and (in secondary education) the examination syllabus and the national examinations. In sum, to a large extent schools are bound by a national curriculum and national quality standards.

The Primary Education Targets Decree describes, for every subject, the level of knowledge and understanding and the skills that pupils should have attained when they have finished their primary education. At the end of primary school, instead of certificates or diplomas, pupils receive a school report showing their progress at school and their learning potential.

Secondary schooling begins with a period of basic secondary education that lasts from two to four years. Its goal is to give pupils a broad, general education. Basic secondary education consists of no less than fifteen compulsory subjects, including technical subjects, information sciences, and "self-sufficiency" (social and practical skills). Attainment targets have been established for the basic secondary education subjects that lay out the minimum level of knowledge and understanding and the skills that students should attain during this time.

The second phase in secondary education was fundamentally changed in 1999–2000. In the second phase, pupils in schools for pre-university education and senior general secondary education have to choose among four "profiles," each of which comprises a range of subjects consisting of three components: a common component, which is similar for all profiles and is obligatory (about 45 percent); a profile component, which is obligatory for the profile in question and which is especially important for transfer to further education (some 30 percent); and an elective component (20 to 25 percent), which allows pupils to choose among the subjects taught at the school.[41] The profiles are Nature and Technology, Nature and Health, Economics and Society, and Culture and Society. This change is linked to a new form of secondary education, the concept of "learning to learn." This project, which has been given the name Study House, allows schools to differentiate between classroom lessons and time during which pupils study on their own.

Half of the examination is determined by the local school board; the other half is a national examination. The average of the marks for the local and the national exam is the final grade.

A more or less similar restructuring has taken place in the second phase of secondary education in schools for general secondary education and preparatory vocational education. These schools have to offer "learning routes:" the theoretical route, the professionally oriented learning route, and the "mixed" learning route. The education offered in each route is divided into four sectors, among which the pupil has to choose: Technology, Care and Welfare, Economics, and Agriculture. In addition to these learning routes and sectors, there also are new examination programs that have been set up by the government.

The Primary and the Secondary Education Acts also contain procedural norms. For instance, the school boards are obliged to develop a policy to increase the quality of education. A school board has to publish a school plan, the basic document of the school's education philosophy, in which the board explains how it plans to achieve the standards set by law and to realize its own pedagogical aims. Furthermore, school boards must publish a school guide, in which they explain to parents and pupils what their educational aims are and how they are going to achieve them.

The legal bases for these quality standards are laid down in article 23, sections 2, 5, and 6, of the Constitution. These provisions declare, on one hand, that the state is authorized to formulate such standards; on the other hand, they require that in doing so, freedom of education should not be hindered.

Freedom of education is protected in several ways. Article 9 of the Primary Education Act and article 11(a) of the Secondary Education Act give the board of a denominational school the right to substitute their own targets for the government attainment targets if they can demonstrate that this is necessary from the point of view of the religion or world view that forms their basic philosophy. Furthermore, article 25 and article 29(6) of the Secondary Education Act give the Minister of Education the authority to allow schools to depart from provisions concerning the curriculum and examination depending on the specific characteristics of their educational program.

This does not mean that there is in fact a great divergence in standards. Only a few school boards have opted for their own attainment targets, and then only in "sensitive" subjects like history and biology. Furthermore, these substitute targets must be equivalent in terms of quality. This implies that a request to drop teaching and examining a vital theory in biology or physics— for example, the theory of evolution—will be refused, because the alternative—for example, creationism—cannot be regarded as equivalent.[42] For the same reason, the Education Council rejected the claim of ten anthroposophic schools, which in fact denied the right of the state to formulate general attainment targets and were willing to accept only process-oriented criteria.[43]

Another guarantee of the freedom of education is the great reluctance in the Netherlands to prescribe moral standards on behalf of the state. There is a general dislike of the state as teacher or as inculcator of virtue. This dislike has its legal foundation in the constitutional safeguard of educational freedom, but it also reflects the feeling that government should not moralize.

It is true that the education acts and the education decrees contain general aims with moral content. For instance, article 8, section 3, of the Primary Education Act and article 17 of the Secondary Education Act demand that schools take into account that pupils "grow up in a multicultural society." These provisions seem to imply that schools should instill in their students a positive attitude toward this multicultural society. The attainment targets likewise contain provisions that call on schools to stimulate their pupils to become responsible, tolerant citizens. But these provisions are vague and imprecise. They address the pupil as an ideal future citizen, consumer, and participant in society, but they do not specifically address the concrete civic virtues and social capacities that young people will need to be good participants in civil society.[44]

It is also true that although they do not specifically address the educational system, general laws such as the Criminal Code and the Civil Code, as well as public order requirements, are applicable to schools. This implies that denominational schools are not free to express racist or antidemocratic opinions, even if such opinions form part of their religion or philosophy. But these prohibitions are only negative minimum norms that describe what should *not* be done or said; they do not specifically identify the positive values that should be actively promoted.

This rejection of the state as moral educator is also reflected in the absence of a separate subject like citizenship education. Citizenship is a subject in the history courses, but it is treated from a theoretical or conceptual point of view, not with an eye to cultivating civic attitudes. There is nothing in the Dutch curriculum like *education civique* in France or citizenship education in England and Wales.[45]

It should be stressed, however, that in recent years a sense of alarm and urgency has arisen concerning the failing integration of religious and ethnic minorities in Dutch society. For a long time it was assumed that integration would be realized within one generation, but that has not been the case. The school results of children of the second and third generation—children and grandchildren of the guest workers that came to the Netherlands in the 1960s and 1970s—are still very much lower than the results of average middle-class Dutch children.[46] This "education gap" is to a large extent transmitted to the next generation because a majority of immigrants marry an uneducated person from their home country (such as Turkey and Morocco). There also are worries about whether Islamic schools foster separatism and hostility. It is suspected that sometimes those schools use religion courses to disseminate anti-Western propaganda. And finally, there are more general fears that Dutch society is disintegrating. In response to these developments, the state will now supervise religion courses (until recently the Education Inspectorate refrained from doing so on the grounds of freedom of education); schools will be urged to promote civic values and social cohesion more actively; and family reunification will be restricted through language proficiency requirements, discussed in greater detail below.

Supervision of primary and secondary public and private schools is the core business of the Education Inspectorate, acting under the authority of the Minister of Education. The tasks of the inspectorate are defined in the Education Inspection Act, which also requires that school boards, teachers, and school management allow the inspectorate access to the school and provide all requested information. The Education Inspectorate has the following tasks:

—Evaluate the quality of education by checking compliance with statutory standards and with other aspects of quality (supervision)

—Promote the development of education through consultation with school boards, school staffs, and regional or local government (promotion)

—Report to and advise the Minister of Education, either at his or her request or on its own initiative (reporting).

Supervision by the inspectorate concerns not only compliance with legally binding provisions such as attainment targets and examination requirements but also with other aspects of educational quality, such as the pedagogical climate and the school "atmosphere." The inspectorate formulates parameters that define these other aspects of quality. These parameters function as guidelines but are not legally binding and do not include funding conditions; nevertheless, the inspectorate is authorized to apply these parameters in evaluating primary and secondary schools. All evaluations are published on the inspectorate's website.[47] In my opinion, the inspectorate is thus allowed to interfere with pedagogical autonomy, even though article 4, section 1, of the Education Inspection Act states that the inspectorate must fulfill its tasks with due observance of the freedom of education.

Finally, there is one other trend yet to be mentioned. Increasingly, parents and students think of themselves and act as "private quality controllers" by adopting the role of critical, well-informed consumers. School plans, school guides, complaint procedures, education contracts, and evaluations of the inspectorate, among other things, give substance to this role. The school board has to publish its plans. The inspectorate now publishes the results of primary and secondary schools, which are compared with each other in quality charts and transformed by newspapers into ranking lists. Sometimes schools make contracts with their "consumers." Finally, since 1998 parents and pupils have a right to file complaints—about poor quality, for example—before an independent commission.

The prevailing presumption is that by strengthening the role of the "consumer" there will be more competition among schools, which in turn will lead to a better "product"—education of a higher quality. It is not yet clear whether this presumption is correct or whether there are no negative side effects, such as stricter selection of pupils by prestigious schools.

Organization

Private schools have the freedom to organize their internal affairs as they see fit. The daily management of primary and secondary schools may be determined by the head teacher, the head of the school, or the school management. The ultimate responsibility remains with the school board itself. The tasks and responsibilities of the boards of public and private schools are very similar. The school board has decisionmaking power concerning the curriculum, choice of teaching materials, school plan, appointment and dismissal of teachers and nonteaching staff, admission and expulsion of pupils, use of school buildings, and management of financial resources.

Freedom of organization applies to both public and private schools but to a different degree. The state may not interfere in private schools when it comes to denominational matters. When it comes to nondenominational matters, the situation of both types of schools is fairly similar. In particular, the state must be cautious not to interfere too much with the pedagogical autonomy of public and private schools.

As stated above, the internal affairs and thus the rules determining the composition of the board of a private school are laid down in its own regulations. In general, a school board consists primarily of parents, although due to the trend toward larger organizations school boards have been in some cases professionalized, leaving parents merely a role on a supervisory board. Nevertheless, many private schools still are able to realize a significant role for parents in the governance of their school and to create a sense of community and commitment. This may have different results. To the extent that unity and commitment lead to involvement in society at large, such schools definitely play an integrative civic role. On the other hand, the stress may be placed on internal unity and adherence to values that lead to voluntary religious and cultural apartheid, a claim made especially against Islamic and orthodox Christian schools.

Under the Education Participation Act of 1992, every primary and secondary school is required to set up a participation council consisting of an equal number of elected staff members and parents or pupils. The participation council has a number of general rights, including the right to give advice or consent and to make proposals, depending on the matter to be decided. In the 1990s, there was much debate on whether the law should prescribe that a majority of the members of the boards of private schools should be parents. The government—the second cabinet (1998–2002), led by prime minister Wim Kok—finally decided that this is as yet unnecessary because there is already sufficient parental involvement in these schools.[48]

Fundamental Issues

Various important issues confront the Dutch educational system. The main question is how the state can implement the principle of equality and the ideals of good citizenship in a multicultural and multiethnic society while respecting educational freedom. These principles—equality, good citizenship, freedom of education, freedom of choice—may strengthen one another; however, they also sometimes contradict one another. It is an important task of the state—but also, to an extent, an important task of schools—to try to reach an optimum point, at which all of those principles are respected as far as possible. But such harmony cannot always be realized, and in that case which principle should prevail over others must be decided.

The Common (State) School System versus a Pluralist School System

A recurrent discussion in Dutch politics is whether the state should fund only the "common," secular state school, the public authority school that provides a neutral curriculum and is equally accessible to all. The argument behind the plea for the common school is that in a society as religiously and culturally differentiated as Dutch society, it is necessary to use the school as an instrument for integration, teaching children of different ethnic, religious, social, and cultural backgrounds to live peacefully together and to respect each other; instilling in them the basic values of democracy and the rule of law; and creating equal opportunities for all. This argument proposes to move the Dutch system in the direction of the American system of common (public) schooling.

Critics of the dual school system argue that the government can and should fund only common state schools. Authorities should expect schools to contribute to eliminating social inequality and religious and cultural apartheid as a precondition for the full participation of all citizens in society. Because private, and especially denominational, schools are established to perpetuate rather than to diminish group loyalties, they cannot adequately contribute to cultural integration; therefore they should give up their distinctive character. When they do, they thereby lose their right to independence from the public school system and should simply be taken over by the state.[49]

This argument puts denominational schools in an impossible position. It is asserted that as long as they are truly distinctive and religious, they cannot fulfill their integrative tasks and should therefore not be funded by the government. But as soon as they begin to fulfill these tasks and contribute to social integration, they give up their religious characteristics and can claim no reason to stay outside the state school system.

This proposal, though attractive to some politicians, is problematic.[50] According to provisions of the various international documents described earlier, individuals, groups, and legal persons have the right to freedom of education, by which they are free to establish private schools and to base their curriculum on a distinct religion, philosophy, or pedagogical theory. It is true that from this freedom they cannot derive an enforceable claim to public funding. Nevertheless, such funding is in fact a necessary precondition for effective educational freedom. Without the financial support of the state there would be only a few independent schools for the elite, who can afford to pay for them. Most parents would be deprived of a real opportunity to choose a school of their liking. Finally, it would destroy one of the main virtues of the Dutch school system—its openness to private initiatives, which made it possible for the majority of school board members to consist of parents.

The plea for the common state school is inspired by the presumption that a pluralist school system in fact leads to divisions among schools along ethnic and religious lines. It has to be admitted that freedom of education has as a side effect the existence of mono-religious and mono-ethnic schools. However, a large majority of denominational schools (mainstream Catholic and Protestant schools) do not select on the basis of religion, and only a limited number of schools do so consistently. It should be stressed once again that a denominational school that is not consistent in its selection criteria thereby forfeits its right to refuse pupils on religious grounds.

Furthermore, it is true that for some fifteen years now there has been a trend toward a division between "white" and "black" schools. It is debatable, however, whether the Dutch school system is the primary cause of this trend, which seems to a larger extent to merely reflect demographic and housing patterns. Such trends also can be found in countries where the model of a common secular school system is strongly favored, as in the United States and France. In general, a school in a "black" neighborhood is "black," whereas a school in a "white" neighborhood is "white," *irrespective* of whether it is a public authority school or a private denominational school.[51]

The debate concerning the legitimacy of the dualistic school system has recently been triggered by the growth in the number of Islamic schools and the suspicion that they are financed and influenced by government organizations from Muslim countries to resist integration and to propagate fundamentalism. But recent reports on this issue by the Netherlands's Internal Security Service and the Education Inspectorate do not support those suspicions.[52] The debates in Parliament nevertheless made clear that all schools and all courses should remain within the boundaries of the law and should respect the principles of democracy and rule of law.[53] As a result, even religious courses will now be supervised by the Education Inspectorate.[54]

It should be stressed once more that freedom of education does not confer absolute educational autonomy. For instance, the state is allowed to establish certain minimum educational standards. These standards may also prescribe that all lessons—including religious instruction in Islamic and other denominational schools—take into account minimum standards of tolerance and respect for other views.[55] However, the state is not allowed to lay down a detailed ethical and pedagogical curriculum to which all schools must adhere. Freedom of education allows only for minimum requirements, leaving denominational schools a fair amount of freedom to define their own religious, moral, and philosophical views and their own educational goals.

It is still unclear to what extent government in the Netherlands has the authority to prescribe positive educational standards in terms of social cohesion, civic virtues, and the like. The Education Council has advised the government to take steps to strengthen the integrative functions of schools, recommending that the education acts and attainment targets should explicitly mention the active promotion of citizenship as one of the key goals of education.[56] In a policy document of April 2004, the government endorsed the recommendation and announced that it would introduce a bill to that effect.[57]

It should also be noted that a system in which only public authority schools are funded may lead to the growth of private commercial schools—at this moment the number of such schools is negligible—thereby creating a division between private schools for the rich and public schools for the rest. Of course, there is some division along socioeconomic lines in the current system. But it is probable that government funding of private schools minimizes the socioeconomic divide and prevents it from getting worse. Private government-funded schools must be free: admittance may not depend on the financial contributions of the parents.

Finally, it seems to me that the critics of the Dutch school system create a false opposition. It is not true that a denominational school is by definition unable to fulfill civic integrative functions. Indeed, I believe that many denominational schools are able to create a sense of community based on Christian humanism, characterized by an open atmosphere in which civic virtues can effectively be cultivated. But maybe this is a subjective observation. Some data suggest better results from Christian schools than non-Christian schools in this respect, although they are not conclusive. Unfortunately, there are as yet but few objective empirical studies on the relation between integration and denomination.[58]

The Status of the Public School

Given their level of prosperity, all Western states are obliged to provide at least free primary education and free secondary education (at the first stage) to all (article 13(2)(a) and (b) of the ICESCR; article 4(a) of the CDE). In my opinion, these human rights provisions, requiring free primary and first-stage secondary education for everyone, presume that there is a neutral, pluriform public school accessible to all who opt for nondenominational education. To guarantee that there is real freedom to choose such schools, the state must fully fund them. These fundamental guarantees are explicitly formulated in article 23, sections 3, 4, and 7, of the Dutch constitution.

In order to fulfill its function as "the school for all," public school education must be religiously neutral. A public authority school must not have a specific denomination or philosophy; nor may it select teachers and pupils on the basis of their religion or lack of it. For instance, a public school may not reject a Muslim teacher on the grounds of his or her belief. Recently, however, the question has been raised of whether, on the basis of the neutrality principle, Muslim women explicitly expressing their faith by the clothing they wear should be allowed to teach in public schools. In two cases the CGB, monitoring the observance of the General Equal Treatment Act (AWGB), had to rule on regulations forbidding head scarves.[59] They concerned Muslim women who were prevented from teaching at public authority schools because their head scarves were regarded as symbols of faith that were incompatible with the neutrality clause in the Constitution. The commission decided in both cases that the decision did not comply with the AWGB. The mere fact that these women wore clothing expressing their religious beliefs did not justify the conclusion that the content of their lessons would not be neutral. The school boards had not given them the opportunity to express themselves on this matter; therefore, the decisions were presumed to be based on a rejection of the religious views implicitly expressed by the teachers' head scarves. Although these decisions are in accordance with the AWGB, they are nevertheless problematic. One should keep in mind that quite often liberal Turkish and Moroccan parents favor the public school in order to be sure that their children will not be exposed to religious influences.

How far should public authority schools go to accommodate religious minorities? Should they allow prayers, religious ceremonies, and the like? The CGB has decided that a public authority school is neither obliged to provide—nor prohibited from providing—Muslim pupils with a classroom to enable them to pray during breaks.[60] But many aspects of this question—to what extent the public school should be allowed or required to give room to religion—remain unanswered.

There are other tendencies that make this question relevant. Recent developments in law and policy promote cooperation between public and private education. Since 1996 it has been possible for public and private schools to be placed under one school board. Furthermore, a change of section 4 of article 23 of the Constitution has been proposed to create a legal basis for a cooperative structure, the so-called *samenwerkingsschool*, a school that provides for public authority education *and* private denominational education within the same organization.[61] This construct is regarded as a solution for areas in which a public or private school faces closing because it does not have enough pupils. By merging into a *samenwerkingsschool,* both types of school can survive.

This constitutional change undoubtedly will blur the distinction between public neutral education and private denominational education. Whether this will in time lead to a common pluralistic school system is debatable. I believe that the *samenwerkingsschool* will remain an exception to the binary rule that public education is provided in a public school and private denominational education is provided in a private denominational school.

Forced Desegregation, Freedom of Education, and Freedom of Choice

In the last twenty-five years, the ethnic and cultural composition of the Dutch population has changed considerably. The number of so-called ethnic minorities—persons coming from countries other than those of western Europe and North America, as well as their children—has risen continuously. In 1999 they numbered approximately 1.35 million of 16 million residents. The four largest ethnic minority groups—Turkish, Moroccan, Surinamese, Antillean—together comprise some 1 million persons. In recent years there also has been substantial growth of the number of asylum seekers from Asia and Africa, notably from Afghanistan, Iran, Iraq, Somalia, and Sri Lanka.

These demographic changes obviously have had an impact on the composition of the school population. The percentage of ethnic minority children in primary schools has risen from 11 percent in 1990 to 14 percent in 1998. Furthermore, the number of so-called black schools has also risen considerably. In 1999, 7 percent of primary schools were "black" schools (500 of 7,100)—that is, schools in which more than 50 percent of students are from ethnic minorities and because of that may be presumed to have learning disadvantages. These schools therefore require additional funding.[62]

A further consequence has been a moderate growth in the number of denominational schools based on a minority religion, especially Islamic schools. At the moment there are approximately forty Islamic schools, including two Islamic secondary schools, in the Netherlands, and that number is expected to rise sharply in the next few years. These developments have created a lively political debate about whether the trend toward further segregation between "white schools" and "black schools" should be countered by legal measures. There are several arguments about why this trend is problematic.

One argument often made is that Islamic schools, which are always "black" schools, are based on a religion that is to a certain extent opposed to

Western society and liberal values and that in general they are detrimental to integration. In my opinion, these schools—as long as they fulfill the funding criteria, operate within the limits of the law, and respect the fundamental values of democracy and the rule of law—have a constitutional right to exist. Whether they impede the integration process is difficult to say. However, it may be useful—as the Education Council has proposed and the government has endorsed—to define furtherance of civic virtues and citizenship more explicitly as a basic goal of primary and secondary education.[63]

Two other arguments seem to be more plausible. One argument is that it is surely more difficult to realize a minimum of communication and social integration between "black" and "white" children in ethnically segregated schools than it is when the school population consists of an adequate ethnic mix.[64] Given such a mix, it is more probable that Dutch will be the main language spoken on the playground and that friendships between "black" and "white" children will develop. In addition, there is some empirical evidence that pupils with learning disadvantages benefit from the presence of pupils without such disadvantages.

One way to counter the tendency toward segregation is to enact a government policy requiring schools to achieve an adequate mix of "black" and "white" pupils. In my opinion, however, such a policy must be voluntary to be compatible with human rights provisions.[65] One has to keep in mind that the existence of "white" and "black"schools is to a large extent due to the ethnic composition of the district in which the school is located. Countering segregating tendencies by imposing quotas and the like—a solution that would certainly lead to the rejection of some pupils merely because they would disturb the required ethnic mix—probably would be regarded as a breach of the principle of parental choice and furthermore would be incompatible with the constitutional requirement that the public school system has to admit every child. And allocating pupils to a specific school also would violate the rights of parents as guaranteed in article 2, protocol 1, of the ECHR. Finally, when based on ethnic quotas, such a policy would contravene the AWGB and international instruments; a quota system, however well intentioned, would amount to prohibited direct differentiation based on racial or ethnic origin.[66] It is true that the CERD and Directive 2000/43/EC of the Council of Ministers of the European Union allow for compensating measures favoring ethnic minorities in order to realize full equality, because this qualifies as positive action. But a compulsory mixing policy would quite often be *disadvantageous* to individuals belonging to ethnic minorities, since it would frequently hinder their choices.[67] It should be observed that Moroccan and Turkish parents quite often prefer a nearby "black" school, not only for practical reasons but also because such schools specialize in teaching minority children and receive more funding than the average school.[68]

Another option put forward is to strengthen the position of pupils and their parents.[69] Quite often it is assumed that denominational schools abuse their right to select in order to refuse minority children, leading to the concentration of a disproportionate number of these children in public authority schools, which do not have that right. By giving parents a legal claim to have their children admitted to the school of their choice, a desirable mix will come about, or so it is supposed.

I have serious doubts about such a policy. First, unconditional freedom of choice would be inconsistent with freedom of education—the right to select on denominational grounds—which is enshrined in article 23 of the Dutch constitution. It is true that this right may be restricted. But a legal measure that denies that right even to the small number of denominational schools that consistently apply religious criteria when admitting pupils would surely be unconstitutional; it would surely be incompatible with freedom of education as it is understood in the Netherlands.

Furthermore, proponents of this option seem to believe that strengthening parental choice would result in an adequate ethnic mix. That belief is incorrect. The existence of segregation between "white" and "black" schools is largely the result of housing patterns and not of school boards' efforts to frustrate parental choice; it is in part also the result of parental choice, so-called white flight, and the preference of large numbers of Moroccan and Turkish parents for public and Islamic schools in their neighborhood that has led to segregation.[70]

Maybe a more effective course of action would be to strengthen local education authorities. According to the historical interpretation of sections 5 through 7 of article 23 of the Constitution, which until recently was predominant, the educational system had to be regulated and funded exclusively by the central government. That was thought to be necessary to guarantee the equal status of private and public authority schools and to ensure a sufficient level of quality and adequate funding. However, under the Socialist-Liberal governments that were in power from 1994 to 2002, that interpretation was modified. The view currently prevailing, which is based on a "dynamic" reading of the Constitution, is that regulation and funding of primary and secondary education may, to a certain extent, be left to decentralized authorities, especially to municipal councils.

Since 1997, local authorities have been responsible for planning, coordinating, and funding school buildings and facilities.[71] Furthermore, in 1998 an act of Parliament came into force that assigned to local authorities the power to determine how schools spend the funds they have received to assist pupils with educational disadvantages.[72]

This policy of delegating vital powers to municipalities was inspired by the idea that it is necessary to take an integral approach to related problems—socioeconomic inequality, segregation of cultural minorities, juvenile delinquency, early school leaving—and to coordinate youth and welfare work, job placement assistance, and education. Coordination could not take place at the level of the central government or the school; it was best realized by local government.[73] Especially in the major cities, local authorities are worried by the tendency toward "ghettoization" and hope that educational policies, such as strengthening the community-building capacities of "magnet schools," may counter that tendency.

Recently the Education Council has suggested that the cabinet and Parliament discuss the question of local desegregation policies.[74] It may be that there are sufficient reasons to spread pupils across all schools within the municipality. The Education Council stipulated, however, that any coercive arrangement should

—explicitly be declared by an act of Parliament to be legitimate

—be justified by fundamental interests

—not be based on ethnic criteria, because that would be incompatible with human rights provisions, but on educational criteria related to learning advantages and disadvantages of the pupils, determined for instance by home language or the level of parental education[75]

—leave intact the freedom of the "strict" confessional (denominational) schools to refuse pupils on denominational grounds

—be decided at the local level.

In its policy letter of April 2004, the cabinet seems to have accepted this view. It has proposed requiring school boards to negotiate desegregation schemes with the municipal board, but it has not yet clarified to what extent school boards can be obliged to participate in such schemes.[76]

Conclusions

It is not easy to decide what educational policy should be adopted in the Netherlands—or in the United States—in order to promote civic values. What is clear, however, is that fears that a system like that of the Netherlands, which is based on freedom of education and school choice, is detrimental to social cohesion and integration are unjustified. For instance, worries concerning anti-integrative tendencies in Islamic schools seem to be unfounded.

This does not automatically imply that in the near future the Dutch system is the most fit to cope with segregation, fundamentalism, individual isolation, and other possible problems. It is not implausible that the current trends toward stronger consumerism, religious pluralism, and multiculturalism will continue. In response, schools probably will be summoned by central and local government to reinforce civic values and social cohesion. This is not a task that the state, or the schools themselves, at the moment regard as part of the core business of primary and secondary education. It should be stressed, however, that freedom of education in the Dutch system is not unlimited; on the contrary—both public and private schools have to fulfill many standards. And while at the moment these standards primarily focus on the intellectual level of curricular content and on assessment, it is probable that there will be a reorientation in the near future toward more instruction to promote civic values—which until now has been avoided due to its perceived incompatibility with the constitutional freedom of education and to a general Dutch reluctance to moralize.

The trend toward further segregation between "black" and "white" schools is problematic from the perspective of improving social cohesion and the educational achievement of minority pupils. It seems that this trend is not caused primarily by the binary school system but by housing patterns and parental choice. Under certain conditions a local desegregation policy nevertheless might be allowed, even under the current constitutional provisions.

What I expect is that future governments will insist on integration and even assimilation of cultural and religious minorities more persistently than in the past. The autonomy of religious schools and the maintenance of their minority culture will be regarded as less important and sometimes even counterproductive. For this reason, education in minority languages is to be removed from the curriculum as of August 2004.

I also think that, in the long run, education and immigration policies will be combined, in that spouses and children from third world countries wanting to come to the Netherlands to reunite their families will have to show that they speak Dutch (or English?) and have some basic knowledge of Dutch society before they can obtain visas. And when they want permanent residency permits, they probably will need to fulfill even stricter requirements.[77]

It may be that the United States can learn something from the Dutch education system. But I believe that the Dutch, in developing policies linking integration, education, and immigration, can probably learn something from the United States.

Notes

1. See also Henk J. M. Hoefnagel and Ben P. Vermeulen, "Recent Developments in Dutch Legislation on Education," *European Journal for Education Law and Policy*, no. 1 (1997), pp. 155 ff.

2. Figures are for 1999–2000; Ministry of Education, Onderwijs *Cultuur en Wetenschappen in kerncijfers 2001* (The Hague, 2000), pp. 37, 47.

3. I will not address here the difficult question of which provisions are self-executing and which are not.

4. "No person shall be denied the right to education."

5. "The States Parties to the present Covenant recognize the right of everyone to education." This right is further developed in article 13, section 2, of the International Covenant on Economic, Social, and Cultural Rights: "The States Parties to the present Covenant recognize that, with a view to achieving the full realization of this right: (a) Primary education shall be compulsory and available free to all; (b) Secondary education in its different forms . . . shall be made generally available and acessible to all by every appropriate means, and in particular by the progressive introduction of free education."

6. "1. States Parties recognize the right of the child to education, and with a view to achieving this right progressively and on the basis of equal opportunity, they shall, in particular: (a) Make primary education compulsory and free to all; (b) Encourage the development of secondary education . . . , make [it] available and accessible to every child, and take appropriate measures such as the introduction of free education."

7. "States Parties undertake to prohibit and to eliminate racial discrimination in all its forms and to guarantee the right of everyone, without distinction as to race, colour, or national or ethnic origin, to equality before the law, notably in the enjoyment of the following rights: . . . (e) economic, social, and cultural rights, in particular: . . . (v) the right to education and training."

8. "In order to eliminate and prevent discrimination within the meaning of this Convention, the States Parties thereto undertake: . . . ; (b) to ensure, by legislation where necessary, that there is no discrimination in the admission of pupils to educational institutions."

9. "The States Parties to this Convention undertake . . . (a) to make primary education free and compulsory; make secondary education in its different forms generally available and accessible to all."

10. See my "Commentary on Article 2, Protocol 1, of the ECHR," in P. van Dijk and G. J. H. van Hoof, eds., *Theory and Practice of the European Convention on Human Rights* (The Hague: Kluwer Law International, 1998), pp. 647–48.

11. President Rechtbank Alkmaar, January 22, 1982, *NJCM Bulletin* (1982), pp. 134ff.

12. Hoge Raad, January 22, 1988, *Administratiefrechtelijke Beslissingen (AB)* (1988), no. 96 (Maimonides).

13. Nathan Lerner, *The U.N. Convention on the Elimination of All Forms of Racial Discrimination* (Alphen aan den Rijn: Sijthoff and Noordhoff, 1980), pp. 39, 59.

14. *Official Journal of the European Communities* L 180, July 19, 2000, pp. 22–26.

15. Article 1 and article 2(1) and 2(2) of Directive 2000/43/EC read as follows:

"Article 1: The purpose of this Directive is to lay down a framework for combating discrimination on the grounds of racial or ethnic origin, with a view to putting into effect in the Member States the principle of equal treatment."

"Article 2: 1. For the purposes of this Directive, the principle of equal treatment shall mean that there shall be no direct or indirect discrimination based on racial or ethnic origin.

"2. For the purposes of Section 1: (a) direct discrimination shall be taken to occur where one person is treated less favourably than another is, has been, or would be treated in a comparable situation on grounds of racial or ethnic origin; (b) indirect discrimination shall be taken to occur where an apparently neutral provision, criterion, or practice would put persons of a racial or ethnic origin at a particular disadvantage compared with other persons, unless that provision, criterion, or practice is objectively justified by a legitimate aim and the means of achieving that aim are appropriate and necessary."

16. Article 5 of Directive 2000/43/EC reads as follows: "With a view to ensuring full equality in practice, the principle of equal treatment shall not prevent any Member State from maintaining or adopting specific measures to prevent or compensate for disadvantages linked to racial or ethnic origin."

17. See the European Commission of Human Rights in application 11533/85, *Ingrid Jordebo Foundation of Christian Schools and Ingrid Jordebo* v. *Sweden, Decisions and Reports* 51 (1987), p. 128; and in application 23419/94, *Verein Gemeinsam Lernen* v. *Austria, Decisions and Reports* 82-A (1995), p. 45. Article 2, protocol 1, of the ECHR guarantees the right to establish and run a private school, but does not contain a positive obligation for the state to fund it.

18. Charles Glenn and Jan de Groof, *Finding the Right Balance: Freedom, Autonomy, and Accountability in Education*, vol. 2 (Utrecht: Lemma, 2002), pp. 251–52.

19. Afdeling Geschillen van Bestuur Raad van State, November 10, 1992, *AB* (1993), no. 88.

20. Afdeling Bestuursrechtspraak Raad van State, February 11, 1997, *AB* (1998), no. 28 (primary school).

21. Afdeling Bestuursrechtspraak Raad van State, January 15, 1998, *AB* (1998), no. 173 (secondary school).

22. Afdeling Bestuursrechtspraak Raad van State, August 5, 1997, *AB* (1998), no. 64.

23. Afdeling Bestuursrechtspraak Raad van State, July 3, 1997, *AB* (1998), no. 63.

24. Afdeling Bestuursrechtspraak Raad van State, July 3, 1997, *AB* (1998), no. 63; and August 5, 1997, *AB* (1998), no. 64.

25. Onderwijsraad, *Richtingvrij en richtingbepalend* (The Hague, 1996).

26 "De identiteit van de school in een pluriforme samenleving," *Kamerstukken II,* 25167, no. 1 (1996–97); "Naar een flexibeler scholenbestand," *Kamerstukken II,* 25167, no. 5 (2000–01) (available at www.overheid.nl).

27. *Kamerstukken II,* 29200 VI, no. 84 (2003–04).

28. *Handelingen II* (2003-04), pp. 2163–69.

29. "Onderwijs, Integratie en Burgerschap," *Kamerstukken II,* 29536, no. 1 (2003–04), p. 10.

30. Kantongerecht Wageningen, December 23, 1996, *AB* (1997), no. 218.

31. Article 1 of the Dutch constitution reads: "All persons in the Netherlands shall be treated equally in equal circumstances. Discrimination on the grounds of religion, belief, political opinion, race or sex or on any other grounds whatsoever shall not be permitted." Article 3 reads: "All Dutch nationals shall be equally eligible for appointment to public service."

32. Commissie Gelijke Behandeling (CGB), April 29, 1999, *AB* (2000), no. 71.

33. See, for instance, CGB, December 23, 1996, oordeel 96-118.

34. Hoge Raad, January 22, 1988, *AB* (1988), no. 96.

35. CGB, August 5, 2003, *AB* (2003), no. 375.

36. Voorzieningenrechter Rechtbank Haarlem, March 21, 2003, *AB* (2003), no. 234.

37. Hof Den Bosch, September 5, 1989, *Rechtspraak Vreemdelingenrecht* (1989), no. 96.

38. Hof Den Haag, October 27, 1992, *Nederlandse Jurisprudentie* (1993), no. 680.

39. CGB, September 6, 2000, oordeel 2000-63.

40. CGB, March 20, 2003, *AB* (2003), no. 233.

41. In response to the protests of schools and pupils, these standards have been lowered.

42. See *Aanhangsel Handelingen II* (1994–95), p. 1120.

43. Onderwijsraad, March 28, 1997, *Nederlands Tijdschrift voor Onderwijsrecht en onderwijsbeleid (NTOR)* (1997), pp. 147ff.

44. Andries Tj. de Jong and Nina A. Stegerhoek, "Onderwijs en civil society", in Onderwijsraad, *Rondom onderwijs* (The Hague, 2002), p. 77.

45. D. Kalb and B. van Steenbergen, "Civil society en educatie: sociaal-wetenschappelijke startpunten", in Onderwijsraad, *Rondom onderwijs,* pp. 102–03.

46. When a child of Turkish or Moroccan descent leaves primary school at the age of twelve, his or her command of the Dutch language is on average equivalent to that of a ten-year-old Dutch child. See Paul T. M. Tesser and others, *Rapportage minderheden 1999* (The Hague: Sociaal en Cultureel Planbureau, 1999), p. 156.

47. See www.owinsp.nl.

48. *Kamerstukken II,* 27680, no. 1 (2000–01), pp. 17–18.

49. Fons P. M. van Schoten and Harm A. Wansink, *De Nieuwe Schoolstrijd: Knelpunten en Conflicten in de Hedendaagse Onderwijspolitiek* (Utrecht: Bohn, Scheltema and Holkema, 1984).

50. See Onderwijsraad, *Vaste grond onder de voeten. Een verkenning inzake artikel 23 Grondwet* (The Hague, 2002), pp. 48ff.

51. Sjoerd Karsten and others, *Schoolkeuze in een multi-etnische samenleving* (Amsterdam: SCO Kohnstamm Instituut, 2002).

52. Binnenlandse Veiligheidsdienst (BVD), *De democratische rechtsorde en islamitisch onderwijs. Buitenlandse inmenging en anti-integratieve tendensen* (2002). See further, *Aanhangsel Handelingen II* (2001–02), nos. 892 and 894, as well as the response of the Minister of Home Affairs in *Kamerstukken II*, 28006, no. 7 (2001–02); Onderwijsinspectie, *Islamitische scholen en sociale cohesie* (Utrecht, 2002), as well as the response of the Minister of Education in a letter of October 25, 2002 (stuk ocw 0200837); Onderwijsinspectie, *Islamitische scholen nader onderzocht* (Utrecht, 2003), as well as the response of the Minister of Education in *Kamerstukken II*, 29200 VIII, no. 5 (2003–04).

53. *Kamerstukken II*, 28600 VIII, no. 115 .

54. *Kamerstukken II*, 28600 VIII, no. 123 (2002–03).

55. See the Minister of Education in *Kamerstukken II*, 28600 VIII, no. 115 (2000–03), p. 9; cf. article 13(3) and (4) of the ICESCR; article 5(1)(b) of the CDE.

56. Onderwijsraad, *Onderwijs en burgerschap* (The Hague, 2003).

57. "Onderwijs, Integratie en Burgerschap," *Kamerstukken II*, 29536, no. 1 (2003–04), p. 15.

58. Anne Bert Dijkstra, "Opbrengsten van onderwijsvrijheid. Over de effecten van verzuild onderwijs", in Tijmen J. van der Ploeg and others, eds., *De vrijheid van onderwijs, de ontwikkeling van een bijzonder grondrecht* (Utrecht: Lemma, 2000), pp. 243–60.

59. CGB, February 9, 1999, in Titia Loenen, ed., *Gelijke behandeling: oordelen en commentaar 1999* (Deventer: Kluwer, 2000), pp. 152ff; CGB, December 22, 1999, *AB* (2000), no. 72.

60. CGB, August 3, 2000, *Jurisprudentie Onderwijswetten* (2000), pp. 142–45.

61. *Kamerstukken II*, 28726, nos. 1–3 (2002–03).

62. This category of pupils can be roughly defined as children (a) with at least one parent from Southern Europe, Turkey, Morocco, Tunesia, Surinam, the Netherlands Antilles, or another non-European non-English-speaking country; and (b) who have at least one parent with only lower education.

63. Onderwijsraad, *Onderwijs en burgerschap*; "Onderwijs, Integratie en Burgerschap," *Kamerstukken II*, 29536, no. 1 (2003–04), p. 15.

64. I must emphasize that in the Dutch context the term "segregation" merely has a factual connotation, meaning a situation of mono-ethnic and/or mono-religious schools. Unlike in, for instance, the United States or South Africa, it has nothing to do with a racist state policy, but merely refers to the current situation, which is primarily the result of housing patterns and parental choice.

65. Ben P. Vermeulen, *Witte en zwarte scholen* (The Hague: Elsevier, 2001).

66. As decided by the monitoring body, the Commissie Gelijke Behandeling, in CGB, November 6, 2001, *AB* (2002), no. 48.

67. The use of ethnic quota systems in order to reach an adequate mix in the larger cities was declared unlawful, violating the CERD: Koninklijk Besluit, July 19, 1974, *Staatsblad* (1974), no. 496; Koninklijk Besluit, September 10, 1974, *Staatsblad* (1974), no. 556; President Rechtbank Rotterdam, March 10, 1981, *Rechtspraak Vreemdelingenrecht* (1981), no. 113. See also Kantongerecht Eindhoven, March 28, 1984, *Rechtspraak Vreemdelingenrecht* (1984), no. 122; *Aanhangsel Handelingen II* (2003–04), no. 154.

68. Until now these "black" schools in general have not been able to develop into magnet schools that are also attractive to white parents and pupils.

69. *Kamerstukken II*, 28000 VIII, no. 71 (2001–02).

70. Karsten and others, *Schoolkeuze in een multi-etnische samenleving*; Onderwijsraad, *Vaste grond onder de voeten*.

71. "Wet van 4 juli 1996 inzake de decentralisatie van huisvestingsvoorzieningen," *Staatsblad* (1996), p. 402.

72. "Wet van 15 mei 1997 inzake het gemeentelijk onderwijsachterstanden-beleid," *Staatsblad* (1997), p. 237.

73. It may ring odd to U.S. ears that strengthening local authority will help ease segregation, while desegregation in the United States was accomplished through federal intervention against states and local authorities. It must be stressed once again that in the Netherlands segregation is not the product of local government policies, but the result of housing patterns and choices of individuals.

74. Onderwijsraad, *Vaste grond onder de voeten*; Onderwijsraad, *Onderwijs en burgerschap*. In the 2003–04 school year a system was introduced in Flanders that combines the principle of parental choice with the right of schoolboards to refuse pupils when the relative percentage of non-native-language-speaking pupils is 10 percent higher than in other schools in the same district. See A. Overbeeke, "Non-discriminatie en gelijke kansen inzake schoolkeuze in het Vlaamse onderwijs— requiem voor het toelatingsbeleid van identiteitsgebonden instellingen?" in Jan Velaers/ Jochem Vrielink, eds., *Vrijheid en gelijkheid. De horizontale werking van het gelijkheidsbeginsel en de nieuwe antidiscriminatiewet* (Antwerpen-Apeldoorn: Maklu, 2003) pp. 707–53.

75. Probably a change of the AWGB will be necessary. The CGB has recently ruled that an integration policy developed by a Christian school board for its fourteen schools, according to which no more than 15 percent of an individual school's student population should consist of students whose home language is not Dutch, was not justified by compelling reasons and thus was in breach of the AWGB (CGB, 29 July 2003, *AB* [2003], no. 376).

76. Onderwijsraad, *Onderwijs en burgerschap*; "Onderwijs, Integratie en Burgerschap," *Kamerstukken II*, 29536, no. 1 (2003–04), p. 15.

77. The policy document of the current government (the second Balkenende administration), which contains the main political targets for the next four years, states: "He who wants to settle in the Netherlands must actively participate in society and acquire the Dutch language; he must have knowledge of the basic norms of

Dutch society, and obey the legal rules. Immigrants . . . must already have a basic command of the Dutch language when they want to come to the Netherlands. Once having arrived they will have to further integrate in Dutch society. . . . Certain groups of immigrants . . . as well as asylum seekers will have to pass an 'integration exam' before they will get a permanent residence permit." *Kamerstukken II*, 28637, no. 19 (2002–03), p. 14. A more detailed plan is outlined in the policy statement of the Minister of Immigration, "Herziening van het inburgeringsstelsel," *Kamerstukken II*, 29543, no. 2 (2003–04).

3

Private Schools as Public Provision for Education: School Choice and Market Forces in the Netherlands

ANNE BERT DIJKSTRA, JAAP DRONKERS,
AND SJOERD KARSTEN

U nlike parents in most areas of the United States, parents in different European societies have a real choice of comparable schools, both public and private, and they can exercise their options without paying very high fees. Most often the private schools are Catholic or Protestant schools that operate within the national educational system and receive state grants.

In international discussions on the expansion of parental choice and the private delivery of education, the Dutch arrangement quite often is regarded as "unique." Central to the Dutch arrangement are two constitutional rights: the right of freedom of education and the right of public and private institutions to equal public funding. As a result, approximately 70 percent of Dutch parents send their children to schools that, although established by private associations and managed by private school boards, are nonetheless fully funded by the central government. In the opinion of national interest groups as well as national experts, this freedom of education and equal financing of public and private education from public funds makes the Dutch system exceptional.[1] Foreign observers have tended to agree with this assessment, as illustrated by a review of the Dutch education system by the Organization for Economic Cooperation and Development and by the remarks of other international observers who have said, among other things, that "the evolution of the Dutch system of education is unique in the Western World."[2] Therefore, the argument goes, the Netherlands offers an "experiment" in the private production of education on a national scale, a century-old experiment that includes the entire education system. As Brown so concisely puts it, "The Netherlands is the only country with a nationwide school choice program." [3]

These statements, however, are exaggerated. The Dutch educational system is not too far removed from the systems of other countries, as one can see in Dronkers's analysis of European public and religious schools in chapter 11 of this volume. Religious schools in some other European countries also have a constitutional right to state financial support. Still, although these observers are exaggerating the uniqueness of the Dutch educational system, school choice in the Netherlands differs in several respects from school choice in other European countries, such as Germany and Belgium, with similar state-subsidized religious and public school sectors.

First, in most European countries with school choice, the religious schools are of *one* denomination, operated mostly by the Catholic Church or one of the Protestant churches, which at one time may have been the state church. This is not the case in the Netherlands, which was created in the religious wars of the sixteenth century and, as a result, became home to a large Catholic minority within an ultimately moderate Protestant state. The religious diversity of Dutch society promoted an early de facto neutrality of the Dutch Protestant state in relation to most Christian religions and thus to an early de facto separation between the dominant Protestant church and the state. Consequently, there was hardly a political battle on the juridical separation of the church and the state, as there was in France or Germany. Nor did the link between church and state linger on in the Netherlands during the twentieth century, as it did in the United Kingdom. The taken-for-granted neutrality of the Dutch state therefore owes itself to something other than the juridical separation of church and state.

Since the 1920s, in the wake of political struggles the century before, the Netherlands has had—in addition to the locally run public education sector—three main private sectors: Catholic, Protestant, and a smaller, religiously neutral sector, all with independent private school boards. The three main private sectors have been joined by other, smaller religious sectors—first Jewish, later Islamic and Hindu—and some small, private nonreligious sectors with a special didactic, first Montessori and Jena, later Steiner. Within the Catholic and Protestant school sectors there are national umbrella organizations that also function as lobbies. But they do not replace the autonomous school boards, nor do they coordinate all Protestant or Catholic schools. These school boards have the juridical form of a foundation (predominantly in the Catholic sector) or an association (predominantly in the Protestant sector), both with a high degree of self-selection of new board members.

Second, the equal subsidizing of all religious and public schools has promoted a diminution of prestigious elite schools outside the state-subsidized sector. As a consequence of equal subsidies and prohibition of the use of extra funds for teacher grants, smaller classes, and the like, there is not an institutionalized hierarchy of schools within each school type. In the Netherlands, you do not see the equivalent of the so-called public schools or independent grammar schools in England, nor do you see versions of the prep schools in the United States or the differences in quality that exist there between schools in the poor inner cities and those in the wealthy suburbs.

The distinctive situation in the Netherlands, in terms of the size of the private sector and the context in which private schools operate, provides a favorable setting for testing many of the arguments in the school choice and voucher debates. First, one can test the hypothesis that providing subsidies to private schools will make them more effective competitors of public schools and that the strengthened competition will force public schools to become better.[4] In order to test that hypothesis, the barriers to attending a school other than the one closest to a student's residence must be low. That is the case in the Netherlands, where schools are numerous, population density is high, public transportation is generally available, spending per pupil varies little, and money follows the student. Second, it must be possible to test the interaction of school choice, private schools, and external examinations. According to Bishop, private schools, being more sensitive to market pressures, will respond more radically to an external exam system than public schools will.[5] In the Netherlands, the government sets the examinations for each type of school—these exams influence access to tertiary education and job opportunities—while leaving schools a good deal of freedom to choose course materials and teaching method. And finally, the practice of repeating grades, *redoublement*, as a way of allowing some students extra time to achieve very demanding learning goals, can be examined. This practice is widespread in some European countries, and schools differ in their rates of *redoublement*, but by American standards the rates are very high in the Netherlands.

Religious Schools in a Secular Society?

Since the middle of the twentieth century, the religious pillars in Dutch society have broken down rapidly. In 1947, only 17 percent of the population did not officially belong to any church; by 1995, that proportion had increased to 40 percent. The same trend can be seen in the votes for Christian Democratic candidates in national elections: in 1948, they gained 55 percent of the vote;

in 1994, less than 30 percent. The Netherlands is considered one of the most secularized of Western societies.[6] It would seem likely, then, that there would have been a decline in institutions such as religious schools, which depended on religious affiliation to recruit students. In the 1960s and 1970s, many experts anticipated precisely such a decline.[7] However, although a decline did occur in a number of organizations and institutions—unions, journals, clubs, and hospitals—related to or affiliated with particular religious groups, religious schools did not have the same problem. In 1950, 73 percent of all pupils in primary education were attending a nonpublic school; in 2000, the figure was 68 percent, although in recent decades Protestant and Catholic schools lost some of their share of the total private school market to other nonpublic schools. Specifically, the Catholic market share diminished from 65 percent of private schools in 1980 to 59 percent in 2000.

How, then, can one explain the nondisappearance of religious education or the failure of public schools to attract the growing number of children of nonreligious parents?[8] A temporary explanation is the strong involvement of the public school sector in the proposed but never realized educational reforms of the 1970s, which had two major effects. First, they hampered the ability of public schools to attract the majority of more traditional nonreligious pupils and parents. In addition, the political battles around these unrealized reforms—which aimed at creating a comprehensive high school similar to high schools in the United States and doing away with the existing hierarchy of different school types—gave religious schools enough breathing space to redefine themselves as schools based not only on religion but also on educational quality. But this temporary explanation needs to be supplanted by more permanent ones because the strong involvement of the public school sector in educational reform did not last long.

The issue of religious schools prospering in a secular society might be of interest to other modern societies characterized by an increasing number of religious schools and increasing pressure for public funding—and it might be even more interesting in societies with a less active religious population. The Dutch case might offer some insights into the mechanisms underlying the stability or increase in religious schooling in societies that are not particularly religious. Several explanations and theories attempt to explain this paradox.[9]

Certainly, the increasing irrelevance of church and religion in everyday life is not unique to the Netherlands; it is apparent in most European societies. And as in the Netherlands, the religious schools in these other societies did not dwindle away. On the contrary, the religious school sector in European societies with less active religious populations is either growing or is disproportionate to the percentage of religious citizens. This is true not only for places that traditionally have had such schools, such as Austria, France, the Netherlands, and the old German *Länder* (states), but also for places such as Hungary and eastern Germany in which nonpublic schools were abolished under communist regimes.

One of the possible explanations for the popularity of religious schools even in secularizing societies is that nonpublic schools are generally more effective in their teaching than are public schools. Their better educational administration, stronger value-oriented relationship among parents and schools, and more deliberate self-selection process might be the most important mechanisms in producing their average higher effectiveness in Europe. Chapter 11 in this volume reviews the available evidence on differences in the effectiveness of public and religious state-funded schools in Belgium, France, Germany, Hungary, the Netherlands, and Scotland.

Various Explanations for the Survival of Religious Schools after Secularization

There are a number of possible explanations for the survival of religious schools after the secularization of a society. Nonpublic schools may or may not promote the separation of affluent from nonaffluent students. National examinations may reduce the differences in content and quality of public and nonpublic schools, making the latter more attractive. In the Netherlands, religious schools may enjoy a political advantage, and even nonreligious parents may appreciate the moral education that religious schools offer. Various explanations are examined below.

Segregation of Public and Religious Schools

A possible explanation for the attractiveness of nonpublic schools is that they can promote the segregation of more privileged or affluent students from less privileged or affluent students. This might be an important explanation for the stability of religious schools in irreligious societies, which still might desire such segregation.

Although both public and private schools take a fair—more or less equal—share in educating children from minority backgrounds, Karsten and other researchers have shown that segregation of children of immigrant workers and children of Dutch-born parents sometimes occurs along lines of nonpublic and public schools.[10] Some of this segregation can be explained by the concentration of both immigrant workers and public schools in the big cities.

Still, many children of immigrant workers would prefer religious to public schools. This preference for religious schools is due in part to the greater openness of Catholic and Protestant schools to accommodating religious values, even those of religions other than their own, such as Islam. The importance of Islam to large groups of workers from Turkey, Morocco, and Suriname led to the establishment of state-funded Islamic primary schools in the Netherlands during the 1990s. It is still too early to evaluate the effectiveness of these schools, but they seem already at least as effective as (if not already more effective than) non-Islamic schools in comparable circumstances. Moreover, the early dropout rate is significantly lower in Islamic schools than in comparable non-Islamic schools. However, it is clear that these Islamic schools attract children of parents who are less integrated in Dutch society than parents from the same group who send their children to comparable non-Islamic schools.[11] The problem is comparing the costs and benefits of a possibly lower level of integration with those of a possibly higher level of scholastic attainment. Indeed, in the public debate, there has already been much opposition to Islamic schools on the grounds that segregation will hamper the integration of Islamic children into Dutch society. The strongest opposition comes from advocates of public rather than Catholic and Protestant schools, since the integration of all religious groups into one school has always been the ideal of public schools in the Netherlands.

Differences in the backgrounds of students admitted to the schools in the various sectors explain, on average, only one-third of the outcome differences among the schools. After controlling for differences in student background, the differences in effectiveness among public, Catholic, and Protestant schools are roughly the same as before controlling, a point that we elaborate on below. Religious schools do not, on average, have a better-qualified student body, so the social composition theory does not explain the attraction and the greater effectiveness of religious schools. However, when the number of pupils increases while the number of available good teachers decreases, some nonpublic schools can become more attractive for both teachers and parents. Nonpublic schools are better equipped legally to attract more and better-qualified teachers than their public counterparts. The attraction is not due to higher salaries but to advantages in working conditions, like smaller class sizes and less bureaucracy. In a situation in which there is an abundance of students, this difference might lead to a more discerning selection of entering pupils and thus to stronger social segregation among schools.

National Examinations

The mandatory national examinations in the Netherlands may have decreased the differences between public and religious schools in terms of both content and quality and thus made the latter more attractive to secular parents. Bishop compared the degree of segregation in educational systems in America, Europe, and Asia and formulated interesting conclusions.[12] The use of national diploma exams at the end of secondary education raises scholastic achievement in both public and private schools. National exams also make the differences in quality between private and public schools more open to public inspection and debate, and therefore the differences tend to be smaller, especially if public and private schools both are funded by the state on a comparable basis. According to Bishop, private schools, being more sensitive to market pressures, will respond more radically to an external exam system than public schools will. As a consequence of these two factors, national diploma exams are an important means of decreasing school segregation. Nationally organized exams take place in the Netherlands both at the end of primary school and at the end of secondary school, as they have since 1968. Also, the results of these exams have been open to the public since the late 1990s.[13] National exams, together with fair publication of the results, can avoid strong social segregation of Dutch private and public schools.[14] However, even in an educational system with a strong tradition of national exams, schools are able to manipulate the grading of these exams by being more or less strict in their grading of the school part of the national exams.[15]

Competition and School Sector Size

Another explanation for the popularity of religious schools is that competition between schools—within and between the different school sectors for the best pupils or the most highly motivated parents—can make religious schools attractive to secular parents. The size of the private school sector is linked to the ability of private schools to select the most able pupils: the larger the private sector, the lower the possibility that private schools can skim only the cream of the crop and thus promote social segregation. This is an obvious explanation for the virtual lack of student background differences among the major public, Protestant, and Catholic school sectors in the Netherlands. Thus, Roeleveld and Dronkers found evidence that the effectiveness of all schools was the highest in districts in which no group of schools—public, Protestant, or Catholic—attracted a majority of the students but in which the size of all sectors was substantial.[16] Another finding that reinforces the competition argument is the lack of effectiveness of private religious schools that serve a student body with a very specific religious orientation.[17] The schools of religious minority groups like the orthodox Protestants attract their students because of religious considerations and do not need to compete with other schools. In general, their parents or students do not really consider other options in choosing a school.

But the relation between the size of the private sector and segregation among schools also depends on the rules governing admission to public schools and the opportunities for parents to choose within the public school sector. The less choice parents have in choosing a public school (due to required assignment to a neighborhood school, for instance), the higher parental demand will be for a private sector alternative to the assigned public school. When parental demand is stronger, nonpublic schools can be more selective in their admission policies. Therefore more parental choice among public schools also can decrease social segregation of public and private school students. But at the same time, increased choice can also increase the social segregation of *schools*, within both the public and the private sectors, as we discuss later. Another important aspect of greater parental choice is that social segregation of neighborhoods is not further enhanced by forced school assignment.

The smallest private school sector (besides the orthodox Protestant and the Islamic sectors) is the neutral private sector, which is still growing in the Netherlands. Often these neutral private schools are the more established and traditional schools or ones that offer specific pedagogical approaches (Montessori, anthroposophy). Here we find the highest degree of social and ethnic segregation—both among schools of this sector and between schools in this and other sectors—in accordance with Bishop's hypothesis.[18] The higher scholastic achievements of schools in the neutral private sector can be fully explained by the elite social composition of the student body.[19] If one controls for the social status of the student body, the neutral private schools tend to achieve less academically than comparable schools outside this sector. The lower effectiveness of the neutral private schools does not diminish their attractiveness, however, because their lower effectiveness is neutralized by their social composition. An explanation for this neutralization is that in the Netherlands admission to higher levels of education depends only on having a diploma, which Dutch students are more likely to obtain if they are educated alongside students from elite social circles.

Political Protection of Religious Schools and Support for School Choice

An oft-suggested explanation for the religious schooling advantage in the Netherlands is the strong position of religious schools, which enjoy the political protection of the Christian Democratic party through laws protecting freedom of education and which benefit from the dense administrative network of religious school organizations. This hypothesis has some validity. The central position of the Christian Democratic party on the Dutch political map until the mid-1990s made it possible to maintain the "pillarized" school system[20] and the religious schools within that system—despite Dutch society's increasing secularization—and even to establish new religious schools in areas with low numbers of active church members. Nevertheless, active support from the Christian Democrats cannot fully explain the flourishing private religious school sector.

Much of the success of religious schools hinges on the fact that Dutch policymakers have made it easy for parents to "vote with their feet." Despite many regulations and the strong formal position of religious schools, parents can favor other school sectors without facing serious geographical or financial barriers because of the free choice of schools—the Dutch public system, among other things, no longer contains catchment areas—and equal government funding of public and private schools. Schools are financed according to the number of pupils enrolled, and the way to establish a new school is to find enough parents who will send their children to that school. Several less powerful groups of parents—orthodox Protestant, Evangelical, Islamic, and Hindu—have recently used this mechanism of "voting with their feet" with success against the powerful, long-established organizations of private religious schools, founding schools of their own religious preference.

The essential question here, therefore, is why nonreligious parents did not use the same mechanism to increase the number of nonreligious schools or the number of pupils attending them. In the Dutch case, it is hard to argue that these nonreligious parents are less powerful or less numerous than the orthodox Protestant, Evangelical, Islamic, or Hindu parents and their organizations—in fact, the opposite might be true. Nonreligious parents are on average better educated and have more links with the established, large, and powerful political parties than the groups mentioned before. What we conclude is that nonreligious parents no longer feel deterred by the religious socialization of religious schools—that is, to the extent that religious schools still offer such socialization—and therefore do not see the need to change to nonreligious schools. [21]

Higher Quality of Nonpublic Administration

There exist slight differences in educational administration in public and religious schools that can explain some of the differences in academic outcomes, despite enforced financial equality and strong state control.[22] It is not the formal differences in educational administration but the stronger informal relations between board and teachers in the religious schools that in part explain the better performance of their pupils and therefore the attractiveness of religious schools for nonreligious students and parents.[23]

A Conservative, Value-Oriented Education

Another possible explanation is that irreligious parents prefer religious socialization because they still appreciate the moral values taught by their no-longer-adhered-to religion. However, it is clear from longitudinal research that the number of adherents to religious values among Dutch adults is decreasing, which contrasts with the stability of religious school recruitment. Only a minority of parents (about 30 percent, depending on the local situation) gives religious reasons for choosing a religious school for their children. If the appreciation of religious values by irreligious parents was an effective explanation of their choice of a religious school, that reason should show up in surveys more frequently. An important consideration, however, is that the values-oriented character of religious schools leads them to stress secular, nonreligious values (for instance, tolerance of homosexuals) as a significant aspect of schooling in the broader sense (Germans would call this *Bildung* and the French *éducation*). Public schools, with their religiously neutral status, tend to avoid discussion of value-oriented topics and instead stress instruction. Irreligious parents who think schooling should have a broad educational scope rather than only a narrower instructional purpose therefore choose the modern religious school for its expansiveness, which they consider an aspect of educational quality, rather than for the specific religious values that it teaches.

Today neither the Catholic Church nor the Protestant churches have a major influence on the curriculum of most religious schools, and—especially in the Catholic schools—religious education has decreased to the point that it involves simply the dissemination of factual information on various world views.[24] Several studies have shown in particular that the religious identity of Catholic schools has become very weak.[25] There are few traces left of specifically Catholic elements either in entry requirements for pupils or in the selection of personnel. One good reason for the breakdown of religious socialization is the increasing scarcity of teachers who are themselves religious, a lack that in the Netherlands can be explained by the negative relationship between level of education and degree of traditional religiousness. A majority of pupils in religious schools do not have an active religious background, and their parents do not want them to be heavily socialized in an outdated religion, but they do not object to having them learn factual information on various world views.[26] So there is a happy conjunction of the fact that it would be difficult for religious schools to provide strong religious socialization and the fact that only a small number of parents still want it. These schools offer, as the next-best alternative, factual information on different world views, which a teacher who is not religious can relate as part of students' cultural education although such courses are often still known under the old title of religious education. The forced neutrality of public schools in relation to different world views and the moderate, secular values orientation of religious schools explain, in part, the attractiveness of the latter schools. Also, most nonreligious parents prefer a values-oriented education to strict neutrality, because they believe that becoming educated implies learning values.

Another explanation offered for the attractiveness of religious schools was their (on average) mild educational conservatism compared with the (on average) more progressive tendencies of public schools from the 1960s until the 1990s. Among the reasons for this mild conservatism were the differences in the exposure of public and private schools to social policy initiatives. The board of a public school was the municipal council. Because education is one of the major instruments that policymakers have to effect change, such councils might favor implementing educational experiments in order to accomplish political goals. In contrast, the boards of religious schools felt less need to embark on politically motivated educational experiments. This difference between the two might be changing due to the increasing scale of religious school boards and the delegation of the administration of public schools to more or less independent committees.

Another difference between public and private schools is that the former have less opportunity to avoid pressure from the national government because they cannot use the principle of freedom of education to shield themselves. Religious schools, on the other hand, can be obliged to conform to educational experiments only if they are forced to by a national law that declares the educational experiment a condition necessary to qualify for public funding. In all other cases, religious schools' participation in educational experiments is voluntary.

Higher Cognitive Effectiveness of Religious Schools

Dutch research contains ample evidence of the positive effects of Catholic and Protestant schooling on academic achievement.[27] These findings, all adjusted for differences in the backgrounds of students in public and private schools, are reported in terms of educational outcomes measured as dropout rates, test scores, degrees, attainment, and so forth, for both primary and secondary schools. However, there are a number of deviant results that defy easy explanations. The first deviation from the average higher effectiveness of Dutch religious schools is that public schools in regions where there is a majority of Catholic or Protestant schools have higher effectiveness than do public schools in regions where there is a majority of public schools, while

Catholic or Protestant religious schools in these regions are not more effective than public schools. Second, schools that are both nonreligious and private have, on average, lower effectiveness than public and religious schools, after controlling for the social composition of the student body.[28] This second deviation shows that it is not the private nature of the administration of religious schools that makes them more effective, but their religious background. The third deviation from the average higher effectiveness of Dutch religious schools is that orthodox Protestant schools do not have higher effectiveness than public schools or less strict Protestant schools.[29] The fourth deviation is that the higher effectiveness of religious schools might be restricted to a certain historical period (the late 1960s to the 1990s). If this is correct, a possible explanation is the dominance of religion as the basis of school choice before the 1960s[30] and the disappearance of the small-scale advantages of religious schools during the 1990s due to large-scale reorganization of the religious school sectors.

The reputation of religious schools for academic quality may be closely related to the exercise of deliberate educational choice. Because of the selection effect, parents' deliberate choice of an "unconventional" school (compared with a "default" choice for a common school) will increase the possibility that this "unconventional" school will become a community with shared values and dense social ties in which students perform better. The selection effect can apply and affect student achievement in either a religious or a public school. Roeleveld and Dronkers[31] found evidence that in districts where public, Protestant, and Catholic schools each failed to attract a majority of students, the effectiveness of all schools was the highest, after taking student composition into account. In districts without a dominant type of school, there is no such thing as a "default" school choice, and thus parental choice has to be more deliberate. In districts in which public, Protestant, or Catholic schools had either a very small share of the market (less than 20 percent) or a very large one (greater than 60 percent of all students), the effectiveness of these small schools was lower. In districts with a dominant share of one school sector, the "conventional" school choice is most common and parental choice is more by default. A practical consequence of these findings is that public schools in the two southern provinces of the Netherlands, where the large majority of schools are Catholic, are more effective than the Catholic schools; they also are more effective than the public schools in the two northern provinces, where public schools dominate.

Especially given the high secularization of Dutch society since the 1960s, religious schools have been forced to compete for students for motives other than religious ones, and they have been unable to rely on the religious segmentation of society for new students. For religious schools, the notion of deliberate educational choice became important. Religious schools were, on average, better equipped for this competition partly because of their history. During the nineteenth century, Dutch religious schools won the struggle to attract the most students. They also have won the battle for students because of the relative flexibility of their private governance and administration.[32] Finally, religious schools have remained popular in secularized Holland because of their reputation for educational quality.[33] Perhaps public schools lost this battle because their leading advocates expected the religious school sector to break down automatically as a consequence of the growing secularization and irreligiousness of Dutch society and were far too optimistic about the attractiveness of the schools' "neutral" identity.[34]

Questions about the extent to which these differences between public and religious schools are permanently important are unsettled, in the Netherlands and elsewhere. Most studies show differences in school effectiveness that vary with denomination, even after taking into account differences in pupil characteristics and student body composition. As far as these differences follow a regular pattern, the average effects are mainly negative for public schools, positive for private religious schools, and negative for nonreligious private schools. It seems that Catholic schools in particular—and to a lesser degree, Protestant schools—have distinguished themselves favorably. These results seem slightly more pronounced in primary education than in secondary education. Dutch religious schools do distinguish themselves by a reputation for offering educational quality, which, as research shows, is an important factor for parents who are choosing among schools.

Higher Noncognitive Effectiveness of Religious Schools

Most of the studies on school effectiveness are limited to the effects of a particular sector on the cognitive aspect of learning. Much less research has been undertaken to investigate possible differences between sectors in other, noncognitive domains. These are at least as interesting, particularly in the light of the pillarized history of the current Dutch school system, which is linked to the different religious socialization processes of the main religious denominations in Dutch society.[35] Education officials may only be paying lip service to the importance of the noncognitive results of education, however, as the Dutch Education Inspectorate measures only the cognitive, not the noncognitive, outcomes of schools.[36]

Van Marwijk Kooy conducted one of the first Dutch education studies that included outcomes in noncognitive domains.[37] Despite several differences in pupils' attitudes toward their school, the author concluded that there are no great differences with respect to those attitudes among secondary schools of various denominations. In the early 1990s, Wittebrood analyzed approximately sixty secondary grammar schools on student attitudes like political interest and cynicism, political participation, authoritarianism, and ethnocentrism.[38] Although there were differences among sectors, most of the effects could be attributed to the religious, social, and ethnic composition of the school population. The sector of the school adds only some explanatory power and shows only slight effects of private religious schools on political interests. Vreeburg and Dronkers pay attention to possible lifestyle differences among students of secondary schools of various denominations.[39] Among other things, they investigate whether students at religious schools have more sober spending habits (for clothes, entertainment, and so forth), spend their time differently (reading, small jobs), and spend less money on gambling and drugs. Their analysis, based on data on more than 13,000 students from the *National School Survey* of 1994, shows that substantial differences between students of religious and public secondary schools do not exist, after controlling for individual student characteristics including the religiosity of the individual students.

Knuver investigates the relationship between class and school characteristics and the affective functioning of pupils, based on data collected in some 200 primary schools.[40] The study shows that the affective functioning of pupils—which includes their attitudes toward language and arithmetic, performance motivation, self-image, and attitude toward the school—is somewhat higher in Catholic schools than in public and Protestant schools. Hofman's analysis of private nonreligious schools, based on the same data, shows that the score for attitude toward the school is higher in Catholic schools than in Protestant schools.[41] Jungbluth, Peetsma, and Roeleveld also investigated pupils' assessment of their own well-being in primary education; they did not find systematic differences related to the sector of the primary school.[42] Driessen and van der Slik also found no differences in the self-confidence and well-being of pupils in primary schools related to school religious status, after controlling for the social and ethnic background of the pupils.[43] Braster compared the religious, social, and political value orientations of 2,087 youngsters (fifteen- to twenty-four-year-olds) who attended different types of schools. After controlling for background characteristics such as religion, church attendance, educational level, age, and gender, he found that most effects of the denomination of schools disappeared.[44] Only attending an orthodox Protestant school showed any effect in terms of religious orientation. So in the three most important groups of schools in the Dutch education system—public, Catholic, and Protestant—no reliable differences in the value orientation of their pupils could be found. Findings based on national survey data collected in 1999 show that this conclusion might be true to a larger extent.[45] Even for students in a small, orthodox religious school sector, no substantial attitudinal or behavioral effects of attending a religious school were found. A comparison of sector effects in a broad range of life-style domains showed no substantial differences among sectors, except for attitudes and behavior closely related to the religious sphere of life.

The picture of the nonacademic effectiveness of religious schools is far less clear than the picture of their academic effectiveness. Sometimes denomination-specific differences are apparent, but mostly they are not, especially after controlling for the individual characteristics of the pupils and their parents. On the whole, one cannot find evidence that Dutch religious schools are substantially more effective in the noncognitive domain, despite their claims along those lines.

Negative Side Effects of School Choice in a Secular Society

Any social system has negative side effects, and that is also true for school choice in the Netherlands, which may contribute to educational differences between religious and public schools and to ethnic and social segregation. In addition, maintaining a dual system may increase the total cost of providing education.

More Segregation of Schools

As stated, the equal funding of private and public schools has reduced the number and size of prestigious elite schools. The equal financing of religious and public schools has prevented either from skimming off the best students. Before the 1970s, the choice of religious or public school generally was made not on educational but on religious grounds; therefore the long-standing existence of parental choice did not increase educational inequality in Dutch society. The educational differences between religious and public schools are recent and could be the start of a new form of inequality, despite efforts of the Dutch administration to diminish unequal opportunities for education. Differences in parents' knowledge of school effectiveness, which correlates with their own educational level, can perhaps be seen as the basis of this new form of inequality.[46] In the Netherlands as well as in other European countries, the importance of deliberate parental choice in promoting children's educational opportunities seems to be an important element in the persistence of educational systems with a substantial religious school sector, despite secularization. But in a school system without a sizable private religious sector, parents' knowledge of school effectiveness can be an important factor in choosing the right school and neighborhood for their children.

Recent studies on the relation of school choice and ethnic segregation show clearly that ethnic and social segregation in primary schools is a general phenomenon in the Netherlands. This is the case for the education system on a national scale, as well in the large metropolitan areas in the western and southern parts of the country.[47] In the big cities the religious character of schools is not really an important factor in the segregation of students.[48] Protestant elementary schools in Amsterdam, for instance, have more children from non-Western families and also more children from Dutch families with a low level of education than the average for the city's schools as a whole. Only the populations of Islamic and Hindu schools are composed almost entirely of children from ethnic minority families with a low level of education. That contrasts with the private nondenominational schools, which have the lowest percentage of these children and often are completely white middle-class schools. They request a relatively high parental financial contribution and adopt a specific, often freer teaching method (for example, Montessori, Steiner, Jena), in this way ensuring that they select pupils from the "better circles." Ethnic and social segregation in primary schools is caused mainly by parental choice of school and aggravated by "gatekeeping" activities of school principals. The important point here is not that the distinction between "socially undesirable" and "socially desirable" schools is more or less equal to that between public and religious private schools. The main point is that the current, nonreligious interpretation of the constitutional right to freedom of education means free school choice by parents, both within and between the public and private sectors. This free school choice opens the possibility of ethnic segregation in primary schools, not necessarily only between school sectors, but more often among schools within the same school sector and neighborhood. The existence of free school choice, although beneficial even to public schools under certain conditions, thus can deepen the social and ethnic inequality of schools within the same neighborhood and thus in society at large.[49] This deepening of social and ethnic segregation of schools in the Netherlands might be neutralized by a less strong social segregation of neighborhoods, because free school choice does not force parents to find a house in a particular catchment area in order to obtain the right to enroll their children in a desired school located there. The net effect of school choice in the Netherlands on social integration—stronger school segregation but weaker neighborhood segregation—is impossible to know with certainty.

Lower Costs per Religious School but also Reduced Economy of Scale

Another explanation for the demand for private schooling may be the financial differences between school sectors. Dutch schools do not differ greatly in their fees. Religious schools charge certain extra fees, which are mostly used for extracurricular activities, but the choice of parents here can hardly be influenced by financial considerations. This irrelevance of financial criteria for school choice has been shown in various educational attainment studies.[50] Financial differences are not a good explanation for the existence of religious schools.

A dual educational system, however, is not less expensive than a single public system. Koelman estimated the extra costs of the Dutch system of public and religious schools at about 631 million Dutch guilders (about $400 million) a year for primary education.[51] The extra costs come from maintaining the many small schools of different sectors in one community, given the small minimum number of pupils necessary to maintain a school. The government is making efforts to reduce these costs by increasing the minimum number of pupils in a school. In secondary education, this has led to a fusion of schools into larger units, but the mergers have been mostly within the public and religious sectors, with some tendencies to merge Protestant and Catholic schools into one Christian school. Moreover, there are indications that these mergers of nonpublic schools might have diminished their effectiveness advantage.[52] This fusion movement has partly collapsed in primary education because the government could not raise the minimum number of pupils to a sufficient level. The main cause of the failure has been pressure from smaller communities, which fear losing their only school. In contrast to the higher cost of maintaining small schools—public or religious—are the lower overhead costs of most religious schools, which are not obliged to use the more expensive municipal services but can shop around to obtain the cheapest and most effective assistance for administration, repairs, building, cleaning, and so on. Religious schools also use more voluntary help, owing to their more direct link with parents, which also lowers overhead costs. A total balance sheet of the lower overhead costs of religious schools and the higher costs of maintaining a multisector school system has never been agreed on, however, since all sides dispute the figures.

Toward a Policy of Demand-Driven Nonreligious School Choice in the Public and Private Sectors

An important recent development in education in the Netherlands is a proposal for a demand-driven policy that would not take the religious charter of a school into account in deciding whether to approve an educational establishment but would base decisions on quantitative criteria, like the number of prospective students. Such a change would have various ramifications.

A Nonreligious Basis for School Choice

Recent developments suggest that the disparity between the supply of schooling (organized around religious diversity) and demand for schooling in a predominantly secular society might lead to some adjustment in the regulations regarding the establishment of private religious schools in the near future. Notably, an advisory report published by the Netherlands's influential Education Council might become the marker of an important change in the current system of choice. The Education Council, commonly seen as a powerful watchdog for freedom of schooling, is proposing to adjust the educational system to fit the new social realities of Dutch society. In effect, the report radically reinterprets the design of the system of choice in education.[53] The Council argues that the government should no longer take the religious charter of a school into account when planning an educational establishment but should base such decisions solely on quantitative criteria (like number of students). This would remove from legislation all criteria regarding the need for a religious or philosophical foundation for a school. In practice, this would not necessarily result in the founding of new schools. In the current system, the denomination of the school also plays a part in the funding of a school that wishes to change or merge its religious direction. This school has to prove that there exists a demand for this changed religious direction that is not met by other schools in that region. If other schools already meet the demand, a change of the religious direction is not allowed. In a system in which a religious or philosophical charter is no longer a criterion for state funding, it is becoming easier to realize parental preferences through adaptation of the school's religious charter.[54] So, by providing for diversity along dimensions other than religious or philosophical, according to parental demands, it is hoped that the system would allow for more of a link between changing parental preferences and teaching. Furthermore, the system would be more consistent, no longer having as its rationale the religious diversity that Dutch society no longer exhibits.

With the adaptation of an educational infrastructure based on religion to a demand-driven system, the evolution of the current religiously based system to a system based on preferences other than religious ones—be they ideological, pedagogical, educational, or based on any other principle—could lie ahead. By basing the founding and closing down of schools on quantitative criteria, the proposal is expected to tip the balance between educational consumers and suppliers in favor of the first.

This would mean that educational supply is based on actual parental needs and demands. The decreased importance of religion in Dutch society and the enlargement of cultural diversity is reason to rid the school system of as many impediments as possible to creating maximal freedom for whoever manages to mobilize sufficient support for a school, no matter what the grounds.

Bureaucratically Disguised Religious Schools

What does this mean for the future of Dutch school choice? Most likely it will continue to exist, but in a transformed shape. The importance of the ideological and religious legitimacy of private nonprofit organizations increasingly will move to the background. That will happen, however, without any public renouncing of their ideological and religious identity, because religion and ideology still form the building blocks of society. In those cases in which a religious identity is abandoned, it will be traded in for one based on the effectiveness of the education offered. This effectiveness need not relate only to school results, but also to the extent to which the school offers students protection against the dangers of modern society (for example, dropping out of school, drugs). The legitimization of this efficiency will probably be rather multiform, ranging from ideological attention to certain didactics to religious identity or to a certain sociocultural composition of the student population. Because private nonprofit organizations may provide adequate surroundings more easily, there will not be a movement to increase the number of state-run schools. To the contrary, schools that are at the moment being managed by a local or national government might increasingly become schools managed by private nonprofit organizations or something similar. In short, the most likely development would be a transformation toward a type of nonreligious or nondenominational education.

This transformation of private production of education based on religious and ideological organizations to a system based on private nonprofit organizations might also create new problems. The private delivery of education by nonprofit organizations does not automatically lead to economically efficient educational organizations. A situation in which there are too many small schools governed by too many private nonprofit organizations leads to inefficiencies of scale and therefore to an overly expensive educational system. On the other hand, large nonprofit organizations, each managing many large schools, will not be very efficient either, because frequent and intensive involvement in the internal affairs of the school and with external authorities will diminish.[55] The cause of this is the necessary increase of bureaucracy and legal rigmarole. Therefore it will remain the task of the government, as provider of the collective means for education, to continually strive to strike a balance between efficiency and effectiveness.

Private nonprofit organizations have another classical drawback: they may fall into the hands of a certain elite in society. The managerial control of education may, in such a situation, become an uncontrollable instrument of power. The current structuring of education on denominational grounds is a good illustration of just such a situation: there is a close bond between the administrators of denominational education and the Christian Democratic political party, which took up a central position in the Dutch political landscape for a long time. This classical drawback makes an active national government necessary in order to prevent unproductive concentrations of power in education. If the transformation of the education system toward a more private production of education takes place too quietly or is dominated by rhetoric and symbolism, this disadvantage might be even more serious. Any solutions, such as handing administrative power to parents or schools, also must indicate which groups will receive this power in situations in which parents or schools do not have adequate administrative or market resources at their disposal (for example, in poor neighborhoods). Given the inequality among schools and parents, it is unlikely that all schools and groups in society will be able to summon the resources to administer a school effectively.

Discussion

The Dutch case shows that promoting more parental choice in education and more competition among schools can be a means to improve the quality of teaching, to decrease the level of bureaucracy in and around schools, and to reduce the costs within schools. The Dutch case also shows that it is possible to strike a fair balance between parental freedom of school choice and the aims of a national educational policy. It assumes, however, the equal funding and treatment of public and private religious schools by the state. Advocates of a strong market orientation and the absence of the state in education tend to forget these important conditions. Without these conditions, the introduction of religious schools will result in lower-quality teaching for the average student, more educational inequality, and a less balanced provision of education. A balanced combination of market forces and state involvement produces a better education for a larger part of the population than reliance on either the state or the market alone. Alone, either a powerful state or an almighty market inevitably will produce certain negative outcomes in education. For example, recent developments within the Dutch system show that free parental choice of public and private schools can increase social segregation among schools within the different school sectors, although parental choice does not necessarily increase the social segregation of different school sectors and can even soften the social segregation of neighborhoods.

The developments outlined earlier make the Dutch experiment interesting because they raise questions about why parents in a secularized society do not favor education that is managed by the government on behalf of that society but instead favor education managed by private organizations. Schools run by private nonprofit organizations will have, on average, more chances to achieve more effective management and to create a social network around those schools than schools that are run by local or national governments. This explanation of the existence of religious schools in a secular society cannot be seen as separate from explanations of the problems governments have in allotting quasi-collective services in other areas, such as health, social services, and the arts. In particular, the importance of maintaining face-to-face communication between parents and teachers while producing these quasi-collective services requires a less bureaucratic form of governance and administration. Private nonprofit organizations seem to be able to deal better with the two-sided, face-to-face demands of supplying quasi-collective services than private, profit-seeking organizations or public organizations. Therefore the former can produce quasi-collective services, under equal circumstances, more effectively and efficiently than the state or business organizations.

Notes

1. J. A. van Kemenade, P. L. M. Jungbluth, and J. M. M. Ritzen, "Onderwijs en samenleving," in J. A. van Kemenade and others, eds., *Onderwijs: bestel en beleid* (Groningen: Wolters-Noordhoff, 1981), pp. 95–242; C. Hermans, *Vorming in perspectief. Grondslagenstudie over identiteit van katholiek onderwijs* (The Hague: ABKO, 1993).

2. OECD, *Reviews of National Policies for Education* (Paris, 1991); E. James, "The Netherlands: Benefits and Costs of Privatized Services," in G. Walford, ed., *Private Schools in Ten Countries: Policy and Practice* (London: Routledge, 1989), p. 179.

3. F. Brown, "The Dutch Experience with School Choice: Implications for American Education," in P. W. Cookson Jr., ed., *The Choice Controversy* (Newbury Park, Calif.: Corwin Press, 1992), p. 177.

4. J. H. Bishop, "Privatizing Education: Lessons from Canada, Europe, and Asia," in C. E. Steuerle and others, eds., *Vouchers and the Provision of Public Services* (Brookings, 2000), pp. 292–335.

5. Bishop, "Privatizing Education."

6. A. M. Greeley, "Religion around the World Is Not Dying Out," *Origins*, vol. 23 (1993), pp. 49–58.

7. J. A. van Kemenade, *De katholieken en hun onderwijs. Een sociologisch onderzoek naar de betekenis van katholiek onderwijs onder ouders en docenten* (Meppel: Boom, 1968).

8. J. Dronkers, "Blijvende organisatorische onderwijsverzuiling ondanks secularisering. Een onbedoeld effect van overheidsbeleid?" *Beleid & Maatschappij*, vol. 19 (1992), pp. 227–37.

9. J. Dronkers, "The Existence of Parental Choice in the Netherlands," *Educational Policy*, vol. 9 (1995), pp. 227–43; A. B. Dijkstra, J. Dronkers, and R. Hofman, eds., *Verzuiling in het onderwijs. Actuele verklaringen en analyse* (Groningen: Wolters-Noordhoff, 1997).

10. S. Karsten, "Policy on Ethnic Segregation in a System of Choice: The Case of the Netherlands," *Journal of Education Policy*, vol. 9 (1994), pp. 211–25; A. B. Dijkstra, P. Jungbluth, and S. Ruiter, "Verzuiling, sociale klasse en etniciteit. Segregatie in het Nederlandse onderwijs," *Sociale Wetenschappen*, vol. 44 (2001), pp. 24–48.

11. G. Driessen and P. Valkenburg, "Islamic Schools in the Netherlands: Compromising between Identity and Quality?" *British Journal of Religious Education*, vol. 23 (2000), pp. 14–25.

12. Bishop, "Privatizing Education."

13. J. Dronkers, "Het betere is de vijand van het goede. Een reactie op de commentaren over het Trouw rapportcijfer," *Pedagogische Studiën*, vol. 75 (1998), pp. 142–50; D. R. Veenstra and others, "Scholen op rapport. Een reactie op het Trouw-onderzoek naar schoolprestaties," *Pedagogische Studiën*, vol. 75 (1998), pp. 121–34.

14. A. B. Dijkstra and others, eds., *Het oog der natie: scholen op rapport. Standaarden voor de publicatie van schoolprestaties* (Assen: Van Gorcum, 2001).

15. J. Dronkers, "Is het eindexamen wel gelijkwaardig tussen scholen? Discrepanties tussen de cijfers voor het schoolonderzoek en het centraal examen in het voortgezet onderwijs," farewell address as chair of Educational Sciences, University of Amsterdam, November 25, 1999 (www.iue.it/Personal/Dronkers).

16. J. Roeleveld and J. Dronkers, "Bijzondere of buitengewone scholen? Verschillen in effectiviteit van openbare en confessionele scholen in regio's waarin hun richting een meerderheids- of minderheidspositie inneemt," *Mens en Maatschappij*, vol. 69 (1994), pp. 85–108.

17. A. B. Dijkstra, *De religieuze factor. Onderwijskansen en godsdienst: een vergelijkend onderzoek naar gereformeerd-vrijgemaakte scholen* (Nijmegen: Instituut voor Toegepaste Sociale Wetenschappen, 1992).

18. Bishop, "Privatizing Education."

19. P. Koopman and J. Dronkers, "De effectiviteit van algemeen bijzondere scholen in het algemeen voortgezet onderwijs," *Pedagogische Studiën*, vol. 71 (1994), pp. 420–41.

20. "Pillarization" refers to the segmentation of Dutch society in separate networks of organizations and institutions (unions, hospitals, journals, schools, clubs, libraries, and so forth) on the basis of religion and ideology (Catholic, Protestant, social-democrat, neutral).

21. B. A. N. M. Vreeburg, *Identiteit en het verschil. Levensbeschouwelijke vorming en het Nederlands voortgezet onderwijs* (Zoetermeer: De Horstink, 1993).

22. R. H. Hofman, *Effectief schoolbestuur. Een studie naar de bijdrage van schoolbesturen aan de effectiviteit van basisscholen* (Groningen: RION, 1993).

23. R. H. Hofman and others, "Variation in Effectiveness between Private and Public Schools: The Impact of School and Family Networks," *Educational Research and Evaluation*, vol. 2 (1996), pp. 366–94.

24. A. W. M. Claassen, *Schipperen tussen school en kerk. Een onderzoek bij onderwijsgevenden van katholieke basisscholen naar de situatie van de hedendaagse schoolkatechese tegen de achtergrond van haar geschiedenis* (Nijmegen: Dekker & van de Vegt, 1985); E. Roede, Th. Peetsma, and F. Riemersma, *Betrokkenheid bij godsdienstonderwijs. Evaluatie van de lesmethode "Levende Godsdienst"* (SCO-Kohnstamm Instituut, Universiteit van Amsterdam, 1994).

25. S. Karsten, J. Meijer, and T. T. D. Peetsma, "Vrijheid van inrichting onderzocht," *Nederlands tijdschrift voor onderwijsrecht en onderwijsbeleid,* vol. 8 (1996), pp.101–10; Consultatiecommissie Katholiek Onderwijs 2000+, *Is het katholiek onderwijs millennium-bestendig?* (Nederlandse Katholieke Schoolraad, 1999).

26. A. B. Dijkstra and S. Miedema, *Bijzonder gemotiveerd. Een onderzoek naar de ideale school volgens dragers en vragers van confessioneel basisonderwijs* (Assen: Van Gorcum, 2003).

27. For reviews of this research, see Dijkstra, Dronkers and Hofman, *Verzuiling in het onderwijs*; A. B. Dijkstra, G. Driessen, and R. Veenstra, "Academic Achievement in Public, Religious, and Private Schools: Sector and Outcomes Differences in Holland," paper presented at the annual meeting of the American Educational Research Association, Seattle, April 11, 2001.

28. Koopman and Dronkers, "De effectiviteit van algemeen bijzondere scholen."

29. Dijkstra, *De religieuze factor.*

30. J. Dronkers, "Schoolkenmerken en individuele prestaties," in P. Vogel and others, eds. *De school: keuzen en kansen. Onderwijssociologische studies* (Muiderberg: Coutinho, 1989), pp. 60–76.

31. Roeleveld and Dronkers, "Bijzondere of buitengewone scholen?"

32. Hofman, *Effectief schoolbestuur.*

33. Dijkstra, Dronkers, and Hofman, *Verzuiling in het onderwijs.*

34. C. Felix, S. Karsten and L. van de Venne, *De positie van het openbaar onderwijs* (SCO-Kohnstamm Instituut, Universiteit van Amsterdam, 2002).

35. A. B. Dijkstra, "Opbrengsten van onderwijsvrijheid. Over de effecten van verzuild onderwijs," in T. J. van der Ploeg and others, eds., *De vrijheid van onderwijs, de ontwikkeling van een bijzonder grondrecht* (Utrecht: Lemma, 2000), pp. 243–59.

36. Dijkstra and others, *Het oog der natie: scholen op rapport.*

37. L. Van Marwijk Kooy-von Baumhauer, *Scholen verschillen. Een verkennend vergelijkend onderzoek naar het intern functioneren van vijfentwintig scholengemeenschappen voor vwo-havo-mavo* (Groningen: Wolters-Noordhoff, 1984).

38. K. Wittebrood, *Politieke socialisatie in Nederland* (Amsterdam: Thesis Publishers, 1995).

39. B. Vreeburg and J. Dronkers, *Effecten van denominatie op tijdsbesteding en uitgavenpatroon van scholieren in het voortgezet onderwijs* (SCO-Kohnstamm Instituut, Universiteit van Amsterdam, 1995).

40. J. W. M. Knuver, *De relatie tussen klas- en schoolkenmerken en het affectief functioneren van leerlingen* (Groningen: RION, 1993).

41. R. H. Hofman, *Algemeen bijzondere schoolbesturen en hun basisscholen* (Groningen: RION, 1994).

42. P. Jungbluth, T. Peetsma, and J. Roeleveld, *Leerlingprestaties en leerlinggedrag in het primair onderwijs* (Nijmegen/Amsterdam: ITS/SCO-Kohnstamm Instituut, 1996).

43. G. Driessen and F. van der Slik, "Religion, Denomination and Education in the Netherlands: Cognitive and Noncognitive Outcomes after an Era of Secularization," *Journal for the Scientific Study of Religion*, vol. 40 (2001), pp. 561–72.

44. J. Braster, "De effecten van verzuild basisonderwijs op de waardeoriëntaties van Nederlandse jongeren," *Sociale Wetenschappen*, vol. 44 (2001), pp. 49–69.

45. A. B. Dijkstra, *Werelden apart? Leefstijlen van middelbare scholieren* (Assen: Van Gorcum, 2002).

46. A. B. Dijkstra and P. Jungbluth, "The Institutionalization of Social Segmentation? Segregation of Schooling in the Netherlands," paper presented at the 33rd World Congress of the International Institute of Sociology, Cologne, July 1997.

47. Dijkstra, Jungbluth, and Ruiter. "Verzuiling, sociale klasse en etniciteit."

48. S. Karsten and others, "School Choice and Ethnic Segregation," *Educational Policy*, vol. 17 (2003), pp. 452–77.

49. Although not convincing, due to a lack of necessary research sophistication, see David Rusk, Dirk Frieling, and Leon Groenemeijer, *Inside Game/Outside Game: Segregation and Spatial Planning in Metropolitan Areas* (Delft: ABF Strategie, 2001).

50. P. de Graaf, *De invloed van financiële en culturele hulpbronnen in onderwijsloopbanen* (Nijmegen: Instituut voor Toegepaste Sociale Wetenschappen, 1987).

51. J. B. J. Koelman, *Kosten van verzuiling; een studie over het lager onderwijs* (Den Haag: VUGA, 1987).

52. Dijkstra, Driessen and Veenstra, "Academic Achievement in Public, Religious, and Private Schools."

53. J. M. G. Leune, "The Meaning of Government Legislation and Funding for Primary and Secondary Schools with a Religious Character in the Netherlands," paper for a colloquium on "The Ambiguous Embrace of Government," Erasmus University, Rotterdam, November 1996; Onderwijsraad, *Advies Richtingvrij en richtingbepalend* (1996).

54. T. Netelenbos, *De identiteit van de school in een pluriforme samenleving* (Den Haag: OCW, 1997).

55. Hofman and others, "Variation in Effectiveness between Private and Public Schools."

4

Regulation, Choice, and Basic Values in Education in England and Wales: A Legal Perspective

NEVILLE HARRIS

The political, economic, and philosophical underpinnings of the development of school choice in England and Wales have been well covered by scholars.[1] Less attention, however, has been paid to the role of law. The educational policy literature understandably adopts a broad-brush approach to the legal dimension of policy implementation—not least because the increasing volume and complexity of the law make any other approach appear impractical. This is doubly problematic because of the importance of the role of law in shaping not only the educational system itself but also the relationships among the various interested individuals and institutions.

The framework of rights that is developing around these relationships has increased the importance of paying close attention to the legal dimension. The 1998 Human Rights Act, which came into full operation in England and Wales in October 2000, incorporates into national law the key articles of the European Convention on Human Rights and Fundamental Freedoms (referred to in this chapter as the European Convention on Human Rights). Particularly relevant are those providing for respect for private and family life, freedom of religion, nondiscrimination in relation to the rights and freedoms protected by the convention, and the right to an education respectful of parents' religious and philosophical convictions.[2] So far as possible, the courts must construe U.K. legislation in a way that is compatible with the rights guaranteed in the convention and may strike down secondary legislation that is incompatible with the convention or issue a declaration of incompatibility to the government regarding acts of Parliament. Public authorities (a term that includes the courts for the purposes of this duty) must act in a way that is compatible with convention rights. [3] The rights framework is now particularly pertinent to any evaluation of the place of choice or civic values in the educational context, in addition to being relevant to wider social and political participation. [4]

Education is one of the most heavily regulated public sectors in the United Kingdom, irrespective of recent efforts by the government to reduce red tape and bureaucracy in the school system and to deregulate certain areas. [5] It is perhaps ironic that the freeing up of state schools to form companies under the 2002 Education Act is being accomplished through a detailed set of new regulations! [6] Regulation was used during the 1980s and 1990s to reconstitute the power relationships within the education system, adopt elements of market choice and competition, and transform the institutional framework. While elements of institutional autonomy considered necessary for choice and competition to flourish were introduced, central regulation enabled the government to exert considerable control over the flow of resources and to ensure the implementation of policy goals. Key landmarks included the 1980 Education Act, which introduced a presumption in favor of parental preference regarding school choice and requirements for publishing school information (including examination results); and the 1988 Education Reform Act, which provided for a national curriculum and pupil testing, leading in turn to the compilation and required publication of further school performance information. Delegation of budgets to individual schools, with funding allocations linked to pupil recruitment, was also introduced, and capping the number of pupils at a level below school capacity was banned.

With the enactment of the 2002 Education Act, legal regulation of the English and Welsh education systems reached an important stage. [7] It followed more than two decades of increasing centralization of power under a succession of legislative measures covering the organization and content of state education—a process that the election of the Labour government in 1997, after eighteen years of Conservative administrations, failed to halt despite changes in policy emphasis. The 2002 act provides for the selective relinquishment of central power in key areas. In particular, markedly successful state schools are now able to "earn" autonomy and freedom in relation to teaching the statutory national curriculum, and legislative barriers to collaboration between schools have been eased so that two or more schools can develop joint working arrangements and delegate certain decisions to joint committees, without becoming fully federated under a single governing body. Yet it would be a mistake to see the 2002 act as a major turning point. Indeed, regulation has increased in general and in several specific areas—for example, in relation to independent schools.[8] One of the dominant forms is the legislative power conferred on ministers of state by primary legislation (that is, an act of Parliament).[9] One of the purposes of the 2002 act is to effect the modernization of education law by shifting various details, such as regulatory orders, from primary legislation into secondary legislation, with the ostensible purpose of speeding up the process of reform and innovation.[10]

Against the background of pervasive state regulation outlined above, this chapter explores the ways in which choice and basic social and cultural values are promoted within the school system. To put this analysis into proper context, it is first necessary to explain the diverse school system itself.

The Developing School System

To understand the current school system in England and Wales it is necessary to be aware of some features of its historical development, starting with the landmark 1944 Education Act.

Categories of Schools after 1944

The current state school system originated with the 1944 Education Act. Leaving aside the standard categorization of schools based on student age[11] or on whether students are selected on the basis of their academic ability,[12] the essential division was between schools established by religious bodies, which were denominational, and schools that were essentially secular. This arose from the skillful balancing of interests under the act by R. A. Butler, the minister of education. In order to assist the wider policy goal of education for all, Butler sought to support, in the state sector, schools run by the Church of England and the Catholic Church, many of which were struggling to maintain their school buildings and meet operating costs. In many cases these schools were not in a strong position to adapt to a newly reformed education system. Around half the schools in England and Wales were run by the churches at the outbreak of World War II, although they provided for less than one-third of the total school population.[13] The Catholic Church wanted to retain control of its own schools, while the Church of England recognized that a shortage of funds put the future of its schools in jeopardy.

The 1944 act offered most of these church schools a choice between "controlled" or "aided" status. The former meant that the school would retain its religious character but would be funded entirely by the local education

authority (LEA), which would have control over staff appointments—strictly
speaking, this is no longer the case—and would generally follow a locally
agreed syllabus for religious education.[14] Aided status, on the other hand,
would give the school's foundation body (its founders or their successors)
much more control over staff appointments and the content of religious education, plus majority membership in the school's governing body (namely, a
"board of managers" in primary schools or a "board of governors" in secondary schools, both known today as the "governing body"). Although the LEA
would meet the aided school's operational costs, the foundation body would
have to meet 50 percent of the capital costs (this was later reduced in stages
to 15 percent and recently to 10 percent).[15] While aimed primarily at the
Catholic sector, aided status also was chosen by some of the Church of
England schools, although controlled was the preferred status for the majority. A small number of church schools were in a third category—"special
agreement" schools—under the 1944 act. Their status was very similar to
that of aided schools, but their funding arrangements were based on an
agreement between the school and the LEA. They have since been designated
as aided schools under the 1998 School Standards and Framework Act. The
other mainstream schools were "county" schools—nondenominational and
controlled and funded entirely by the LEA. County schools were redesig-
nated under the 1998 act as "community" schools.

Under a range of statutes from 1986 to 1993 the government passed significant decisionmaking power and authority, including management of
school budgets, from the LEAs to schools.[16] Concomitantly, the structure
and role of school government was changed to reduce the influence of local
government and give parents greater representation. Institutional autonomy
within the state sector, part of the process of creating a market among competing institutions, reached a new height with the "grant-maintained" school,
a category introduced under the 1988 Education Reform Act. Grant-maintained schools were outside LEA control and received their budget directly
from the central Funding Agency for Schools.[17] Most county and voluntary
(aided and controlled) schools were eligible for grant-maintained status, and
it later became available to special schools (schools specializing in educating
students with learning difficulties). To acquire grant-maintained status, a
school first needed to receive the formal approval of the school's governing
body.[18] Then parents voted, but the secretary of state for education had the
final say on the matter. A number of legal battles were fought in the courts as
LEAs attempted to halt this undermining of their power.[19] Grant-maintained
status was promoted by central government as a means of giving parents further choice. In reality, though, it was an ideologically grounded device for

weakening further the hold of LEAs over the school system, part of a more general centralization of national government power.[20] The Conservative government continued to expand opportunities for schools to acquire grant-maintained status by streamlining the acquisition procedure and enabling groups of schools, including small primary schools, to apply jointly for grant-maintained status and by allowing new schools to be established with this status.[21] However, only about 1,200 schools (far fewer than the government had predicted) had become grant-maintained by 1998, when that type of school was abolished by statute.[22]

The enhancement of parental choice as a result of the creation of grant-maintained schools was probably overstated. Whether greater autonomy, the transfer of both property and staff employment contracts from the LEA to the school, the higher funding allocations (through capital grants), and the far greater representation of parents on the school's governing body—not to mention the absence of LEA appointed governors—really gave these schools a distinctive character is unclear. The content of education did not change, as schools that acquired grant-maintained status were still bound to follow the national curriculum and relevant religious education requirements. Although in some cases the schools that applied for grant-maintained status saw it as a means of preventing their closure by the LEA, in many other cases applications were made by schools that were already the most popular or successful, reinforcing a false perception that grant-maintained status per se was precipitating improvements in educational standards. Nonetheless, the autonomy enjoyed by grant-maintained schools was highly favored by their head teachers and arguably strengthened the schools' internal government. In this regard, it is significant that the legislation abolishing grant-maintained status and creating "foundation school" status in its place provided for only minimal LEA representation on these schools' governing bodies and preserved elements of autonomy—for example, in the use of school facilities.[23] The recent legislative provision under the 2002 Education Act for "earned autonomy" from some areas of regulation for any high-achieving school provides some potential for another distinct cadre of more-autonomous schools within the state system.

Along with the introduction of grant-maintained status came a new form of school, the city college, of which there were two categories—the "city technology college" and the "city college for the technology of the arts." These urban secondary schools—there are only fifteen of them—are established with the aid of private sector sponsorships and public money, although in practice less of the former than was envisaged has materialized. They must cater to pupils of "different abilities"—in other words, not

Table 4-1. *Number of Primary and Secondary Schools in England, 2003*

School type	Primary schools	Secondary schools	Total
Community	11,153	2,248	13,401
Voluntary aided	3,729	551	4,280
Voluntary controlled	2,614	127	2,741
Foundation	365	510	875
Total	17,861	3,436	21,297

Based on the figures in Department for Education and Skills, *Statistics of Education: Schools in England, 2003* (London, 2003), table 21.

merely to the academically most able—but, since a change made in 2002, no longer do the children have to be age eleven or over.[24] What is unique about these schools is that they were categorized as independent schools from the start, but they are nonetheless subject to a certain degree of control by the secretary of state.[25] The colleges are exempt from the statutory requirements concerning the national curriculum and religious education and worship that apply to mainstream state schools, and they regulate their own admission procedures. Nonetheless, under the funding agreement between the central government and the proprietor or promoter, the colleges are subject to minimum curriculum requirements consistent with a school's statutory duty to offer a broad curriculum.

Rather than abandon this hybrid, public-private model, the Labour government has extended the concept by adding another type, the "city academy," specializing in modern foreign languages, visual/media arts, sport, or other prescribed subjects.[26] In addition, it is in the process of renaming city academies and both types of city technology college as "academies," with planned links to the rest of the school system for the purposes of the organization of school admissions.[27] Private sector involvement in state schools and LEAs has also developed in other ways—particularly in the construction or alteration of school buildings, grounds, and facilities.

Numbers and Designation of Schools

According to the most recent official figures, there were 21,297 maintained primary and secondary schools in England as of January 2003. The numbers in each category are shown in table 4-1.[28] The religious affiliation of voluntary and foundation schools is shown in table 4-2.[29] Most foundation schools have no religious affiliation. In January 2003 there were also 1,160 special schools and 2,178 independent schools.[30] Approximately 7.5 million children were registered at community, voluntary, or foundation schools; 96,000 at special schools; and 590,000 attended independent schools.[31]

Table 4-2. Foundation and Voluntary Schools in England by Religious Affiliation, 2003

Religious affiliation	Primary schools			Secondary schools			Total
	Aided	Controlled	Foundation	Aided	Controlled	Foundation	
Church of England	1,933	2,522	38	126	63	8	4,690
Roman Catholic	1,724	0	0	351	0	1	2,076
Methodist	3	24	0	0	0	0	27
Other Christian	20	28	1	21	6	1	77
Jewish	28	0	0	5	0	0	33
Muslim	2	0	0	2	0	0	4
Sikh	1	0	0	1	0	0	2
Other	1	0	0	1	0	0	2
No affiliation	17	40	326	44	58	500	985

Based on the figures in Department for Education and Skills, *Statistics of Education: Schools in England, 2003*.

Choice of School and Schooling

The earliest mention of school choice under education law in England and Wales is in the 1944 Education Act, which required those exercising statutory functions—the secretary of state for education and LEAs—to "have regard to the general principle that pupils are to be educated in accordance with the wishes of their parents, so far as that is compatible with the provision of efficient instruction and training and the avoidance of unreasonable public expenditure."[32] This was only a general principle, however, and it did not give parents a guaranteed choice. But the 1980 Education Act promised what one judge subsequently referred to as an "enhanced principle of parental choice."[33] The law is now to be found in the 1998 School Standards and Framework Act, as amended. Parents must be granted an opportunity to express a preference for a state school.[34] Their preference must be upheld, subject to exceptions that reflect the fact that admission authorities often cannot "give effect to every preference which has been expressed" because popular schools tend to be oversubscribed.[35] Applicants are at the mercy of the local admissions policy and the categories for admission within it. One of the most important factors for admission typically is residence in a school's catchment area or neighborhood zone, although sibling attendance, distance from home to school, and medical or substantial social factors also are typical criteria. Catchment areas often are used as a rationing device by LEAs, but they are potentially problematic because they may maintain social divisions and limit the choice of particular ethnic groups that are concentrated in particular areas.[36] Nevertheless, they have been deemed legitimate by the courts.[37] All things being equal, it is unlawful to discriminate against applicants for a school simply because they live outside the LEA's boundary,[38] but otherwise the catchment area criterion tends to prevail. [39]

Both the framing of local admissions policies and the decisionmaking process are guided by the statutory Code of Practice.[40] The admissions policy interacts with the grounds set out in the 1998 School Standards and Framework Act for denying preference—namely, that the admission of a child would "prejudice efficient education or the efficient use of resources" or, if the school is permitted to use academic selection, that there are academic grounds for refusing admission.[41] In one leading case, the parents sought a place at a girls-only Catholic secondary school in London.[42] The school's admissions policy permitted priority for admission to be given to Catholics. In this case one Muslim girl and one Hindu girl were refused admission. In the House of Lords, Lord Browne-Wilkinson recognized that "[v]iews may differ as to whether the religious leaning of the school or parental preference should prevail."[43] The court held that the law sanctioned the use of religious criteria in admissions to a religious school, as they formed a rational basis for determining priority in the selection of pupils for a place if the school was oversubscribed.

It is clear that there is no right of choice as such.[44] For example, an Audit Commission survey of ten local authorities revealed that one of every five parents had not obtained his or her genuine first preference of state secondary school.[45] To claim, as governments have done, that parents have a choice of state school is somewhat disingenuous in any event, given that many choices are excluded by reasons of religion or geography. Gorard, Taylor, and Fitz found that LEAs using catchment areas to determine admissions have above-average levels of socioeconomic segregation among pupil intakes to schools.[46] The Audit Commission report concluded that in the purportedly marketized system, the reality was that choice tended to be exercised by the schools themselves, through the admissions policy, rather than by parents. Since then, the introduction of a statutory maximum class size for five- to seven-year-olds has probably restricted primary school choice still further for some parents by limiting places at some schools. The Office for Standards in Education has noted how attempts to adjust the market by facilitating the expansion of popular schools may help some parents but can threaten the viability of less popular schools that still have an important role in advancing social cohesion in communities.[47]

Since 1980, parents have had the right to appeal a denial of school admission, and increasing numbers of parents have exercised that right.[48] Appeals increased from 25,203 in 1991 to 41,389 in 1994—a 64 percent increase over just three years.[49] But the latest statistics show that they reached a staggering annual total of 94,900 in 2001–02.[50] Of the appeals lodged that year, 66,100 appeals were heard, of which 21,700 were upheld, meaning that one-third of parents won their case. A substantial body of case law, legislation, and official guidance now govern the appeal process and have rendered it a legal minefield for admission appeal panels.[51]

As demonstrated, the school admissions process is heavily regulated in England and Wales. Indeed, regulation and choice interact in important ways. What values are in play? Despite the apparent moral neutrality of markets, the process of regulation was not and is not value free. Regulation can, for example, be used to promote social values within a market-based process. In the context of choice in education, this can be seen in attempts to ensure that, however competition and choice operate, greater equality of access and social inclusion are promoted. Examples of intervention in the United Kingdom include extending the 1995 Disability Discrimination Act to educational institutions and affirming the value of mainstreaming children with special educational needs.[52] Another relevant development is the proposed creation of an Office for Fair Access, under a Director of Fair Access to Higher Education, whose role the government is aiming to establish through the higher education bill that currently is being debated in Parliament. The aim is to help widen participation in higher education.[53] Similarly, legislative reform of the school curriculum, under a succession of statutes, has injected a range of values into the provision of education.[54] To take one example, sex education must be "given in such a manner as to encourage . . . pupils to have due regard to moral considerations and the value of family life," and central guidance to schools must aim to ensure that pupils learn "the nature of marriage and its importance for family life and the bringing up of children."[55] To take another value-laden example, "citizenship" has recently been added as a compulsory subject under the national curriculum.[56] In that subject, the prescribed attainment targets for students of age fourteen to sixteen refer not only to knowledge and understanding of legal and political institutions and the rights and responsibilities of citizens, but also to a critical appreciation of "different ways of bringing about change at different levels of society." They also require that pupils take part in "school and community-based activities, showing a willingness and commitment to evaluate such activities critically" and demonstrate "personal and group responsibility in their attitudes to themselves and others."[57]

Education law also promotes parental responsibility through home-school agreements and strict enforcement of school attendance.[58] Good behavior by pupils is emphasized within the disciplinary framework established by statute and statutory guidance, recently amended to enhance the power of schools to exclude violent or persistently disruptive pupils.[59] New powers have been introduced to enforce parental responsibility for truancy and expulsions (referred to as "exclusions") through the 2003 Anti-social Behaviour Act.[60] These provisions apply irrespective of the state school that is selected by parents or pupils.

Parents seeking further choice over educational content or values may look to independent schools. Opportunities to exercise such a choice were enhanced by the "assisted places" scheme introduced by the Conservative government under the 1980 Education Act. The scheme was designed to enable academically able children from poorer backgrounds to receive an independent education, thereby extending a choice to their parents otherwise denied them because of their income level. Independent schools were able to enter into agreements with the Department of Education and Science (now the Department for Education and Skills), enabling them to participate in the scheme. The secretary of state could terminate an agreement if educational standards were not being maintained at the school or if conditions of the agreement or the relevant regulations were not met. Under the scheme, the school fees and incidental expenses of an eligible child would be wholly or partly met by the department. Eligibility for an assisted place was limited to low-income students who met the school's entry requirements. In one sense, the scheme represented a partial privatization of education, since without this support the pupil would be educated in a state school. Approximately 40,000 children obtained an assisted place each year the scheme was in effect, and it became very important to the independent sector in maintaining enrollments and resource levels during times of economic recession. In some schools, up to 40 percent of pupils had an assisted place.[61]

In 1997, the new Labour government decided to end the assisted places scheme, arguing that it cost the state £145 million (equivalent to around $250 million at the time) annually and that the funds could be put to better use, such as by facilitating the government's plan to reduce class sizes in state-run primary schools.[62] The 1997 Education (Schools) Act subsequently provided for phasing out the scheme by excluding any new school entrants. However, the exclusion of assisted primary-stage children when they transferred up to their secondary stage at an "all-through" (ages five through eighteen) school resulted in litigation, because it conflicted with preelection reassurances given by members of the new government. The court, however, held that the preelection promises were not legally binding.[63]

Regulation of Independent Schools

In its first major policy paper on schools, in 1997, the newly elected Labour government stated that "[t]he educational apartheid created by the public/private divide diminishes the whole education system."[64] The official line seems to have softened considerably since then and currently projects no ideological concern about private education. Indeed, the government has articulated its approval:

> The independent sector is diverse, with schools that cater for a wide range of faiths, philosophies and family circumstances. A flourishing independent sector provides stimulus and challenges to maintained schools, and we hope that the sector will retain its tradition of providing distinctive education that reflects the unique ethos of individual schools.[65]

So enamored does the Labour government now appear to be with private schools that it is encouraging them to collaborate with state schools and share good practices and facilities with them.[66] To this end, it has set up the Independent/State School Partnership scheme. Since 1997, 220 partnerships have been funded and a further sixty will be funded during 2004 and 2005 at a cost of £1 million.[67] The government also has established a more rigorous regime of registration and monitoring of independent schools, which is likely to have a further legitimizing effect by countering some of the traditional opposition to these schools based on their freedom from control, which contributed to their privileged status and enhanced their exclusivity.

Inspection

An important aspect of the regulation of *all* schools has been the school inspection regime, which was radically reformed in 1992.[68] A chief inspector of schools—one for England and one for Wales—reports on educational standards and the quality of management in schools and administers the system of school inspections, which are carried out mostly by inspectors registered with the Office for Standards in Education. Public expenditures on the regulation and inspection of education and child care by the office ran to £155 million (equivalent to $280 million) in 2001–02 and were estimated to increase to £195.5 million ($350 million) in 2002–03.[69] Independent schools other than city technology colleges or academies and approved special schools are, however, excluded from this education inspection regime. It was envisaged at the time of the 1992 reforms that a parallel system for independent school inspections would develop, and until recently around 80 percent of these schools were being inspected, at a charge to the school, under arrangements made by the Independent Schools Council (ISC).[70] The chief inspector nevertheless had to mandate inspection of an independent school when directed to do so by the secretary of state.[71] In addition, the chief inspector had (and still retains) the power to require *any* school in England, including an independent school, to be inspected.[72] All *provisionally* registered independent schools and the 20 percent of independent schools that were not ISC-inspected were inspected by the Office for Standards in Education. Since the 2002 Education Act, however, inspection of *all* registered independent schools is carried out at the instigation of the registration authority under the aegis of the Office for Standards in Education by Her Majesty's inspectors or by a registered inspector as arranged by the chief inspector.[73] In the *Talmud Torah School* case, one of the objections to the inspectors' findings raised by the school was that the inspection team was not qualified to judge this Hasidic Jewish school because it lacked the necessary special cultural and linguistic expertise.[74] This is likely to remain a problem for the Office for Standards in Education when conducting inspections under the new arrangements.

Unlike state schools, private schools are now required to pay for inspections. Rates, which are related to the number of pupils, are set by regulation.[75] Reports of inspections will be published by the registration authority on its website. The Office for Standards in Education expects an independent school to be inspected at least once every six years, a more regular cycle than at present.[76] Enforcement measures can be taken when the school is deficient, but independent schools are outside the strict enforcement regime covering state schools that are failing or otherwise giving cause for concern.[77]

Registration and Standards

The registration system dates back to the 1944 Education Act. The statutory framework was consolidated in the 1996 Education Act but did not change in substance. However, a major change occurred in 2003.

Under the 1944–2003 system a register of independent schools was kept by the registration authority.[78] A school could not become registered if, by virtue of an order, the proprietor or premises were disqualified or the premises were used or proposed to be used for any disqualified purpose.[79] It was an offense to run a school or to seek or accept employment at a school while any disqualification was in force.[80] Initial registration was provisional, but by 2003 there was concern that some seventy of the 2,200 registered independent schools had been provisionally registered for more than two years.[81] It was a criminal offense to conduct an independent school that was not registered or provisionally registered or to engage in any act calculated to lead to the belief that a provisionally registered school was fully registered.[82] All the above offenses attracted a maximum fine of £2,500 or imprisonment for a term not exceeding three months, or both.[83]

The principal quality control mechanism was the secretary of state's duty to serve a statutory "notice of complaint" if the school premises or any parts of them were unsuitable; if accommodation provided was inadequate or unsuitable; if the proprietor or a member of the staff was not a "proper person" to undertake his or her role; if efficient and suitable instruction was not being provided at the school; or if there was a failure in the statutory duty to safeguard the welfare of a child boarding at the school.[84] Unless the faults were irremediable, the notice had to specify the measures necessary to remedy the deficiencies and the time (a minimum of six months) allowed for taking them. There was a right of appeal against the notice to an Independent Schools Tribunal.[85]

An important judgment under the old law has continuing relevance. The High Court accepted that, in the case of an independent school catering to the special traditions and characteristics of a particular religious group, the school might be "suitable" if it primarily equipped the children for a place in their own particular religious community rather than in the wider community, provided they were left with the capacity to choose some other way of life later on.[86] Nevertheless, Justice Woolf said that although the secretary of state for education had a duty, when considering the suitability of provision, to take account of parental wishes, particularly with regard to matters of religion, he was "perfectly entitled to have a policy setting down a minimum requirement which he will normally apply to all schools irrespective of the background of the children sent to that school." Despite dismissing the legal challenge of the plaintiff—a Hasidic Jewish school—to the secretary of state's notice of complaint, the judge was critical of the secretary's prescription of a minimum number of hours for secular subjects and his expectation that music and drama would be part of the curriculum of this school: "drama is not acceptable to the community on religious grounds and instrumental music is only tolerated on special occasions, such as weddings." Aside from this judgment, there has been no wider judicial guidance on "suitability" in this context.

It was reported in 2003 that, according to the ISC's inspectors:

In a minority of independent schools with a religious basis there is still insufficient time allocated to the secular curriculum and the balance is unsatisfactory. Many of these schools have a pattern of religious studies in the morning, with a secular curriculum delivered in as little as two hours in the afternoon and with limited learning resources. The creative and aesthetic areas of the curriculum are often poorly represented.[87]

Striking an appropriate balance between respecting the autonomy and values of religious minorities and applying the necessary social and educational standards in registering and inspecting independent schools remain problematic. The new standards for independent schools, described below, are unlikely fully to resolve this difficulty.

According to the chief inspector of schools in England, speaking in April 2003, "the . . . system of registration, deriving largely from the 1944 Act, has not done enough to force [the worst independent] schools to improve, or close."[88] The government had already acknowledged the need for stricter enforcement of standards and provided for a new regulatory regime under part 10 of the 2002 Education Act. This part of the Act, along with separate regulations, came into force in September 2003. Standards relating to the quality of education and matters such as premises and accommodation, pupil welfare, pupil development, the suitability of proprietors, and the handling of complaints are all prescribed.[89] One of the specific areas covered is "the spiritual, moral, social and cultural development of pupils." The government's consultation paper on the standards sees these as matters largely for schools and parents to determine, however, and there is an aim "to minimize regulation." At the same time, though, it recognizes a need to ensure that "on leaving independent schools, pupils are likely to become well adjusted citizens."[90] This arguably reflects Justice Woolf's reference to ensuring that a curriculum enables students from all religious minority backgrounds to participate in wider society and clearly was applied by the inspectors in one of the first inspections under the new system.[91] In a similar vein, the regulations require that if English is not the principal language of instruction, the curriculum must include lessons in written and spoken English.

The regulations prescribe educational content in very general and rather utilitarian terms, referring to such matters as well-planned lessons, attention to the intellectual development of pupils, preparation for adult life, and the acquisition of mathematical skills. The regulations also place an emphasis on values such as tolerance for others, knowing right from wrong, taking initiative, behaving well, and understanding different cultures and the working of public institutions and services. These prescribed civic and moral values are clearly uncontroversial; many of them reflect the broad curricular duties imposed on state schools.[92] But there is certainly a lack of detailed prescription. In contrast to the detailed content of the national curriculum in subjects such as mathematics, history, and technology, set out in separate publications and statutory orders, there is more general terminology: "full-time supervised education for all pupils of compulsory school age, which gives pupils experience in linguistic, mathematical, scientific, technological, human and social, physical and aesthetic and creative education" and "subject matter appropriate for the ages and aptitudes of pupils, including those pupils with a statement [of special educational needs]." Sex education, compulsory for all secondary school pupils in state schools and subject there to detailed statutory guidance, is not mentioned specifically.[93] Instead, there is "personal, social and health education which reflects the school's aims and ethos"—an apparent bow to the sensitivities of particular religious and ethnic groups. In the light of such sensitivities, the standard requiring "aesthetic and creative education" may be more problematic in some schools than the one regarding personal education.

Under the new registration system, maximum penalties for running an unregistered school—a £5000 ($9000) fine, up to six months in prison, or both—are higher than they were before.[94] The chief inspector of schools has powers of investigation, and there is a separate offense of willfully obstructing his or her officers.[95] A "material change" to a school after registration requires approval by the registration authority.[96] A school's failure to meet the prescribed education standards could lead to immediate removal from the register if there is a risk of serious harm to pupils or if remedial work identified by the registration authority is not made in a timely fashion. Other orders that could be issued include a direction to close off part of its premises or not admit new pupils, and noncompliance is an offense.[97] A school also may be removed from the register if it employs an unsuitable person as proprietor, teacher, or other worker.[98] Strict regulations regarding the provision of information by proprietors may be imposed, with a criminal offense of noncompliance.[99] Appeals in respect of registration and other decisions now lie to a tribunal established under the 1999 Protection of Children Act; the Independent Schools Tribunal has been abolished.[100]

One can see, therefore, that registration requirements and enforcement powers, combined in relevant cases with the contractual framework of the city technology college arrangements, set in place controls to preserve the autonomy of independent schools while providing some basic safeguards for parents and children. Moreover, antidiscrimination legislation applies to independent schools as well as to others. Independent schools also must operate in accordance with the terms of any trust deeds under which they were established and, for the approximately 50 percent of independent schools that have charitable status, in compliance with charity law.[101] Nonetheless, there is only "light touch" regulation of management structure, curriculum, and discipline. The disciplinary power to expel a pupil, for example, is subject to appeal and prescribed procedures in state schools but is essentially unregulated in independent schools, where the only remedy for a parent or child is through court action for breach of contract.[102] Similarly, there is little control over staff appointments on religious grounds, unlike in the public sector.[103] However, prohibitions on the employment of teachers for reasons of poor health, misconduct, unsuitability for working with children, or inclusion on a particular list (known as List 99) appear to apply to all schools, including independent schools.[104]

It is important to see the relative freedom of independent schools against the background of a heavily regulated state school system. The contrast between the public and private sectors in regulatory terms is still considerable. To the Conservatives, the essential rationale for an autonomous independent school system is to accommodate parental choice and promote high educational achievement. Independent schools on the whole still cater to the academically able and the socially and economically privileged (although, even if they enjoy charitable status giving them tax concessions, they still need to charge substantial fees to parents, save for the few parents whose child is awarded a scholarship). Recently, however, some parents have begun to question the merits of choosing an independent school due to perceived discrimination by some U.K. universities against applicants from independent schools in favor of public school students who have lower grades but suitable potential. The Labour government too supports efforts by universities to promote wider access to higher education in this way— comparable to "affirmative action" in the United States—and intends to set indicators of access that take into account family income, average school results, and even parents' educational background.[105] This has led to suggestions that the demand for private education might wane.

However, for those parents who still see advantages to private education and for the politicians and others who regard independent schools' freedom as contributing unfairly to the uneven playing field on which state and private schools compete, there is the reassurance that the new, more strict regulatory regime may to some extent even things out. Under the new system, outlined above, the status of the independent sector as a whole is likely to become more robust politically, thereby consolidating parental choice in favor of private education. The Labour government appears to regard the independent sector as contributing to the realization of its ideological commitment to plurality and respect for cultural diversity in the educational context, combined with high levels of academic attainment. Within this ideological framework, there also must be an underlying recognition of human rights and fundamental freedoms, especially since the implementation of the 1998 Human Rights Act. Yet the actions of private schools could lie largely outside that framework of protection, as discussed below.

Personal Integrity and Respect for Personal Beliefs

Ensuring respect for personal integrity enables individuals to make a choice that reflects their personal beliefs. Such a choice might be linked to religious identity, but it also could reflect personal philosophical convictions. The way in which personal integrity and respect for personal beliefs are recognized under education law is changing because of the 1998 Human Rights Act.

The 1944 Education Act obliged the secretary of state and local education authorities to have regard for parents' wishes, as noted earlier.[106] The courts confirmed, however, that even in relation to a choice of state school on religious grounds, this section provided no guarantees; it merely established a general principle while enabling an authority "to have regard to other things as well, and also to make exceptions to the general principle if it thinks fit to do so."[107] This general principle, now found in the 1996 Education Act, is still pleaded in cases involving parental choice regarding special education and school placement.[108] It has not, however, gained potency. In a 1999 decision, for example, the judge said, "It is well established that section 9 does not require the LEA to give priority to parental wishes, so long as they are properly considered and taken into account."[109]A similar approach has been taken in relation to a parallel provision that requires an LEA to fund a child's transport to school, paying due regard to (among other things) the parent's desire that the child attend a school providing religious education consistent with the parent's religion or denomination.[110]

The contrast was repeatedly drawn when the national curriculum was first introduced in England and Wales in 1989 that while parents had acquired a degree of choice over the school their children attended, they had no influence over the content of their education.[111] The national curriculum aims to standardize provision and assessment so that the relative progress of individual children and the overall attainment within schools can be monitored. The only effective choice for parents who disagree with all or part of the national curriculum remains private schooling, as independent schools are not bound to follow it, although many in fact do.

Over the ensuing years, regulation has remained tight, but the greater flexibility that is currently being introduced to education for fourteen- to nineteen-year-olds should mean more choice for that age group.[112] Even in relation to collective worship and religious education, which are not part of the national curriculum but are part of the prescribed "basic curriculum" that all state schools have to follow (although in fact three-quarters of state schools fail to comply with the law requiring a daily act of collective worship), the only aspect of individual choice that is sanctioned is the right to withdraw a child or to cause the child to be absent from school to receive religious education elsewhere.[113] Most acts of collective worship in nondenominational public schools must be "wholly or mainly of a broadly Christian character" by reflecting "the broad traditions of Christian belief without being distinctive of any particular Christian denomination."[114] This has caused some controversy due to its possible conflict with the European Convention on Human Rights, despite the fact that individual schools are able to apply to a local committee for an exemption from broadly Christian collective worship.[115] The main concern is that the requirement is possibly discriminatory and fails to respect religious minorities.[116] But in one case, a group representing persons with fundamentalist Christian views challenged (albeit unsuccessfully) collective worship at a nondenominational school because it was insufficiently devotional to God.[117] Religious education and collective worship in independent private schools are not legislatively controlled, which illustrates the wider disparity noted earlier.

The right to withdraw was also attached to sex education when it was added to the required basic curriculum in state schools in 1994.[118] However, the inclusion of sex education as a compulsory component of the school curriculum is not inconsistent with the state's obligations under the European Convention on Human Rights to respect parents' religious or philosophical convictions (see below). Individual parental choice over sex education illustrates well that the rights attached to choice in education have been enjoyed exclusively by parents rather than by children, representing a serious lack of recognition of the independent rights of the child.[119]

The strong emphasis on respect for personal beliefs in the education system that is found in England and Wales is found also in the European Convention on Human Rights, article 2 of protocol 1, which provides that

> No person shall be denied the right to education. In the exercise of any functions which it assumes in relation to education and to teaching, the State must respect the right of parents to ensure such education and teaching in conformity with their own religious and philosophical convictions.

The United Kingdom declared a reservation to the second sentence of the Article, stating that it would apply only when compatible with the provision of efficient instruction and avoidance of unreasonable public expenditure. With that important exception, the right was applied in U.K. law by the 1998 Human Rights Act, which provides that public authorities, including those bodies "certain of whose functions are functions of a public nature," must comply with it and other convention rights.[120] State schools and LEAs are public authorities, but private schools are covered by the act only when exercising particular functions, probably those that the courts would recognize as sufficiently covered by public law to bring an action within the courts' jurisdiction—as, for example, when a school withheld an "assisted place."[121] City technology colleges or academies, although categorized as independent schools, have been held to be exercising public law functions and so would be covered by the Human Rights Act.[122] Equally, it is arguable that in relation to independent schools, inspectors and the registration authority are exercising public law functions. In the *Talmud Torah School* case, Justice Woolf said that the secretary of state, when determining a complaint relating to an independent school, had a statutory duty to take parental wishes into account and that this was "underlined by Article 2 of the First Protocol of the European Convention on Human Rights." Thus it is arguable that today the relevant inspection authorities should not give approval to any school provision that is incompatible with the European Convention on Human Rights as applied by the 1998 Human Rights Act. In relation to the question of whether independent schools themselves are bound by the act, they are not generally thought to be exercising functions of a public nature (see above) although, as one leading lawyer noted recently, "the jury, or rather the High Court, is still out on this issue."[123]

Both the precise weight that article 2 of protocol 1 gives to upholding parental wishes and the nature of parental convictions respected have received increasing judicial attention in the United Kingdom. The decision in *Belgian Linguistics (No. 2)* by the European Court of Human Rights has been particularly influential.[124] The judicial majority in that case held that "the Contracting Parties [states] do not recognise such a right to education as would require them to establish at their own expense, or to subsidise, education of any particular type or at any particular level."[125] The court rejected a claim by French-speaking parents that they were entitled to have their children educated in accordance with their linguistic and cultural preferences. On a similar basis, the Court of Appeal in England held that article 2 of protocol 1 did not guarantee the right to an assisted place at an independent school when public education was available.[126] Meanwhile, in a recent Scottish case, the court noted that the right of parents who objected, on the basis of article 2, to the management system in their child's state school—on the grounds that the school's managers did not have enough autonomy—was not violated because the parents had the option of sending the child to a private and independently governed school instead.[127]

In theory, it is possible for a parent to hold firm convictions or beliefs about any aspect of education, such as teaching methods, textbooks, general curriculum content, disciplinary matters, and so on. There is, for example, opposition by a small number of parents to compulsory assessment of children under the national curriculum, which they see as putting undue pressure on young children. Both the degree of respect to be accorded to various individual views and the extent of individual choice available within the education system will always be conditioned by the overriding duty of the state to maintain an effective and efficient education system for the benefit of young people in general. The way these matters have to be balanced is illustrated, for example, by cases in which a decision must be made on whether a formal "statement" held by the LEA regarding a child with severe learning difficulties should provide for the child to be educated in a mainstream school or educated in a special school, separate from children who do not have special educational needs. There is a statutory right of parental preference over school placement in this context; parents may ask the LEA for a particular school to be named in the child's "statement" and, subject to certain conditions (including the need for it to be an efficient use of resources), the LEA must uphold their selection. The LEA must ensure that the educational provision specified in the statement is made and therefore fund the placement.[128] Parents often dispute the LEA's choice, perhaps preferring an approved independent special school despite the additional expense to the LEA. For some parents this might be a matter of consumer choice per se, but for others personal beliefs often are the driving factor. The LEA has statutory responsibility for the education of all children with special educational needs.[129] Accordingly, there is no question of the 1998 Human Rights Act being inapplicable to its decisions.

In *Simpson* v. *United Kingdom,* the parents of a boy with special educational needs due to dyslexia claimed the right under article 2 of protocol 1 to have their boy educated at a private school at the LEA's expense.[130] The authority believed the child's needs could be met, at lower expense, in one of its own secondary schools. The European Commission of Human Rights recognized that there had to be "a wide measure of discretion left to the appropriate authorities as to how to make the best use possible of the resources available to them in the interests of disabled children generally." Therefore,

> While these authorities must place weight on parents' and pupils' views, it cannot be said that the first sentence of Article 2 of Protocol 1 requires the placing of a dyslexic child in a private specialized school, with fees paid by the State, when a place is available in an ordinary school which has special teaching facilities for disabled children.[131]

This ruling and *Belgian Linguistics (No. 2)* were applied in a U.K. case when the court dismissed an article 2 protocol 1 challenge to an LEA's decision not to carry out a statutory assessment of a ten-year-old girl's special educational needs.[132]

In another case, the mother of a nine-year-old girl with cerebral palsy contended that the girl's placement in a mainstream school would run contrary to her religious and philosophical convictions.[133] This argument was not accepted by the court, which found that the mother was motivated by concern about practical matters such as the size of the class and the disruption that a change of school would cause rather than her philosophical convictions. Such an argument is unlikely to succeed, in the light of previous failures before the European Commission and Court of Human Rights, to overturn special school placements on the ground of philosophical convictions.[134] More recently, in *T* v. *Special Educational Needs Tribunal and Wiltshire County Council*, the parents challenged the LEA's refusal to finance their autistic child's home education Lovaas program before the child's eventual mainstreaming.[135] Justice Richards held that the parents' preference for a certain form of education because it best met the child's needs "seems to me to fall far short of a philosophical conviction in favor of the Lovaas programme."[136]

Where, however, codes of personal or social morality are more closely engaged, the picture is less clear. Take, for example, the question of compulsory sex education. In *Kjeldsen*, the European Court of Human Rights acknowledged that a democratic state might regard it as being in the public interest to require sex education in school even though some individual religious or philosophical views might be overridden, provided that there is no element of indoctrination.[137] The state must ensure that "information or knowledge is conveyed in an objective, critical and pluralistic manner" and not through "indoctrination that might be considered as not respecting parents' religious and philosophical convictions."[138] Yet, as Bradney points out, "in a school serving a multi-religious and multi-ethnic community there may be widespread differences in what various parents will accept in terms of the delivery and content of sex education."[139] The fact that parents in Denmark who objected to compulsory sex education because it conflicted with their Christian beliefs and values had the option to send their children to private schools or to educate them at home was a factor in the *Kjeldsen* decision that there was no breach of article 2 of protocol 1. The provision in England and Wales allowing parents to withdraw their children is perhaps the only way that, in the context of sex education, a religiously and ethnically diverse society can hope to respect the right of all parents to bring their children up in accordance with their own value system. Yet strong arguments against the right of withdrawal have been articulated, particularly with regard to the rights of the child and liberal democratic notions that education should be inclusive and aimed at full and equal social participation.[140] There is, however, common agreement that the issues are difficult to reconcile.

The fact that, as noted earlier, sex education must be "given in such a manner as to encourage . . . pupils to have due regard to moral considerations and the value of family life" is not problematic in human rights terms.

Not only is teachers' freedom of expression (a freedom protected under article 10 of the European Convention on Human Rights) subject to being limited in a proportionate manner by the state when necessary for, among other things, "the protection of health or morals."[141] It is also the case that, according to Feldman, "states are entitled to seek to advance family life over other social arrangements as long as their mode of doing so does not interfere disproportionately with the rights and freedoms of people affected."[142] Feldman argues that the parents' statutory right to withdraw the child from sex education prevents state interference from being disproportionate. However, what about the right to education in accordance with philosophical convictions, as interpreted in *Kjeldsen*? The official guidance on sex education in England and Wales, to which state schools are statutorily required to have regard, must emphasize the importance of marriage for family life and the upbringing of children.[143] This is arguably a doctrinaire approach to human relationships. It might constitute a broadly objective approach, as marriage is still the main social unit for the upbringing of children. Yet given the numbers of children who are raised and cared for by unmarried couples, including some gay or lesbian couples, it cannot be considered particularly pluralistic. The law also requires that the guidance ensure that children are "protected from teaching and materials which are inappropriate having regard to the age and the religious and cultural background of the pupils concerned."[144] Adhered to strictly, this could mean that referring to homosexuality, sexual intercourse outside marriage, or even contraception should be advised against in many urban schools because of their ethnic or religious mix. Controversially, local authorities were banned from intentionally promoting homosexuality, publishing material with the intention of promoting homosexuality, or promoting "the teaching in any maintained school of the acceptability of homosexuality as a pretended family relationship"; however, these statutory restrictions have recently been removed.[145]

Another area involving moral beliefs concerns the use of corporal punishment in schools. Legislation removing the legal sanction for corporal punishment in state and private schools has left parents who believe in its administration with quite limited options, because only children educated at home might lawfully be given it.[146] More than twenty years ago corporal punishment at school contrary to parental wishes was held by the European Court of Human Rights in *Campbell and Cosans* v. *United Kingdom* to constitute a breach of article 2 of protocol 1.[147] The court found that the parents' views concerned "a weighty and substantial aspect of human life and behavior, namely the integrity of the person, the propriety or otherwise of the infliction of corporal punishment and the exclusion of the distress which the risk of such punishment entails."[148] Those views therefore met the test of worthiness of respect in a democratic society, compatibility with human dignity, and absence of conflict with the child's fundamental right to education.

The government subsequently removed the teacher's defense of lawful chastisement (but sanctioned the use of physical force necessary to avert immediate danger to person or property) in state schools and with respect to state-sponsored children in private schools and later extended the ban to cover children in all schools.[149] In so doing the government might claim to have given effect to the moral wishes of the majority, who believe that physical punishment of children is inherently wrong. But recently, in *R (Williamson) v. Secretary of State for Education and Employment*, a challenge to the prohibition was brought by teachers and parents of pupils at an independent Christian school who supported the use of corporal punishment and argued that the ban was not only incompatible with their right to manifest their religious convictions but also with their rights under article 2 of protocol 1.[150] The Court of Appeal held that Parliament had indeed made corporal punishment unlawful in all schools but, unlike the lower court, concluded that the teachers and parents who inflicted or authorized the imposition of physical chastisement of children in their care on the basis of their religious faith were practicing, or manifesting, a religious belief or conviction. The Court of Appeal held that the parents had a religious conviction that was entitled to respect. However, the majority of the judges held that corporal punishment could not be said to be an expression (such as worship or ritual) of religious belief; nor did the ban interfere materially with manifestation of the belief that corporal punishment should be inflicted for breaches of school discipline, because infliction of corporal punishment by the parent, which was permitted by national law, would satisfy that belief. One of the majority judges also made the important point that parental convictions cannot prevail over the child's fundamental right to education.[151]

In another recent (and highly publicized) case, *Begum*, the religious belief of a Muslim girl, Shabina Begum, led her to want to attend school wearing the jilbab (a long gown and headcovering). [152] The school, Denbigh High, refused permission, citing the school's dress code. The girl claimed that the decision amounted to an exclusion from school (the term "constructive exclusion" was suggested) that gave rise to a denial of her right to education under article 2 of protocol 1 of the European Convention on Human Rights. It was also argued on her behalf that her freedom of religion under article 9 was violated. The dress code of this community school, which had been drawn up in consultation with local Muslim representatives, permitted the wearing of the shalwar kameeze (headscarf), which pupils' parents considered appropriate. The pupils at Denbigh High came from twenty-one ethnic groups, and 79 percent of pupils categorized themselves as Muslim. Shabina Begum had attended school from 2000–02 wearing the shalwar kameeze, but her beliefs were reported to have changed, and she now considered it necessary to wear the jilbab. Several other schools across England permitted the wearing of the jilbab, but Denbigh High considered doing so to be potentially divisive. Justice Bennett did not regard the girl to have been "excluded" from school, but noted that even if she had been, "she was excluded for her refusal to abide by the school uniform policy rather than her religious beliefs as such."[153] This opinion was based on the fact that she had originally chosen Denbigh High knowing of its school uniform policy. The judge concluded that "it was not an infringement of Article 9 . . . that the [school] was not prepared to change its policy in order to accommodate the claimant's changed religious beliefs."[154] He appeared to have been influenced by the availability of a place at an alternative school (a girls' school that permitted the wearing of the jilbab to and from school, but not in school, a policy that was said to accord with the girl's religious sensibilities). That, of course, ignores the fact that Shabina Begum wanted to attend Denbigh High specifically. In effect, the judge was saying that she had to decide between her religious beliefs and the school. The legal justification for presenting a person of deep religious convictions with that choice was more easily established with reference to article 9(2), which provides:

> Freedom to manifest one's religion or beliefs shall be subject only to such limitations as are necessary in a democratic society in the interests of public safety, for the protection of public order, health, or morals, or for the protection of the rights and freedoms of others.

Justice Bennett rejected the argument that the ban on the jilbab was justified on health or safety grounds, but he did regard it as necessary "for the protection of the rights and freedom of others," per article 9(2). He observed that the school uniform policy promoted "a positive ethos and a sense of communal identity" and that while the shalwar kameeze enabled Muslim girls to manifest their religion, it was also worn by Hindus and Sikhs, so that there was at the school "no outward distinction" among female pupils of these faiths.[155] He said that the policy protected those Muslim girls who did not want to wear the jilbab from outward pressure from inside or outside the school to do so, thereby protecting their rights and freedoms. He concluded that the school uniform policy at Denbigh High had a legitimate aim and was proportionate:

The legitimate aim was the proper running of a multi-cultural, multi-faith, secular school. The limitation was also proportionate to the legitimate aim pursued. The limitation was specifically divised with the advice of the Muslim community. Although it appears that there is a body of opinion within the Muslim faith that only the jilbab meets the requirements of its dress code there is also a body of opinion that the Shalwar Kameeze does as well . . . . [T]he adoption of the Shalwar Kameeze by the Defendant as the school uniform for Muslim (and other faiths) female pupils was and continues to be a reasoned, balanced, proportionate policy. [156]

He also dismissed the claim that there was a denial of the right to education contrary to article 2 of protocol 1, holding that it was "unrealistic and artificial" to say that her right to education had been denied when the school was able and willing to accommodate her and that she had, in any event, the option of transferring to another school.[157]

Begum was a local dispute about a matter of much wider importance concerning multiculturalism and social cohesion that is part of an ongoing debate in the United Kingdom, as it is elsewhere in Europe and beyond. From the legal perspective, human rights lawyers are likely to be disappointed that the judgment does not contain a more detailed discussion of the basis for not considering the claim that the girl's religious freedom had been infringed by the school, albeit that legal justification was found under article 9(2). In any event, both *Begum* and *Williamson* appear to show that, in the context of education, more extreme or fundamental beliefs that are nonetheless broadly consistent with the tenets of mainstream faiths not only are less able to be accommodated than more moderate beliefs but also are less well protected under the European Convention on Human Rights, as applied in the United Kingdom.

The limits of article 2 of protocol 1 to protect personal beliefs in the context of education were also recently tested in Scotland, in *Dove* v. *The Scottish Ministers*, over the issue of self-governing school status.[158] Self-governing status was the Scottish equivalent of grant-maintained status in England and Wales, discussed earlier. Like grant-maintained status, self-governing status for a school brought direct financing by central government, independence from control of the local education authority (although the school remained part of the state sector), and a governing board with greater parental representation. Some parents challenged the termination of their children's school's self-governing status, claiming, among other things, a violation of their rights under article 2 of protocol 1. They said that the change would alter the method of managing the school and the school's character, with a consequentially detrimental effect on their children's education. However, the court found that the change of status would not affect the curriculum or teaching at the school. Changes to the school's management or administration did not concern the right to education as such and did "not constitute a disadvantage to any of the modalities of the exercise of that right nor are they linked to the exercise of that right."[159]

With regard to their philosophical or religious convictions, the parents had claimed that they held a strong and sincere belief that parental control of the school's management gave the school "its own identifiable ethos and spirit" and a responsiveness to parental wishes that had been beneficial to their children's education, had produced efficiencies, and, by bringing greater diversity to the school's system, had advanced choice in the locality. The court rejected this argument, holding that the parents' asserted convictions amounted "at best to no more than individual opinions relating to the governance of [the school]."[160]

It is reasonable to conclude that personal beliefs about educational practice or policy are unlikely to be recognized for human rights purposes, especially because to do so would interfere with the state's overriding duty to maintain an effective education system[161] or because the courts are reluctant to accept that they are truly based on philosophical or religious convictions under article 2 of protocol 1, the corporal punishment case of *Williamson* being a rare exception. The case of *Begum* also points to some of the limitations to religious freedom for the purposes of article 9 in the context of secular schools.

Conclusion

The increasing regulation of education in England and Wales has now caught up with independent schools. Rather than signifying an attempt to gain greater control over the private sector, perhaps with a view to the eventual absorption of these schools into the state sector, it seems aimed at having a legitimating effect in relation to them.[162] Not only is the independent sector tolerated by the Labour government despite the Labour Party's past hostility toward it, but much of its freedom from control is set to continue. There appears to be not only recognition of the contribution that many independent schools make to increasing levels of attainment (although the overall achievement of sixteen-year-olds in these schools is in fact lower than it is in state schools that select pupils by academic ability), but also the perception that many independent schools, like many faith schools in the state sector, are particularly attuned to civic values as well as to safeguarding minority religious and cultural identities.[163]

The current policy on independent schools also reflects the fact that respect for individual rights has moved up the legal and political agendas since the introduction of the 1998 Human Rights Act. Individual choice is increasingly seen in terms of the right to respect of personal integrity and beliefs rather than merely a facet of consumerism. The chief inspector of Schools in England, one of the most important figures in the educational establishment, said in a recent speech on inspection of independent schools: "It is the right of parents in a free society to make choices about the ways in which their children are educated."[164] Nonetheless, in reality, school choice is still predominantly motivated by overriding concerns for educational quality and social integration or mobility. The latter is especially the case with regard to private schooling. As Timmins says, "Plenty of private education exists elsewhere in Europe, but it is often chosen for religious and cultural reasons, not for the class and opportunity-based divisions that have so marked Britain's public/private split."[165]

The government's abolition of the assisted places scheme has reduced the opportunities for those from socially disadvantaged backgrounds to attend independent schools. Yet the government can point to ways in which features of independent schools are being emulated in the state sector. The 2002 Education Act facilitates earning of autonomy from the national curriculum and increasing the number of specialist schools (schools that specialize in arts, technology, sports, languages, engineering science, or business and are permitted to select up to 10 percent of their new intake of pupils each year on the basis of their aptitude in the area of specialization) as well as faith-based schools in the state sector.[166] This shows that some of the ideals, if not the elitism, that independent schools represent have gained more widespread political acceptance. An argument that by this process greater social inclusion will occur and inequality of opportunity will diminish would, however, be more tenuous. Clearly more direct action by government would be needed, as has been advocated recently in relation to access to higher education in the United Kingdom and is seemingly acknowledged by the government in its plans, noted earlier, for an Office for Fair Access.[167]

Many of the current government's aims for regulating the school sector seem remarkably similar to those of the 1979–97 Conservative governments that preceded it, especially that of maintaining a framework for promoting and enforcing prescribed standards in education while ensuring that choice and diversity are maximized. Nonetheless, there is also an emphasis on inclusiveness, and there has been a subtle shift in the values that form the basis for choice in particular. Values related to personal integrity and respect for personal beliefs, such as respect for philosophical or religious convictions, are now promoted in the matter of education through some of the provisions of the 1998 Human Rights Act. The realization of choice, however, is still based on participation as a consumer within a market or quasi-market for a service, education—whether by the selection of private education or a particular university or college or by selection of a state school under the parental preference provisions of school admissions law. While individual choice might be perceived as a means to self-development and self-fulfilment that reflects basic liberal values, there is nevertheless a limit to the potential of consumerism to satisfy the individual's wants because of the scarcity and competition on which markets function and the inherent social and economic inequalities that influence the realization of choice. Therefore it might in some senses be more appropriate to see consumer choice in relation to public services as a rationing device rather than a form of social participation. The government has sought to use the exercise of individual consumer choice and competitive forces to help drive up standards in schools by allocating resources partly on the basis of enrollment, although targeting of schools that have a high social deprivation quotient—and often relatively low market appeal—also has occurred, through funded initiatives such as education action zones (generally comprising groups of two or more schools that take a larger-than-average proportion of socially disadvantaged pupils for whom special curricular initiatives or facilities are needed) and the Excellence in Cities program. Recent findings suggest that these initiatives have had an uneven impact in terms of raising attainment levels, although they have reduced truancy and school exclusion rates.[168]

Choice in education is also exercised through democratic participation, particularly through the right to vote on whether a school should retain selective academic admission status, to elect parent governors of schools, and to make representations to the authorities when changes to the organization of local schools, such as closures, are planned. Arguably it also is reflected in less formal aspects of democracy, such as policies aimed at greater parental involvement though home-school partnerships; as Fabre states, "Democracy is not reducible to a decision-making procedure: it is a regime where certain decisions are made that treat people in certain ways."[169] This comes closest to acknowledging that rights of choice can be as much a facet of citizenship as of consumerism, because participation brings an extra degree of attachment to the service or institution in question by virtue of the commitment made by the participant.[170]

Choice in education is accompanied by reciprocal obligations reflected in home-school agreements, school rules on matters such as school uniform or behavior, and compulsory school attendance. Representing the liberal value of freedom, individual choice is therefore balanced against the more collectivist values of social responsibility, inclusion, and community. Recent attempts through legislation to promote greater cooperation among institutions or administrative authorities—by, for example, allowing coordinated school admission procedures across an area, formal partnerships for early education, education action zones, and collaboration between schools— might be seen as an attempt to temper the harshness of the market and thereby alter the overall balance between these competing values.[171] The socially segregating effects of parental choice of school in Bradford along ethnic or religious lines remind us of the difficulty of finding an appropriate balance between these two dimensions.[172] Recent debates about the proposed establishment of more faith-based schools in the state sector to meet the collective wishes of particular religious groups have highlighted once again the difficulties of preserving social cohesion in a pluralistic society while respecting different religious beliefs and institutions.

Despite the continuing discrepancy between the statutory curriculum requirements for independent and state schools, there has been a move toward guaranteeing that in both sectors—and thus in all schools—a solid grounding in civic and social values is imparted to all students. Education law is reflecting wider efforts to maintain choice and respect for personal beliefs and autonomy while trying to promote greater social inclusion and cohesiveness, as noted earlier. A difficult balance must be struck in this process. Given, however, that despite the diversity in the state school sector in England and Wales there is a common national curriculum and framework for sex education, justification for the separate statutory curriculum requirements for state and private sectors seems problematic, and the matter warrants reconsideration. If the government wants to make improved social cohesion a key underlying objective of schooling, while at the same time respecting a degree of individual choice and the upholding of minorities' cultural or religious values and rights, it seems appropriate to remove the anomalies between the public and private sectors so that whatever balance between freedom and interference is deemed appropriate is applied universally across schools in England and Wales.

Notes

1. For example, M. Adler, A. Petch, and J. Tweedie, *Parental Choice and Educational Policy* (Edinburgh University Press, 1989); G. Whitty and others, *Devolution*

and Choice in Education (Buckingham: Open University Press, 1998); H. Brighouse, *School Choice and Social Justice* (Oxford University Press, 2003).

2. Respectively, articles 8, 9, and 14 and Protocol 1, Article 2.

3. Human Rights Act 1998, sections 3, 4, and 6. Secondary education legislation consists of regulations or orders made under delegated powers contained with acts of Parliament. See note 7 below.

4. See N. Harris, "Students, Mental Health, and Citizenship," *Legal Studies*, vol. 24, no. 3 (2004), pp. 349–85; N. Harris, *Law and Education: Regulation, Consumerism and the Education System* (London: Sweet and Maxwell, 1993); and J. Ahier and others, *Graduate Citizens? Issues of Citizenship and Higher Education* (London: Routledge Falmer, 2003). As regards rights in this context, see C. Fabre, *Social Rights under the Constitution* (Oxford University Press, 2000), pp. 125–26.

5. As regards reducing bureaucracy, see, in particular, Department for Education and Skills (DfES)/Cabinet Office, *Reducing Red Tape and Bureaucracy in Schools* (London: DfES, 2003), and Department for Education and Employment, *Reducing the Bureaucractic Burden on Teachers* (London, 1998). On deregulation, see the Education Act 2002, part 1.

6. The School Companies Regulations 2002 (SI 2002/2978), made under the Education Act 2002, section 12. In this chapter, the term "state school" refers to schools that are not independent (private) schools (defined in note 8 below). The legislation in fact uses the term "maintained school" rather than "state school," but the latter is used here because it more clearly emphasises their distinction from private schools. In the United Kingdom, the term "public schools" actually refers to private schools.

7. This chapter concentrates on the law applicable in England and Wales. The education systems of both Scotland (see chapter 11, by Jaap Dronkers) and Northern Ireland are entirely distinct and covered by separate legislation. Acts of Parliament applicable to England or Wales are made by the U.K. Parliament in Westminster. Secondary or delegated legislation, which is extensive in the field of education, is made by ministers of the Crown in England and, following the National Assembly for Wales (Transfer of Functions) Orders 1999 (SI 1999/672) and 2000 (SI 2000/253), by the National Assembly in Wales (NAW). In order to avoid too much legal technicality, this chapter will largely relate the law in England only, although the two countries' education laws cover considerable common ground.

8. Education Act 2002, section 157, empowering the making of regulations prescribing standards for these schools. An "independent school" is a school or special school that provides full-time education for five or more pupils of compulsory school age (five through sixteen years) (or for at least one pupil of that age who has a statement of special educational needs or is a child looked after by a local authority) and is not maintained by a local education authority; Education Act 1996, section 463 (as altered by the 2002 act, section 172).

9. See note 3 above. Education is not alone is this respect; see E. C. Page, *Governing by Numbers* (Oxford: Hart, 2001).

10. Department for Education and Skills, *Schools: Achieving Success* (London, 2001), part 9. An example is the power to exclude from school, which the 2002 act vests in head teachers, but the basic procedures and appeal rights and structures are all now prescribed in separate regulations; the Education (Pupil Exclusions and Appeals) (Maintained Schools) (England) Regulations 2002 (SI 2002/3178), as amended in 2004 (SI 2004/402).

11. Namely, nursery (under five), primary (ages five through eleven), or secondary (ages eleven through eighteen). In addition, there are "middle" schools, catering for the eight-through-fourteen age group but classed for official purposes as primary or secondary schools.

12. Secondary schools cover the age ranges eleven through eighteen or eleven through sixteen. "Grammar" schools, today around 164 in number, have selective admissions. "Comprehensive schools," which form the overwhelming majority, do not. An increasing number of these schools, however, are able to select a minority of their pupils on the basis of their aptitude in a particular subject or subjects in which the school has an officially recognized specialization; they are known as "specialist" schools, and the range of permitted specializations is being increased under the 2002 Education Act. In addition there are "special" schools catering exclusively for students with various learning difficulties or disabilities.

13. N. Timmins, *The Five Giants: A Biography of the Welfare State* (London: Harper Collins, 1995), p. 79.

14. In community schools, voluntary controlled schools, community special schools, and maintained nursery schools the local education authority is, for legal purposes, the employer of staff (Education Act 2002, section 35; see also *Green* v. *Governing Body of Victoria Road Primary School* [2003] ELR 455, Employment Appeal Tribunal). But for some years now the school's governing body (board of governors, see note 18 below) has been responsible for making appointments and decisions on dismissals, although curiously the local education authority would be the respondent to any employment tribunal case.

15. School Standards and Framework Act 1998, schedule 3, paragraph 5, as amended.

16. Notably, through the Education (No. 2) Act 1986, the Education Reform Act 1988, and the Education Act 1993.

17. Prior to 1993 funds came directly from the Department for Education.

18. All maintained nursery, primary, secondary, and special schools must have a governing body constituted in accordance with regulations: Education Act 2002, section 19; and the School Governance (Constitution) (England) Regulations 2003 (SI 2003/348). The governing body must be composed of nine to twenty governors; the numerical balance between the different categories (staff, parents, local education authority members, community members, and so forth) must be as laid down in the regulations.

19. See Harris, *Law and Education*, chapter 2.

20. M. Flude and M. Hammer, eds., *The Education Reform Act 1988: Its Origins and Its Implications* (Lewes: Falmer, 1990).

21. Education Act 1993, part 2.

22. School Standards and Framework Act 1998, schedules 30 and 31.

23. Ibid, schedule 13.

24. The Education Act 2002, section 65, amending the Education Act 1996 by inserting a replacement section 482.

25. Ibid., and initially the Education Reform Act 1988, section 105; see also *R* v. *Governors of Haberdashers' Aske's Hatcham College Trust ex parte T* [1995], ELR (Education Law Reports) 350. See note 8 for definition of "independent school."

26. Learning and Skills Act 2000, sections 130, 131.

27. Education Act 2002, sections 65, 67–68.

28. Based on the figures in Department for Education and Skills, *Statistics of Education: Schools in England, 2003* (London, 2003), table 21.

29. Ibid., tables 23a, 23b.

30. Ibid., tables 30, 41.

31. Ibid., tables 23a, 23b, 30, 41.

32. Education Act 1944, section 76.

33. Per Lloyd LJ in *R* v. *Greenwich London Borough Council ex parte Governors of John Ball Primary School* (1989), 88 LGR (Local Government Reports) 589 at 595.

34. School Standards and Framework Act 1998, section 86, as amended (originally the Education Act 1980, section 6).

35. Per Kennedy LJ in *R* v. *Lancashire County Council ex parte F* [1995], ELR 33 (QBD) at 40A. For community schools and, normally, controlled schools, the admission authority is the local education authority; in the case of aided or foundation schools, the school governing body is the admission authority. School Standards and Framework Act 1998, section 88.

36. See *R* v. *Bradford Metropolitan Borough Council ex parte Sikander Ali* [1994], ELR 299 QBD (Queen's Bench Division).

37. *R* v. *Greenwich London Borough Council ex parte Governors of John Ball Primary School* (note 33 above); *R* v. *Wiltshire County Council ex parte Razazan* [1997], ELR 370, CA (Court of Appeal).

38. *R* v. *Greenwich London Borough Council ex parte Governors of John Ball Primary School*.

39. *R* v. *Wiltshire County Council ex parte Razazan*.

40. Department for Education and Skills, *Schools Admissions Code of Practice* (London, 2003). The local "admission forum" advises admission authorities; School Standards and Framework Act 1998, section 85A.

41. School Standards and Framework Act 1998, section 86(3), as amended.

42. *Choudhury* v. *Governors of Bishop Challoner Roman Catholic Comprehensive School* [1992], 3 All ER 277, House of Lords.

43. Ibid. at 285e–f.

44. Chapter 5 in this volume examines this issue further.

45. Audit Commission, *Trading Places–Planning School Places* (London: Her Majesty's Stationery Office [HMSO], 1996).

46. S. Gorard, C. Taylor, and J. Fitz, "Markets in Public Policy: The Case of the United Kingdom Education Reform Act 1988," *International Studies in the Sociology of Education*, vol. 21, no. 1 (2002), pp. 23–41.

47. Office for Standards in Education (Ofsted), *School Place Planning*, HMI 587 (2003), paragraphs 51–57 (www.ofsted/gov/uk [accessed January 2004]).

48. School Standards and Framework Act 1998, sections 94, 95.

49. Council on Tribunals, *Annual Report 1991–92* (London: HMSO, 1992), p.65; Council on Tribunals, *Annual Report 1995–96* (London: HMSO, 1996), p.104.

50. Department for Education and Skills, *Admission Appeals for Maintained Primary and Secondary Schools in England 2001/02* (London, 2003).

51. The official guidance is the Department for Education and Skills, *Admissions Appeals Code of Practice* (London, 2003). Appeal panels are established under the School Standards and Framework Act 1998. See N. Harris, "The Developing Role and Structure of the Education Appeal System in England and Wales," in M. Harris and M. Partington, eds., *Administrative Justice in the 21st Century* (Oxford: Hart, 1999), pp. 296–325.

52. See the Education Act 1996, sections 316 and 316A, as substituted or introduced through the Special Educational Needs and Disability Act 2001, section 1.

53. Department for Education and Skills, *The Future of Higher Education*, Cm 5735 (London: Stationery Office, 2003), paragraphs 6.29–6.31.

54. The relevant statutes include Education (No. 2) Act 1986, Education Reform Act 1988, Education Act 1993, Learning and Skills Act 2000, and Education Act 2002. See further A. Blair, "Negotiating Conflicting Values: The Role of Law in Educating for Values in England and Wales," *Education and the Law*, vol. 14, no. 1 (2002), pp. 39–56.

55. Education Act 1996, sections 403(1), 404(1A).

56. Education Act 2002, sections 84, 85.

57. See www.teachernet.gov.uk.

58. School Standards and Framework Act 1998, sections 110, 111.

59. Education Act 2002, section 52; Department for Education and Skills, *Social Inclusion: Pupil Support*, Circular 10/1999 (London, 1999), as amended.

60. Part 3, from February 27, 2004. The powers do not apply in respect of pupils at independent schools, apart from city technology colleges, city colleges for the technology of the arts, and "academies."

61. R. Boyd, *Independent Schools: Law, Custom, and Practice* (Bristol: Jordans, 1998), p. 32.

62. S. Byers MP, *Hansard, House of Commons Debates*, vol. 295, col. 592 (June 5, 1997).

63. *R* v. *Secretary of State for Education and Employment ex parte Begbie* [2000], ELR 445, CA.

64. Department for Education and Employment, *Excellence in Schools*, Cm 3681 (London: Stationery Office, 1997), p. 72.

65. Department for Education and Skills, *Draft Regulations for Registration and Monitoring of Independent Schools* (London, 2003), p. 3.

66. As regards the current extent of sharing of facilities by independent schools with maintained schools and others, see Independent Schools Council, *Good Neighbours 2003* (London, 2003).

67. Department for Education and Skills, "A £1 Million Boost for Independent/State School Links," press release, November 24, 2003.

68. Education (Schools) Act 1992. See Harris, *Law and Education,* ch. 6. The law is now in the School Inspections Act 1996. Some independent residential schools are classed as children's homes and fall under a separate inspection regime under the Care Standards Act 2000. Independent schools making special provisions for children with learning difficulties are subject to separate approval requirements; Education Act 1996, section 347.

69. Office for Standards in Education, *Departmental Report 2002–03*, Cm 5903 (London, 2003), annex B. Nursery education was brought within Ofsted's remit by the School Standards and Framework Act 1998.

70. Ofsted monitors the quality of Independent Schools Council inspections. See, for example, Office for Standards in Education, *Independent Schools Council Inspections 2001/02* (London, 2003).

71. School Inspections Act 1996, section 2(2)(b).

72. Ibid, section 3.

73. Education Act 2002, sections 163, 164.

74. *R* v. *Secretary of State for Education and Science ex parte Talmud Torah Machzikei Hadass School Trust* [1985], *The Times*, April 12, LexisNexis.

75. The Education (Independent School Inspection Fees and Publication) (England) Regulations 2003 (SI 2003/1926).

76. Office for Standards in Education, *Inspecting Independent Schools: The Framework for Inspecting Independent Schools in England from September 2003. Draft for Consultation* (London, 2003), paragraph 14.

77. School Inspections Act of 1996, Sections 13–22; part 1, School Standards and Framework Act 1998, sections 14–19A.

78. Education Act 1996, section 464.

79. Ibid., sections 470, 471.

80. Ibid., sections 473, 478.

81. Department for Education and Skills, *Regulatory Impact Assessment for the Reform of Regulation and Monitoring of Independent Schools* (London, 2003), paragraph 1.7.

82. Education Act 1996, section 466(1), (3).

83. Ibid., section 478(2).

84. Ibid, sections 468 and 469.

85. Constituted under the Education Act 1996, section 476 and schedule 34: one legally qualified person and two others from an "education panel" formed an Independent Schools Tribunal, as stated in section 470(1).

86. See note 74 above.

87. Office for Standards in Education, *Annual Report of Her Majesty's Chief Inspector of Schools: Standards and Quality in Education 2001/02* (London, 2003), paragraph 445.

88. David Bell HMCI, "Standards and Inspections in Independent Schools," Address to the Brighton College Conference on Independent Schools, April 29, 2003.

89. The Education (Independent School Standards) (England) Regulations 2003 (SI 2003/1910) and the Independent School Standards (Wales) Regulations 2003 (SI 2003/3234 (W.314)). These regulations are pursuant to the Education Act 2002, section 157.

90. DfES, *Draft Regulations for Registration and Monitoring of Independent Schools*, p. 4.

91. Office for Standards in Education, "Akiva School," inspection report, January 28, 2004 (www.ofsted.gov.uk/reports/manreports/1430.htm [May 3, 2004]).

92. The curriculum at a state school must promote "the spiritual, moral, cultural and physical development of pupils at the schools and of society" and must prepare pupils "for the opportunities, responsibilities and experiences of later life"; Education Act 2002, section 78(1).

93. The relevant provision for state schools is the Education Act 1996, section 403, as amended. The guidance is Department for Education and Skills, *Sex and Relationship Education Guidance* (London, 2000).

94. There will continue to be registers of independent schools, one for England (kept by the secretary of state for education) and one for Wales (kept by the National Assembly for Wales); Education Act 2002, section 158. Registration procedure is prescribed by Education Act 2002, sections 160, 161. The registration authority is the secretary of state for education in England and the NAW in Wales. The six-month penalty is likely to be increased to fifty-one weeks under the Criminal Justice Bill.

95. Education Act 2002, section 159.

96. Ibid., section 162. The definition of "material change" is in section 162(2).

97. Ibid, section 165.

98. Ibid., sections 142, 169.

99. Ibid., section 168. Education (Provision of Information by Independent Schools) (England) Regulations 2003 (SI 2003/1934), which came into force on September 1, 2003.

100. Education Act 2002, sections 166, 167.

101. See Boyd, *Independent Schools*; DfES, *Regulatory Impact Assessment for the Reform of Regulation and Monitoring of Independent Schools*, paragraph 1.3. Cabinet Office Strategy Unit, *Private Action, Public Benefit* (London, 2002), calls for a more stringent test of "public benefit" to justify the tax concessions the charitable schools enjoy, reputedly worth £82 million per annum, and new legislation is planned; T. Halpin, "Independent Schools Share More Facilities," *The Times,* June 18, 2003. See also the draft Charities Bill 2004.

102. See N. Harris and K. Eden with A. Blair, *Challenges to School Exclusion* (London: Routledge Falmer, 2000).

103. In maintained schools, such preference or discrimination is not permitted unless the school is a voluntary or a foundation school. However, unless a foundation or voluntary controlled school has a religious character (and is designated as such), the preference, etc., may only be applied to a teacher of religious education. Preference in the appointment or promotion of any teacher at a voluntary aided school, on the other hand, may be based on whether the teacher's religious opinions conform to the tenets of the faith on which the school is founded; School Standards and Framework Act 1998, sections 59, 60.

104. See Education Act 2002, sections 141 and 142; parts of Education Reform Act 1988, sections 218 (mostly now repealed by the 2002 Act) and 218A; and Education (Health Standards) (England) Regulations 2003 (SI 2003/3139). Under the Standards Regulations (note 89 above), proprietors will be expected to carry out checks on such matters and on staff qualifications, previous employment history, and so forth, before confirming an appointment.

105. Department for Education and Skills, *The Future of Higher Education* (London: Stationery Office, 2003), part 6.

106. Education Act 1944, section 76.

107. Per Denning LJ in *Watt* v. *Kesteven County Council* [1955], 1 QB 408, at 424, Court of Appeal. See also *Cumings* v. *Birkenhead Corporation* [1972], Ch [Chancery] 12.

108. Section 9. See, for example, *B* v. *London Borough of Harrow* [2000], ELR 109, HL; *S* v. *Metropolitan Borough of Dudley and Another* [2000], ELR 330.

109. Per Pannick J in *R* v. *West Sussex County Council ex parte S* [1999], ELR 40 at 45A-B. See also *B* v. *Gloucestershire County Council and the Special Educational Needs Tribunal* [1998], ELR 539; *S and S* v. *Bracknell Forest Borough Council and the SENT* [1999], ELR 51; *W-R* v. *Solihull Metropolitan Borough Council and Wall* [1999], ELR 528; *C* v. *Buckinghamshire County Council and the Special Educational Needs Tribunal* [1999], ELR 179.

110. Education Act 1996, section 509(4). *The Queen on the Application of T* v. *Leeds City Council* [2002], ELR 91.

111. For example, L. Bash and D. Coulby, eds., *The Education Reform Act: Competition and Control* (London: Cassell, 1989).

112. See, for example, the Education Act 2002, section 178, providing for work-based training, and the Education (Amendment of the Curriculum Requirements for Fourth Key Stage) (England) Order 2003 (SI 2003/2946), providing for work-based learning and a range of new options (such as drama, dance, or media arts) for this age group.

113. Ibid., sections 80, 99; and School Standards and Framework Act 1998, section 71. As a consequence of this failure (by 76 percent of schools), the chief inspector of schools in England argued in a recent speech that individual schools should be permitted to decide how frequently the act of worship should take place and be given

more freedom "to determine what . . . worship should involve." D. Bell, "Change and Continuity: Reflections on the Butler Act," speech at the House of Commons, April 21, 2004.

114. School Standards and Framework Act 1998, schedule 20, paragraph 3.

115. Education Act 1996, section 394.

116. See articles 9 and 14 of the European Convention on Human Rights; S. Poulter, "The Religious Education Provisions of the Education Reform Act 1988," *Education and the Law*, vol. 2, no. 1 (1990), pp. 1–11; A. Bradney, "Christian Worship?" *Education and the Law*, vol. 8, no. 2 (1996), pp. 127–36; C. Hamilton, "Freedom of Religion and Religious Worship in Schools," in J. De Groof and J. Fiers, eds., *The Legal Status of Minorities in Education* (Leuven: ACCO, 1996), pp. 165–79; P. Cumper, "School Worship: Praying for Guidance" [1998], *European Human Rights Law Review (EHRLR)*, pp. 45–60.

117. *R* v. *Secretary of State for Education ex parte R and D* [1994], ELR 495, Queen's Bench Division.

118. Now in the Education Act 1996, section 405.

119. N. Harris, "Education Law: Excluding the Child," *Education and the Law*, vol. 12, no. 1 (2000), pp. 31–46; J. Fortin, *Children's Rights and the Developing Law*, 2nd ed. (London: LexisNexis U.K., 2003).

120. Human Rights Act 1998, section 6.

121. *R* v. *Cobham Hall School ex parte S* [1998], ELR 389.

122. *R* v. *Governors of Haberdashers' Aske's Hatcham College Trust ex parte T* [1995] ELR 350, Queen's Bench Division.

123. H. Mountfield, "The Implications of the Human Rights Act 1998 for the Law of Education," *Education Law Journal*, vol. 1, no. 3 (2000), pp. 146–58, quote on p. 148; D. Oliver, "Functions of a Public Nature under the Human Rights Act" [2004] Public Law 329–351.

124. *Belgian Linguistics (No. 2)* (1979–80), 1 European Human Rights Reports, 252.

125. Ibid. at p. 281.

126. *R* v. *Department for Education and Employment ex parte Begbie* [2000], ELR 445, CA; [1999] ELR 471, QBD.

127. *Dove* v. *The Scottish Ministers* [2002], Scots Law Times 1296, Extra Division at paragraph 34.

128. Education Act 1996, schedule 27. Parents may select only a state school under this right.

129. Education Act 1996, part 4.

130. *Simpson* v. *United Kingdom* (1989) 64 DR (European Commission of Human Rights Decisions and Reports) 188.

131. Ibid., at paragraph 3.

132. *H* v. *Kent County Council and the Special Educational Needs Tribunal* [2000], ELR 660.

133. *L* v. *Hereford and Worcester County Council and Hughes* [2000], ELR 375.

134. *PD and LD* v. *United Kingdom* (1989), 62 DR 292; *Graeme* v. *United Kingdom* (1990), 64 DR 158; *Klerks* v. *Netherlands* (1995), 82 DR 41. See also *W and KL* v. *Sweden* (1983), Application 14688/83; *Simpson* v. *United Kingdom* (1989) supra note 130; *Cohen* v. *United Kingdom* (1996), 21 EHRR CD 104.

135. *T* v. *Special Educational Needs Tribunal and Wiltshire County Council* [2002], ELR 704, QBD.

136. Ibid, at paragraph 39 (iii).

137. *Kjeldsen, Busk Masden, and Pedersen* (1976), 1 EHRR 711.

138. Ibid. at 731. See also *Campbell and Cosans* v. *United Kingdom* (1982), 4 EHRR 293; *Valsamis* v. *Greece* [1998], ELR 430.

139. A. Bradney, "Ethnicity, Religion and Sex Education," in N. Harris, ed., *Children, Sex Education, and the Law* (London: National Children's Bureau, 1996), pp. 87–98, quote on pp. 96–97.

140. Ibid.; D. Monk, "New Guidance/Old Problems: Recent Developments in Sex Education," *Journal of Social Welfare and Family Law*, vol. 23, no.3 (2001), pp. 271–91, especially at p. 287. Fortin, *Children's Rights and the Developing Law*, pp. 189–91.

141. European Convention on Human Rights, Article 10(2).

142. D. Feldman, *Civil Liberties and Human Rights in England and Wales,* 2nd ed. (Oxford University Press, 2002), p. 790.

143. Education Act 1996, section 403(1A).

144. Education Act 1996, section 403(1A)(b).

145. Local Government Act 1988, section 28, repealed by Local Government Act 2003, section 122.

146. But within limits; see *A* v. *United Kingdom (human rights: punishment of the child)* [1998], 2 Family Law Reports 959.

147. *Campbell and Cosans* v. *United Kingdom* (1982), see note 138 above.

148. Ibid., paragraphs 33–36.

149. Education (No. 2) Act 1986, section 47; School Standards and Framework Act 1998, section 131.

150. *R (Williamson)* v. *Secretary of State for Education and Employment* [2003], ELR 176, CA; [2002], EWCA Civ. 1820. It was also argued that their rights relating to respect for family or private life under Article 8 or of freedom of expression (Article 10, see above) were also violated by the ban. There is an interrelationship among all these provisions, in that "the two sentences of Article 2 [of Protocol 1] must be read not only in the light of each other but also, in particular, of Articles 8, 9, and 10 of the Convention"; *Kjeldsen, Busk Masden and Pedersen* (1976), 1 EHRR 711, paragraph 52; also *Valsamis* v. *Greece* [1998], ELR 430, at paragraph 25.

151. *Williamson*, supra note 150, at paragraph 302, Lady Justice Arden.

152. *R (Shabina Begum)* v. *Head Teacher and Governors of Denbigh High School* [2004] EWHC 1389 (Admin).

153. Ibid, at paragraph 74.

154. Ibid, at paragraph 73.

155. Ibid, at paragraph 90.

156. Ibid, at paragraph 91.

157. Ibid, at paragraph 103.

158. *Dove* v. *The Scottish Ministers,* see note 127 above.

159. Ibid. at paragraph 26.

160. Ibid. at paragraph 30.

161. See U. Kilkelly, *The Child and the European Convention on Human Rights* (Aldershot: Ashgate, 1999), pp. 80–81.

162. On the controversial issue of prohibiting or nationalizing private schools in the past, see H. Dent, *The New Education Bill* (University of London Press, 1944), pp. 20–21; Timmins, *The Five Giants*, p. 95.

163. Ofsted, *Standards and Quality in Education 2001/02,* paragraph 436.

164. Bell, "Standards and Inspections in Independent Schools."

165. Timmins, *The Five Giants,* p. 95.

166. Education Act 2002, section 70 and schedule 8. The schools could include independent schools that want to opt into the state system.

167. L. Archer and others, *Higher Education and Social Class* (London: Routledge Falmer, 2003), ch. 10.

168. Office for Standards in Education, *Excellence in Cities and Education Action Zones: Management and Impact* (London, 2003).

169. Fabre, *Social Rights under the Constitution,* pp. 112–13. See also D. Lewis, *Choice and the Legal Order* (London: Butterworths, 1996), ch. 2.

170. D. Oliver, *Common Values and the Public-Private Divide* (London: Butterworths, 1999), pp. 271–72.

171. These developments are covered by the School Standards and Framework Act 1998 and the Education Act 2002. Section 26 of the latter is headed "Collaboration between Schools." The 2002 act also permits a "federation of schools" (sections 24, 25).

172. See "Apartheid education," *Sunday Times,* July 15, 2001, confirmed in a report for the city by Lord Ouseley, *Community Pride not Prejudice: Making Diversity Work in Bradford* (Bradford: Bradford Vision, 2001).

5

School Choice Policies and Social Integration: The Experience of England and Wales

STEPHEN GORARD

In the United Kingdom, parents may express their preference for any state-funded school that they wish to educate their children, as well as choose to pay for a private school. *All* schools therefore are choice schools, and the range of types of schools within the publicly funded sector is growing, though they have a limited number of places. This chapter considers the impact of fifteen years of school choice and diversity on school composition, standards, cohesion, and justice. It presents a summary of the findings of what so far has been the largest study of a system of school choice, conducted by me and my colleagues Chris Taylor and John Fitz and published in 2003, and concludes with suggested lessons for the future and for other countries, such as the United States.[1]

The emphasis of this chapter is on social cohesion and on changes in the distribution of students among schools, which is termed "segregation" here. These changes are illustrated in terms of student poverty, ethnicity/race, first language, and special educational needs. The levels of and changes in student segregation in schools are largely determined by geographical factors and to some extent by the nature of local schools, rather than by the method of allocating students to schools. Nevertheless, since the introduction of extended choice in the United Kingdom in 1988, the overall level of segregation in the school system has declined. One reason for this is that the process of parental choice *can* override the segregation that routinely takes place when students are simply placed in neighborhood schools. The evidence also suggests that choice and diversity in types of schools are not clearly linked to each other. Choice—pressure from below—appears to drive schools toward uniformity, while such diversity as there is has been largely imposed from above. Choice is, in general, linked to declining segregation while diversity is, locally, associated with increasing segregation. The mix of students within a school also has possible implications for the school's standards of achievement.

This chapter first introduces the nature of school choice in the United Kingdom—and the range of choices—before considering arguments that have been presented elsewhere both for and against choice in education. It briefly discusses how families choose schools in practice and then describes the impact of fifteen years of a national school choice system on the social and economic segregation of schools. It describes in some detail the two most important determinants of school segregation—the nature of local housing and the diversity of local schools—and then ends with some suggestions for ways in which the benefits of choice could be preserved while minimizing its potentially segregating effects.

National Policy Background

The work reported here is an investigation of the long-term impact of market forces on the provision of education for students ages five to eighteen (or in grades K–12, although the chief focus of the study reported here is on secondary students, ages eleven to eighteen, with a less detailed analysis of primary school students). The United Kingdom has become something of a "social laboratory" by virtue of the extent to which policies promoting "competition" and "choice" have been developed. The study provides evidence for the first time concerning the long-term impact of markets in education, markets of a type that some commentators have rightly complained did not exist.[2] This is because elsewhere school choice "has rarely been put into practice in any but the most restricted form, so little has accrued about its consequences."[3] Therefore, "research comparing the distribution of students by social class in a system of choice to the social class distribution that would have existed based solely on neighborhood school assignment is clearly needed."[4] Social class is not the sole area of interest relating to segregation in U.K. schools, but it is the one of most concern to commentators there, whereas segregation by race/ethnicity has been the major concern in the United States. It is also important to note that, whereas official data about the family income of students predates the introduction of choice policies, figures on ethnicity/race have been collected for less than a decade.

The focus here is on changes over time, in order to compare the choice system with the previous system. This is necessary because the United Kingdom, unlike many other countries experimenting with choice, conducted its "experiment" across the entire national school system, leaving no control or comparison group. The emphasis is on public-public choice more than public-private choice.[5] The mix by class, race, and ability of students in a school matters, but primarily for social cohesion rather than school effectiveness.[6] In one sense, what the curriculum states about citizenship does not compare in importance with students' ability to experience mixed ethnic, gender, and religious groups in nonracist and nonsexist settings. The school mix also is closely related to raw-score academic results (note, for example, that all U.K. schools deemed "failing" have high levels of student poverty); however, the emphasis of this chapter is on the mix itself, rather than academic outcomes. In summary, raw scores on examinations have improved in the era of choice; state schools have progressed faster than private schools; and the achievement gap between social groups (as defined by sex, income, and race, for example) has declined overall.

Problems in allocating available school places are not new. The 1944 Education Act underlined the general principle that children were to be educated in accordance with the wishes of their parents and allowed parents to appeal the decisions of their local education authority (LEA) if they wished.[7] The process of allocating places at school had two components. First, an examination at the end of primary school (taken around the age of eleven and known as the "11+") was used to determine a "suitable" type of school within a tripartite system of grammar, secondary modern, and technical schools. The selection was made largely on the basis of academic ability. Second, a specific school was selected within that type, "largely through consultation between parents and primary school and secondary school, under the guidance of general principles laid down by LEAs."[8] The regular use of choice among more privileged families coupled with selection by ability is believed to have limited the role of education in promoting social mobility at that time.[9]

By 1969, the selective tripartite system and the notion of selection at 11+ were disappearing. Most LEAs moved toward a system of comprehensive secondary schools (although these retained considerable diversity in terms of age range, gender composition, and religious affiliation), catering to students across the ability range. In areas with no other system of allocation, a system of neighborhood schools operated automatically. Dore and Flowerdew reported the increasing use from 1968 to 1977 of catchment areas for secondary schools, replacing the use of examination results and other methods.[10] This was supposed to be fairer and to reduce the existing disparities in the standard of education obtained by different students. In practice, evidence arose that the procedure was unintentionally racially discriminatory because local housing was racially segregated.[11]

The 1980 Education Act formally legislated, at a national level, parents' right to a voice in the allocation of school places. It also created the assisted places scheme, which allowed able children from poor families to attend fee-paying schools at public expense.[12] The legislative trend toward explicit parental preference continued with the 1988 Education Reform Act (and subsequent case law), the 1991 Parents' Charter, and the 1992 White Paper. All of these steps represented a shift away from the period before the 1980s when practices were set by individual LEAs and parental preference was, at least according to national legislation, relevant only to selective or single-sex schools, voluntary aided schools, or the fee-paying sector.

Consequently, all publicly funded schools in England and Wales are now "choice" schools, and all of them published raw scores in "performance" tables from 1990–2001 (although in practice these have not generally formed the basis for parental decisions). The 1988 Education Reform Act gave all families the right to express a preference for any school (even one outside their LEA) and denied schools the right to refuse anyone entry until a certain number of students—the standard or planned admission number (PAN)—were enrolled.[13] Most of the funding to schools then was based on number of students enrolled. After 1988 the number of families selecting schools other than the local catchment (neighborhood) school increased substantially. When families are denied access to their selected school (due to oversubscription, for example), they have the right to appeal their assignment. The number of parents exercising this right to appeal also has risen greatly. All of this was designed to produce a situation in which good schools thrived and poor schools either changed or perished. The intrinsically monopolistic state provision of education was supposedly replaced by choice and diversity, although this market is a limited one since, among other things, schools do not operate to maximize their profit and money does not change hands between client and provider.[14]

Considerable powers for self-management were passed to schools, which could, after a ballot of parents, also opt out of LEA control completely to become grant-maintained institutions (now termed foundation schools). These were able to apply their own selection procedures to a significant proportion of their student intake. City technology colleges operated with explicit criteria for the allocation of their limited places, but, in practice, researchers found considerable variation among colleges in how the criteria were applied.[15] Voluntary aided schools had a majority of their governors appointed by a religious foundation and, since the governing body of a school determined admissions, the differences among them in terms of admissions policy were substantial.

Despite the existence of a supposedly national framework of parental choice within an essentially comprehensive system, diversity in admissions also continued for all other secondary schools.[16] Some LEAs still used the 11+ examination; others encouraged individual applications to schools (especially in areas with high proportions of grant-maintained schools or cross-border transfers). Some LEAs asked parents to state a preference, but most authorities merely published their intended allocation and waited for objections, with a null response treated as approval. In the case of oversubscription in any school, a variety of criteria were used to allocate places, including medical and social reasons. The picture of school allocation remained a complex one.

The 1988 Education Reform Act also introduced a compulsory national curriculum, which specified a number of "core" and "foundation" subjects (such as science and history) to be taken by all students and the amount of time to be devoted to each subject. This had the effect of equalizing the opportunities of most children, as well as leaving little time within the normal school day for subjects deemed by some within the government as undesirable (such as sociology or media studies). Therefore the publicly funded schools that parents were now able to "choose" among became more similar in terms of content. The same act introduced compulsory testing at four key stages within the common national curriculum and the publication of raw scores. The curriculum now contains provision for the teaching of "citizenship," still a relatively minor part of schooling, which includes the following themes: civil society; communities, cultures, and identities; personal and social skills; sex and relationships; sustainable development; life, events, and people; health and safety; and careers. For more on these policy enactments, see chapter 4 in this volume.

The 1998 School Standards and Framework Act changed the situation again, perhaps most notably by addressing inequities in school admissions policies, arising in the main from the actions of the former grant-maintained and voluntary schools.[17] Otherwise, the most notable policy of the current U.K. administration has been the state-sponsored encouragement of diversity. School ministers are considering the use of vouchers, subsidies for parent-run private schools, and incentives such as payment by results.[18] Private nonprofit companies are taking over the running of some schools, especially those that have received poor inspections.[19] "City academies" have recently

Figure 5-1. *Percentage of Students in Private Schools in England, 1964–2002*

Percent

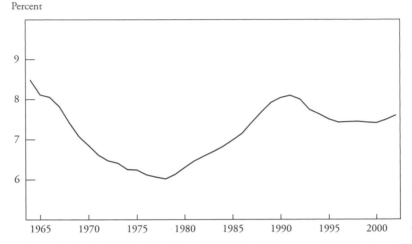

Source: Author's calculations from data published by the Department for Education and Skills (England) and the National Assembly (Wales).

been introduced to solve specific problems in London.[20] A recent Green Paper (government policy paper) on education created a portfolio of diverse schools in England, which includes thirty-three new city academies, 300 advanced schools, and 2,000 specialist schools. According to the minister for education, "The model of comprehensive schooling that grew up in the 1960s and 1970s is simply inadequate for today's needs. . . . The keys are *diversity*, not uniformity."[21]

Types of Schools

A key difference between choice in the United Kingdom and in the United States and elsewhere is that it largely ignores the private sector. Only around 7 percent of students in England attend fee-paying schools, and the figure drops to 2 percent in Wales and 1 percent in Scotland.[22] Many more families than this report that they would consider a private school if they could afford it, so in times of prosperity numbers tend to grow.[23] Figure 5-1 shows the trend in these figures from 1964 (when the tripartite state system was changing to a comprehensive one) to 2002. The highest recorded proportion of fee-paying students was in 1964 (7.9 percent), and it dropped during the comprehensive era to a low of 5.7 percent, in 1978. The causes of the drop are likely to include both economic factors and increasing satisfaction with the state sector. By the time of the 1988 Education Reform Act, the figure had risen to 7.3 percent again, and in the following few years the figure rose again to a mini-peak of 7.5 percent, in 1991. The determinants of this blip probably include the continuation of a trend clearly discernible from 1978 onward (perhaps economic in nature) and temporary suspicion among some middle-class parents about the national curriculum and associated testing regime. By 1995, when all students of compulsory-education age at state-funded schools had entered during the era of choice, the proportion at private schools had stabilized at an even 7 percent, and it remained at 7 percent in 2002.

Private schools were not bound by the terms of the 1988 Education Reform Act and therefore did not have to introduce the national curriculum or take part in the associated testing regime. However, the curriculum was itself largely based on the curriculum already used in top private schools, and private schools were more than happy to take part in the tests. This was partly to ensure ease of transfer between sectors and partly because their results (in terms of raw scores) placed them at the top of all relevant tables. Only a "superclass" defined by wealth and status, plus some professionals, uses private schools only and thus opts out of the state system altogether.[24] The remainder of the more privileged classes have access to the most desirable public schools because of the link between school reputation and the cost of local housing. Only they can afford to buy a house in the catchment area of a "good" school.

The policy changes described above included the 1980 assisted places scheme, whereby the fees of some students at private schools were paid by the state. But this involved a tiny fraction of students in a minority of otherwise very exclusive schools, within a very small private sector. The scheme was means tested, but it did not focus on the very poor or on ethnic minorities, and it never captured the public imagination. None of the assisted places schools in one study actually filled their eligible places.[25] Otherwise, the private sector was largely unaffected by the choice policies described, which amounted to what is effectively a national voucher scheme involving all state-funded schools of whatever type.

In addition to the traditional and less orthodox private schools, there are state-funded but independent city technology colleges and city academies, comprising much less than 1 percent of schools. These are public and private joint-funded independent secondary schools within the state sector, designed to tackle underachievement in urban areas. There are also a somewhat larger number of state-funded schools funded directly by central government rather than through their LEAs. They were originally termed grant-maintained (now foundation) schools and comprise perhaps 8 percent of the schools in England and Wales.

The 2002 Education Act further blurs the distinction between state and private provision by encouraging state schools to form companies and companies to take over failing schools, authorities, and assessment. Private schools can now sponsor city academies partly because take up of sponsorships by traditional industry has been so low, and authorities are being encouraged to pay for children in challenging circumstances to attend private schools. These moves toward greater collaboration between the state and private sectors will lead to the more rigorous monitoring and registration of private involvement in education. However, these changes are very recent and are not reflected in the longitudinal research reported in this chapter.

Another key difference between the United Kingdom and the United States and other countries lies in the relationship between religion and the state. In the United Kingdom, all schools are required by law to provide for a daily communal act of worship and to provide religious education, which is a compulsory part of the national curriculum. Parents are permitted to withdraw their children from this provision, but it is their responsibility to do so, and withdrawal requires formal arrangement. There also is a smaller but stable number of state-funded schools with denominational status, most commonly Anglican but also Catholic, Jewish, and Muslim or affiliated with some other religion. They are termed voluntary aided or voluntary controlled schools and make up approximately one-quarter of all secondary schools. Therefore there is less pressure to attend private schools for religious reasons, and this is probably part of the reason for the relatively small size of the private sector.

Most schools are now coeducational, but a few are still single-sex, particularly girls-only, schools. Most schools are now at least nominally comprehensive, enrolling students of all levels of academic ability, but around 4 percent of students attend selective grammar schools and another 4 percent attend secondary modern schools, which take students who are not eligible to attend grammar schools in areas with a selective system. A growing proportion of schools specialize in one subject (at the time of writing, specialist schools constituted more than one-quarter of secondary-age schools), while some teach in a language other than English. In Wales, for instance, around 10 percent of schools are designated Welsh language schools. There are a very few nontraditional schools (Steiner and Summerhill, for example) and a declining number of schools—now less than 5 percent of all schools—exclusively for children with special educational needs, whose students have been progressively included in mainstream schools. It should be noted that apart from private schools, the school types in the United Kingdom are not mutually exclusive, meaning that the percentages for each sector total considerably more than 100. A foundation school could be selective, single-sex, specialist, *and* denominational, for example.

The Merits of Choice?

School choice is purported to have three main advantages over a system of strict area assignment to school,[26] and the loose alliance of politicians who pushed through the mix of measures in the 1988 Education Reform Act probably represented each constituency claiming one or more of those advantages.[27] First, there is the libertarian notion of choice for its own sake.[28] School choice programs are popular, as evidenced by opinion polls and by the increasing participation of many segments of society (as defined by class, ethnicity, and language) after such policies have been introduced. It is now probably politically unacceptable to take away the right of parents to choose, and it is not clear that opposition to the notion of choice can be sustained logically.[29]

The second argument, which is perhaps the most important for choice advocates, is that market forces will drive up educational standards.[30] Successful schools will be popular, and weaker schools will be unpopular, progressively losing their per capita funding until they either improve or close. Over time, therefore, the general standards of schools will be higher. Evidence on this claim, which is unclear, has been presented elsewhere, but this chapter is more concerned with equity and therefore considers school outcomes only in terms of patterns of polarization by economic status and race.[31] Insofar as it is possible to ascertain, school examination results have risen since 1989 both in absolute terms and in relation to the fee-paying sector. This has had the side effect of reducing differences in attainment among social groups, such as those defined by geography, poverty, and ethnicity.

Finally, there is the argument for equity.[32] Choice of school extends a privilege to all that was previously available only to those able to afford houses in desirable suburban catchment areas or to send their child to a fee-paying school. Markets, by reducing bureaucratic rules and procedures— such as assignment by catchment area— enable poor and ethnic minority families to make choices previously not open to them, including by seeking a better quality of service elsewhere. Markets can be seen as extending a privilege that some members of society already have[33] and therefore as an antidote to social stratification.[34] In the United Kingdom, because the majority of schools are already religious (in name, at least), choice is not for the most part based on arguments about respecting religious pluralism.

Choice might be especially popular with the disadvantaged residents in many communities, such as immigrant, minority, and one-parent families, who have been deserting some large inner-city schools.[35] Witte reported that a Milwaukee voucher scheme attracted very low-income, mainly black or Hispanic families with incomes that were considerably below average.[36] This suggests that choice might lead to successful desegregation by income and ethnicity over time.[37] Other well-founded studies also suggest that choice can lead to greater integration in the United States.[38] Perhaps changing the basis for allocating school places from one based on fixed attendance zones to one based on choice will simply alter the basis for segregation, rather than increase it. A "consequence of the absence of choice in education is that there is extensive stratification of schools" by income and race.[39] Choice could instead lead to a school system stratified by student performance and behavior and therefore lead to overall improvement.

In the United Kingdom, the Performance and Innovation Unit, a temporary nongovernment think tank, cites public school catchment areas as the greatest barrier to social mobility. Instead, it proposes "reducing the weight given to geographical catchment area as a determinant of access to the best State schools."[40] This would counteract the incentive for middle-class parents to "buy" a good education for their children by moving to an area adjacent to desirable schools.

On the other hand, market policies could be said to undermine welfare states. Welfare policies came into existence in the United Kingdom on the premise that state action was necessary in order to achieve social justice within capitalist economies. This was to be achieved through the redistribution of wealth, and the provision of health, education, and social welfare services for free. The policies ensured that those who could not afford to pay could still benefit from such services. Market forces could dismantle the machinery through which equity was to be achieved, increasing the rewards for the already privileged strata of society and reducing them for everyone else. Perhaps school choice will lead to increased selection by ability and social class,[41] and "those endowed with material and cultural capital will simply add to their existing advantages through choice policies."[42] Markets in education apparently lead to wasting effort on marketing instead of teaching and learning and to an increase in selection of students by ability, and their beneficiaries are the middle class rather than the poor.[43] Successful schools are limited by the size of their classrooms and therefore do not generally grow to accommodate demand as a business would. Instead, they become more selective, as data from other countries, such as Chile and Sweden, indicate.[44] Fiske and Ladd, for example, reported that "the most obvious negative consequence of the Tomorrow's Schools reforms is that enrolment in New Zealand . . . became increasingly stratified." Unfortunately, these claims, and those of the Smithfield study in New Zealand cited by Fiske and Ladd, are actually contradicted by the very evidence presented by their authors.[45]

In the United Kingdom, with equally little empirical basis, it has been reported that choice leads to "the polarisation of schools, with those in more working-class areas sucked into a spiral of decline. . . . This polarisation has happened on a massive scale in England, especially in London."[46] In summary, after fourteen years of relatively unrestricted choice policies, many commentators would agree with the *Times Educational Supplement* in concluding that "as every international comparison has shown, English schools are more socially differentiated than any others in Europe. Some hardly warrant the description 'comprehensive' at all, thanks to the parental choice policies pursued by successive governments. They may be even more socially stratified than the old grammar and secondary moderns they replaced."[47] We now have the data to enable us to determine which of the two views outlined above is correct.

Has Segregation Increased?

The evidence from studies on the process of choice is quite clear.[48] Public choice theory does not provide a good description of the process of choice, according to the reports of those involved. The most commonly reported source of information about schools is word of mouth; schools have a widely held local reputation, which explicit marketing is slow to change. Families consider very few alternatives on average—fewer than two schools. Parents and children generally do not emphasize academic standards when selecting a school; rather, they are primarily concerned with safety and happiness. Parents of a four-year-old are generally thinking about the security of their child and the convenience of the school. Parents of a ten-year-old (the oldest cohort in primary schools, commonly 100 to 300 students in size) looking for a secondary school (where their child will be in the youngest cohort in a school that is 1,000 to 3,000 students in size) will naturally be concerned with issues such as bullying rather than academic outcome in six or seven years' time. The children themselves generally want to go to school with their friends. Many families therefore select their nearest school anyway, and most of the rest obtain their expressed preference. Just about all families that do not get their preference then appeal as a matter of course.[49] One would not, under these circumstances, expect the introduction of choice to have made a

Figure 5-2. *Change in Segregation by Poverty over Time in England* [a]

Segregation index

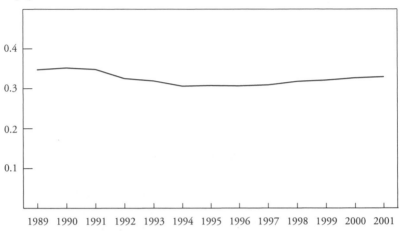

Source: Author's calculations from data published by the Department for Education and Skills (England) and the National Assembly (Wales).

a. This graph shows the proportion of children from families in poverty who would have to exchange schools for there to be a precisely even spread of poverty among schools.

marked and sustained difference in patterns of school use. Indeed, this is what the study described here found.

There is insufficient space here to describe the methods used in this study of the impact of choice in England and Wales. It started with analysis of the annual school census returns for all secondary schools from 1989 to 2001, supplemented with figures from the Programme for International Student Assessment (PISA). From these, around seventy LEAs were selected for further consideration of their published and reported admissions policies. From these, nine LEAs in three contiguous areas and then schools within these areas were selected. Representatives of all these entities took part in taped interviews. The data sets were analyzed using spatial models and a segregation index based on family poverty, ethnicity, first language, and special educational needs.[50]

Figure 5-2 shows the level of school segregation in all state-funded secondary schools in England from 1989 (the last year before open enrollment) to 2001. The first thing to note is that schools in England were, and remain, socially segregated. In any year, around one-third of students would have had to change schools in order for there to be an even spread of "poor" children among schools. The period before open enrollment was not, therefore, some golden age of equity. Some commentators have commenced their analysis as

though the education system in England and Wales was somehow less stratified before 1988.[51] What this research confirms is that, prior to the introduction of market-driven policies, secondary schools in England were already
socially stratified. It appears, however, that whatever the stratifying effects of
market forces may be, the effects of preexisting catchment areas and "selection by mortgage" may have been worse. In fact, the segregation index for
1989–90 is the highest for the years for which school census data still exist.

From 1990 to 1994, segregation in England broadly declined from a high
of more than 35 percent to around 30 percent. The national change for all
primary schools is almost identical to that for secondary schools. Segregation
of all schools in terms of family poverty decreased after 1989–90. Where
other indicators are available, segregation by ethnic group, first language, and
additional educational need also declined after 1989. These changes over
time represent important and long-term shifts in the socioeconomic composition of schools. There is no evidence, in the figures presented here, to link
education markets with increasing segregation. These policies are not necessarily associated with increasing the concentration of disadvantaged children
in some schools and decreasing it in others, rather the reverse. In 1995, 1996,
and 1997, segregation in England stayed at around 30 percent. This suggests
that the imposition of school choice on a system with the level of segregation
found in 1989 led to progressively less segregated schools (in general) as successive cohorts moved from primary to secondary school. Once all of the students in secondary schools had entered after 1989, this trend ceased and the
position stabilized. In essence, the impact of choice policies—if that is what
it is—was limited and relatively short-lived. Subsequently, from 1998 to
2001, segregation in English schools increased every year to around 33 percent, after a change of government in the United Kingdom in 1997 and the
introduction of the 1998 School Standards and Framework Act.

According to the PISA study, by 2001 the United Kingdom still had
lower-than-average segregation of schools on *all* relevant indicators of social
disadvantage and attainment (table 5-1). It was, with Luxembourg, the only
country to be in that position (but it should be noted that the PISA data set
cannot compare in completeness to the one used above). Unlike Luxembourg, however, the United Kingdom also had less-than-average polarization
of reading test scores, by family wealth for example. This polarization, or segregation by outcome, is strongly associated with the degree of selection in any
national school system. After twelve years of public choice, the United Kingdom still had one of the fairest school systems in the European Union.

The overall pattern of reduced school segregation from 1989–94 also
appears in *every* economic region in England and Wales. Schools in Wales

Table 5-1. *Segregation Index (S) by European Union Country*

Country	Parental occupation	Family wealth	Country of origin	Reading score
All EU	33	28	48	49
Austria	36 (+.04)	24 (−.08)	49 (+.01)	62 (+.12)
Belgium	36 (+.04)	26 (−.04)	45 (−.03)	66 (+.15)
Denmark	33	28	42 (−.07)	39 (−.11)
Finland	36 (+.04)	21 (−.14)	55 (+.07)	27 (−.29)
France	31 (−.03)	31 (+.05)	47 (−.01)	56 (+.07)
Germany	36 (+.04)	33 (+.08)	41 (−.08)	61 (+.11)
Greece	43 (+.13)	26 (−.04)	48	58 (+.08)
Ireland	29 (−.06)	30 (+.03)	45 (−.03)	39 (−.11)
Italy	30 (−.05)	27 (−.02)	55 (+.07)	58 (+.08)
Luxembourg	24 (−.16)	23 (−.10)	24 (−.33)	41 (−.09)
Netherlands	30 (−.05)	23 (−.10)	41 (−.08)	66 (+.15)
Portugal	40 (+.10)	36 (+.13)	35 (−.16)	48 (−.01)
Spain	32 (−.02)	28	57 (+.09)	40 (−.10)
Sweden	27 (−.10)	29 (+.02)	40 (−.07)	29 (−.26)
U.K.	31 (−.03)	26 (−.04)	46 (−.02)	43 (−.07)

Source: Author's calculations from data published by the Department for Education and Skills (England) and the National Assembly (Wales).

Note: The values in each cell are for S calculated for the lowest 10 percent of the sample as measured by family wealth, parental occupation, or reading score and for those born outside the test country. The figures in parentheses are the proportionate deviation between S for that country and for the EU as a whole, that is (country score − EU score)/(country score + EU score).

were more mixed in socioeconomic terms than their counterparts in England, and segregation there continued to decline to 2001.[52] Similar trends have emerged in Scotland.[53] The greatest proportionate decreases were in the South East and Outer London. These differences among the four home nations of the United Kingdom and the variation of trends over time within England would suggest that there are several factors affecting school segregation. In accounting for the patterns observed in school segregation over time, both demographic and socioeconomic changes have to be factored into the analysis alongside changes in policy. One should not naively attribute any and all changes in segregation to the introduction of choice and competition in the state-funded education system, as other researchers have done.[54]

The findings also suggest no strong connection between markets and the rate of school closures or between markets and schools going into "spirals of decline." The number of children per secondary school in England has generally been increasing since 1947 (the earliest figures available). This is partly due to population growth and urbanization, partly due to successive raising of the school-leaving age and more recently to school closures. In the period of our investigation (1989–2001), the number of students per school dropped slightly in the first year after the 1988 reforms, but it grew afterward. This would lead us to expect that schools in "spirals of decline" would be rare, since even "'unsuccessful" schools might be expected to grow in number or at least maintain their size. In addition, the closure of schools leads to mixing students from previously distinct catchments and could lead directly to less socioeconomic segregation. Economic growth, in this case growth in the number of schools, would tend to lead to segregation, while declining numbers of schools would lead to desegregation.[55]

Over the period from 1990 to 1994, therefore, when segregation of schools was declining, the number of state schools also was falling and so the school population was divided into fewer units. At the same time, fewer students from higher-income families attended fee-paying schools and fewer students with special needs attended separate schools. These factors, all of which may or may not be related to market forces, may be able to explain much of the drop in segregation.

The Geography of School Placement

Segregation declined in most LEAs, at the district and school level. Areas with a sizable proportion of residents living in poverty were more likely to have such residents evenly distributed among schools than areas where only a small proportion of the population was living in poverty. As overall levels of poverty rise, the population in poverty is likely to be more evenly distributed. Conversely, as overall levels of poverty fall, the population left in poverty is likely to be more concentrated in space, at least in the short term. There was extreme bifurcation of income in some LEAs that lost a large proportion of their population to fee-paying schools. One LEA had 44 percent of students leave the borough to attend faith-based and foundation schools elsewhere. The LEA therefore had a very large proportion of free-school-meal students in its schools and very little LEA-level segregation—"equality of poverty." Where the population is not bifurcated, segregation can still be lower because of the population's uniformity. Segregation is generally lower in the North East and Wales, where the population is less variable in terms of class structure, income, and other socioeconomic indicators. The suggestion here is that segregation depends on the local variability of potential school users as much as their allocation to schools.

However, some LEAs showed little or no change in segregation between 1989 and 1995. In some cases the lack of change was due to a lack of alternative schools (the Scilly Isles has only one school) or low population density (Dyfed has an average of 0.2 persons per hectare). A partial explanation also lies in the LEA procedures for allocating contested secondary school places since 1989. In Cardiff, for example, secondary schools used matched primary schools whose leavers were guaranteed a place. As these primary schools themselves ran a catchment area system, so in effect did the secondary schools. Another example involves the rule that siblings of those already in a particular school take priority. This would lead to a slight inhibition in the year-on-year socioeconomic variation within a school. Similar considerations apply to LEAs that are prepared to fund free travel only to the school closest to a child's home. In effect, these LEAs are saying to poor families that even though the government says that they can choose any school they like, if they choose a nonadjacent school they must pay for the travel themselves. In summary, these stable LEAs are those in which a market for schools cannot operate, for structural, geographic, or political reasons.

A minority of LEAs showed an increase in segregation between 1989 and 1994, but only one showed a regular year-on-year increase. Some of these LEAs, such as those in Bromley and Buckinghamshire, run an overtly selective system of grammar schools, while others, such as in Haringey, are deeply affected by the policy of grant-maintained (foundation) schools. These schools control their own admissions policies and therefore draw their students from wide areas that often extend beyond the boundaries of the LEAs. If these schools are drawing in more privileged students than surrounding neighborhood schools, then that would show up as increasing segregation. Overall, these differences among LEAs highlight the danger of attempting to generalize from a small-scale study in a few areas.

In general, the decline in segregation is greatest in densely populated regions in which the housing for rich and poor is close together, with large numbers of secondary schools and transport links that make choosing from a range of schools feasible for parents from across the socioeconomic spectrum. They are therefore perhaps the most likely to show change in a market-like situation. It would be expected that offering choice of schools—or any other change in the policy of allocating school places—would have less impact on patterns of enrollment in rural areas with fewer candidate schools within a reasonable traveling distance for most families. The largest single factor determining the level of segregation in schools is therefore the pattern of local housing, since even in a system of choice most children attend a school near their home. And the irony of this, as one commentator notes, is that "in Britain, the dominant view . . . is still that selection of students by ability . . . is an insidious route back to elitism . . . , yet selection by residence is acceptable even if it is leading to the concentration of privilege among better-off families living close to more-desired schools."[56]

British cities represent a distinct ecological structure, largely because of the large public housing sector.[57] They are typically characterized by distinct neighborhoods, each with its own sociogeographic dialectic, and different social groups live in distinct areas of the city.[58] This can influence more than variations in housing: "The social geography of the city is itself likely to generate or reinforce differences in values from one neighborhood to another, for the socio-demographic composition of different neighborhoods creates distinctive local reference groups which contribute significantly to people's attitudes to life."[59] Schools and education in urban and even rural life play their own part in generating and reinforcing the differences in values between neighborhoods. Indeed, many schools have been part of the process of creating neighborhoods, as they provide a significant point of community contact.[60] As Robson discovered in a study in Sunderland, parental attitudes toward education were strongly affected by the character of their residential neighborhood.[61] "The *de facto* segregation brought about by concentration of social classes in cities results in schools with unequal moral climates which likewise affect the motivation of the child, not necessarily by inculcating a sense of inferiority, but rather by providing a different ethos in which to perceive values."[62]

In England and Wales, different social classes have long been substantially segregated from each other by residence, which has made any attempt to create a good social mix in local comprehensive schools very difficult. The situation does not seem to be improving. In fact, residential segregation may itself be reinforced by the rising cost of property in desirable catchment areas, leading to selection by postcode and the continuance of educational "ghettoization."[63] Leech and Campos reported that in Coventry there is an estimated premium of 15 percent to 19 percent for neighborhoods surrounding popular schools.[64] This is more significant given that the Coventry LEA operated a "designated" area policy in which oversubscribed schools allocated places by proximity of student residence to the school. Advocates of increased school choice have suggested choice as a partial antidote to this self-sustaining cycle of residential segregation, and there is some, albeit limited, evidence that choice may serve as such. There has been a progressive rise in the use of schools further away from home since 1980, and out-of-catchment schools have been chosen by more children from "struggling" neighborhoods than "prosperous" ones.[65] This is likely to reflect greater dissatisfaction with their local school among those living in poorer areas.[66]

Benn and Chitty report that at the peak of the comprehensive process (sometime around 1968), 62 percent of comprehensive schools drew children mainly from council housing estates or areas of mixed housing with a substandard element.[67] By 1994 that figure had fallen to 31 percent of comprehensive schools. So, if the geographical link between home and school was weakened, even slightly, during the 1990s by a program of school choice, then has residential segregation also declined over time, so reducing segregation at the school level and creating a circle of integrating forces? This is what Taeuber and others described as the "Belfast" model, when they found some evidence that residential segregation by ethnicity declined in Kentucky following the increasing integration of schools.[68] U.K. policies to produce mixed housing schemes providing enough affordable housing in each area are popular with advocacy groups that wish to extend choice to the socially excluded.[69] A similar phenomenon was hypothesized by Goldhaber, who suggested that, paradoxically, increasing choice in urban areas can actually reduce white flight and associated residential segregation, since parents no longer need to move away from city centers in order to use suburban schools.[70] It is certainly the case for a variety of reasons (the nature of travel, for instance) that geographical location is the key to understanding the impact of choice on the school system.[71]

Diversity of Schooling

Choice does not lead naturally to the provision of diverse educational programs in the United Kingdom. All schools are constrained not only by the national curriculum and its testing and inspection regime but also by the more general equal opportunity, racial equality, and human rights legislation in force. The pressure to diversify school provision and move away from what one minister unfortunately referred to as the "bog-standard" comprehensive model (that is, undifferentiated all-ability schools) comes from policymakers and their advocate-advisers rather than from popular demand. The large private schools that were part of the assisted places scheme are very similar in nature to each other.[72] City technology colleges are few in number. Many foundation (previously grant-maintained) schools changed to their current status simply to avoid the threat of closure by their local authority or to retain the right to select their students. Generally, they were not motivated by a different mission (such as religion), and for the majority of schools opting out of LEA control may have seemed too risky. In any case it was possible only when there was considerable local parental support. Parents generally are not calling for expansion of the number of specialist, faith-based, and Welsh-speaking schools because of their sui generis nature but because of their somewhat specious claims to be more effective than standard schools.[73] The heads of schools that seek to become specialist are motivated by the additional £150,000 ($250,000) that they receive initially, plus a further £123 ($210) per pupil per year recurrent funding. Diversification in the United Kingdom is almost entirely top-down in nature.

Local levels of segregation of disadvantaged students are largely determined by noneducational factors, such as the geography of each area. Once these wider factors are accounted for, areas in which there is little diversity in the nature of local schooling (where all schools are LEA-controlled comprehensives, for example) generally have lower levels of segregation and until recently have tended to reduce those levels further. Areas with considerable diversity, on the other hand (where school allocation by selection, faith, fees, or specialism appears), have higher levels of segregation and have tended to maintain these levels over time. Where diversity of schools increases, so too does segregation. This remains the case in the analysis of the national data set whatever the publicized criteria of allocation to schools.[74]

The implications of this for the current expansion of specialist and faith-based schools should be immediately apparent. Whatever merits these schemes have (and the evidence for their merits is far from conclusive), they also present a real danger of creating greater socioeconomic division in the education system. However, the same argument applies to areas with relatively high proportions of foundation schools and to Welsh-language schools in Wales, even when these schools are not specialist, faith-based, or selective. What all of these minority school types have in common is the ability to act as their own admission authority, and perhaps it is this, rather than their marketing identity, that is the chief determinant of increased segregation in their local area. The presence of fee-paying schools also is related to increasingly segregated LEAs. This may be related to the admission arrangements of minority schools, such as the use of selection, and the ability of some parents to express their commitment to a particular religion. Diversity drives segregation by giving people a reason other than perceived quality, rightly or wrongly, to use a school other than the one nearest to them. Diversification of schooling can override fairness in the distribution of school places.

If a policy of increased diversity is deemed desirable in the United Kingdom, and that is present government policy, our analysis argues that it should be organized fairly.[75] If advocates of diversity and specialization are convinced that this is the best route to raising standards then, in all fairness, to test whether this policy is the right one, specialist and the anachronistic faith-based schools should not receive preferential funding. Nor should they be allowed to select students or to use an admissions process that differs from the one used by the schools with which they are in competition. Only then will we be able to see the strength of their advocates' arguments. Two LEAs in our subsample have specialist schools that are based on catchment areas, just like the remaining schools in the LEA.[76] These specialist schools take approximately their fair share of disadvantaged students, and they do not have superior public examination results.

Promoting Equity and Social Inclusion

What this evidence shows is that there are various determinants of school segregation. The most important ones are geography, including population density; the nature of local housing; the diversity of the local population; and local levels of residential segregation.[77] Once geographical and economic determinants are accounted for, there is little variance left in the model, and most of what remains is accounted for by school organization factors, such as the nature and number of local schools. There is almost nothing left for markets to explain, and it is accordingly very difficult to attribute school-level changes to policy changes over time. The local variation in the implementation of national policy and the lack of diversity or even alternative schools in some regions show a simple and universal market model of school choice to be invalid. It depends on the precise nature of the policy and on what that policy replaces.[78] What choice policies may do is change the rules by which segregation takes place, without markedly increasing or eliminating levels of segregation that are largely shaped by structural factors.

Given that the genie is out of the bottle, it is very likely that some measure of parental choice of school will remain part of any future policy. The choice process can be reformed by coordinating the admissions process across and within LEAs.[79] Using a single application form and handling all responses on the same day across the nation would help prevent multiple place allocation and wasted spaces, and it would reduce bureaucracy. Given the limitation of residential segregation and its interaction with school segregation, incentives, such as council-tax exemption, could be provided for high-attaining primary pupils to attend designated secondary schools in poorer areas.[80] Alternatively, schools in difficult areas could receive higher levels of preferential funding. Authorities should be encouraged to fund surplus places, allowing popular schools to grow past their planned admissions numbers, rather than increasing the number of appeals, and they should rationalize school provision through closures where necessary, rather than having a larger number of schools tied to rigidly defined residential areas. The arrangements for free travel should be the same across LEAs and between different school types. A return to all-school banding by ability in urban areas, whereby children are tested before entry to secondary school and each school is then constrained to admit students proportionately across the ability range, would help to further decrease socioeconomic segregation.

Until recently, there has been relatively little diversity within the U.K. school system, in which the national curriculum and associated orders, including those for religious and personal and social education, have constrained differences. Therefore a considerable increase in choice has not led to balkanization of the school system. The biggest differences among types of schools have been in the methods of recruiting and allocating students, and it is difficult to untangle these from their claims to a different ethos and greater effectiveness. The implication of this for those wishing to see greater equity is that *all* schools should be allowed to recruit across larger areas (and appropriate free travel should then be provided for the poorest segments of society). Most crucially, diversity of provision should stem from demand and should take place in a clear culture of different but equal treatment for all school types—with equal funding and identical procedures for application, allocation, and appeals. Only then will we be able to see whether, for example, it is the specialization that makes specialist schools special and whether it is the religious ethos that leads voluntary aided and voluntary controlled schools to better examination results. My own suspicion is that neither proposition holds and that schools are, quite rationally, using the rules of school choice to improve the nature of their annual student intake as well as attempting to improve the nature of their outcomes.

Notes

1. S. Gorard, C. Taylor, and J. Fitz, *Schools, Markets, and Choice Policies* (London: Routledge, 2003).

2. D. Archbald, "Measuring School Choice Using Indicators," *Education Policy*, vol. 10, no. 1 (1996), pp. 88–101; W. Jeynes, "Assessing School Choice: A Balanced Perspective," *Cambridge Journal of Education*, vol. 30, no. 2 (2000), pp. 223–41.

3. C. Weiss, "Foreword," in B. Fuller and R. Elmore, eds., *Who Chooses? Who Loses?* (New York: Teachers College Press, 1996), p. 8.

4. E. Goldring and C. Hausman, "Reasons for Parental Choice of Schools," *Journal of Education Policy*, vol. 14, no. 5 (1999), pp. 469–90.

5. But see S. Gorard, *School Choice in an Established Market* (Aldershot: Ashgate, 1997).

6. Gorard, Taylor, and Fitz, *Schools, Markets, and Choice Policies*.

7. A. Stillman, "Legislating for Choice," in M. Flude and M. Hammer, eds., *The Education Reform Act 1988: Its Origins and Implications* (Lewes: Falmer Press, 1990).

8. National Foundation for Educational Research, *Trends in Allocation Procedures* (London: 1969), p. 1.

9. V. Pohlmann, "Relationship between Ability, Socioeconomic Status, and Choice of Secondary School," *Journal of Educational Sociology*, vol. 29, no. 9 (1956), pp. 392–97.

10. C. Dore and R. Flowerdew, "Allocation Procedures and the Social Composition of Secondary Schools," *Manchester Geographer* (new series), vol. 2, no. 1 (1981), pp. 47–55.

11. Commission for Racial Equality, *Secondary School Allocations in Reading* (London: 1983).

12. T. Edwards, J. Fitz, and G. Whitty, *The State and Private Education: An Evaluation of the Assisted Places Scheme* (London: Falmer Press, 1989).

13. In practice, popular schools generally seek to admit students above their planned admission number when allowed to do so, presumably because it increases their funding. It is more often the LEAs that wish to restrict entry in order to balance numbers among schools in the area, irrespective of parents' wishes.

14. J. Le Grand and W. Bartlett, *Quasi-Markets and Social Policy* (Basingstoke: Macmillan, 1993).

15. R. Murphy, P. Brown, and J. Partington, *An Evaluation of the Effectiveness of City Technology Colleges' Selection Procedures* (University of Nottingham, School of Education, 1990).

16. S. Jowett, *Allocating Secondary School Places: A Study of Policy and Practice* (Slough: National Foundation for Educational Research, 1995).

17. A. West and D. Ingram, "Making School Admissions Fairer? 'Quasi-Regulation' under New Labour," *Educational Management and Administration*, vol. 29, no. 4 (2001), pp. 459–72.

18. C. Canovan, "Minister Adds Vouchers to List of Options," *Times Educational Supplement*, March 8, 2002, p. 2.

19. M. Shaw, "Private Leeds Firm Tries to Win Over Hostile Schools," *Times Educational Supplement*, July 12, 2002, p. 14.

20. A. Kelly, "Academies Are No Panacea," *Times Educational Supplement*, July 5, 2002, p. 10.

21. Department for Education and Skills, *Education and Skills: Investment for Reform* (London, 2002).

22. C. Benn and C. Chitty, *Thirty Years On: Is Comprehensive Education Alive and Well or Struggling to Survive?* (London: David Fulton, 1996); S. Gorard, "Fee-Paying Schools in Britain: A Peculiarly English Phenomenon," *Educational Review*, vol. 48, no. 1 (1996), pp. 89–93.

23. F. Abrams, "Comprehensive Exodus?" *Times Educational Supplement*, April 20, 2001, pp.18–19.

24. A. Adonis and S. Pollard, *A Class Act* (Harmondsworth: Penguin, 1998).

25. Gorard, *School Choice in an Established Market.*

26. J. Witte, "Choice and Control: An Analytical Overview," in W. Clune and J. Witte, eds., *Choice and Control in American Education,* vol. 1, *The Theory of Choice and Control in Education* (London: Falmer Press, 1990), p. 40.

27. S. Gorard, *Education and Social Justice* (University of Wales Press, 2000).

28. D. Erickson, "A Libertarian Perspective on Schooling," in W. Boyd and J. Cibulka, eds., *Private Schools and Public Policy* (London: Falmer Press, 1989).

29. H. Brighouse, *School Choice and Social Justice* (Oxford University Press, 2000).

30. J. Chubb and T. Moe, *Politics, Markets, and America's Schools* (Brookings, 1990).

31. S. Gorard and C. Taylor, "Market Forces and Standards in Education: A Preliminary Consideration," *British Journal of Sociology of Education*, vol. 23, no. 1 (2002), pp. 5–18.

32. P. Cookson, *School Choice* (Yale University Press, 1994).

33. J. Coons and S. Sugarman, *Education by Choice: The Case for Family Control* (University of California Press, 1978).

34. J. Spring, "Dare Educators Build a New School System?" in M. Manley-Casimir, ed., *Family Choice in Schooling* (Toronto: Lexington, 1982).

35. H. Levin, "Market Approaches to Education: Vouchers and School Choice," *Economics of Education Review*, vol. 11, no. 4 (1992), pp. 279–85.

36. J. Witte, "The Milwaukee Voucher Experiment," *Educational Evaluation and Policy Analysis*, vol. 20, no. 4 (1998), pp. 229–51.

37. See also C. Cobb, G. Glass, and C. Crockett, "The U.S. Charter School Movement and Ethnic Segregation," paper presented at the annual meeting of the American Educational Research Association, New Orleans, April 2000.

38. J. Greene, "Choosing Integration: Presentation to School Choice and Racial Diversity Conference," Occasional Paper 12 (New York: National Center for the Study of Privatization in Education, Teachers College, 2000).

39. J. Coleman, "Some Points on Choice in Education," *Sociology of Education*, vol. 65, no. 4 (1992), pp. 260–62.

40. Performance and Innovation Unit, *Social Mobility: A Discussion Paper* (London, April 2001), p. 39.

41. H. Glennerster, "Quasi-Markets for Education," *Economic Journal*, vol. 101, no. 408 (1991), pp. 1268–76.

42. S. Waslander and M. Thrupp, "Choice, Competition, and Segregation: An Empirical Analysis of a New Zealand Secondary School Market," *Journal of Education Policy*, vol. 10, no. 1 (1995), pp. 1–26, quote p. 21.

43. N. Finkelstein and N. Grubb, "Making Sense of Education and Training Markets: Lessons from England," *American Educational Research Journal*, vol. 37, no. 3 (2000), pp. 601–31.

44. M. Carnoy, "National Voucher Plans in Chile and Sweden: Did Privatization Reforms Make for Better Education?" *Comparative Education Review*, vol. 42, no. 4 (1998), pp. 309–29.

45. E. Fiske and H. Ladd, *When Schools Compete: A Cautionary Tale* (Brookings, 2000). The writing of Fiske and Ladd has had considerable international impact, even though their central claim about increased stratification as a result of choice is not upheld by their own data. All of their key tables (such as 7-2 to 7-4) present data for the years 1991, 1996, and 1997 and show a slight increase in segregation from 1991 to 1996–97. However, 1990 was the last year before the reforms, whereas 1991 was the first year *after* the new policy and the only year in which contested school places were allocated by lottery. As Fiske and Ladd admit in a footnote on page 194, "the indexes fell substantially between 1990 and 1991." By 1997, segregation in New Zealand was still substantially lower than in 1990. By not publishing the prechoice levels of segregation, the analysis by Fiske and Ladd makes it look as though segregation increased as a result of choice, whereas it actually fell substantially and then crept up again just as it did in the United Kingdom. The Smithfield study in New Zealand, cited in support by Fiske and Ladd, did publish figures for 1990 showing the same large drop in segregation, but then misreported its own tables (see note 52 below).

46. D. MacLeod, "Perils of the School Run," *Guardian*, August 3, 2001, p. 7.

47. "Light beneath the Rhetoric," *Times Educational Supplement*, June 28, 2002, p. 20.

48. See, for example, S. Gorard, "'Well, That About Wraps It Up for School Choice Research': A State of the Art Review," *School Leadership and Management*, vol. 19, no. 18 (1999), pp. 25–47.

49. Gorard, Taylor, and Fitz, *Schools, Markets, and Choice Policies*.

50. The figures were obtained from the annual school census. The level of segregation for any area of analysis is defined as the proportion of disadvantaged students who would have to exchange schools for there to be a proportionate spread of disadvantage. More precisely, where A_i and C_i represent the number of pupils in the minority group and total number of pupils in each school, respectively, and X and Z are, respectively, the total number of pupils in the minority group and the total number of all pupils sampled in each country, $S = 0.5 \times \Sigma |(A_i/X) - (C_i/Z)|$.

51. S. Gorard and J. Fitz, "Under Starter's Orders: The Established Market, the Cardiff Study, and the Smithfield Project," *International Studies in Sociology of Education*, vol. 8, no. 3 (1998), pp. 299–314.

52. S. Gorard and J. Fitz, "The More Things Change . . . : The Missing Impact of Marketisation," *British Journal of Sociology of Education*, vol. 19, no. 3 (1998), pp. 365–76.

53. L. Paterson, "Education and Inequality in Britain," paper presented to the British Association for the Advancement of Science, Glasgow, September 4, 2001.

54. See, for example, S. Gewirtz, S. Ball, and R. Bowe, *Markets, Choice, and Equity in Education* (Buckingham: Open University Press, 1995).

55. E. Kacapyr, "Are You Middle-Class?" *American Demographics*, vol. 18, no. 10 (1996), pp. 30–35.

56. D. Hirsch, "What Can Britain Learn from Abroad?" in R. Glatter, P. Woods,

and C. Bagley, eds., *Choice and Diversity in Schooling: Perspectives and Prospects* (London: Routledge, 1997) p. 163.

57. D. Herbert and C. Thomas, *Cities in Space: City as Place* (London: David Fulton, 1990).

58. F. Reynolds, *The Problem Housing Estate* (Gower: Aldershot, 1986).

59. P. Knox, *Urban Social Geography* (Essex: Longman, 1995), p. 62.

60. W. Davies and D. Herbert, *Communities within Cities: An Urban Social Geography* (London: Belhaven Press, 1993).

61. B. Robson, *Urban Analysis: A Study of City Structure with Special Reference to Sunderland* (Cambridge University Press, 1969).

62. A. Wilson, "Residential Segregation of Social Classes and Aspirations of High School Boys," *American Sociological Review*, vol. 24 (1959), pp. 836–45, quote on p. 845.

63. Association of Teachers and Lecturers, "Social Selection," *Report*, vol. 22 (2000), p. 5.

64. D. Leech and E. Campos, "Is Comprehensive Education Really Free? A Study of the Effects of Secondary School Admissions Policies on House Prices," Economic Research Paper 581 (University of Warwick, 2000).

65. Stillman, "Legislating for Choice."

66. E. Parsons, B. Chalkley, and A. Jones, "School Catchments and Student Movements: A Case Study in Parental Choice," *Educational Studies*, vol. 26, no. 1 (2000), pp. 33–48.

67. Benn and Chitty, *Thirty Years On*.

68. K. Taeuber and others, "A Demographic Perspective in School Desegregation in the USA," in C. Peach, V. Robinson, and S. Smith, eds., *Ethnic Segregation in Cities* (London: Croom Helm, 1981).

69. J. Sutcliffe, "Home Front in War on Poverty," *Times Educational Supplement*, March 10, 2000, p. 24.

70. D. Goldhaber, "School Choice: Do We Know Enough?" *Educational Researcher*, vol. 29, no. 8 (2000), pp. 21–22.

71. C. Taylor and S. Gorard, "The Role of Residence in School Segregation: Placing the Impact of Parental Choice in Perspective," *Environment and Planning A*, vol. 30, no. 10 (2001), pp. 1829–52.

72. There *are* some very small private schools, arising largely from home schooling arrangements, usually with a minority religious basis. These are very cheap and economically unstable in nature, usually providing their own curricula and tests and so not appearing in league tables of results.

73. S. Gorard, "International Comparisons of School Effectiveness: A Second Component of the 'Crisis Account'?" *Comparative Education*, vol. 37, no. 3 (2001), pp. 279–96.

74. S. Gorard and J. Fitz, "Investigating the Determinants of Segregation between Schools," *Research Papers in Education*, vol. 15, no. 2 (2000), pp. 115–32.

75. R. Smithers, "Church Plan for 20 New Schools," *Guardian*, June 15, 2001, p. 12.

76. S. Gorard and C. Taylor, "Specialist Schools in England: Track Record and Future Prospect," *School Leadership and Management*, vol. 21, no. 4 (2001), pp. 365–81.

77. See also D. Willms and L. Paterson, "A Multilevel Model for Community Segregation," *Journal of Mathematical Sociology*, vol. 20, no. 1 (1995), pp. 23–40.

78. Carnoy, "National Voucher Plans in Chile and Sweden"; M. Narodowski and M. Nores, "Socio-Economic Segregation with (without) Competitive Education Policies," *Comparative Education*, vol. 38, no. 4 (2002), pp. 429–51.

79. J. Sutcliffe, "The Market Has Lost Its Appeal," *Times Educational Supplement,* September 14, 2001, pp. 28–29.

80. N. Schoon, "Making the Best of the Worst," *Times Educational Supplement,* October 5, 2001, p. 15.

6

Regulating School Choice in Belgium's Flemish Community

JAN DE GROOF

The framing of education legislation and chiefly the question of school choice were historically and remain today among the key political issues in Belgium. In 1830 Belgium became an independent unitary and centralized state. Between 1970 and 1993, the 1831 constitution was reformed in several steps to develop a federal system in which there are three policy levels, each with its own legislative and executive bodies and responsibilities: the federal state, the linguistic and cultural communities, and the regions. There is no hierarchy of these three policy levels.[1]

The principle of "federal loyalty" was enshrined during the most recent phase of institutional reform. What this means is that the federal authority, communities, and regions not only adhere to their respective areas of responsibility but also act so as to avoid all conflicts among themselves, the objective being to ensure that the various institutions function as a balanced whole.

The three communities in Belgium—the Flemish (Dutch-speaking) community, the French-speaking community, and the German-speaking community—have, among other functions, responsibility for the cultural and individual affairs within a certain linguistic area. The four linguistic areas are the Dutch-speaking area, the French-speaking area, the German-speaking area, and the bilingual (Flemish- and French-speaking) area (the capital, Brussels). The Flemish community, which is the focus of this chapter, is fully responsible for the Dutch-speaking area and partly for the metropolitan area of Brussels.

Regions divide the country along strictly geographical lines, whereas communities are based on both geographical and linguistic characteristics. In practice, this dual structure means that people living in the Brussels region, the bilingual area, may opt into either the French-speaking or the Flemish community; similarly, people living in the Walloon region may belong to the French-speaking community or the German-speaking community (in the municipalities of Ambleve, Bullange, Burg-Reuland, Butgenbach, Eupen, La Calamine, Lontzen, Raeren, and Saint-Vith). Residents of the Flemish region automatically belong to the Flemish community.

Belgium took shape as a federal state in the wake of quasi-permanent tension between the two major communities, the Flemish and the French-speaking Walloons. An important element of the agreement that founded Belgium was the recognition of Dutch as a national language in administration and justice and as an eligible language of instruction at all educational levels. Separatist movements at present have little popularity since state reforms have guaranteed full autonomy on a wide range of matters related to education, culture, and welfare at the community level. The regions are in charge of economic policy, the environment, urban development, housing, traffic, public construction, and investment, among other things.[2] Quite correctly, the basic report of the review by the Organization for Economic Cooperation and Development (OECD) of national policies for education was entitled *Education in Belgium: The Diverging Paths.*[3]

Educational freedom has been one of the pillars of the Belgian legal, political, and social order since the country gained its independence from France (1815) and from the Netherlands (1830). The education policy of the government during the French and Dutch occupation, in the eighteenth and nineteenth centuries, was the immediate reason for the independence movement. Freedom of education was considered one of the cornerstones of the Belgian nation, constructed as it was of different linguistic communities, and this principle was put into practice by the Church in response to Catholic concerns about one's right to receive an education based on one's personal religious and philosophical convictions.[4]

While historically the overwhelming majority of Flemish Belgians have been Roman Catholic, in the Walloon part of Belgium there have always existed strong socialist and Freemason elements and a high percentage of public schools. At the time when Belgium began to create its own education policies, it was increasingly accepted that nonbelievers had the right to non-religious education. The "public" schools organized by municipalities and provinces at that time were open to all but often embedded in the Catholic Church. There is no established church in Belgium. Church and state are considered independent, but there is no wall of separation between them preventing their cooperation. Several religious denominations are officially recognized by the state.[5] Belgian patriots have long perceived a close connection between political liberties—freedom of association, of the press, of conscience, of opinion, and of speech—and the liberty to provide confessional (denominational) schooling.[6] As a result, they anchored educational freedom in the Constitution, and this guarantee continues today, amended most recently in 1988.

Intermittent political conflict over the independence and public funding of nonstate, predominantly Catholic schools during the nineteenth and twentieth centuries was finally laid to rest by the School Pact of 1958, an interparty agreement that continues to serve as the framework for law and policy in the nonuniversity educational sector. Secularists and Catholics put aside their struggles for hegemony and returned to the earlier emphasis on freedom of choice and democratization of education, establishing the ensuing "School Peace." The focus was no longer on protecting the rights of the Church but instead on protecting the rights of parents to determine the philosophical basis of the education of their children.

The key term in the School Pact is *free choice*. Politicians, however, realized that free choice in education was a dead term without the necessary subsidies. Indeed, the financial situation was no longer tenable; many parents who wished to send their children to Catholic schools could not bear the costs. The School Pact not only introduced the principle of *nondiscrimination* but also of the *democratization* of education—free, compulsory education in the philosophical tradition preferred by the parents.

The political agreement among the three big ideological groups (Catholics, socialists, and liberals) in Belgium was initially at risk of being merely a temporary compromise. If one ideological group were to lose power, a majority in Parliament could change the consensus unilaterally. The fear of this possibility was one of the most important reasons that Belgium amended its constitution, coupling a robust federalism with a unitary state.[7]

Belgians are guaranteed the right to establish and operate nonstate ("free") schools that meet basic quality standards set by public authorities and to choose such schools for their children. In order to ensure that the latter right may be exercised by all, approved nonpublic schools receive public funding at quasi-parity with the schools operated by community, provincial, and municipal governments. In 2001, 68.8 percent of all pupils in Flanders (Flemish Belgium) were in subsidized private ("free") schools, 14.6 percent in Flemish community schools, and 16.5 percent in municipal or provincial government schools.

In Flanders there is a high degree of distrust with regard to institutions. This is not exceptional. Data from the *Eurobarometer* show that the whole of Europe, which generally has less trust in public than in private institutions, is facing a crisis of trust.[8] However, among all the member states of the European Union, the Flemish community shows the greatest distrust of public institutions. In Flanders, only one-third of the population trusts public institutions, while half trusts or has a great deal of trust in private institutions, which is almost the European average.

Only public schools have the trust of a large majority of the population. Presumably, the direct contact of individuals and families with schools, teachers, and educational institutions has an influence on public trust in public education.[9]

The Structure of Schooling

Since the constitutional revision of 1988,[10] schooling has been partly the responsibility of the linguistic communities and partly of the regions.[11] Up to 1961, a single government minister was in charge of state education, with powers in matters concerning administration, programs, and policy. From 1961 to 1980, there were two national ministers of education, one for the French- and German-language communities and one for the Dutch-language community. The language laws had already established the principle that the language of the region would be the language of education for those municipalities whose administration was conducted in one language. The European Court of Human Rights formulated no objections to this proposal in its decree of July 23, 1968.[12]

The division of educational matters and the transfer of responsibility for education to the communities had been prompted to a great extent by the fact that the two ministers of national education each had restricted authority: one for the Dutch-speaking schools, the other for the French- and German-speaking schools. It is not an exaggeration to say that each educational policy was heavily mortgaged by the incoherent and inadequate distribution of authority. The transfer of authority to the communities and the regulation of educational matters by the communities occurred before the required legal framework had been set up. However, some of the authority for education still is exercised at the national level in order to guarantee common regulations with respect to the definition of compulsory education, the retirement scheme for teachers, and the recognition of degrees, in particular the minimal conditions for awarding degrees to students.

Each community has its own education system. Within the ministry of the Flemish community, the education department is responsible for nearly all aspects of community education policy, from nursery school to university. The Flemish minister of education heads the department. Primary and secondary education in Flanders is provided by three "networks." "Public" education can be divided into community education (*Gemeenschapsonderwijs*) and official education (*Officieel gesubsidieerd onderwijs*). Community education is fully organized and financed by the community. Official education is sponsored and controlled by local authorities—provinces and municipalities—but subsidized by the community. "Private" (free) educational institutions (*Vrij gesubsidieerd onderwijs*) are set up by private persons or institutions, mainly the Catholic Church, and subsidized by the community.

Traditionally, three educational levels exist: elementary education, secondary education, and higher education. Within primary and secondary education, special education also exists. Elementary education includes nursery school and primary education. Nursery school is provided free of charge for children ages two and a half to six years, but it is not compulsory. Primary education, which consists of six consecutive years, is for children ages six to twelve years. When they finish this cycle, they are given an elementary education certificate. The "unified" system of secondary education is meant for youngsters ages twelve to eighteen and consists of six years, divided into three cycles of two years each. Great weight is attached to basic skills, and academic electives are postponed in order to expose students to as many subjects as possible in the first year of secondary schooling. Part of the program of study is standard for all pupils of the same year thereafter as well, but students also have a choice of several specific elective subjects. According to the liberal education regime of Belgium, secondary school graduates can begin higher education without entrance exams, except in a few art programs and in medicine, dentistry, and applied sciences. Secondary school graduates also can opt for vocational training.

The Constitutional Framework

Article 24 of the revised constitution (formerly article 17), which is the constitutional basis of educational freedom and justice in Belgium, states the following:

> (1.1) Education is free; any preventative measure is forbidden; the punishment of offenses is governed by law or decree.

(1.2) The community offers free choice to parents.

(1.3) The community organizes neutral education. Neutrality implies notably *respect for the philosophical, ideological, or religious conceptions of all parents and pupils* [emphasis added].

(1.4) The schools organized by the public authorities offer, until the end of mandatory schooling, a choice between the teaching of one of the recognized religions and nondenominational moral teaching.

(2) If a community, in its capacity as an organizing authority, wishes to delegate authority to one or several autonomous bodies, it can only do so by decree adopted by a two-thirds majority vote.

(3.1) Everyone has the right to education that respects fundamental rights and freedoms. Access to education is free until the end of mandatory schooling.

(3.2) All pupils of school age have the right to moral or religious education at the community's expense.

(4) All pupils or students, parents, teaching staff, or institutions are equal before the law or decree. The law and decree take into account objective differences, notably the characteristics of each organizing authority, that justify appropriate treatment.

(5) The organization, recognition, and subsidizing of education by the community are regulated by law or decree.

There are two reasons why these fundamental rights were taken up in the Constitution.[13] The first was to guarantee respect for fundamental rights in spite of the fragmentation of authority. The transfer of educational authority from the national to the community level avoids the need for political consensus at the national level, which in the past always sought to balance the interests of the Catholic majority of the northern section of the country and those of the non-Catholic majority of the southern part. With the insertion of constitutional rights into education laws, each citizen has recourse to a legal remedy to an action (or inaction) of the executive power of a community that conflicts with the Constitution. The second reason was that it was found that *social equality*, that is, fully respected nondiscrimination, was not attained with the School Pact and the Constitution as originally designed.[14] To remedy this problem, the right of the individual to education is now guaranteed by the Constitution. The theoretical freedom of education, however, would be meaningless if the authorities did not also guarantee the material right to education through public subsidy.

All these principles are enforceable, not only before an ordinary court but also before the Court of Arbitration, which can examine all decrees or laws for compatibility with articles 10, 11, and 24 of the Constitution and annul decrees or laws that it rules unconstitutional. This modification was a sine qua non for the transfer of authority in educational matters to the communities in order to grant the ideological minorities true guarantees, which beforehand they had drawn only tentatively from the School Pact.

The right of the state to provide its own education is recognized by the Constitution, the outcome of a long period of evolution. As recently as the second "School War" (1950–58), Catholic authorities were still vehemently asserting that state education was merely a complement to the superior, freely chosen education provided in Catholic schools. They urged that state schools not be created unless freedom of educational choice was in danger.

A second historical moment in the evolution of school choice in Belgium was the constitutional confirmation of the right to free choice of religious or nonreligious education, the issue that was the origin of the first School War (1879–84). Successive laws over the course of the twentieth century brought other solutions to the problem of the relations between church and state. The law of August 5, 1948 (one of the numerous pacts the country has known!), was the first to introduce nonconfessional moral instruction in secondary education. The same issue was not regulated for primary education until passage of the law of May 29, 1959.[15]

The same is true for the inclusion in the Constitution of the obligation for the government to subsidize all educational bodies that meet the basic legal conditions to provide education. It was the last phase in the long history of school choice policy, which started with the decree of January 13, 1831. In implementing this decree, the provisional government put state equipment and school premises at the free (Catholic) schools' disposal.

Although the most important regulations of the School Pact are taken up in the Constitution, article 24 also adds an essential principle, namely the coercive force of equality. Unequal treatment is permitted only when it serves the public interest and is grounded in objectives that are legally acceptable. Different treatment has to be necessary to attain the goals pursued, and there has to be a reasonable correlation between the goals to be attained and the means used. These criteria must be applied in unison. Only different treatment based on a different objective, reasonable and justified, is legally acceptable. In this way, the Belgian constitution goes further than the European Convention on Human Rights in promoting equality.

The Constitution obliges the community to guarantee freedom of parental choice.[16] To do this, the community organizes education neutrally, respecting the philosophical, ideological, or religious views of all parents and students (article 24, section 1.3), and subsidizes educational institutions that express a particular religious, philosophical, or educational point of view.

With all official education, religious instruction is offered in all federally recognized denominations, namely Catholic, Protestant, Jewish, Muslim, Greek and Russian Orthodox, and Anglican. For those parents who do not opt for religious instruction, a course providing "nonconfessional moral education" is substituted. All these norms reflect the explicit commitment of public officials to respecting the specific philosophical and religious convictions of parents and pupils. The fact that the majority of schools in the nation are "free Catholic" rather than community, provincial, or municipal educational institutions indicates the longstanding preference of parents for education in the Catholic context.

In practice, freedom of education presupposes that the organizing authorities that do not directly depend on the community can claim community subsidies under certain conditions. According to the Court of Arbitration, the right to subsidies is restricted on the one hand by the authority of the community to make schools first meet requirements of general importance—such as providing instruction of an appropriately educational nature and meeting certain standards regarding student numbers and equal access to education—and, on the other hand, by the need to spread the available financial resources over the community's various individual responsibilities.[17]

Parental freedom of choice cannot be seen as separate from an educational institution's right to admit students or from the right to subsidies enjoyed by those institutions. In any case, parental freedom of choice can apply wholly only if the ability to organize education and the right to educational subsidies are not restricted unlawfully.[18]

The rulings of the Court of Arbitration—the quasi-constitutional court in Belgium—safeguard the principles regarding education and explicitly state that the principle of equality is intrinsically interrelated with the other guarantees contained in article 24 of the Constitution, particularly with regard to freedom of education. The first constitutional norm, namely freedom of education, colors the detailed constitutional provisions on education in article 24.[19]

Freedom of education has long been defined, on one hand, as the freedom of parents and students to choose and, on the other, as the freedom to offer education based on one's own philosophical, ideological, or religious outlook. Both are in effect dependent on each other and have been mentioned explicitly as such in article 24.[20] The Court of Arbitration formerly referred to the right to establish schools based on a certain "denominational or nondenominational philosophy of life."[21] The court obviously also granted such a right of establishment, direction, and organization to schools characterized by certain "pedagogical or educational views,"[22] but at the same time it accepted the old "denominational/nondenominational" divide for selecting schools[23]—a questionable method that is a relic of the School Pact era.[24] Selecting a particular kind of education or teaching method might result in greater expenditures for the educational establishment than it would incur with the usual teaching methods.[25]

The Court of Arbitration has made it clear in previous judgments that freedom of education means having education organized and provided according to one's own outlook by a teacher who acts as a "mediator" in terms of both the form and the content of the curriculum.[26] Pedagogical freedom defined at the institutional level is, despite all nuances and regulatory provisions, the very essence of pluralism in education.[27] The teacher's role is to implement the particular pedagogical mission chosen by the parents, but teachers also derive from their position the right to adopt their own teaching style.

Before 1989, state education in Belgium was fully under the authority of the minister of education, a fact that guaranteed a significant degree of politicization of the office and discontinuity in administration. The decree of July 14, 1988, created an autonomous body that organizes the education of the Flemish community, the Autonomous Council for Community Education (*Autonome Raad van het Gemeenschapsonderwijs*, or ARGO).[28] Its autonomy was strengthened in the decree on community education (*Decreet gemeenschapsonderwijs*).

The revised constitution has confirmed rather than replaced the detailed provisions of the School Pact, which contains the basic legal norms governing subsidies and recognition of independent schools.[29] The law of May 29, 1959, which has since been revised repeatedly, must be taken into consideration in its entirety because the organization of independent schools is referred to in several places either directly or indirectly, and it serves as the basis for much that follows.

The right to autonomy can be derived from the articles in the decree on primary education (*Decreet Basisonderwijs*), the decree on measures in secondary education (*Decreet Maatregelen Secundair Onderwijs*), and the decree on nonuniversity higher educational institutions (*Hogescholendecreet*). Several reports and reviews have shown the opportunities and limits of the proclaimed division of responsibilities and (relative) autonomy of schools.[30] This division of responsibilities should lead to intensified cooperation among institutions and networks.[31]

Freedom to Establish Nonstate Schools

As noted, the freedom to establish nonstate schools has long been guaranteed in Belgium and given force by carefully negotiated administrative arrangements. In addition to the freedom to provide education, the Constitution guarantees the parents' freedom of choice. Belgian parents are allowed to school their children at home or in unsubsidized private schools, though the great majority choose schools that are publicly funded.

Any naturalized citizen or legal immigrant has the right to provide education and can establish institutions for that purpose. The "organizing authority" is therefore a key concept in the organization of education in Flanders. An authority is a legal entity "taking up responsibility for an educational institution."[32] The individual right to open a school may not, the Constitution insists, depend on prior authorization by government. Neither the legislative nor the executive power may promulgate any measure that would hinder the freedom to provide education. Those who drafted the Constitution feared, even more than the disadvantages that can be associated with this principle, the dangers of a system of prior authorization. The government has the power to impose conditions on schools—for example, on their use of funds—only if a school asks for community support, and it can impose conditions regarding the recognition of certificates. Therefore the Flemish community can set certain standards as to quality of the education provided, a power that places definite limits on the possibility of operating a school that has not obtained official approval.

The Constitution fully protects freedom of education but also protects citizens from the possible abuse of that freedom, as it protects them from the possible abuse of the freedom of the press or the freedom to express an opinion. For this reason, it provides for the restraint of criminal abuses committed in the exercise of freedom of education. The sole restriction provided for by article 24 itself is against the repression of educational freedom.

The Constitution makes the organization of educational networks possible, under the communities, provinces, municipalities, and other public law authorities and also under private persons, de facto associations, and nonprofit organizations. There are three networks of organizing authorities. *Community education* is organized by the Autonomous Council for Community Education on behalf of the Flemish community. The Constitution requires community education to be neutral; this means that the religious, philosophical, and ideological convictions of all parents and pupils must be respected. *Subsidized official education* includes education organized by provincial authorities and by municipal authorities; a school in this network can be denominational or not. Finally, *subsidized private education* is education provided by private initiative—a private person or a private organization. It includes denominational and nondenominational private education and independent schools that apply specific instructional methods. Of the non-public schools in Flemish Belgium, more than 90 percent are Catholic. There are also a few Protestant, Jewish, and secular humanist schools, as well as twenty Waldorf schools (Steiner schools), fourteen Freinet schools, and a handful of schools offering other alternative pedagogies. The education organized by the first two networks (the authorities) is called "official" education; the education provided by the third network is called "free" education.

The networks have extensive autonomy. They are free to develop their own curriculum and schedule, subject to approval by the minister of education. They are free to choose their instructional methods. There are a few truly private institutions that receive no government subsidies whatsoever; however, they are not entitled to award officially recognized certificates if they do not accept the conditions of article 24 of the School Pact Law, and most of these types of schools do not.[33]

School Choice Is Not Limited by Family Income

The Constitution imposes on education, in explicit words, *the principle of equality*. It guarantees that every educational institution will be treated equally. All receive money from the community in relation to the number of students. Unequal treatment is allowed only when objective differences exist. As the Constitution is currently understood, an "adapted" treatment authorizes study grants or loans for financially weaker families, more flexible standards for schools in rural areas (and for that reason with fewer students), facilities for handicapped students and immigrant children, and different financial treatment according to the level and form of education, the geographical place, and the distance between schools of the same network. In all of these cases there is an objective reason that fully justifies different funding by the authorities.

The School Pact of 1958 states that "the right of parents to choose the education given to their children implies the possibility of having available, at a reasonable distance, a school corresponding to their choice."[34] Since parents are not equally able to pay for schooling, this requires that public funds be provided to cover the costs, a principle enshrined in the Constitution, which guarantees that compulsory schooling will be free. With regard to freedom of choice, the community is even compelled either to subsidize a "free" confessional or public school or to subsidize the transportation costs to such a school on request of the parents of sixteen pupils who do not find a public or a free school within a range of four kilometers.[35] Tuition fees in all types of primary and secondary education are prohibited. However, a contribution can be requested from families for educational materials for specific activities.

The resources of free schools consist largely of community subsidies. The school boards mostly have endowments and some private benefits. The public subsidy to nonpublic free schools includes three types of financial support by the government: salaries of teachers, a per-pupil fixed sum for operational costs, and a per-pupil contribution for capital costs. Public funds pay for administrative and support staff as well as for teachers, and they receive their salaries directly from the government on a monthly basis.

The subsidy of operational costs is intended to cover replacement of equipment and provision of textbooks to pupils. This subsidy varies by school level—secondary schools receive more than twice as much per pupil as elementary schools—and is adjusted annually for inflation. Competition among schools is inevitable in a system of funding based on the number of pupils attending each school, but it is forbidden to engage in unfair competition.[36]

Approved nonpublic schools also receive support for facilities costs. The Subsidized Education Infrastructure Department (*Dienst voor Infrastructuurwerken van het Gesubsidieerd Onderwijs,* or DIGO) is a government agency that subsidizes the purchase, construction, and renovation of buildings for municipal, provincial, and private institutions. It grants subsidies of up to 60 percent of total construction costs for primary education and 70 percent for secondary and higher education; the costs must not exceed the maximum legal standards for educational buildings. Demand for state aid in financing educational infrastructure has been increasing for some years, and the funds available are far from sufficient.

Recently, some advocates have called for "network blurring" to remove traditional religious and sociopolitical barriers in education and to promote more cross-network cooperation.[37] The proposal is to treat schools and students on an equal basis, regardless of the network. In all respects, this trend has already taken root. In recent years, the network factor has not been structurally incorporated into new initiatives and regulations on educational priority policy, broader remedial and supplemental education programs, postgraduate education, European education exchange projects, pupil transport in special education, the development of final attainment targets, and the reorganization of school inspection programs. Nevertheless, there remain significant differences among the various networks.

A report, commissioned by the government and produced by Deloitte and Touche, contains the following summary of the principal differences between networks with respect to the resources available:[38]

—Community education has structurally higher public operational and investment resources from the Flemish community than the other two networks, for both levels of education. The additional permanent appointment of Teacher Service personnel magnifies still further the difference with subsidized private education.

—Schools in subsidized official education often have quite considerable supplementary resources at their disposal from their organizational powers, as a result of which they have even more options open to them on average than community education. Consequently, schools in subsidized private education have significantly fewer resources at their disposal than those in official education and have to appeal more to parents and other private sources.

—Generally speaking, private primary schools are in the most unfavorable situation financially.

—Differences arise in the treatment of schools, particularly with respect to the provision of resources, that cannot, or cannot completely, be justified by differences in needs or requirements.

To create a level playing field would mean transferring operational resources from community education to the two other networks.[39] This concerns some 31 percent of the present operational resources in community education, which is considerable. To achieve greater equality of the networks, the report proposes to increase the coverage of facilities and infrastructure costs to 85 percent (primary education) and 80 percent (secondary education) in subsidized private education and to lower it to 50 percent in subsidized official education. The results of this study were discussed in the Roundtable Conference, which was sponsored by the Flemish government and which, with the cooperation of all the education partners, hopes to outline the broad structure of future education policy.

School Distinctiveness Protected by Law and Policy

Constitutional law completely concurs with the legislative bodies that describe freedom of education from the perspective of "character," "tendencies," and "pedagogical method."[40] Such freedom is not found or at least is not found to the same extent in the case of official education. Next to the fulfillment of the obligation of neutrality, the theory of the uniformity of the pedagogical concept of community education currently prevails in education organized by each of the three communities in Belgium. Nevertheless, the purpose of such uniformity will be questioned more frequently in the future, and differentiation of the pedagogical missions in the different communities could be pursued by the local community, in consultation with parents and without infringing the rights of parents who have a different perspective.[41]

The pedagogical freedom granted *official* education was previously described as being "anchored in the legislation governing education" but with the reservation that it was to be combined with the requirements of a public service organized by public authorities.[42] All, or at any rate most, experts subscribe to this interpretation, certainly after the revision of the Constitution in 1988.[43]

The Court of Arbitration linked freedom of education to freedom of association,[44] and the Council of State has raised the possibility of excessive interference by the government in the composition and activity of private nonprofit associations.[45] The council has on several occasions referred to the less flexible rules of decisionmaking that exist in the official education sector compared with those in the free education sector and has assumed that such rigidity could mean that community education takes place amid more difficult working conditions. It has consequently suggested that schools organized under community education have the guaranteed right to establish a separate decisionmaking structure.[46]

Community organizations that provide the public service of subsidized free education do not lose their usually nonprofit legal status as a result. The recognition of a private law institution as a "nongovernmental public service" further guarantees the labor relationship between the staff and the board under private law, though not in public law.[47] Such educational establishments are free to choose their staff.[48]

Government is required to provide subsidies to any school that meets the objective criteria of quality, number of pupils, and so forth; officials may not exercise discretion about which schools they fund. The criteria for approval and therefore for subsidy include compliance with the language laws, adopting an approved grade structure, having the required number of pupils and an adequate facility and school equipment, following the curriculum guidelines set by the government for all schools of that type, and accepting state inspection to ensure that all other requirements are met.[49]

Each school may employ its own curriculum and pedagogy in meeting the government guidelines and arrange for staff development and consultation services. The community sets forth a set of final attainment targets (*eindtermen*) and development goals (*ontwikkelingsdoelen*). No government-prescribed goals exist for religion courses. The schools work out a curriculum by themselves in relation to the final attainment targets and development goals and a school action plan (*schoolwerkplan*) that reflects among other factors the individual school's pedagogical mission. Schools organized on a certain methodological or ideological basis that cannot function within this system may ask for exemption from the final attainment targets and development goals. In the process, they must identify their own attainment targets, which are subject to approval by the Flemish government and ratification by the Flemish parliament. Final attainment targets have been developed by schools at the primary education level, but they are still being developed at the secondary education level. Government inspection does not extend to the pedagogical methods used.[50]

The legal significance of a school's distinctive character makes it essential that the school's governing board explain its pedagogical mission clearly, along with any philosophical basis, and update it regularly if necessary. Parents have a right to this information as they choose their children's schools, and school staff have a right to know to what pedagogical mission they are committing themselves.

Also, before the "federalization" of the Belgian system of government, a long-standing tradition of consultation with educational networks and stakeholders characterized state education policy and strengthened respect for education freedom. For example, the Flemish Education Council (*Vlaamse Onderwijsraad*)—composed of representatives of the networks and trade unions, parents and students, economic and social experts, and ministry officials—has broad authority to advise on all preliminary draft laws and policy documents. Parent and student associations are supported by the government.[51]

In subsidized education, every school has to set up a participation council, either individually or with other schools, which usually is chaired by the head of the school. The participation council is authorized to give advice relating to the general organization, operation, and schedule of the school and the general criteria regarding the guidance and evaluation of students. It also has the power to consult on specific subjects. In addition, a number of other rights or powers also can be granted, such as the right to obtain information on all matters that have repercussions in school life in general and the right to consent. The participation council does not restrict the authority and responsibility of the school head and organizing authority but provides a forum for consultation among all the participants in school life. However, in subsidized official education and subsidized private education, approximately two-thirds of the parents have asked for the participation council to have more influence. Note with regard to this that the parents adopt a slightly less critical attitude than the teachers do.[52]

Distinctive Character

Oversight by the Flemish community of subsidized private education is essentially identical to that of public education. It takes various forms, including ensuring that a school satisfies health and safety requirements, meets the requirements for the receipt of public funds, meets the requirements for awarding certificates and diplomas, complies with Belgian language laws, and satisfies the compulsory school attendance law. School inspectors are not qualified to evaluate the teaching methods or the school work plan of the educational institution, which are protected by the principle of educational freedom, or to inspect religion or nondenominational moral education courses. The legal representative bodies of each recognized philosophical and religious community themselves organize the pedagogical inspection and support process for the philosophical and religious courses taught at school.

These requirements are to be interpreted and applied, however, in a manner that does not force subsidized nonpublic schools to become identical with municipal and provincial public schools. The board responsible for a school, whether public or nonpublic, is free to express its distinctive character in its methods of teaching and to a considerable extent in the content of teaching, as well as in other aspects of school life.

In practice the right of parental choice in Belgium is defined largely in terms of the alternatives of secular or Catholic schooling. There are, however, a number of non-Catholic subsidized free schools that have either a religious or a pedagogical distinctiveness. Schools inspired by secular humanism are distinguished from "neutral" public schools, as are a number of "pluralistic" schools that seek to provide a place for students to encounter diverse perspectives. In a 1985 decision about pedagogically distinctive schools, the Council of State upheld the rights of "parents with a personal philosophy of life that lies outside the traditional spectrum, from which views on upbringing and thus on education, teaching methods and educational organisation have evolved."

The category of pluralistic schools was introduced by the law of July 14, 1975. Such schools need to be recognized by the Committee for Pluralistic Education, on which no philosophical or religious tendency can have the majority. The charter of a pluralistic school defines the legal requirements regarding the pluralistic character of such schools and must be signed by each member of the staff. The law itself defines pluralistic education as based on "an open mind which acknowledges and respects a diversity of opinions and attitudes, and which, despite this diversity, emphasizes common values . . . denounces all proselytism, and . . . respects the development of the personality of the pupil and the freedom of the teaching staff to have his or her personal commitment known, as far as this complies with the nature of the assigned task." The number of "pure" pluralistic schools remains extremely limited.

The law of July 14, 1975, which created the possibility of pluralistic schools, introduced into Belgian law the concept of the "mission" of a school.[53] Each independent school is supposed to develop and guarantee its mission.[54] Educational freedom applies, in the first instance, to the school and thus to the parents who have a right to select a distinctive school. Freedom of organization is a fundamental component of educational freedom that applies to school curricula, schedules, teaching resources, objectives, evaluation techniques, disciplinary procedures, criteria for relationships within the school, and all the other ways in which social and philosophical values and interests are expressed.

The federation of Steiner Schools contested the attainment targets, which they believed to conflict with freedom of education as they reduced the "zone of autonomy" of the pedagogical concept and as they imposed a certain world view. The Court of Arbitration complied with this demand, since the large number of targets could hardly be seen as only setting a minimum standard. The government responded by reducing the number of targets and by introducing a special evaluation procedure for those schools in a unique position.[55]

Linguistic distinctiveness is not considered a basis for claiming a subsidy under the principle of educational freedom. The language laws, designed to protect the position of the three official languages (Dutch, French, German) in their respective territories by requiring schooling to be provided through the locally dominant language and by carefully defining the schooling choices in the Brussels conurbation, were upheld in a 1968 suit before the European Court of Human Rights and Fundamental Freedoms.

Decisions about Admitting Pupils

As in most other European states, ethnic and cultural pluralism in Belgium is growing, beyond its traditional status as a trilingual state. Immigration from Italy and Spain in the 1950s, from the Maghreb countries (chiefly Morocco) and Turkey in the 1960s and 1970s, and from Eastern Europe and member states of the European Union in the 1970s and 1980s has provoked tensions. The arrival of refugees and the international status of Brussels strengthened further the multiethnic character of a country that had always been a special meeting spot of the Latin and Germanic cultures and a world center of Jewish culture. But integration problems affecting the education sector exist mainly vis-à-vis Muslim immigrants.

In theory, foreigners have the same legal right to education as Belgian people.[56] But different studies show significant disparities in practice, and the statistics on student performance at school point to two handicaps among foreign students: on average, more foreign than Belgian students fall behind in their work, and they remain behind for longer periods. In the Flemish community, the largest concentration of foreigners, mostly Muslims, and highest level of social polarization are in the major urban centers.

Since the early 1990s the Flemish community has implemented a target group–oriented education policy, with a twofold approach. First, in 1993 the Flemish minister of education and the relevant coordinating bodies signed the Declaration on a Nondiscrimination Policy in Education.[57] Second, schools also are given support through a range of projects to help them handle differences between pupils better. On the basis of the nondiscrimination declaration, cross-network agreements were reached in a number of selected areas to prevent segregation and to work toward a nondiscriminatory learning environment.[58]

Since 1991 the Educational Priority Policy has been implemented in primary and secondary education to promote the integration of underprivileged immigrant children. In primary education a program has been underway since 1993 to offer a broader range of remedial and supplemental education services for educationally deprived and underprivileged pupils. In both programs schools with a given percentage of target group pupils get extra teaching periods or supplementary classes in a number of fields of activity, much like U.S. schools under the Title I federal education program.

A recent draft decree on the equal admission rights of pupils starts from the principle of the unconditional right to attend the financed or subsidized school of one's choice. This draft decree allows all pupils and parents in "our pluralistic knowledge society" an "unrestricted choice of education" and establishes a fundamental right "to attend a given school." This right is seen as a central element in the 1999–2004 Official Government Policy Memorandum: "The Flemish government considers the right of attendance as a fundamental and in principle unconditional right which is guaranteed in every educational establishment."

In view of the altered social reality it is the responsibility of the government and the school authorities to ensure that every student is able to enter a school with an educational mission that meets his or her preferences. To promote diversity in schools, the approach taken hitherto has been one of desegregation. This policy has obligatory consequences for the pupil and for education providers.

The draft decree hence chooses to seek cultural differentiation in education on the basis of encouragement and provision of information. Binding arrangements are made under the "consultative platforms" detailed in the nondiscrimination declaration, which may, for example, incorporate an obligation for a school to accept a minimum number of underprivileged pupils. Within some constraints a pupil can be transferred to another school, without prejudice to the pupil's right to an education. The pupil must be registered at the original school until he or she is registered at another school under a local consultative arrangement.

The general character of the right of attendance prevents the organizing authority of a school from making decisions on its own about who is suitable for admission under the rules and within the school's educational mission. Each pupil thus has a fair chance of being educated within the pedagogical and educational structure selected by his or her parents, and a child is considered to be registered only if the parents approve the school regulations and the school's pedagogical mission. Following registration the pupil and his or her parents are obliged to comply with the pedagogical mission and school regulations. The organizing authority determines how documentary evidence of parental consent is obtained.

An organizing authority can decide not to register a pupil for either of two reasons. First, students may be excluded when a school or the branch of study in question does not have the physical space available to take on more pupils without compromising student health and safety.[59] The organizing authority itself assesses when the school is at capacity. Second, students may be denied admission if they have been removed from school during the preceding two academic years for disciplinary reasons. In the *Mossaïd* ruling the Council of State endorsed a refusal to accept a pupil suspended for disciplinary reasons in official education.[60] This judgment is based on the belief that an exception can be vital in order to protect the rights of the other members of the group.[61]

Accountability for School Quality

Despite the extensive protection given educational freedom as expressed in the autonomy of individual schools with distinctive missions, Belgium is not exempt from the general tendency of governments to extend their involvement in the details of school life. It is very tempting to use subsidies as a way to make nonpublic schools into instruments of public policy.

Originally, the system of quality control within Belgian education was predominantly characterized by a division between educational content and pedagogic methods. The government dictates the curriculum and the schedule, to a minimal extent. The organizing authorities thus have a limited autonomy with regard to curriculum and schedules, but they are free to choose the method of implementing the selected educational content and their didactic methods. There are no standardized government tests. Schools have complete freedom to develop and draft tests, implemented within the networks of organizing authorities.

In 1991 the concept of final attainment targets was introduced within a completely revised "monitoring and inspection system for schools." Previously, state education was used as a benchmark for subsidized schools in regard to the approval and monitoring of the curriculum and timetables. In practice, this meant that approval of the curriculum was subject to its compatibility with the syllabi used in state education.

The Autonomous Council for Community Education is an implementing body that exercises on behalf of state official schools the same didactic and organizational authority that the other school organizers exercise—for example, the power to independently decide on a general pedagogic policy and curriculum. When ARGO was established (1989), government responsibility with respect to general educational policy was redesigned for all schools of whatever denominational or other sponsorship. In this way, government has adopted an even-handed approach to all sponsors of schools, including denominations.

Since state education was no longer the benchmark, it was necessary for the government to draw up minimum requirements for the curriculum as well as for schedules for all schools. From then on, the government had its own instruments to control educational quality, expressed in different ways: in terms of targets, results, learning processes, the extent of the educational and vocational services offered, or achievement measured in relation to the prior level of the pupil. The concept of final attainment levels provides a legal foundation for a goal-oriented approach to education. The old wording in the School Pact with regard to the mandate of the inspectorate—that is, "to monitor the level of learning"—has been replaced by "to verify whether the final attainment targets are achieved."

Since 1991, final attainment targets have been a new legal concept of quality control that refers to the minimum aims and objectives (knowledge, understanding, attitude, and skills) that should be attained by the majority of students at a particular level of education. The final attainment targets were formulated by the government in accordance with expectations within the global community that governments should provide a legal foundation for the schedule and curriculum drawn up by the implementing bodies and monitor the quality of the education that they fund.

Schools are free to determine the way in which they implement the final attainment targets, just as the organizing authorities are free to shape specific types of education according to their own requirements. In addition, they may add their own final attainment targets to the curriculum. Nevertheless, attainment targets require the full duration of the time set aside for education; as mentioned, this might mean that pedagogic goals that are specific to the school may not be realized.

The Educational Development Authority (Dienst voor Onderwijsontwikkeling, or DVO), a part of the Education Ministry, is a scientific research and implementation body consisting of educational experts and scientists who develop instruments to review and assess schools.[62] The DVO is to prepare a report on the final attainment targets to be put before the Flemish Education Council for approval. The council has to draft a unanimous proposal on this subject and put it before the Flemish government, which will refer the final paper to the Flemish parliament for ratification. This ratification procedure is necessary to guarantee an adequate differentiation between the various levels of education. Following ratification, the final attainment targets will become operative and can be altered when the legislature initiates new changes.

Education Inspectorate

For the community education inspectorate, half of the staff is recruited from the official network, the other half from the subsidized private education network. The affiliation of inspectors is determined by the school where each was teaching before he or she started working as an inspector. Equal representation in the inspectorate corps is intended to guarantee objectivity. The inspectorate has a mandate to evaluate all Flemish educational institutions and centers, from nursery schools to institutions of higher learning, over a single cycle of two or three years of study leading to graduation. Schools that remain approved by the inspectorate may give out certificates at the end of the school year, after monitoring of their achievement of the final attainment targets and execution of all organizational requirements.

The final attainment targets and development goals must be incorporated into the curriculum, which is a systematic inventory of the academic content and aims to be achieved in a subject or subject area. The instructional method also is part of the curriculum. The inspectorate evaluates whether the institution has implemented its curriculum and succeeded in guiding its pupils to achieve the final attainment targets and development goals. The inspection is less concerned with detailed control of the educational process than with a global quality-control approach to each institution. It examines whether the attainment targets and development goals are effectively realized and whether the other organic obligations (among other things using a minimum schedule) are correctly met. If the pupils of a certain school do not reach the attainment targets and after a warning there is no improvement, the community can stop or reduce funding for the school.

Inspections are conducted according to a model that uses contextual and input data as well as procedural and output indicators that can be analyzed in relation to each other. The choice of this model implies first of all a resolute decision to take a systematic approach to evaluating schools. This means, for example, that the arrangements in a school are interpreted in relation to each other; it also involves viewing the operation of the teaching staff and the head of the school within the context of the school and locality.

The inspectorate is not authorized to monitor a number of important educational factors. First, inspectors cannot monitor the instructional methods used by schools and teachers. The relationship of the pedagogic mission, the ideological or religious curriculum, and the school work plan is based on a delicate balance of the rights of the acknowledged denominations and the constitutional rights of all citizens. Second, inspectors cannot assess and approve individual teachers. The inspectorate does not assess the teacher's teaching, only achievement of the final attainment targets. Finally, inspectors do not determine the graduation or failure of individual students, which remains within the exclusive authority of the school, more specifically of the deciding class council.

Researchers in nine primary schools have investigated how schools experience inspections and how they deal with the recommendations of the inspectors. From this, it can be seen that an investigational report has results only if the directorate or an internal supervisor acts on it systematically.[63] The existence of an internal network to ensure the success of the proposed improvements also is extremely important. This new style of investigation was evaluated through a survey of heads of schools.[64] More than 98 percent of the headmasters or headmistresses and 89 percent of the teaching staff agreed with the principles of the investigation. In particular, the fact that it involves a global assessment of the school was appreciated. Equally, the schools regretted that the inspection took the educational misson or vision of the school into account, because they felt that the school, not the inspectors, has full authority regarding the mission. In addition, the investigation was felt to be administrative first and foremost, based chiefly on review of documents.

A decree from the Flemish government (February 2, 1999) emphasizes the public nature of investigational reports, obligating schools to make them available to members of staff, pupils, and parents.[65]

Pedagogic Supervisory Services

The different educational networks have school advisers, who provide external counseling for schools and staff members. They have the task of giving general pedagogic and methodological assistance to teachers and schools.

These pedagogic supervisory services are provided through nonprofit organizations responsible for the external supervision of schools, centers, and staff members. For each cluster of organizing authorities and networks, a provision is made within the grant regulations for one pedagogic supervisory service provider. Thus, supporting pedagogic tasks are clearly separated from monitoring tasks carried out by the inspectorate.

The special decree of December 19, 1988, and the decree of July 17, 1991, state that a number of tasks are assigned to pedagogic supervisory service providers, among them providing external support to the educational institutions involved based on their specific pedagogic concept—for example, assistance in drafting the school work plan. They also help to develop initiatives for improving educational quality within the institutions involved, and they encourage initiatives for reinforcing the professional skills of staff members. Finally, the service providers prepare an annual supervisory plan and an annual report on current activities.

No framework exists for obligatory consultation between the inspectorate and the supervisory service providers; therefore it is up to the organizing authority responsible for the quality of each school to assess whether the providers should be called in, and if so, to what extent they should be involved. The relationship between the inspectorate and the service providers may be explained in the annual report and in the supervision plans. The aim is to avoid a discrepancy between the pedagogic concept and the minimum final attainment targets. The inspectorate assesses the educational process in relation to its attainment of the minimum aims and objectives, while supervisory service providers try to enhance educational quality based on maximum pedagogic goals. The points of view are different, but the actions of both groups should become visible in the end product.[66]

In accordance with the logic of the system, whereby the organizing authority carries the responsibility for the quality of education provided, sanctions with respect to final attainment targets are implemented at the school level.[67] When the educational institution complies with the final attainment targets, it is approved and may give out accredited certificates and diplomas. The old sanctioning system was replaced by an approval procedure that ensures the required level of quality of the institution that is issued a certificate.

Attainment Targets and Development Aims

In 1995 the concept of final attainment target was further refined and a new legal concept, "development aims," was introduced, distinguishing between final attainment targets that are linked to a specific subject or learning area and those that are not. The latter type of aims refers to the development of attitudes and values—which implies that the government's influence should be limited in order to fully allow for the pedagogic freedom of the education provider. Obviously, this has an impact on the assessment procedure.

It was decided that a school's results on certain subjects or attitudes—for example, creativity, patriotism, helpfulness, civic spirit, and so forth—would not be assessed . Instead, the inspectorate investigates the extent to which the school has made an effort to achieve the skills and objectives that relate to these subjects, while taking the school population into account. In practice, this means that the assessment takes place through a dialogue between inspectors and school staff, with clear "human" and "interactive" aspects.

It could be said that final attainment targets lead to a commitment by the school to achieve results with respect to three-quarters of its students, while development aims lead to a commitment by the school to make an effort with respect to an individual student or group of students. When a school is committed to achieve results, the school has to make sure that its students achieve the final attainment targets. This way, identical certificates for primary education, given out by different schools, ensure that an identical level of skills and knowledge was achieved.

Conclusion

Conflicts regarding the choice of school were effectively resolved by the constitutional revision of 1988. The constitutional prescriptions dealing with education reinforce school choice and equality among educational institutions, whatever the character of the instruction. Nevertheless, the future will focus on the ideological characteristics of official schools, the relationship between free schools and official schools, the role of the state, and the consequences of multiculturalism for the school. The outcome-driven approach and the autonomy of free schools still guarantee the exemplary position of Belgium, and chiefly its educational sector, across Europe.

Notes

1. The Constitution, as it stands today, stipulates that the federal authority has only the powers that are formally attributed to it by the Constitution or by legislation enabling provisions of the Constitution and that the communities and regions, each in its own field of concern, have power for other matters, as stipulated by law. The federal authority has jurisdiction over provincial and municipal law.

2. Flanders merges the Flemish community and region, and it has a single parliament and government. Under the Belgian constitution, as revised in 1993 and coor-

dinated in 1994, "Belgium is a federal State made up of Communities and Regions" (article 1). Belgium "is made up of three Communities: the French Community, the Flemish Community, and the German-speaking Community" (article 2), as well as "three Regions: the Walloon Region, the Flemish Region, and the Brussels Region."

3. *Education in Belgium: The Diverging Paths* (Brussels: Organization for Economic Cooperation and Development, 1991).

4. Michel Leroy, "La liberté d'organiser un enseignement et la liberté de choisir un enseignement," in Jean Bourtembourg and others, eds., *Quels droits dans l'enseignement? Enseignants, parents, elèves* (Bruges: La Charte, 1994), p. 12; Els Witte, Jan De Groof, and Jeffrey Thyssens, *40 jaar schoolpact 1958–1998* (Brussels: VUBPress, 1999).

5. Jan De Groof, "De herziening van het art. 117 van de grondwet en de erkenning van de vrijzinnigheid" (The revision of article 117 of the constitution and the recognition of free-thinking), *Tijdschrift voor Bestuurswetenschappen en Publiek Recht*, no. 6 (1986), pp. 469–81.

6. Jan De Groof, "De bescherming van de ideologische en filosofische strekkingen—Een inleiding" (The protection of ideological and philosophical trends—An introduction), in André Alen and Louis-Paul Suetens, eds., *Zeven knelpunten na zeven jaar staatshervorming* (Seven pressure points after seven years of state reforms) (Brussels: Cepess, 1988), pp. 239–331.

7. As a side remark: education at universities followed another track. This is due to the historical equilibrium between two free universities on one hand and between two state universities, a French-language one and a Dutch-language one, on the other hand. The two free universities had for a long time received equal treatment as far as their finances went. Both also had the right to grant academic grades.

8. The Public Opinion Analysis sector of the European Commission (http://europa.eu.int/comm/public_opinion/index_en.htm [June 17, 2004]).

9. Education Department, *Flemish Educational Indicators in an International Perspective* (Brussels: Ministry of the Flemish Community, 2001), pp. 38–39. Jan De Groof and others, eds., *De school op rapport. Het Vlaams onderwijs in internationale context* (Grading schools: Flemish education in an international context) (Kapellen: Pelckmans, 1993); Jan De Groof and Tony Van Haver, *Het Vlaams onderwijs in de kijker: Internationale vergelijkingen* (Flemish education in detail: International comparisons) (Brussels: Ministry of the Flemish Community, Education Department, 1995).

10. Partly after the constitutional revision of 1968–71; see Jan De Groof, "De bevoegdheidsverdeling van 1970 inzake onderwijs: zienswijzen van de Raad van State en lessen voor de Constituante," *Tijdschrift voor Bestuurswetenschappen en Publiek Recht*, vol. 8 (1988), pp. 391–405; Raf Verstegen, "De gemeenschappen bevoegd voor het onderwijs," *Tijdschrift voor Bestuurswetenschappen en Publiek Recht*, vol. 1 (1990), p. 22; Ludo Veny, "Onderwijs en Grondwet. De nieuwe grondwetsbepalingen inzake onderwijs," *Tijdschrift voor Bestuurswetenschappen en Publiek Recht*, no. 11 (1988), p. 594.

11. Since the 1988 revision of the Constitution, a few functions, chiefly dealing with social security, labor organization, and pensions, have been federal. Jan De

Groof and Hilde Penneman, "Artikel 127, § 1, eerste lid, 2 van de Grondwet. Een overzicht van de bevoegdheidsverdeling in onderwijsaangelegenheden" (An oversight of the distribution of authority regarding education), *Tijdschrift voor Onderwijsrecht en Onderwijsbeleid,* nos. 5–6 (1997–98).

12. A decree is a law established by a community parliament; it has the same legal value as national law. The Court of Arbitration is in charge of judging conflicts between laws and decrees.

13. See Jan De Groof, *De grondwetsherziening van 1988 en het onderwijs* (The revision of the Constitution in 1998 and education) (Brussels: Story Scientia, 1989), and in French, *La révision constitutionnelle de 1988 et l'enseignement* (Brussels: Story Scientia, 1989); Jan De Groof, "The Belgian Model for Constitutional Rights on Education," in Jan De Groof, *Subsidiarity and Education: Aspects of Comparative Educational Law. First Report of the European Educational Law Association* (Leuven: Acco, 1994), p. 305.

14. The mechanisms of consultation and pacification, which had been installed by the School Pact, no longer functioned. The threat that the government would fall and the right of each traditional ideological group to veto legislation obstructed any reliable guarantees. The Catholic community realized that the School Pact was only an agreement of fact, only a *modus vivendi.* Furthermore, it was clear that neither the Dutch-speaking nor the French-speaking party would abandon their ideological position. Therefore the amendment of the Constitution became indispensable.

15. Jan De Groof, *Recht op en vrijheid van onderwijs* (Right to and freedom of education) (Brussels: Cepess, 1994).

16. Constitution of Belgium, article 24, sec. 1, para. 2.

17. Court of Arbitration, ruling no. 25/92 (April 2, 1992), ground 4.B.2 (see, in particular, the French, Dutch, and German text of this ruling published in the *Moniteur Belge,* June 10, 1992) and ruling no. 85/98 (July 15, 1998), ground B.3.7. See also ruling no. 28/92 (April 2, 1992), ground 6.B.3; ruling no. 18/93 (March 4, 1993), ground B.3.4; ruling no. 85/95 (December 14, 1995), ground B.2.5; ruling no., 76/96 (December 18, 1996), ground B.4.3, in which rulings the words "and of equal access to education" do not appear.

18. See the rulings cited in the note 17.

19. See Court of Arbitration, ruling no. 66/99 (June 17, 1999); Francis Delperée, *De l'interpretation de la loi* (Brussels: Publications des Facultés Universitaires Saint-Louis); See Jan De Groof, *De overheid en het gesubsidieerd onderwijs* (Government and grant-aided education) (Brussels: Cepess, 1985).

20. De Groof, *Recht op en vrijheid van onderwijs.*

21. Court of Arbitration, judgment no. 25/92 (April 2, 1992), consideration B.4.l; judgment no. 76/96 (December 18, 1996), consideration B.4.2; judgment no. 110/98 (November 4, 1998), consideration B.2.2. Regarding jurisprudence on educational freedom, see also Jan De Groof, "On Pedagogical Freedom: Some Legal and Policy Considerations," in Jan De Groof and Jan Fiers, eds., *Minorities in Education* (Leuven: Acco, 1996), p. 246.

22. De Groof and Fiers, eds., *Minorities in Education,* p. 246.

23. Court of Arbitration, judgment no.85/96, preambles B.5.7.1, B.5.7.2.

24. On rationalization and programming, see Jan De Groof, *Het levens-beschouwelijk karakter van de onderwijsinstellingen* (The ideological character of education) (Bruges: die Keure, 1985). On the developments in legislation and case law in this area, see Jan De Groof, *Het regime van de vrije keuze tussen de confessionele en de niet-confessionele school* (The system of free choice between denominational and non-denominational schools), part 3 (Leuven: K. U. Leuven, 1983-84).

25. Court of Arbitration, judgment no. 28/92 (April 2, 1992).

26. Court of Arbitration, judgment no. 18/93 (March 4, 1993); See also Court of Arbitration, judgment no. 76/96 (December 18, 1996).

27. From the ruling of the Court of Arbitration and the recommendations of the Court of State, it appears that the communities must act "cautiously" with regard to this.

28. Jan De Groof, "Hoe bijzonder is het bijzonder decreet in uitvoering van het artikel 24, § 2 G.W.?" (How special is the special decree for the execution of article 24, § 2 G.W.?), *Tijdschrift voor Onderwijsrecht en Onderwijsbeleid*, no. 1 (1995-96).

29. On the involvement of the School Pact principle in the Constitution, see De Groof, *De grondwetsherziening van 1988 en het onderwijs.*

30. Jef Verhoeven and Mark Elchardus, *Onderwijs een decenium Vlaamse autonomie* (Education: a decade of Flemish autonomy) (Kapellen: Pelckmans, 2000); Jef Verhoeven, Guy Fosty, and Roland Gaignage, "Federalisering, decentralisatie, deconcentratie, en deregulering" (Federalization, decentralization, deconcentration, and deregulation), in Department of Education, *Het Educatief bestel in België, van convergentie naar divergentie OESO. Doorlichting van het educatief overheidsbeleid* (The educational establishment in Belgium, from convergence to divergence, country report of Belgium, OECD: Investigation of government educational policy) (Brussels: Ministry of the Flemish Community, 1991) pp. 380–402; Jan De Groof and others, "Responsabilisering van de school" (Making schools accountable), *Cahiers voor onderwijsrecht en onderwijsbeleid*, vol. 3 (Antwerp: Kluwer, 1998); Jan De Groof and others, "Optimalisering van beleidsbeslissingen in het hoger onderwijs" (Optimising policy decisions in higher education), *Cahiers voor onderwijsrecht en onderwijsbeleid*, vol. 4 (Antwerp: Kluwer, 1998), p. 8; Johan L. Vanderhoeven, "Medezeggenschap: een duik in de locale autonomie," *Tijdschrift voor Onderwijsrecht en Onderwijsbeleid*, no. 3 (1991–92), p. 157.

31. Geert Devos, Piet Vandenberghe, and Jef Verhoeven, *Schoolbeleid: mogelijkheden en grenzen. Een empirisch onderzoek* (Leuven: ACCO, 1989); Geert Devos, Herman Van den Broeck, and E. Bracke, *Samenwerkingsverbanden en enveloppefinanciering: mogelijkheden en knelpunten van bestuurs- en directiestructuren*, (Ghent: Mys & Breesch, 1996); Kurt De Wit, Geert Devos, and Jef C. Verhoeven, "Op weg naar samenwerking. Vier casestudies uit het secundair onderwijs," *Tijdschrift voor onderwijsrecht en onderwijsbeleid*, no. 1 (1998–99), pp. 56–65; Walter Nonneman and Mike Smet, *Financiering secundair onderwijs* (University of Antwerp, 1996); Jef Verhoeven and Mark Elchardus, *Onderwijs een decenium Vlaamse autonomie* (Kapellen: Pelckmans, 2000).

32. School Pact Law, article 2, sec. 3.

33. Jan Adé, "Juridische regeling van het privé-onderwijs in Vlaanderen" (Legal framework of purely private education in Flanders), *Tijdschrift voor Onderwijsrecht en Onderwijsbeleid*, nos. 5–6 (1997–98), p. 357.

34. School Pact Law, article 4, sec. 1.

35. Implementation of Article 24 of theConstitution, Decree of February 25, 1997; De Groof, *Recht op en vrijheid van onderwijs.*

36. Catharina Offeciers, "De positie van het officieel secundair en basisonderwijs binnen het Vlaamse onderwijsaanbod en de (her)definiëring van het grondwettelijk gegarandeerde beginsel van de vrije keuze," *Tijdschrift voor Onderwijsrecht en Onderwijsbeleid*, no. 4 (1995–96), p. 199; Frank Ornelis, "De identiteit van het gemeentelijk en provinciaal onderwijs," *Tijdschrift voor Onderwijsrecht en Onderwijsbeleid*, no. 4 (2000–01), p. 281.

37. Most recent policy document, under the authority of Minister-President Patrick Dewael and the Flemish Government, *Kleurrijk Vlaanderen als levend trefpunt*, March 4, 2001, p. 12. This document, however, stressed the opportunities of *pluriformity* in education, rather than defending monopolies of state schools.

38. Deloitt and Touche, *Inkomsten en uitgaven van scholen in Vlaanderen: Kwantificering van de objectiveerbare verschillen* (Brussels: July 11, 2001).

39. For the sake of convenience, the report leaves aside special education where, making the same assumptions, a transfer would be sure to arise in primary education.

40. Document, Belgian Parliament, Senate, extraordinary session 1988, no. 100-1/1, p. 2.

41. See Jan De Groof, "Onderwijs en regelgeving. Enkele notities. Lezing in de Commissie 'Onderwijs' van de Vlaamse Raad op 22 januari 1997" (Education and regulations: Some notes: Version of the 'Education' Committee of the Flemish Council on 22 January 1997) *Tijdschrift voor Onderwijsrecht en Onderwijsbeleid*, no. 4 (1996–1997), p. 201–08.

42. De Groof, *Het levensbeschouwelijk karakter van de onderwijsintellingen.*

43. See De Groof, *De grondwetsherziening van 1988 en het onderwijs.*

44. Court of Arbitration, judgment no. 65/95 (September 28, 1995).

45. See, for example, Document, Parliament of the French Community of Belgium, session 1993-94, no. 171/1.

46. Document, Parliament of the Flemish Community of Belgium, session 1990-91, no. 548/1.

47. See, for example, Mauric-André Flamme, *Droit administratif* (Brussels: Bruylant, 1989). On "recognition," see, for example," De Groof, *De overheid en het gesubsidieerd onderwijs.*

48. In the same sense: "This must ultimately allow significant scope for standards which the authorised authority of the school sets itself or which are voluntarily accepted in the social exchange with bodies other than the authority which provides the finance for maintenance. Both assume a private law form of organisation for 'special' (Dutch terminology for 'denominational') education within which decision-making primarily takes place in accordance with the principles (party autonomy, reci-

procity) and rules of private law. Were it otherwise, there would be no workable framework within which to shape one's own direction according to one's own standards." Paul J. J. Zoontjens, "De smalle ruimte: Enige opmerkingen over privaatrecht en publiekrecht, bezien vanuit de positie van de bijzondere school" (The narrow scope: Some comments regarding private law and public law as seen from the perspective of the special [denominational] school), *Nederlands Tijdschrift voor Onderwijsrecht*, vol. 1 (1999), p. 32.

49. De Groof, *De overheid en het gesubsidieerd onderwijs*.

50. School Pact Law, art. 24, sec. 2.

51. Decrees of June 5, 1996, and March 30, 1999, issued by the Flemish Government; see Ilse Van Heddegem, Jef C. Verhoeven, "Gesubsidieerde oudervorming in Vlaanderen," *Tijdschrift voor Onderwijsrecht en Onderwijsbeleid*, nos. 5–6 (1998-99), p. 317.

52. Jef C. Verhoeven, Marc Jegers, and Ilse Van Heddegem, *Participatieraden en lokale schoolraden in Vlaanderen: de eerste jaren* (Leuven: Garant, 1997); Jef C. Verhoeven, "Leerkrachtenparticipatie en schoolbeleid. Een appreciatie door directie en leerkrachten," *Tijdschrift voor Onderwijsrecht en Onderwijsbeleid*, no. 3 (1993–94), p. 162. There seems nevertheless no unanimity on teachers' positions: Geert Devos, *De flexibilisering van het secundair onderwijs in Vlaanderen* (Leuven: Acco, 1995), p. 67.

53. For schools recognized as such by the Hoge Raad voor het Pluralistisch Onderwijs (High Council for Pluralistic Education).

54. See Wim Vertommen, "De school tussen droom en daad. Opvoedingsproject en samenhang. Een begrippenanalyse," *Tijdschrift voor Onderwijsrecht en Onderwijsbeleid*, no. 4 (1992–93), p. 211.

55. See Raf Verstegen, "Eindtermen getoetst aan de grondwet," *Tijdschrift voor Onderwijsrecht en Onderwijsbeleid*, no. 4 (1996–97), p. 223; De Groof, "On Pedagogical Freedom."

56. See Marie-Claire Foblets and Bernard Hubeau, *Migratie- en migrantenrecht: recente ontwikkelingen* (Bruges: die Keure, 1995); Jan De Groof and Frank Ornelis, "Recht op onderwijs, ook voor 'illegalen'" (A right to an education for everyone, including "illegals"), *Tijdschrift voor Onderwijsrecht en Onderwijsbeleid*, no. 5 (1999–2000), p. 333.

57. See Raf Verstegen, ed., "De non-discriminatieverklaring in het onderwijs. Moeilijkheden en mogelijkheden," *Cahiers voor onderwijsrecht en onderwijsbeleid*, vol. 5 (Antwerp: Kluwer, 1998); Adriaan Overbeeke, "Netoverschrijdend spreiden van migrantenleerlingen. Het non-discriminatiepact in het Vlaamse onderwijs," *Tijdschrift voor Onderwijsrecht en Onderwijsbeleid*, no. 4 (1993–94), p. 220; Paul Mahieu, "Eén leerling op vier. Een tussentijdse verkennende evaluatie van de eerste proefprojecten in het kader van de non-discriminatieverklaring," *Tijdschrift voor Onderwijsrecht en Onderwijsbeleid*, no. 1 (1998–99), p. 21.

58. Patrice Caremans, "Over de doelstellingen, het ontstaan, de inhoud en de praktische uitvoering van de gemeenschappelijke verklaring inzake een non-discriminatiebeleid in het onderwijs," *Tijdschrift voor Onderwijsrecht en Onderwijsbeleid*, no.

2 (1996–97), p. 90. Compare Ben Vermeulen, "Concentratiescholen, spreidings-beleid en keuzerecht in het Nederlands onderwijs," *Tijdschrift voor Onderwijsrecht en Onderwijsbeleid*, no. 4 (2000–01), p. 261.

59. See Raf Verstegen, "De non-discriminatieverklaring in het onderwijs. Moeil-ijkheden en mogelijkheden," p. 104 .

60. *R. v. St.*, Mossaïd, case no. 67.287 (July 2, 1997).

61. *R. v. St.*, Pesch, case no. 26.749 (August 12, 1991). On independent educa-tion, see Liege, April 23, 1987, *Journal des Tribunaux* (1987), pp. 446–47.

62. Decrees of July 17, 1991, and April 13, 1999, of the Parliament of the Flem-ish Community of Belgium.

63. Roland Vandenberghe and others, *Evaluatie van het beleid inzake kwaliteit-szorg. Analyse en effecten van begeleiding, nascholing en doorlichting* (Evaluation of pol-icy with respect to quality care: Analysis and effects of supervision, postgrade educa-tion, and investigation), 2 parts (Leuven: K. U. Leuven, 1997).

64. Jean-Pierre Verhaeghe, Tammy Schellens, and Lieve Oosterlinck, *Kwaliteit-szorg in het secundair onderwijs* (Quality care in secondary education), 2 parts (Ghent: RUG, 1998).

65. Jean-Marie Marchand, "The Educational Inspection and the Public Nature of Administration," *Journal for Educational Law and Educational Policy*, vol. 1 (1997–98), p. 8.

66. Peter Michielsens, "De groei van een kwaliteitscultuur. Vragen over school en overheid, ervaringen met schooldoorlichtingen, uitdagingen voor kwaliteitszorg op school," *Tijdschrift voor Onderwijsrecht en Onderwijsbeleid*, no. 3 (1993–94), p. 180; Peter Michielsens, "De werking van de gemeenschapsinspectie. Een stand van zaken, een perspectief en een antwoord op sommige mythen," *Tijdschrift voor Onderwijs-recht en Onderwijsbeleid*, no. 4 (1991–92), p. 233; Geert Kelchtermans and Luc Van de Poele, "De vernieuwde gemeenschapsinspectie en pedagogische begeleiding," *Tijd-schrift voor Onderwijsrecht en Onderwijsbeleid*, no. 1 (1995–96), p. 43; Geert Kelchtermans, Roland Vandenberghe, and Inge Devis, "De effectiviteit van inspectie, pedagogische begeleiding en nascholing. Determinanten en micropolitieke verklar-ing," *Tijdschrift voor Onderwijsrecht en Onderwijsbeleid*, no. 3 (1999–2000), p. 153.

67. This means also that in addition to the external evaluation of schools by the community inspectorate (school audits), schools are expected to carry out their own internal evaluation. School audits and internal evaluation are complementary strate-gic instruments for quality assurance and should therefore not duplicate each other. Differences in the profiles of the types of secondary schools do not permit conclu-sions about differences between individual schools. The latter appear to vary a great deal. In other words, this instrument can easily discriminate between individual schools. See Peter Van Petegem, *Scholen op zoek naar hun kwaliteit. Effectieve-scholenonderzoek als inspiratiebron voor de zelfevaluatie van scholen* (Ghent: RUG, 1997); Geert Devos and Jef C. Verhoeven, "Het proces van zelfevaluatie. Een verken-nend onderzoek in secundaire scholen," *Tijdschrift voor Onderwijsrecht en Onderwijs-beleid*, no. 6 (1999–2000), p. 425.

7

The Civic Implications of Canada's Education System

DAVID E. CAMPBELL

I n 2001, the government of the Canadian province of Ontario announced that it would grant tax credits for tuition paid to private—including religious—elementary and secondary schools. The policy detonated an explosive debate within Ontario over the role of private, particularly religious, schools in a pluralistic democracy. Public support for private schools, critics argue, will only splinter Ontario's increasingly diverse population—an outcome antithetical to Canadians' collective vision of their nation as a harmonious blend of different cultures. For example, the head of Ontario's Human Rights Commission (a body funded by the Ontario government) has described the policy as having the "potential to result in racial, ethnic and religious apartheid in our educational system, as well as intolerance and ignorance."[1] For anyone following the debate over private school vouchers in the United States, the rhetoric in Ontario should sound familiar. Like a voucher, the Ontario tax credit is a means of subsidizing private school tuition. And in both the United States and Ontario, opponents of public subsidies for pri-

I would like to thank Earl Fry and Paul E. Peterson for their assistance as I sought to educate myself about Canada's education system. My thinking on the subject was honed also by my interaction with the participants at "Regulating School Choice to Promote Civic Values: What Can the U.S. Learn from the Experience of Other Nations?" a conference sponsored by the Brookings Institution/Gates National Working Commission on School Choice and held at the University of London. All errors, of course, are mine.

vate schools criticize private education as being in tension with democratic ideals. Consider the words of Justice John Paul Stevens, dissenting in the 2002 decision in *Zelman* v. *Simmons-Harris*, in which the U.S. Supreme Court ruled vouchers to be constitutional. Stevens provocatively suggests that public funding for religious schools will "increase the risk of religious strife and weaken the foundation of our democracy."[2]

There is, however, a fundamental distinction between Ontario and the United States. In Ontario, religious schools already are funded directly with public dollars. Or at least Catholic schools are. Thirty percent of Ontario students attend Catholic schools that are fully supported with revenue from the public treasury. Notwithstanding the rhetorical similarities between the voucher debate south of the 49th parallel and the contretemps over tax credits north of it, the educational environments in the two places are actually quite different.

These differences are relevant for policymakers contemplating the implementation of greater school choice in the United States. Recently, some policy analysts have argued that Canada's experience with public funding for religious and other independent schools is useful for understanding the potential consequences of a voucherized education system. For example, a 2002 report on the subject published jointly by the Fraser Institute, a Canadian think tank, and the Milton and Rose D. Friedman Foundation concludes that "the evidence from Canada presents a compelling case for increasing educational choice in the United States."[3] Marvin Olasky similarly writes that "Canadian school choice has helped all students, and particularly the poor. . . . [S]chool choice contributes to the pursuit of educational equity rather than takes away from it."[4] While these authors are correct to note that Americans can learn from the Canadian example, they have perhaps been too quick to gloss over the significant differences between the educational systems of the two nations. In contrast, this chapter explores how Canada's educational environment—actually, its environments—can inform the debate over school choice in the United States, but with an eye toward noting both the similarities and the differences in the nations' systems. Specifically, it focuses on the Canadian educational landscape to assess its implications for civic—or democratic—education.

It is important to note that nowhere in Canada is there a system that resembles a voucher system as it is commonly understood. But, as noted above, there are places where religious schools are directly subsidized with public funds, an arrangement with obvious parallels to a voucher system. Because of these parallels, American policymakers considering the potential consequences of school choice (of vouchers in particular) can benefit from examining the civic implications of Canada's various education models.

In spite of, or perhaps because of, the pervasiveness of government funding for religious schools, its civic consequences have largely escaped the attention of social scientists studying civic education in Canada. Even though scholars and citizens alike often express concern over the development of Canadians' national identity, the research literature reveals very little discussion of the role of either private or religious education in that process. One exception is the Fraser/Friedman report cited above, which briefly addresses the civic side of funding for religious schools. The report is sanguine about the civic implications of publicly funded religious and private schools:

> There is no evidence that support for independent schools has harmed Canadian social cohesion. Funding for private, independent schools has existed for decades with no discernable adverse impact on citizenship. There is no sense among Canadians that British Columbia, Alberta, Manitoba, and Quebec, the provinces that fund independent [private] schools, are more balkanized than the rest of the country.[5]

The fundamental assertion here is that Canadians do not perceive public funding for private schools as having harmed the preparation of Canadian youth for civic life. Proving a negative is difficult, but the silence in the research literature on the subject gives the claim prima facie validity. However, the recent controversy in Ontario over tax credits for private school tuition also suggests that Canadians are far from unanimous in their opinions about the role of religious schools in a pluralistic democracy.

This chapter begins with a synopsis of the Canadian education system in general. Next, it turns to the specific institutional arrangements in different Canadian provinces, of which there is a wide array. It concludes with a discussion of what aspects of the Canadian experience are most readily applicable in U.S. policymaking. Specifically, the chapter argues that the most applicable element of Canada's experience with funding independent schools is not a specific institutional arrangement but rather a model for evaluating the civic impact of *any* education system. For all of the ink spilled on the subject of school choice in the United States, there is a relatively small body of evidence evaluating the impact of increased choice on any aspect of education. And the studies that have been done focus on a relatively narrow definition of academic performance. The empirical evaluation of civic education has been largely ignored, in both the school choice literature specifically and scholarship on education more generally. Thus the debate over the civic consequences of public funding for private education has proceeded largely in a vacuum of data, making it difficult if not impossible to evaluate the claims made on either side of the issue. American policymakers should take note of the fact that the province in Canada that has most fully embraced school choice—Alberta—also has implemented a systematic means of evaluating students' civic capacity: a curriculum-based exit exam in social studies. In Alberta, therefore, the debate over whether school choice will weaken the civic dimension of education is informed by an evaluation of the civic education provided by different types of schools. If the United States adopted a similar system, it would be possible to add what has been missing from the debate over the civic impact of school choice—evidence.

Similarities and Differences in the Canadian and the U.S. Education Systems

Superficially, the education systems of Canada and the United States have much in common. Both nations have a federal form of government, and consequently both have a decentralized education system in which the national government plays a minimal role. In fact, Ottawa plays a smaller role in education than does Washington, as there is no Canadian equivalent of the U.S. Department of Education. Each province has almost total autonomy in determining its education policies. There are local school boards, as in the United States. All of the provinces provide funding for schools from the provincial treasury; in most, these provincial funds are augmented with revenue from local property taxes. Canadian public schools generally have geographically defined catchment areas from which they draw their students. As explained later, however, geography is not the only factor determining who attends which school. In some places, religion and language matter too. The organization of Canadian high schools generally resembles that of their American counterparts. Pedagogical techniques, length of the school day and year, school size, extracurricular activities, and parent-teacher organizations all are similar.

But these surface likenesses are deceiving. A closer look reveals that the two nations have fundamental differences in terms of the relationship of church, state, and school. In the United States, jurisprudence regarding the role of religion in public institutions has been dominated by Jefferson's metaphor of a wall separating church and state; that same wall also separates church and school. The last forty years have seen a long line of Supreme Court decisions banning school-sponsored religious expression in the public schools. Over the same period, the Court also has been wary of channeling public money to religious schools, although that has been permitted when the money is to be used for a primarily secular purpose. The difficulty in distinguishing a religious from a secular purpose has resulted in the Court's palpable ambivalence on the question of whether and how public money can be used for private, particularly religious, schools. The *Zelman* decision divided the Court, since only five justices supported the conclusion that the purpose of Cleveland's voucher program is primarily secular in nature. Similarly, in *Aguilar* v. *Fenton*, the Court ruled that publicly funded special education teachers could not provide remedial instruction for struggling private school students on the grounds of their school, but then reversed itself just over a decade later in *Agostini* v. *Felton*, declaring such instruction to be constitutional after all.[6]

In sharp contrast to the constitutional legacy of the United States, Canada's does not include a wall separating church and state; therefore there has been no barrier between church and school. To the contrary, from Canada's beginnings in 1867, religious schools have received government funding. The Canadian constitution—section 93 of the British North America (BNA) Act of 1867—specifically stipulates that any province joining Canada must preserve the religious character of its schools as they existed at the time of union. This constitutional provision was crafted as a compromise between Ontario and Quebec, the two largest provinces at the time Canada was founded.

> In nineteenth-century Ontario and Quebec religious differences marked deep political fissures, and a common education that prescinded from religious conviction was acceptable to scarcely anyone. Common schools in both provinces would cater to the creed of the majority. But since the religious majority in each was the minority in the other, almost everyone had reason to support a *modus vivendi* that would cater to minority demands in both provinces. Agreement on school rights for the Protestant minority in Quebec and the Catholic minority in Ontario was critical to the very creation of the Canadian state.[7]

As each of the provinces joined Canada, historical contingencies led to different institutional arrangements for education, which today have resulted in wide variation in whether and how religious schools receive public monies. Some provinces resemble the U.S. model and provide no funding for religious schools. Other provinces fully fund a Catholic school system, and some provinces also fund other religious schools. So while Canadians do not employ Jefferson's metaphor of a wall between church and state, Canada is a case study in support of Justice Louis Brandeis's metaphor for the virtue of federalism: the states (provinces) are laboratories of democracy. Rather than a single institutional model, Canada presents us with multiple templates for the relationship between church and school.

The backdrop for Canada's constitutional provision preserving the religious schools within a province is the enduring challenge of accommodating both its English- and its French-speaking populations. While section 93 of the BNA Act is literally phrased in terms of religion, it was really about language. In 1867, when the first four provinces came together in the Canadian confederation, schools were either Protestant or Catholic, which generally meant that they were either English or French, respectively. Section 93, therefore, is a fulcrum for balancing the rights and prerogatives of the two primary groups, English and French speakers, who initially forged the nation of Canada out of disparate British colonies. In other words, while the U.S. Constitution was eventually interpreted as forbidding the racial segregation of schools, the Canadian constitution has always mandated separation along religious lines.[8] Furthermore, some provinces fund schools based on their linguistic (English or French) rather than religious character.

The constitutionally mandated religious or linguistic segregation of Canadian schools notwithstanding, Canadians speak of the democratic purposes of their schools much as Americans speak of those of theirs. In a review of civic education in Canada, Alan M. Sears and his colleagues note that "a concern for citizenship education figures in the policy of all jurisdictions. . . . Across the country there is acknowledgment that citizenship education is the responsibility of schools as a whole."[9] For example, a royal commission on education in British Columbia recently issued a final report containing the uncontroversial statement that Canadians "have long expected schools to serve as agencies for civic and democratic development."[10]

While Americans and Canadians share sentiments regarding schools as institutions to both educate young people and prepare them for engagement in democratic life, they nonetheless have very different perspectives on the accommodation of cultural differences within their nation's collective civic identity. The royal commission cited above went on to describe the criteria that schools should use to prepare their students to become members of a democracy, using language that focuses more on preserving cultural distinctiveness than the language in similar documents south of the 49th parallel: "Today we turn to schools to help us enshrine language rights, to preserve diverse cultural heritages, to promote social equality and justice through recognition of individual differences."[11] If American schools seek to balance *pluribus* and *unum*, then Canadian schools put a thumb on the scale so that it tilts toward the former. Canadians historically have been more comfortable than their American neighbors with the conception of rights granted to groups or communities, and Canada officially embraces multiculturalism as a national ideal. "Whether it is accurate or not, Canadians view the diverse peoples of the United States as having a far more homogeneous sense of civic identity than do the peoples of Canada."[12] The religious and linguistic diversity among schools that receive public funding reflects this Canadian vision of pluralism—the state recognizes and even facilitates diversity among groups qua groups, not just among individuals.

The different perspectives on religious education in the United States and Canada fall into sharp relief when the legacies of Catholic education in the two nations are compared. In the United States, Catholic schools were founded in response to the rise of the common school. Common school advocates crafted the public education system ostensibly as a means to make loyal Americans out of immigrants; Catholic leaders saw these new schools as designed to make Protestants out of Catholics.[13] Rightly or wrongly, therefore, Catholic schools have long been viewed with suspicion as teaching values antithetical to the "American creed," a suspicion evident in the Blaine amendments in numerous state constitutions. In Canada, by contrast, Catholic education is a complement, not a counterweight, to the common school. In many provinces Catholic schools have been woven into the fabric of the public education system.

Canada's Laboratories of Democratic Education

As mentioned, the combination of Canada's federalism and its constitutional requirements for funding religious schools has resulted in a wide variety of education environments in its provinces. Some provinces fund only secular public schools; these include New Brunswick, Nova Scotia, Prince Edward Island, Newfoundland, and Quebec. Some provinces use public revenue to fully fund a Catholic school system whose students pay no tuition (Alberta, Saskatchewan, and Ontario). Some fund private schools through grants designed to cover a portion of their operating costs; these schools still charge tuition for expenses not covered by the provincial subsidy (British Columbia, Alberta, Saskatchewan, Manitoba, and Quebec). Ontario also subsidizes private schools but does so with a newly introduced tax credit for the amount spent on tuition. Table 7-1 displays the specific funding arrangements in each province and shows, unsurprisingly, that provincial funding for the private sector leads to greater private school enrollment.

Table 7-1. *Canada's Educational Systems*

Province	Full public funding for Catholic schools?	Public subsidies for independent schools?	Percent in "public" Catholic schools	Percent in independent schools
British Columbia	No	Yes	n.a.	8.5
Alberta	Yes	Yes	23	4.5
Saskatchewan	Yes	Yes	21	2.0
Manitoba	No	Yes	n.a.	6.7
Ontario	Yes	Yes[a]	30	4.6
Quebec	No	Yes	n.a.	9.1
New Brunswick	No	No	n.a.	0.7
Nova Scotia	No	No	n.a.	1.7
Prince Edward Island	No	No	n.a.	0.9
Newfoundland	No	No	n.a.	0.8

Sources: Data in third column are from Federation of Independent Schools in Canada, (www.independentschools.ca/trend.htm [January 2004]); data in fourth column are from William Robson and Claudia Hepburn, *Learning From Success: What Americans Can Learn from School Choice in Canada* (Indianapolis: Milton and Rose D. Friedman Foundation and the Fraser Institute, 2002).

a. As discussed at length in the paper, the subsidy comes in the form of a tax credit granted to parents for private school tuition.

This chapter examines a few of these provincial models in depth in order to understand their consequences for civic education. Regrettably, however, it is difficult to make an empirically grounded assessment of civic education within these different systems, with one notable (and replicable) exception. It is this exception, found in the province of Alberta, that offers a lesson for the United States.

Quebec and Newfoundland: Schools in Transition

Quebec and Newfoundland are of particular interest, as they have recently undertaken significant reforms of their respective education systems. Both provinces had a system in which the schools were defined exclusively along religious lines, and each has now shifted to a secular orientation in its schools. The specifics of the reforms vary, however, in ways that are germane to the consideration of their civic implications.

Newfoundland

Newfoundland was the last province to join Canada, waiting until 1949 to do so. Owing to its separate historical trajectory, Newfoundland long had a unique education system. Prior to its recent systemic reforms, all of the province's provincially funded schools were governed by one of four religious groups: Roman Catholics, Integrated (Anglican, United Church of Canada, Presbyterian, Moravian, and Salvation Army), Pentecostals, and Seventh-Day Adventists. Parents could send their children to a school run by one of these groups or choose one of a small number of private schools (which received no provincial funding then and do not now). There were no secular public schools. This unusual arrangement was specifically protected in the Canadian constitution under a provision governing Newfoundland's union with Canada.

Because parents could choose to send their children to a school governed by any of the sponsoring religious groups, enrollment was not based on geography. Therefore children in a given neighborhood might attend any of four different publicly funded schools. As a result, this sparsely populated province had a large number of schools in overlapping districts, each with its own bureaucratic apparatus, transportation system, and so on. The provincial government—which provides all of the funding for these different school systems—saw this as grossly inefficient, especially given declining enrollments and the soft economic foundation of the province.[14]

After unsuccessful negotiations with the religious groups governing the schools, the provincial government under Premier Clyde Wells brought the matter of school reform to a referendum in 1995. Specifically, the referendum asked Newfoundland voters whether the province's four existing school systems should be consolidated into a smaller number of interdenominational districts. It did not, however, eliminate schools run by a single religious group ("unidenominational" schools). Where there was enough demand, unidenominational schools would have been maintained, although the province left unclear how strong that demand had to be. The referendum passed with the support of 54 percent of Newfoundland voters. Following the vote, Parliament amended the Canadian constitution in order to allow the change to occur, although not before the unelected and typically docile Senate stalled the amendment for six months.[15] However, momentum for the reform slowed when the Newfoundland supreme court issued an injunction halting its implementation. In response the newly elected premier, Brian Tobin, put a more sweeping referendum question before the Newfoundland electorate in 1997. While the reform proposed in the first referendum would have retained religious schools where numbers warranted, the second referendum asked voters whether the province should abandon denominational schools altogether. In an interview, an official in Newfoundland's department of education described the referendum question as "Schools in or schools out?" The second referendum passed by a much larger margin than the first, garnering 73 percent of the vote.

There is a sharp contrast between Newfoundland's reformed system and a voucher system. In Newfoundland, a system totally defined along religious lines was transformed into a secular system, while voucher programs take a totally secular system and divert funds to religious schools. At first glance, it would appear that Newfoundland's pre-reform, denominational system was a Solomonic compromise between two conflicting priorities in civic education, one to preserve parents' right to select an educational setting for their children that upholds their values, the other to ensure that all students receive an education that meets widely accepted standards (particularly in the area of citizenship training). An education system designed to emphasize parental autonomy has received the support of Terry Moe, who proposes that parents be given maximum freedom to choose schools that embody their values. Such a system, Moe writes, "allows ordinary people . . . to make their own decisions about what values their children should be taught, how they should be socialized, and what democratic purposes their schools ought to be pursuing."[16] On the other hand, Amy Gutmann articulately defends the position that public money should fund only schools that endorse widely held civic values. For Gutmann, the problem with a system like that advocated by Moe is the absence of public deliberation over school policies and curriculum. Essentially, her objection is that schools in such a system could end up teaching values antithetical to the civic aims of the wider society.[17]

Newfoundland's denominational schools, it would seem, strike a balance between the positions of Moe and Gutmann. On one hand, parents could choose among schools run by different faith communities and that therefore espoused different values, thus satisfying Moe's criteria. At the same time, Gutmann's concerns would seem to be met because these schools were governed by elected boards, thus introducing democratic control of the schools. But, in fact, a look below the surface of Newfoundland's denominational system reveals it to be unsatisfactory from both perspectives. In Newfoundland's system, contrary to Moe's model, parents' choices were quite constrained. Most notably, perhaps, there was no secular option, as all primary and secondary education was provided by religious organizations. It is difficult to believe that no parents in Newfoundland would have preferred a secular education for their children. The glaring absence of secular schools, therefore, falls short of Moe's proposal for a full-fledged system of choice among school communities. Nor did the system allow new groups to establish schools, at least not without considerable effort. While Pentecostals were granted official recognition in 1987 and thereby allowed to run their own schools, it required amending the Canadian constitution—hardly a recipe for innovation.

The system was equally unsatisfactory according to Gutmann's criteria. She too would presumably object to the absence of a secular option, less because it represents a lack of choice and more because compulsory religious education limits students' exposure to different ways of life (a key criterion for her model of democratic education). Also, in practice the system fell short of fostering the deliberation over policies that Gutmann argues is essential to ensure that schools teach the collective values of the polity. Under New-foundland's denominational system, the democratic dimension of school governance was actually very thin. The school boards had a combination of elected and appointed members, with the appointed positions filled by the churches sponsoring each school. Furthermore, voting in each school board election was limited to members of that denominational group, precisely counter to Gutmann's ideal of deliberation among "citizens who disagree on many moral and political issues."[18] In sum, far from successfully accommo-dating the two competing priorities in civic education, Newfoundland's denominational system of school governance failed to satisfy either one.

Quebec

Like Newfoundland, the province of Quebec also has recently eliminated its religion-based school system, and again Parliament had to amend the Cana-dian constitution to allow the change, as it did in December of 1997. Unlike Newfoundland, however, Quebec replaced a school system defined by religion with one defined by language. Whereas it previously had school districts des-ignated as Catholic and Protestant, they are now defined as French or English.

The only province in Canada with a French-speaking majority, Quebec has long had an uneasy relationship with the rest of Canada. Twice Quebe-cers have voted on secession from Canada, with the second referendum (in 1995) falling short by an extremely narrow margin. Quebec did not sign the Canadian constitution of 1982, and efforts since to incorporate Quebec for-mally into Canada's constitutional framework have been unsuccessful. Within the province's borders, the Quebec government has adopted many measures to promote the French language and culture, including making education in French mandatory for all but a very small percentage of stu-dents. There is not space here to detail all of the pressure points over lan-guage policies in Quebec, but suffice it to say that just as there is tension between Quebec and the English-speaking provinces over Quebec's place in Canada's federation, there is tension between Quebec's francophones and anglophones over the latter's place in the province.

It is in that context, therefore, that religion, language, and education have always been tightly intertwined in Quebec. Since 1875, students could choose between Catholic and Protestant school systems only; there were no secular public schools. In fact, until 1964 there was not even a provincial ministry of education overseeing the schools. And even with the establishment of a provincial education bureaucracy, the schools retained their denominational status. The fact that the province maintained schools defined by religion until just recently suggests the strong institutional legacy of any well-entrenched education system, as it ran counter to the general trend toward secularization that characterized Quebec during that period. Indeed, the Quebec government felt that it had to explicitly exempt its denominational schools from the religious freedom guarantees of its own provincial Charter of Human Rights and Freedoms, which was enacted in 1975.

In 1995–96, Quebec convened the Estates General on Education—essentially, a blue-ribbon commission—to examine the denominational status of Quebec's schools. The commission concluded that the system then current was an anachronism inconsistent with a "pluralistic, secular society" and therefore recommended that the churches no longer play a primary role in running the schools. The provincial government received the recommendation favorably, and in 1997 it took steps to implement the proposed changes. Rather than hold a referendum, as in Newfoundland, members of the provincial legislature simply voted on the reform, unanimously approving the change.

The reform in Quebec consisted of ending the denominational nature of school boards, converting them to boards based on language. Religion was not immediately excluded from the classroom, however; individual schools could retain their denominational status during a transitional period of at least two years. Furthermore, in the wake of the reforms Quebec introduced a new curriculum for moral education in the schools. This program offers a choice of courses grounded in a particular religious perspective (primarily Catholic or Protestant, but where numbers warrant, schools also can offer instruction based on other faiths). Alternatively, students can take a course in secular moral education.

While both Newfoundland and Quebec went through a similar process to change their schools and did so at roughly the same time, the two provincial governments justified the changes for very different reasons. In Newfoundland, the primary rationale for creating secular schools was simply efficiency—the elimination of overlap and duplication in a province that is thinly populated, predominantly rural, and economically beleaguered. In Quebec the rationale was couched in civic terms, as a means of ensuring that Quebec's schools fully prepare their students for engagement in a democracy rich with diversity. For example, consider the words of an official publication of the Ministry of Education, written in preparation for the end of denominational schools. Here the government of Quebec explains what the change means, and in so doing, implicitly criticizes what was wrong with an education system whose contours were shaped solely by religion.

> Within the framework set out by the law, all will now be called upon to contribute to the educational project, free of the discomfort associated with having to comply with the values of a specific religious tradition. Everyone, without restriction, will be able to participate in creating a common school that serves all the children in a given area. An inclusive school that takes into account the social, cultural and religious background of its students as well as their talents and limitations. A democratic school that educates students in shared civic values. An open school that gives students access to the world of knowledge and a broad-based culture and that is responsive to the community it serves.[19]

The rhetorical justification for secularizing Quebec's schools seems consistent with the language generally used in both the United States and Canada to define the civic purposes of public schools. By separating church and school, Quebec's education system will be "inclusive," "democratic," and "responsive to the community"—all terms consistent with the ideal of the common school.

However, it is important to note that the inclusiveness of Quebec's schools applies only to religion. Recall that there are still two school systems in Quebec, one for French-speaking students, the other for English speakers. For virtually every resident of Quebec, the assignment to one or the other is not a matter of choice. Under Quebec's Charter of the French Language (Bill 101), all but a small percentage of students in public and subsidized private schools must be educated in French. Exceptions are granted only for those few students whose parents were educated in English.[20] It seems ironic that the government of Quebec would invoke an image of the public school as an institution designed to foster mutual understanding among people of diverse backgrounds when the linguistic segregation in its schools means little interaction between students on opposite sides of the province's most salient social division.[21]

From Quebec's perspective, requiring students to receive an education in French is justified by the province's self-defined mission of protecting the French minority in Quebec from the English-speaking majority in the rest of North America. Quebec's efforts to promote the use of French within the province extend beyond education, and they have been a flashpoint of controversy within Canada for decades. Presumably because of the ongoing debate over language issues in Quebec, the report of the task force on the place of religion in Quebec's schools provides a lengthy justification for the policy of religious integration but linguistic segregation. The task force, which was formed to address whether the denominational system should continue, specifically grapples with the question of whether compulsory French education runs contrary to the principles of a liberal democracy:

> [T]o justify policies aimed at protecting and promoting the French lan-guage, do we not have to renounce the liberal framework and accept the community standpoint, at least to some extent? We do not think so. We do not need to abandon liberal democracy's normative frame-work to justify such measures. Indeed, to live in a culture that is not constantly threatened with imminent extinction is a necessary condi-tion for individual fulfillment. Individuals cannot exercise their ability to choose and deliberate in a vacuum. They need resources rooted in a culture—to such an extent that we could say they have a right to a cul-ture. A culture that is in the minority on a given continent, as is the case for Québec, can guarantee this right for its citizens only if it adopts measures to protect itself from the pressure to assimilate that is exercised by the continental English-speaking majority. The mainte-nance of a French-speaking cultural milieu in which every citizen is able to take full advantage of a right enjoyed automatically by the members of the majority continental culture is therefore justified within a liberal-democratic normative framework.[22]

This chapter's purpose is not to determine whether Quebec's policies on mandatory French education are justified; as noted, this is a perennial issue of considerable controversy in Canada, and one that is far beyond the scope of this chapter. Instead, interested parties can learn from the aspects of Que-bec's institutional innovation that speak to the civic purposes of schools in general.

The discussion of Newfoundland's pre-reform system contrasted the views of Moe and Gutmann, since those scholars stress opposing priorities in civic education. By way of comparison, their approaches also can be used to evalu-ate Quebec. First of all, there is little to meet Moe's call for a choice-based system, since a complex set of provincial regulations govern who is eligible to attend which type of school. The same rules also apply to students attending private schools, at least if the schools wish to receive a provincial subsidy, which equals roughly half of the per-pupil expenditure in the public schools.

In at least one respect, however, the process by which Quebec has designed its education system seemingly conforms to Gutmann's call for public deliberation over education policy. Before enacting the reform, the provincial government facilitated considerable discussion within the province by forming a parliamentary committee to study the issue. This committee held thirteen days of public hearings and received 254 briefs by interested parties. Nonetheless, even if this process seems consistent with Gutmann's model, the outcome falls short of what she describes as the ultimate objective of a public school: "to reap the benefits of social diversity."[23] To the contrary, Quebec's education system seems to irritate rather than soothe the social division between the province's two historically antagonistic linguistic groups. Like Newfoundland's system, then, the system in Quebec fails to satisfy either of the competing priorities in civic education.

Ontario: Controversy over a Tax Credit for Private School Tuition

While Newfoundland and Quebec have been secularizing their schools, Ontario has moved in the opposite direction by introducing a tax credit for tuition at private, including religious, schools. While the provision is relatively modest, it nonetheless has generated tremendous controversy within Ontario.[24] That controversy, however, should be seen in the context of the international criticism that Ontario received for its inequitable treatment of schools before the introduction of the tax credit, when the province funded a secular public school system as well as a quasi-public Catholic system but provided no financial support for private religious schools. In contrast, the other provinces in Canada with a publicly funded Catholic school system also provide some measure of funding for private schools run by other religious groups (although none provide funding on par with that received by Catholic schools). Because of the special treatment of Catholics under the province's system, in 1999 the United Nations Human Rights Committee (UNHRC) ruled that Ontario, and by extension Canada, was in violation of the International Covenant on Civil and Political Rights, which guarantees freedom from religious discrimination. The Canadian federal government chose not to exert any pressure on Ontario to reform its education system to conform to the UN decision, and in the immediate aftermath of the ruling, the Ontario provincial government did nothing to respond either.

In 2001, the Ontario government announced that it would provide a tax credit for parents who pay tuition at private, including religious, schools. While the motive for the tax credit seems rooted in the governing Conservative party's ideology rather than in compliance with the UNHRC, it nonetheless has the effect of changing Ontario policy to assuage the commission's concerns. Within Ontario, though, the tax credit has met with a lot of criticism, most notably from the head of the provincial Human Rights Commission, Ken Norton. Ironically, perhaps, while the UN Human Rights Committee has criticized Ontario for not funding religious schools other than those in the Catholic system, the province's own human rights commissioner has criticized it for doing exactly the opposite.

The UNHRC case was not the first time that Ontario's Catholic-only funding had been brought before the courts. In 1996, the Canadian supreme court heard a case regarding the same issue, but with the opposite result. In *Adler* v. *Ontario*, Jewish and Protestant parents sued the Ontario government over its singular treatment of Catholic schools, arguing that funding a Catholic system violates the guarantee of nondiscrimination on the basis of religion found in the Canadian Charter of Rights and Freedoms.[25] Their argument basically boiled down to "The Catholics have publicly funded schools, so why can't we?" And the court's answer was, essentially, "Because the constitution says so." The majority of the court ruled that because Ontario's education system was itself a product of another provision of the Canadian constitution (section 93 of the BNA Act), it could not be ruled unconstitutional.

Ontario is thus caught between the proverbial rock and a hard place. On one hand, its current Catholic-only system has brought censure from an international monitor of human rights while the introduction of partial funding for other religious schools has brought harsh criticism from within the province. What, then, is one to make of Ontario's dilemma? It seems that the plaintiffs in the Adler case had a legitimate complaint strictly on the grounds of equitable treatment. While perhaps the Canadian supreme court was correct to note that there is a constitutional rationale for singling Catholic schools out, that hardly means that Ontario's system is immutable. With enough political will, Ontario's system could be changed. After all, both Newfoundland and Quebec were able to have the Constitution amended in order to reform their schools. Furthermore, other provinces subsidize private religious schools, so a precedent clearly has been established.

A close reading of the arguments in the debate over Ontario's tax credit suggests a means of accommodating both sides. Grounds for a compromise can be found in the fact that the human rights commissioner is not critical of religious schools per se, as he is not calling for an end to Ontario's publicly funded Catholic system. Indeed, the commissioner's official statement regarding the tax credit makes a point of noting that in stating his opposition to the plan, he is "not referring to any existing private schools." Rather, the concern is that the tax credit will lead to a proliferation of new private schools, subject to little or no regulation.

> The Commissioner's main concern is that a financial incentive is being offered which might be expected to lead to a proliferation of small independent schools without sufficient regulation to ensure that the curriculum and values that are taught will be consistent with public policy in Ontario as expressed in the Ontario Human Rights Code. Unlike the public school system, including the publicly funded Catholic system, which is highly regulated, at present private schools operate with a high degree of autonomy and little government supervision.[26]

If one takes the human rights commissioner at his word, his concerns over public funding for private schools would be met if private schools were subject to a higher level of government scrutiny. A naïve response to the commissioner's criticism of the tax credit, therefore, would simply be a call for greater regulation of Ontario's private schools. If Ontario were to regulate its private schools as it does its Catholic schools, there would be no reason to question the civic commitment of the private sector. This "solution," however, is unrealistic because of the constitutionally unique status of Ontario's Catholic schools. Given that the province's Catholic schools are fully funded from public funds, they are inherently subject to as much provincial regulation as the secular public schools. In many respects, these schools have sacrificed a measure of their religious autonomy in exchange for a guaranteed revenue stream from the public purse. While Ontario's Catholic schools are permitted to take religion into account when making hiring decisions and to offer courses in religion, the content of their religious education courses is subject to approval by the provincial ministry of education. Undoubtedly, most religious educators, whether in Canada or the United States, would be reluctant to embrace a system that put their religious education under government control (notwithstanding the obvious constitutional difficulties that would cause in the United States). After all, the raison d'être of private schools, particularly those with a religious character, is to provide an alternative to the public school. The perverse result of too much regulation is that they lose their distinctiveness. The challenge, therefore, is to find a method of regulation that ensures that students in all schools are learning the skills of good citizenship and does not impede the organizational mission, educational innovation, and distinctive moral climate of any school. Accountability must be balanced with autonomy.

Evaluating Civic Education

The competing objectives of accountability and autonomy can be met with an examination system through which the civic education of every student in every school is gauged according to the same standard. With such a system, the obtrusiveness of government oversight can be minimized. Government regulators need not monitor private schools to ensure that they meet vague notions of appropriate civic education, impeding these schools' ability to distinguish themselves from the public sector. Instead, they need only to ensure that students can demonstrate competency in specific components of civic education identified by the province's elected representatives.

Any call for more testing is not likely to be greeted with enthusiasm by most American readers, given the growing prevalence of standardized testing in the United States. This proposal, however, is substantially different from a call for the typical testing regimen found in an American state. Admittedly, because of its normative overtones, civic education usually is not described as something that can be the subject of an exam, like chemistry or mathematics. To the contrary—only a systematic evaluation of those elements of civic education that enjoy broad public support can answer the critical question of whether students are being prepared to become engaged citizens. In fact, any understanding of schools' success in civics instruction has been thwarted precisely because of a reluctance to consider civic education worthy of rigorous, systematic evaluation.[27]

It is important to note that the type of examination system recommended here is not merely a matter of theory; it has been successfully implemented in a number of Canadian provinces, including Alberta, British Columbia, Manitoba, New Brunswick, Newfoundland, and Quebec. The model of greatest relevance, though, is found in the province of Alberta. While the other provinces have similar exams, Alberta is the only province that combines exams, a publicly funded Catholic system, and subsidies for private, including religious, schools. Alberta also has recently created charter schools based on the U.S. model, and the province is permissive regarding home schooling. In Alberta, all students in the province take the same exams, regardless of the type of school they attend—that is the critical feature of the system.

Alberta has what is known as a curriculum-based external exit examination system (CBEES). Unlike the testing typically found in American states, Alberta's exams do not determine simply whether students have achieved a minimal level of competence in math and reading.[28] Rather, they are comprehensive exams with a substantial written component, each on a specific subject. In the senior year of high school, the exam is worth 50 percent of a student's final grade in a course. Preparatory exams are administered in third, sixth, and ninth grades as well.[29] There is compelling evidence that academic achievement is higher in provinces with a CBEES than in those without, controlling for myriad other factors. An exam system like this also appears to equalize the quality of education across demographic groups.[30]

There are civic ramifications of both the quality and equity of education in all subjects, for as William Galston notes, "all education is civic education."[31] By that standard alone, a CBEES appears to enhance the civic dimension of a province's schools. This is a different matter, however, from that of whether an exam can adequately evaluate the components of the curriculum specifically designed to prepare students to be good citizens. The difficulty in answering that question lies in the very ambiguity of the term. What exactly *is* civic education? How can one judge, for example, whether religious schools are or are not fostering democratic values when there is no consensus on what those values are? Ontario's human rights commissioner contends that religious schools might lead to an apartheid-like system. Ann Bayefsky, the legal scholar who argued the case against Ontario's education system before the UNHRC, contends that private schools do just as well as their public counterparts in preparing students to be informed, engaged citizens.[32] Without some method of evaluating the civic content of students' education, these competing claims are simply unverifiable.

Alberta offers a compelling model for just such an evaluation, as one of its exams is in the subject of social studies—a sequence of courses specifically designed to prepare students to be active, engaged, and informed citizens. In the words of the provincial curriculum guide,

> The ultimate goal of social studies is responsible citizenship. The responsible citizen is one who is knowledgeable, purposeful and makes responsible choices. Basic to the goal of responsible citizenship is the development of critical thinking. The inquiry process, communication, participation, and technological skills are emphasized in order to foster critical thinking. . . . Citizenship education is based on an understanding of history, geography, economics, other social sciences and the humanities as they affect the Canadian community and the world. Current affairs add considerably to the relevance, interest and immediacy of the material and help to foster lifelong learning skills.[33]

In the curriculum guide for Alberta's Catholic school system, identical objectives are identified. They are supplemented, however, with a description of how the curriculum is shaped by Catholicism. For example: "In Catholic

schools, social studies encompasses a view of the person and society as perceived through the eyes of Christ and His Church. . . . It is recognized that
with the gift of free will, individual and communal choices are made. In many
instances our choices help build a better world, but in many other circumstances they lead to a breakdown in relationships, sometimes on a catastrophic
scale."[34] Under Alberta's system, no one in the province need question
whether the application of Catholic teachings to the social studies curriculum
inhibits the civic education of students in the Catholic schools. Those students are held to the same standards as students in private schools (which are
partially funded by the provincial government), students in publicly funded
charter schools, and students schooled at home. Most important, the curriculum guide is not merely "boilerplate"; the exams administered to determine
whether students have met state standards are rigorous.

One can certainly quibble over the specifics of Alberta's objectives for civic
education or over how they are evaluated in Alberta's exams. The key point,
however, is that there is something specific to quibble over. If another jurisdiction were to implement a system like Alberta's, the objectives of the civic
component of education might be defined differently. The critical aspect of
Alberta's system is that it has established a model to emulate by democrati-
cally choosing a particular set of standards and evaluating those standards in
a transparent way.

Critics of this proposal might raise objections over whether the substance
of civic education can be assessed by an exam. Is preparation for active citizenship not more than just the assimilation of information or the ability to
score well on an exam? One should be suspicious of any claims regarding
civic education—or any aspect of education, for that matter—that, by definition, cannot be systematically evaluated. Nonetheless, there is a legitimate
concern that civic education could become a matter of rote learning that is
regurgitated on a standardized test. To avoid this outcome, the design of the
exam is critical. A properly executed evaluation can determine whether students have mastered the critical skills necessary to become active, informed
citizens. A recent study on civic education in twenty-eight nations is instructive in this regard. The International Association for the Evaluation of Educational Achievement (IEA) has conducted a mammoth project to compare
the extent to which students across the globe are prepared for active citizenship. The study included input from researchers in many nations across different disciplines who developed an exam, not unlike Alberta's exam in social
studies, to evaluate the students.[35] Advocates of private and religious education may chafe at the requirement that their students take exams of this sort,
on the grounds that they represent a constraint on their curriculum. How-

ever, it seems reasonable to hold a school receiving public money accountable for maintaining public standards, especially in the area of civic education. Indeed, private schools should welcome the opportunity to demonstrate that they can successfully prepare their students for citizenship in a pluralistic democracy.

While not satisfying either completely, Alberta's system goes a long way toward accommodating the fundamental concerns of the two competing priorities in civic education. At their root, the two perspectives diverge on the issue of the nature of democratic control of the schools. Choice advocates envision a system in which the schools are largely freed from top-down control and government oversight. Defenders of a public-only system are concerned that allowing schools too much autonomy will mean that instruction will be at cross-purposes with widely embraced democratic values. In Alberta, there is considerable choice and a relatively unobtrusive method, subject to democratic oversight, of evaluating the civic consequences of the choices available.

As noted above, Alberta joins other Canadian provinces in providing funds for private schools. The funding arrangements differ slightly in each province, but the essentials are the same: private schools receive a per-pupil grant that is equal to a percentage of the mean per-pupil expenditure in the province's public schools. In Alberta, for example, it is 60 percent.[36] For the purposes at hand, the critical question is whether these independent schools are graduating students who are ill-prepared to function in a liberal democracy. Is public money being used to produce "bad" (or, perhaps, "less good") citizens? Only Alberta provides the means to answer that question, as it is the only province that evaluates the civic education provided by its private schools. The evidence suggests that they do as well as and perhaps a little better than their public and quasi-public (that is, Catholic) counterparts. According to test scores made available by Alberta's department of education, 88 percent of students in Alberta's private schools met the "acceptable" standard on the ninth-grade social studies exam, compared with 81 percent of secular public school students and 82 percent of Catholic school students. Twenty-six percent of private school students met the "standard of excellence," compared with 18 percent of public school students and 19 percent of students in the Catholic system. Students in other alternatives to the public schools also came out well. One hundred percent of home-schooled students met the acceptable standard, while 15 percent achieved excellence. Ninety-two percent of students in Alberta's charter schools had an acceptable score; 27 percent scored in the excellent range. While these results do not necessarily settle the question of whether private education leads to undemocratic attitudes, they would seem to put the onus on those who question the civic competence of students educated outside of the traditional public school.

Conclusion

The problem with discourse on the civic implications of school choice, whether in the United States or Canada, is the dearth of evidence on the subject. As a result, the conversation is riddled with unsubstantiated, hyperbolic claims about the consequences of transferring public money to private, particularly religious, schools. This situation should be familiar to anyone who has followed the issue of the impact of school choice on academic performance, as the debate regarding vouchers and civic education is where the debate on vouchers and academic performance was roughly a decade ago. In the past, the absence of empirical data led to extreme claims on both sides of the debate over academic performance. Over time, however, empirical evidence from participants in voucher programs has been gathered. While research is still under way, at this point there is nonetheless what Jay Greene describes as a "hidden consensus" among researchers studying the effects of school choice: multiple studies employing various methodologies to evaluate different voucher programs have concluded that vouchers lead to improved academic performance among minority, particularly African American, students.[37] To be sure, this research has not settled the debate over vouchers (and probably never will), but it does force both advocates and opponents of vouchers to reconcile their claims with the existing evidence. The proposal to implement an exam system to gauge the civic output of schools in both the public and private sectors has the potential to similarly inform the debate over the civic consequences of school choice.

If the skepticism expressed about the civic education provided by private schools is rooted in a genuine desire to see schools educate young people for engagement in a pluralistic democracy, then it seems logical for the skeptics to support some means of systematically evaluating young people's preparation for civic life. Either their skepticism will be borne out by the evidence, or it will show that private schools do just as well as public schools. Whatever the outcome, it will lead to greater understanding of what constitutes an effective civic education. Just as important, it would also provide a benchmark by which to measure the civic impact of any future education reform in either the public or private sector.

While the type of exam system proposed here would be something new for American education, it would not be totally unfamiliar. There already is a civics test that is administered periodically as part of the National Assessment of Educational Progress (NAEP), the only large-scale civics evaluation conducted in the United States. However, by design the NAEP test does not allow for comparisons across individuals or schools. Furthermore, the NAEP exam has been administered only roughly once a decade (in 1988 and 1999), and because of differences in the design of the exams, comparisons across years are difficult, if not impossible.

Besides allowing for monitoring of the civic impact of increased school choice, an additional positive outcome of evaluating civic education as proposed here is the renewed attention citizenship education would receive in all schools, public and private, religious and secular. John Bishop's research on the effects of curriculum-based testing indicates that it serves as an incentive for schools to prioritize the subjects in which students are examined. For example, in British Columbia, which does not have an exit exam in social studies, a recent provincial report concluded that civic education was in a "state of crisis," largely because social studies is shunted aside as a peripheral subject that does not require any particular expertise.[38] Similarly, a recent report by the Center for Information and Research on Civic Learning and Engagement and the Carnegie Corporation concludes that in the United States "school-based civic education is in decline."[39] With such limited attention paid to citizenship education, it is perhaps not surprising that the level of political engagement among young people in the United States is dismally low and declining.[40] Taking citizenship training seriously has the potential to stem—and even reverse—the decline in political involvement among young people.

This proposal shares the general perspective of the "standards movement" in American education. Essentially, the standards movement is being asked to take civics seriously. Currently, it is a glaring omission among the subjects recommended for testing. However, a curriculum-based external exit exam system like Alberta's avoids a negative consequence of standardized testing as it is typically implemented in American states: the phenomenon disparaged as "teaching to the test." With rigorous, curriculum-based exams, "teaching to the test" is not a concern; rather, it is exactly what teachers would be expected to do. While the focus here has been on civic education, the same point applies to every subject. Indeed, existing research indicates that exams like these boost academic performance generally and equalize performance across race and class lines.[41] That alone is an outcome with positive consequences for civic life in America.

In conclusion, when we look to Canada for insight into the possible consequences of increased school choice, it is unrealistic to think that its educational institutions can be exported wholesale to the United States. Canada's constitutional legacy has shaped the relationship between church and school in Canada so that it is profoundly different from the relationship that exists in the United States, making it difficult to see how Canadian institutions could blossom in American soil. What *can* be exported, however, is the system of rigorous evaluation of educational outcomes pioneered by the province of Alberta.

Notes

1. "Schools That Divide," editorial, *Toronto Star,* July 7, 2002, p. A12.

2. *Zelman, Superintendent of Public Instruction of Ohio, et al.* v. *Simmons-Harris et al.,* 536 U.S. 639 (2002).

3. William Robson and Claudia Hepburn, *Learning from Success: What Americans Can Learn from School Choice in Canada* (Indianapolis: Milton and Rose D. Friedman Foundation and the Fraser Institute, 2002), p. 1.

4. Marvin Olasky, "Canada's Experience Shows That School Choice Works," July 30, 2002 (www.townhall.com/columnists/marvinolasky/mo20020730.shtml [May 10, 2004]).

5. Robson and Hepburn, *Learning from Success,* p. 2.

6. *Aguilar* v. *Fenton*, 473 U.S. 402 (1985); *Agostini et al.* v. *Felton et al.*, U.S. 521 U.S. 203 (1997).

7. Eamonn Callan, "Discrimination and Religious Schooling," in Will Kymlicka and Wayne Norman, eds., *Citizenship in Diverse Societies* (Oxford University Press, 2000), p. 47.

8. In fact, publicly funded Catholic school systems are often officially designated as "separate" systems.

9. Alan M. Sears, Gerald M. Clarke, and Andrew S. Hughes, "Canadian Citizenship Education: The Pluralist Ideal and Citizenship Education for a Post-Modern State," in Judith Torney-Purta, John Schwille, and Jo-Ann Amadeo, eds., *Civic Education across Countries: Twenty-Four National Case Studies from the IEA Civic Education Project* (Amsterdam: International Association for the Evaluation of Educational Achievement, 1999), p. 128.

10. British Columbia Ministry of Education, *Diversity in B.C. Schools: A Framework* (Victoria, B.C.: 2001), p. 7.

11. Ibid.

12. Sears, Clark, and Hughes, "Canadian Citizenship Education," p. 118.

13. Stephen Macedo, *Diversity and Distrust: Civic Education in a Multicultural Society* (Harvard University Press, 2000).

14. Gary Hatcher, senior director, School Services and Facilities, Newfoundland Department of Education, telephone interview with author, March 11, 2003.

15. Because this particular amendment applies to Newfoundland exclusively, it requires only the approval of the two chambers in Parliament, the House of Commons and the Senate.

16. Terry M. Moe, "The Two Democratic Purposes of Education," in Lorraine M. McDonnell, P. Michael Timpane, and Roger Benjamin, eds., *Rediscovering the Democratic Purposes of Education* (University Press of Kansas, 2000), p. 144.

17. Amy Gutmann, *Democratic Education*, 2nd ed. (Princeton University Press, 1999); "Why Should Schools Care about Civic Education?" in McDonnell, Timpane, and Benjamin, *Rediscovering the Democratic Purposes of Education*.

18. Gutmann, "Why Should Schools Care about Civic Education?" p. 78. Regardless of their religious affiliation, parents could vote in the school board elections of any school their children attended.

19. Quebec Ministry of Education, *Quebec's Public Schools: Responding to the Diversity of Moral and Religious Expectations* (Montreal: 2000), p. 7.

20. Actually, the exceptions are a little more complex. To be educated in English, students must have parents who were educated in English, in Canada; have a sibling who received most of his or her elementary education in English within Canada; have been educated themselves in English, in Canada; or have parents who attended school after 1977 in Quebec and could have been declared eligible to be educated in English.

21. Note that Quebec's policy of compulsory French education is qualitatively different from policy in the English-majority provinces that provide French schools. There, parents decide on the language of instruction for their children.

22. Quebec Task Force on the Place of Religion in Schools, *Religion in Secular Schools: A New Perspective for Quebec* (Montreal: Quebec Ministry of Education, 1999), ch. 4.

23. Gutmann, *Democratic Education*, p. 33.

24. At its maximum, the tax credit will equal 50 percent of the cost of tuition, with a ceiling of $3,500 (Canadian). The credit is to be phased in gradually, starting at 10 percent and increasing in 10 percentage point increments annually.

25. *Adler et al.* v. *Ontario* [1996] 3 S.C.R. 609 (Canadian Supreme Court).

26. Ontario Human Rights Commission, "Private School Tax Credit" (www.ohrc.on.ca/english/publications/private-school-fact.shtml [May 10, 2004]).

27. Macedo, *Diversity and Distrust*.

28. John H. Bishop, "Nerd Harassment, Incentives, School Priorities, and Learning," in Susan E. Mayer and Paul E. Peterson, eds., *Earning and Learning: How Schools Matter* (Brookings, 1999).

29. Alberta's system actually entails three series of courses in social studies, with varying levels of academic rigor. Students decide which sequence to take.

30. John H. Bishop, "Privatizing Education: Lessons from Canada, Europe, and Asia," in C. Eugene Steuerle and others, eds., *Vouchers and the Provision of Public Services* (Brookings, 2000).

31. William A. Galston, "Political Knowledge, Political Engagement, and Civic Education," *Annual Review of Political Science*, vol. 4 (2001), pp. 217–34.

32. Ann Bayefsky, "Catholic Funding Is Unfair Discrimination," *Toronto Star*, September 24, 2000, p. 1.

33. Alberta Learning, *Curriculum Handbook for Parents: Senior High School* (Edmonton, Alberta: 2002).

34. Alberta Learning, *Curriculum Handbook for Parents: Senior High School*, Catholic School Version (Edmonton, Alberta: 2002).

35. Judith Torney-Purta, "The School's Role in Developing Civic Engagement: A Study of Adolescents in Twenty-Eight Countries," *Applied Developmental Science*, vol. 6, no. 4 (2002), pp. 203–12.

36. British Columbia is the only province that has two levels of grants, with greater regulation accompanying greater funding. Schools at the first level of funding receive 50 percent of the per-pupil operating costs of the local public district. At the second level, they receive 35 percent of the per-pupil costs.

37. Jay P. Greene, "The Hidden Research Consensus for School Choice," in Paul E. Peterson and David E. Campbell, eds., *Charters, Vouchers, and Public Education* (Brookings, 2001).

38. British Columbia Ministry of Education, *Diversity in B.C. Schools*.

39. Carnegie Corporation of New York and Center for Information and Research on Civic Learning and Engagement, *The Civic Mission of Schools* (College Park, Md.: 2003), p. 14.

40. Robert D. Putnam, *Bowling Alone: The Collapse and Revival of American Community* (Simon and Schuster, 2000).

41. Bishop, "Nerd Harassment" and "Privatizing Education."

8

School Choice and Civic Values in Germany

LUTZ R. REUTER

O ver most of its history, Germany has had a dual system of public and private educational institutions, though the emphasis of this system has shifted through the centuries. The history of institutionalized schooling in Germany began in the eighth century with the establishment of monastery and church schools. Five centuries later, municipalities first established "public" Latin schools, mostly following the educational pattern of the existing religious schools; thereafter, various kinds of public and private schools came into being. It was not until the Protestant Reformation, when monastery and church schools began to secularize, that any major changes in schooling took place, and in the 1600s, licensing of private schools began.

A coherent system of public schooling emerged a century later—in Prussia, for example, in 1717—with the introduction of compulsory education. A public school system no longer supervised by the church materialized gradually but spread widely after the adoption of the Prussian Land Law in 1794. Although traditional private schools continued to exist and new ones were established, particularly for girls and disadvantaged children, the requirements for obtaining private school licenses were tightened and non-licensed schools were phased out. The system, having become more formalized over the years, became official in the nineteenth century, when the framework for public and private schools was laid down in constitutional and school law.

Though the emphasis of the system has changed over the years, one fact has remained the same. At all times, the school system straddles the conflicting spheres of interest of three main players: government, parents, and society. The government's interest lies in developing the abilities of all members of society and in granting everyone equal opportunities in education. This allows citizens to succeed in their social and working lives and to integrate into society, and it ensures social cohesion by facilitating the transmission of the basic principles and values of democratic citizenship to the next generation. Parents, meanwhile, see their stake in education as a matter of natural right, the right to teach their children their own principles and values. They demand qualified schools but are anxious that schools might attempt to indoctrinate their children. Choice, therefore, is a primary constituent of parental rights. Finally, democratic society is inherently pluralistic—that is, composed of numerous groups that may differ with respect to culture, language, ethnicity, religion, values, and needs. Public schools must therefore teach tolerance and remain neutral regarding group interests.

Understanding each of these three areas—state responsibility, parental rights, and social pluralism—is central to understanding education under the German constitutional system. In order to analyze this triangle of interests, this chapter raises three central questions: first, what kind of options are available in the school system? Second, does school choice harm social cohesion? Third, how does the school system impart civic values to students under the existing system, and what kind of civic values does it impart? To answer these questions, the chapter first examines the fundamental principles on which the school system is based. In order to do so, it is necessary to clarify which school regulations are fixed in the constitutional and legal framework, what civic principles and educational objectives underlie that framework, and how those principles and objectives can be instantiated. The chapter then focuses on questions of school choice. The spectrum of options within the public school sector is described, both in terms of the structure of the school system as a whole and the broader political setting. Against this background, the chapter discusses the effects of school choice on social cohesion and the status of civic education.

For the purpose of making international comparisons, private sector choices will be studied more in detail, although for historical and constitutional reasons choices in this sector play a lesser role than choices in the public sector. The chapter focuses throughout on questions of legal standards, funding, and administrative regulation.

Fundamental Principles of Schooling

National and state constitutions and state education acts lay down certain basic principles of public and private schooling. Educational objectives such as fundamental personal, social, and civic values are determined by state school acts while subject-related goals are laid down in the school curriculum.

Constitutional and Legal Setting

Five concepts—democracy, republic, social state, federalism, and rule of law—underlie the basic guidelines for the German school system.[1] Education is a public responsibility under the primary administrative authority of regional and local governments, and it is open to everyone, free of charge. Parents participate in institutional decisionmaking, and the rights of the students are protected by the courts. The state's educational responsibilities are determined by the federal system. The exercise of government powers and the discharge of government functions are incumbent on the sixteen states (*Länder*) unless the Basic Law (*Grundgesetz*, the national constitution) indicates otherwise (articles 30 and 70 and following). Within the education system, only a few legislative powers remain at the national level. The right of the *Länder* to legislate applies to preschool education, primary education, higher education, and adult and continuing education; with the exception of private educational institutions, administration of education is exclusively a matter for the regional governments. Schools are owned by municipalities and counties; specialized vocational or professional schools may be run by *Länder* governments. Municipalities bear responsibility for school development, funding, and the transportation of pupils. The responsibilities of the federal government as defined by the Constitution include child and youth welfare, legal aspects of distance learning, in-company vocational training and vocational further education, framework legislation for higher education, regulations regarding educational and training grants, promotion of research, regulations for entry into the legal and medical professions, professional education and training as employment promotion measures, and, finally, pay and pensions for civil servants, including teachers and university staff. With the exception of some schools in Bavaria, the municipalities bear no responsibility for hiring teachers or for curriculum development.

Schooling in Germany is compulsory, and compulsory schooling is permitted under the Constitution because social integration, or social cohesion, is understood to be the core function of the school system. Consequently, home schooling for religious or other reasons is not permitted; exceptions are allowed only for medical reasons.[2] Compulsory schooling begins at the age of five or six, although children under school age may be admitted. Schooling lasts full-time for either nine years (in ten states) or ten years (in six states); an additional two to three years of part-time vocational schooling is required for youths who do not attend a three-year, full-time general education program or at least a two-year, full-time vocational program at the upper secondary level. This part-time vocational schooling involves training in a recognized occupation with formal in-company training.

Public schools are responsible not only for transmitting knowledge to students but also for educating them; the state's educational goals are considered equivalent to parents' rights.[3] Legislation has set general educational targets that are grounded on basic constitutional rights, principles, and values. Religious instruction on a denominational basis is an ordinary subject of the public school curriculum in most *Länder*, but attendance is voluntary. Two *Länder* (Bremen and Brandenburg) offer nondenominational instruction on major world religions, and one *Land* (Berlin) allows religious groups to hold denominational classes in public schools outside official lessons. School curricula on denominational instruction must be "in accordance with the tenets of the religious communities" and are drafted by the school authorities in agreement with representatives of the respective religious groups (article 7, section 2). These curricula are creed based, but as "ordinary subjects" they must reflect the basic values of the Constitution. They include a broad range of philosophical ideas and humanist values, and consequently, several *Länder* require students who do not participate in religious instruction to take substitute classes in ethics or philosophy.[4]

The constitutional provision for religious instruction in public schools essentially permits different denominations to offer such instruction or not. Some religious groups have chosen not to do so. For instance, Jewish instruction is not available at public schools since the Jewish community, which enjoys the same legal status as the Christian community, has not asked the state for it.[5] Classes are available for Catholic, Protestant, Russian and Greek Orthodox, and, most recently, for Muslim students.[6] General arrangements on voluntary religious instruction, including the curricula, are made between the regional government and the respective religious group. When parents of different religious denominations request religious instruction in the local school, separate classes will be taught simultaneously, for example for Catholic, Muslim, and Protestant pupils.

National and *Länder* constitutions, state acts, statutory instruments on public and private schooling, and precedents of regional and federal courts constitute the legal platform of the school system. The Basic Law does not provide a general framework for education; it establishes only general standards for state legislation (article 28, sections1–3) and provides little specific guidance on education. Included are statements on the comprehensive authority of the *Länder* to supervise the schools (article 7, section 1); the educational rights of the parents (article 6, section 2; article 7, section 2); equality before the law and prohibition of discrimination (article 3, sections 1 and 3); basic provisions regarding private schooling (article 7, sections 4 and 5); freedom of faith and creed (article 4); freedom of teaching and research (article 5, section 3); and freedom to choose an occupation or profession (article 12, section 1).

Civic Values and Educational Objectives

Traditionally, German public schools were based on clear-cut religious beliefs ("confessions"). This tradition is reflected in article 7, section 5, of the national constitution, which authorizes *Länder* or municipal authorities to establish public confessional (denominational) schools (*Konfessionsschulen*) upon the application of parents.[7] But, of course, the old situation, in which regions tended to be dominated by one Christian denomination, either Catholic or Protestant, is not the current situation. As a result of the great waves of immigration in the last century, the old status quo was overwhelmed by increasing religious pluralism and secularization. Today, nationwide, 21.8 percent of fifteen-year-old students have a foreign background—that is, at least one parent was born abroad.[8] As a result of this shift, denominational public schools have faded in significance, replaced mostly in the 1960s by nondenominational Christian schools. The official legal provision allowing the creation of confessional schools was intended to pacify the Catholic Church, which wanted to have a hand in public schooling but remained unsuccessful in halting the trend toward an educational climate in public schools that was pluralistic, nonreligious, and often indifferent to religious issues.[9]

In reaction to secularization, religious and ethnic pluralism, and decreasing parental influence in education, politicians and the public at large revived the conviction that state schools have a genuine responsibility not only to transmit knowledge, but also to educate—to teach ideas, norms, and values—whether in liberal arts, social studies, or religious instruction or ethics as its substitute.[10] Exactly what the substance of those values should be, however, has not been a matter for easy agreement. One of the fiercest constitutional conflicts in recent educational politics, for example, revolved around the Life-Formation, Ethics and Religious Knowledge program in the widely secular, eastern state of Brandenburg. Surprisingly, the litigation was not about the religious topics in the curriculum, but the churches' worry that the "substitute" courses might replace confessional instruction.[11]

The Basic Law itself has no express educational goals but provides for a framework of fundamental obligations and civic values the schools are supposed to transmit. This framework includes the first nineteen articles of the Constitution on Human Rights and Civil Liberties, such as human dignity (article 1), the right to free development of the personality (article 2), the freedoms of faith, conscience, and creed (article 4), the freedoms of information and speech (article 5), the freedoms of assembly, association, and movement (articles 8, 9 and 11), and equality before the law (article 3); it also applies to the basic principles of republican, democratic, social, and federal order and the rule of law (article 20, section 1, and article 28, section 1).

Finally, as already mentioned, compulsory schooling is constitutional only because of its integrative function. Most of the sixteen *Länder* constitutions and school acts include provisions on fundamental "educational goals." On the basis of the democratic and rule-of-law principles, everything important to the constitutional rights of a student must be regulated by law; this includes, among other things, certificates, sanctions, and fundamental educational objectives. The school acts cover a broad range of educational principles and values related to Western religious and philosophical ideas, values, and customs; the international community of nations; politics; economics; society, communes, and social groups; the family; and individual attitudes and virtues. They include, to mention a few, respect for God;[12] religious, political and social tolerance; (Christian) charity; patriotism; willingness to help and to serve in public office; social reliability; responsibility toward oneself, family, and society; openness to the interests and needs of minorities; responsibility for nature; love of peace; and international responsibility.[13] Because of the variations in curricula among the regional authorities, the Conference of State Education Ministers (KMK) has agreed on a common set of nine fundamental educational objectives for schooling:

—to transmit knowledge, readiness, and skills

—to develop independent critical judgment, responsible action, and creative activity

—to educate for freedom and democracy

—to educate for tolerance, esteem for the dignity of other people, and respect for others' convictions

—to develop a peaceful attitude and a spirit of understanding among peoples

—to ensure understanding of ethical norms and cultural and religious values

—to develop readiness for social action and political responsibility
—to enable students' acceptance of their rights and duties in society
—to provide an orientation on the demands of work life.[14]

These fundamental educational objectives affect schooling on different levels and in many ways. They serve as guidelines for curriculum construction, and they bind members of curriculum commissions and education ministers, who approve curricula and textbooks. Textbooks produced by private publishers have to comply with the appropriate subject curricula, and only when they correspond with the curricula are they included by the ministers on a list of admitted textbooks, from which schools and teachers choose. Framework curricula include general and subject-specific educational objectives and content regulations; as a rule, the former are binding; the latter give teachers latitude to choose. In general, educational objectives are final guidelines for teaching, but they may function as sanctions to make sure that the teaching staff pursues the fundamental goals.[15]

Civic values are embedded throughout the curriculum. They are taught explicitly in subjects like social studies, civic education, and history; they appear also in religious instruction or its substitutes, philosophy and ethics. Certain "cross-section" topics—such as health, law, and environmental education—which are taught in various subjects, are particularly important for transmitting civic values. Some KMK issuances and *Länder* curricula specify objectives and content along these lines, emphasizing intercultural education and "one-world/third-world" education (a cross-section topic area in which civic values are taught with respect to the third world and now to all other countries) to prepare students for life in a multicultural social environment, both national and global.[16] Students are assessed through oral exams, written tests, and course work. The grading system also applies to subjects like social studies, religious instruction, and ethics, and grades play a role in determining whether students move up or down. But this does not guarantee, of course, that students are developing healthy civic attitudes; unquestionably, assessing civic attitudes is less feasible than testing knowledge about good citizenship and democratic politics.

Public Schooling

As mentioned above, because Germany is a federal republic, there are sixteen different education systems within the nation.[17] A certain measure of uniformity and coordination is provided by the KMK, which, among other things, has set common standards for types of schools, compulsory schooling, duration of schooling, examinations, and degrees.[18] All the education systems share an age-distribution scheme. Schools are grouped into preschool institutions (under age five), primary schools (ages six to ten), lower and upper secondary schools (ages ten to fifteen and fifteen to nineteen), tertiary education institutions, and continuing adult education institutions (figure 8-1).

Structure of the School System

Elementary education is provided by crèches, day care institutions, kindergartens, and preschools, which are either publicly or privately owned. Preschool attendance is voluntary, except for children of school age who are not yet ready to go to school or who have below-average German language skills. Primary education is provided by primary schools (*Grundschule*), which cover either first through fourth grades (as in fourteen *Länder*) or first through sixth grades (as in Berlin and Brandenburg).

The lower secondary stage of education (fifth through tenth grades) is "tripartite," split into basically three types or levels of schools that differ in academic program, student achievement level, duration, and diploma. In a five-year program (fifth through ninth grade with an optional tenth year), the lower level of lower secondary school (*Hauptschule*) enrolls 20.8 percent of lower secondary school pupils. It covers the minimum requirement for compulsory schooling, and the diploma allows admission to vocational or technical education and training without excluding access to academic education. The middle level of lower secondary school (*Realschule*) enrolls 23.8 percent of lower secondary school pupils; it covers six years of general education and allows access to either vocational/technical or academic programs. The upper level of lower secondary schools (*Gymnasium*) also covers five to six years; it enrolls 30.2 percent of lower secondary school pupils. The subject requirements are the most stringent and include two foreign languages. Apart from these three tracks, almost all *Länder* have comprehensive schools (*Gesamtschulen*, fifth through tenth grades), although in some they have a fairly low number of pupils (9.5 percent of students overall). Several *Länder* have introduced new types of lower secondary schools that combine or integrate the lower and middle levels of lower secondary schools (15.7 percent of students).[19]

The upper secondary stage (grades 11 through 13 or 14) offers a wide range of part-time and full-time academic, vocational/technical, and comprehensive courses. Besides educational establishments that are available only regionally, all *Länder* offer four different options:

—full-time general education in three- to four-year schools (upper stage of *Gymnasium* or *Gesamtschule*), which allows unrestricted access to all establishments of higher education

Figure 8-1. *Education System of Germany*

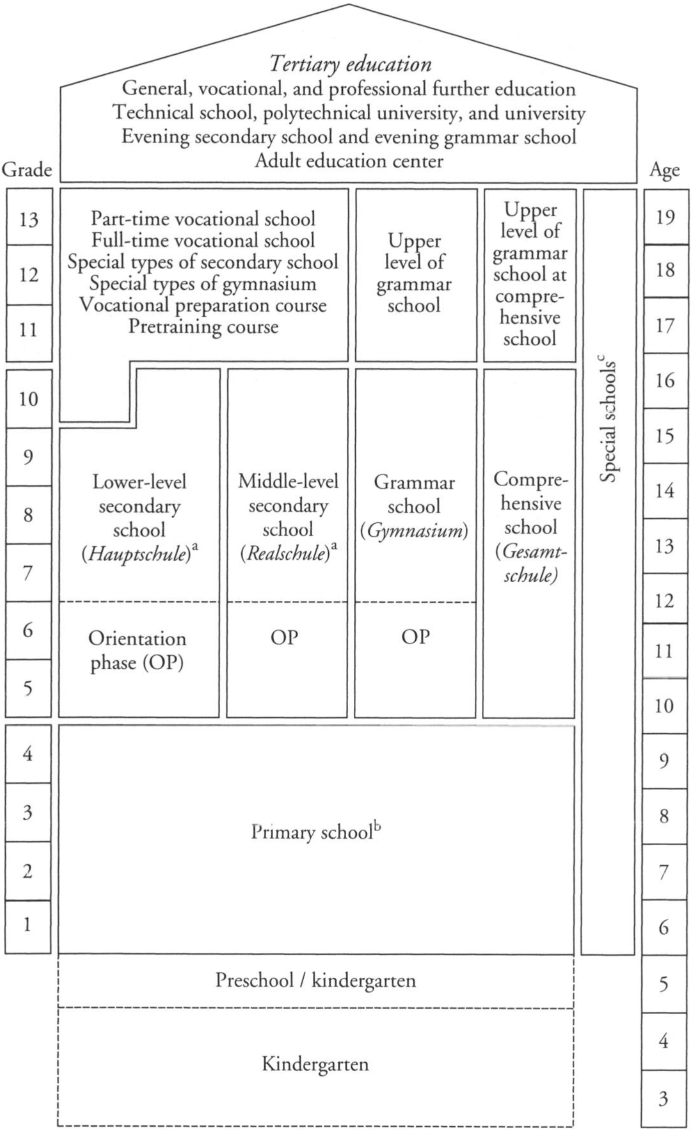

a. In some *Länder*, a branch of the integrated secondary school.
b. Six-year primary school in Berlin and Brandenburg.
c. Different types of general and vocational schools for pupils with special needs.

—two-year schools (*Fachoberschulen*), which combine general and technical education and prepare students primarily for polytechnical universities
— three-year, part-time vocational schools (*Berufsschulen*) combined with
company-based training
—one- to five-year, full-time vocational/technical schools (*Berufsfach-
schule, Fachschule*).[20]

School Choice

The Basic Law stipulates the primacy of public schools, but it recognizes
individual school choice as a constitutional right (article 6, section 2). Consequently, all *Länder* constitutions and school acts allow parents to choose
among different options in schooling, whether between public and private
schools or among schools within the public sector. Choices within the public
sector play by far a greater role than those within the private sector.

At the primary education level, parents have no legal right to choose a particular public school; they have to enroll their children at the school within
their home school district, and they may apply for a primary school outside
the district only for significant reasons. Still, parents are able to circumvent
this provision by applying for a second legal residence for their child with rel-
atives outside the district. This kind of choice is illegal, and it is practiced
only by small numbers of middle-class parents; socially viewed with indiffer-
ence, it is possible only in populated areas with several primary schools. The
motives for doing this vary: parents may want to avoid enrollment in a
school with a high number of immigrant pupils, enroll at a school with a better reputation, or find a primary school with lower standards in order to
increase the likelihood that their child will avoid being recommended for
placement in a lower- or middle-level lower secondary school. School district
regulations are established to ensure short walking distances to school, but
these policies have, at least in bigger towns and cities, certain segregating
effects based on class.

At the secondary level, parents may choose among the different levels of
public schools, depending on the abilities and achievement of their child.
Parents also may choose among different schools of the same type or level. In
most *Länder*, geographical school districts still exist not only for elementary
but also for lower-level lower secondary schools (*Hauptschulen*), but for
important reasons (for example, physical disability) access to a public school
outside the district is not a problem. In most *Länder*, geographical school districts do not exist for middle- and upper-level lower secondary schools.[21] The
choice of an out-of-state school is possible, but this sometimes depends on
interstate financial agreements. Some *Länder* (for example, North Rhine–

Westfalia, Bavaria) allow parents to choose between public interdenominational Christian common schools (*Christliche Gemeinschaftsschulen*) and public denominational schools or denominational classes within a public nondenominational school. Finally, parents can elect to have their children take extra classes in different subjects, such as additional foreign languages or native language classes for immigrant children.

Another aspect of school choice is related to the variations in secondary schools, particularly of the upper-level lower secondary school (*Gymnasium*). Academic programs—in classical or modern languages, mathematics and science, music and arts, economics, and social sciences—have always played a significant role. In some *Länder*, variations among school programs have been limited since the 1970s in order to facilitate school change and to ensure comparable standards, but the major program variations, depending on the *Land*, are still available. And since the 1990s, schools have had to develop individual school programs, which have fostered a growing variety of public schools (for example, UNESCO schools and Europe schools, whose programs focus on UNESCO objectives or European topics; bilingual schools; and schools focused on arts or sports). Besides traditional decision-making factors like geographic proximity and academic mission, school performance and prestige influence school choice, particularly among middle- and upper-class parents.

The traditional self-segregating effect of school choice within the tripartite public system disappeared after the 1970s when blue-collar workers stopped enrolling their children at the *Hauptschule*; there is no longer a significant psychological distance between upper-level lower secondary schools and everything below them. But while educational aspirations among poor and working-class parents, including immigrants, are relatively high, the representation of lower-class and immigrant students in upper-level schools is far below average. About 52 percent of middle- and upper-class students are enrolled in upper-level and 13 percent in lower-level secondary schools, compared with 11 percent of students with an unskilled-worker family background in upper-level and 41 percent in lower-level secondary schools.[22] The tripartite system, which is supposed to offer pupils an education appropriate to their level of ability and performance, still contributes to reinforcing social class distinctions. This finding, although not new, has been rejected by the conservative political parties.[23] They refer to recent German survey data for Bavaria's strict tripartite system, which correspond to the high results of Sweden's comprehensive system, while the data for Bremen's mostly comprehensive system are the worst in the country.[24]

In contrast to most European countries, where the traditional multitrack systems were replaced by comprehensive school systems, in Germany the attempt to switch along these lines failed during the 1970s, despite the efforts of the Social Democrats. That communist East Germany had a system of comprehensive "uniform polytechnical schools" allowed the Christian Democrats in West Germany to denounce comprehensive school systems altogether as purveyors of "socialist egalitarianism." Meanwhile, conservative parent groups, supported by constitutional lawyers, claimed that parents were entitled not only to a choice between public and private schools, but also to a choice of public secondary schools. The same groups, pushing for the preservation of multitrack schools, even fought the introduction of an integrated "orientation phase" for fifth and sixth graders. The groups received support from the courts when the Federal Constitutional Court ruled in the *Hesse* case that parents had the constitutional right to choose among different educational tracks. Although the court allowed the establishment of the integrated school in fifth and sixth grades and avoided any obiter dictum about the constitutionality of a fully unified school system,[25] it observed that parents would have no choice if there were only one form of compulsory school.[26] Since then, constitutional lawyers have argued that only a comprehensive system offering different course levels in lower secondary schools would be constitutional.[27]

Private Schooling

Private schools offer different religious, philosophical, societal, or pedagogical concepts of education; these include Catholic, Protestant, Jewish, or Muslim schools and Waldorf, Hermann-Lietz, or Montessori schools, among others. Private schools address certain special pedagogical interests of parents and the educational needs of national or ethnic minority groups (Danish and Greek schools, for example); they also serve those parents who for some reason want or need boarding schools.

Private school associations prefer the term "free school," which denotes independence. But this wording is not quite accurate since the entire school system—and all private schooling—is subject to state supervision.[28] In international terms, most German private schools are not independent schools because they are bound, one could even say subordinate, to the public school system that they are supposed to serve. This role is clearly addressed in article 90 of the Bavarian School Act: "Private schools serve to complete and enhance the state system. Subject to the law, they enjoy freedom of choice with regard to educational, religious, or ideological inclinations, methods of teaching and education, subject matter, and forms of organization." The

Länder school law and policy documents adhere to this "justification" for private schooling; choice between public and private educational programs and institutions, as the Conference of State Education Ministers kindly puts it, "promotes competition and innovation in education."[29] In fact, private schools lay at the center of the Reform Pedagogy movement between 1880 and 1930, but despite this and the postwar ascription that they are "competitive and innovative" institutions, they are primarily perceived by educational authorities and the public as "particular," serving only a certain segment of the population and not challenging the public school system as a whole. This is clearly reflected in constitutional and private school law and also in statistical data: German private schools are middle-class institutions.

Privately owned schools exist at all levels of education. To a greater extent, they are available at the preschool, vocational, and professional education levels; to a smaller extent in secondary and higher education; and to a very small extent in primary education. Of a total of 12.6 million pupils at public primary and secondary general and vocational schools, 739,200, or 5.8 percent, attended nearly 4,100 private schools in 2000. In absolute figures, there has been a continuous increase of pupils in private schools since 1960 (1960: 277,000 [3.3 percent]; 1970: 407,400 [3.6 percent]; 1980: 546,000 [4.6 percent]; 1990: 539,000 [5.9 percent]; 1999: 545,500 [5.1 percent]). The decrease in percentage from 1990 to 1999 is due to the fact that East Germany under communism had nearly no private schools, and the share of pupils at private schools in the east is still significantly below the western standard.[30] At 8.9 percent, the proportion of pupils attending private schools was highest in Bavaria.[31] Figures differ significantly when one distinguishes among the different types of schools. The percentage of pupils at private primary schools was 1.2 percent; at lower-level secondary schools, 1.9 percent; and at medium- and upper-level schools, 7.5 percent and 10.5 percent, respectively. Private full-time secondary vocational schools and professional schools enrolled 17.9 percent and 34.1 percent of students at those levels, respectively.[32]

Legal Framework and Funding

Under constitutional law, the right to establish private schools is an individual right and the existence of private schools as an institution is guaranteed. Individuals have a constitutional right to establish and operate private schools, and the *Länder* have to ensure the existence and foster the development of private schools as an institution; therefore, for example, a private school may replace an existing public school. Freedoms in private schooling include the right to found and maintain a school, to establish its mission, to design the curriculum, and to select teachers and pupils. Correspondingly, the right to teach and to enroll at a private school is guaranteed.[33]

Sources of German private school law are the constitutions of the *Länder*, school acts, and statutory orders. But the general standard for private schooling is laid down in article 7, sections 4-5, of the Basic Law. Its five principles are as follows:

—The right to establish private schools is guaranteed.

—Private schools as a substitute for, or alternative to, public schools shall require the approval of the state and shall be subject to the laws of the *Länder*.

—Approval of private schools must be given when they are not inferior to public schools in terms of their educational aims, facilities, and the professional training of their teaching staff and when segregation of pupils according to the means of the parents is not thereby promoted.

—Approval of private schools must be withheld if the economic and legal position of the teaching staff is not sufficiently ensured.

—A private elementary school[34] shall be approved only if the educational authority finds that it serves a special pedagogical interest, or if, on the application of parents or guardians, it is to be established as a denominational or interdenominational school or as a school based on a particular philosophy and no public elementary school of that type exists in the municipality.

On the basis of this standard framework, the *Länder* education ministers adopted an agreement on private schools in 1951 specifying the constitutional requirements.[35] Consequently, the private *Länder* school laws are widely uniform; this applies particularly to the legal requirements for licensing private substitute schools.

There are, however, significant differences across Germany with respect to the regulation of public funding for private schools. There is no explicit provision for public funding under constitutional law. Instead, following Federal Constitutional Court precedents, the right to establish private schools and the prohibition against segregating children by the economic status of their parents require the *Länder* "to protect and to support private substitute schools," but the states must act only if the existence of substitute private schools as an institution is otherwise in danger.[36] In contrast to the Federal Administrative Court, the Federal Constitutional Court avoids recognizing a constitutional right to state funding.[37] Generally speaking, the condition for public funding of a private school is a means test; therefore only nonprofit schools may be subsidized. Due to the lack of federal regulation, *Länder* funding conditions differ widely. Some *Länder* subsidize all substitute schools;[38] some support only recognized substitute schools[39] and require a "special pedagogical profile"; and some give voluntary payments to complementary schools (described below).[40] Most *Länder* have introduced two- to three-year—and in two cases, six-year—waiting periods before public subsidies are paid.[41] The idea behind this "seriousness test" is that state governments want to force private schools to look for matching funds from private donors.

The percentage of costs for private schooling covered by the respective *Land* differs widely; as a rule, private substitute schools are entitled by school law to receive a general allowance for the annual expenses for salaries, teaching materials, and school maintenance, either at a data-based, flat-rate approach (for example, Bavaria) or on a proved deficit basis (for example, North Rhine–Westphalia). Depending on the *Land* and the type of primary or secondary school, the substitute schools may receive as much as 60 percent and even up to 100 percent of the amount that public schools spend per student on staff or general costs; schools for handicapped children, denominational schools, or schools with a special educational profile may get a higher percentage of their costs covered than do other substitute schools.[42] In addition, most *Länder* provide cost-free schoolbooks or reimburse schools for expenses for books and student transportation services; some transfer state-employed teachers to substitute schools, with the assent of both teacher and private school; cover pension contributions; or even reimburse salary expenses. Finally, private nonprofit schools enjoy tax benefits.[43]

Regulatory Framework: Admission and Control

Basically, one has to distinguish between two types of private schools: "substitute" or "alternative" schools (*Ersatzschulen*) and "complementary" schools (*Ergänzungsschulen*). The former correspond to the existing state-run schools; they serve as substitutes for existing public establishments and fulfill compulsory school attendance requirements. The latter offer programs and degrees that have no equivalent in the public system, which they complement. A substitute school owner is required to apply for approval to the school authority, which is bound to the aforementioned constitutional conditions, which are enforced by the legal and administrative provisions of the *Länder*. Owners of complementary schools, on the other hand, have to comply only with general law requirements such as those pertaining to safety standards, the suitability of facilities, and the reliability of owners and management staff. In international terms, substitute schools are private dependent schools and complementary schools are private independent schools.

The approval of a substitute school is granted on the condition that it is not inferior to the corresponding type of public school. Five major criteria apply:

—*Equivalence of educational aims.* Private schools must observe the basic constitutional principles, civic values, general educational goals, and general subject structure laid down in constitutional and school law, and they must fulfill the overall standards of the given type of public school, including those pertaining to promotion, examination, and certification. However, strict adherence to public school curricula, teaching hours, schoolbooks, or teaching methods is not required.

—*Equivalence of facilities.* The standards for public schools apply to substitute schools with respect to buildings, equipment, teacher-student ratio, maximum number of students per class, and vacations; however, exceptions may be tolerated. Differences are permitted with respect to school organization, management, and parent and student participatory rights.

—*Equivalence of teacher training.* Teachers must have an academic education and a teaching certificate that comply with the standards for public teacher education and training. Since comprehensive private teacher training facilities are not yet available, nearly all substitute school teachers have passed at least the first academic stage of public teacher education.

—*Economic and legal security of teaching staff.* Working conditions, including salaries, job security, and teaching load, need not be the same as in public schools, but the position of substitute school teachers must not be significantly worse. A contract of employment must cover duties, conditions for dismissal and resignation, salary, vacation, and retirement benefits.

—*No socioeconomic segregation of pupils.* School fees may be charged, but they must be socially equitable. Private schools may select their pupils freely, but segregation according to the financial means of parents is prohibited. Fees therefore must be moderate or fee-reduction regulations for low-income parents must apply; offering a limited number of stipends or scholarships does not satisfy this requirement.

Since basic compulsory education is under closer control of the school authorities than the intermediate and upper tracks, private schools are the exception at that level; they may be established only under very strict conditions. Private primary and lower-level secondary schools may be established only as denominational or ideological schools when public schools of that type do not exist or when the school authorities find that they serve "a special pedagogical interest" (article 7, section 5, of the Basic Law). This provision, which goes back to the Primary School Act of 1920, sticks to the democratic-egalitarian denial of social differentiation, whether related to income, rank, status, or social class, and it is relevant today for primary schools. An exception to the school-for-all principle requires, as the Federal Constitutional Court puts it, "a reasonable alternative to public and already existing private schools which enriches pedagogical experiences and supports the development of the school system."[44] The pedagogical concept does not have to be new or unique; it is sufficient when an existing pedagogical concept is combined with a serious new approach.[45] But a claim that an approach has special pedagogical value will be recognized only when it outweighs the general priority of the public primary school. A denial may be subject to judicial review, but a certain freedom of decisionmaking remains with the state school authority.[46] The admission of new primary schools is the main focus of litigation in private schooling; in numerous cases private school initiatives have tried to break the almost monopolistic position of public primary schools.[47] But while the courts were willing to narrow the discretionary powers of the educational authorities, it remains that all supreme, administrative, and constitutional courts, both in the *Länder* and at the federal level, keep a firm hold on the constitutional provision that the state shall have the final say on whether a new private school is in the public interest and should be admitted to the overall system.

Private schools are not created through contract but by virtue of application and approval. Once approved, they are supervised by the school authorities only insofar as the conditions of approval are concerned. Private schools have to inform state authorities, for example, about changes in the curriculum or the teaching staff insofar the changes might affect the civic purpose or overall pedagogical mission of the establishment. The authorities may impose compliance with basic educational objectives or dismissal of a non–academically trained teacher as a condition of continued approval. Principals and owners of private schools who infringe regulations or conditions can be sanctioned; in serious cases, the school may be closed.[48] In all *Länder* except North Rhine–Westphalia, state approval of a private substitute school does not include the right to award certificates and degrees corresponding to those of public schools. To receive valid diplomas, students have to pass an examination before a state examining board at a public school. Only through the act of official recognition are private schools entitled to hold examinations and to award certificates or degrees, and these have to comply with existing regulations. In some *Länder*, substitute schools can claim official recognition when the conditions for approval are met over a certain period of time; in others they must also comply with certain public school regulations, about curricula, for example. Consequently, the act of recognition extends public control over substitute schools.

Complementary private schools offer a variety of programs, including foreign languages as well as vocational and professional education; some do private tutoring. Complementary schools do not correspond to existing types of public schools; therefore their programs do not fulfill compulsory schooling requirements. School authorities, however, may exempt students from compulsory vocational schooling if they choose suitable alternative institutions and programs at complementary schools.

Private Schooling and the State: a Final Valuation

The current system is based on a set of fundamental principles. Schooling is understood to be a public good that serves the needs and interests of both individuals and society at large. In a democratic and social state, it is a primary task of the government to provide schools for all and to transform constitutional principles and values into binding general educational goals. Compulsory schooling, though it restricts certain parental prerogatives, is constitutional since social integration is the uppermost task of public schooling. Private schools are an exception to the primacy of public schooling; they serve particular interests and needs that are recognized and protected as basic human rights. The primacy of public schooling requires private schools to comply with certain minimum standards; among them is the condition that private school educational objectives and programs must observe fundamental constitutional values and principles, including democracy, human dignity and basic rights, equality, and tolerance. Since substitute schools are not allowed to charge financially segregating tuition fees, the *Länder* have to subsidize them.

By and large, the current system of public and private schooling seems to be accepted; there is no significant public discourse or political pressure to change it. It is surprising that when recent international school data were published, private schools were not able to reap the benefits of public frustration over the below-average quality of German lower secondary schooling. Private schools have seen a steady increase in public support, but there is no sign of a paradigm shift from public to private schools; all debates and reform measures focus on increasing the quality of the public system.[49] It appears that in the public at large, certain traditional social prejudices about private schools still linger, be they prejudices about socioeconomic elitism, ideological particularism, or the "cramming" nature of private schools—what is called "drill and kill" in the United States. But without question, there also is criticism—particularly, of course, among adherents and associations of private schools—about the precedence that the public sector takes over the private. This applies, for example, to the criteria that bind substitute schools to the standards of public schools and to the insufficient funding of private schools, which nevertheless serve the public interest. Insufficient funds may drive private schools to reduce services and thereby lose students or to charge higher fees and thereby endanger their approval. In fact, overall public support for private schooling declined over recent years because of general budget constraints.[50] As a consequence, private schools, caught between a rock and a hard place, can escape only by looking for private donors or asking for voluntary parent contributions.

There is an ongoing movement to remove the interpretation of article 7, section 1, of the Basic Law from its Prussian state-oriented context and to reassess the formula for "state supervision of the schools."[51] Courts and constitutional lawyers agree that private schools fulfill a public task and consequently are "public" schools in their own right. It is argued that the state should refrain from running schools altogether and instead fund schools of different ownership; according to proponents of this idea, such a system would allow parents to choose freely among different concepts of schooling.[52] The main counterargument in this debate, which is upheld by all major political parties[53] and the courts, is that parents have a constitutional right to public schooling that is primarily neutral toward different world views and bound to pluralistic educational values and subject content, while private schools are encouraged to be "alternative"—in other words, one-sided—with respect to philosophical concepts and values. Consequently, in the framework of existing German constitutional law, a system of exclusively private schools would serve neither the individual's right to a philosophically neutral education nor the public interest.

Conclusions

The German national constitution is based on values (human dignity, human rights and freedoms, equity, tolerance, nonviolence) and political concepts (republic, democracy, social state, federalism, rule of law) that are unalterable (article 79, section 3); these values and principles underlie fundamental educational aims that are to be achieved in school, either public or private. Every child and young person has a right to education, which is ensured through public schooling. Schooling is compulsory, and home schooling is not admitted since school education is meant to integrate all pupils into society regardless of sex, social class, language, ethnicity, or cultural background.

Constitutional law and school law enact and regulate school choice. All major schooling options have been available to all German students since 1949. School choice exists in the public and in the private sector, but it plays a bigger role in the former. The framework for regulating private schooling is integrated into the national constitution. The Constitution recognizes the individual's right to establish and maintain private schools; while it ensures plurality in education, it gives public schools priority over private schools. The constitutional regulation about private schooling in article 7, section 5, is clear, and there is no majority support for a constitutional amendment.

German private schools can be divided into private independent and private dependent schools. Private independent schools are so-called complementary schools, which are not subject to approval or to any kind of contractual regulation. They may be run for profit or as nonprofit institutions. Within the general legal framework, school owners are free to decide on the mission, goals, programs, standards, and certificates of complementary schools. They do not fulfill compulsory schooling requirements and may not award the certificates or degrees that public schools award. But school authorities are free to bestow certain rights on complementary schools and may support them financially; depending on the conditions of approval, state support may partly do away with the character of an independent school. Private dependent schools are so-called substitute or alternative schools, subject to approval by *Länder* school authorities. Conditions of approval require that substitute schools not be "inferior" to public schools in terms of educational aims and facilities or professional training and economic and legal position of the teaching staff. Substitute schools must teach the basic principles and values promulgated by the Constitution and the school act of the given state, and they must not segregate pupils according to parental income or property. Beyond these conditions, substitute schools may develop their own educational philosophies and profiles. Approved substitute schools may offer examinations and diplomas only when formally recognized. Recognition is awarded by *Länder* school authorities on the ground of various criteria, such as the length of time that the school has existed, a special pedagogical concept, or compliance with public school curricula. Substitute schools relieve the public school budgets of the financial burden of educating some children. Consequently, Federal Administrative Court and Federal Constitutional Court precedents require the partial financial support of substitute schools because their cost-related fees would tend to segregate pupils by the means of the parents, which is prohibited by the Constitution. Behind the state-oriented German concept of private schooling is a philosophical commitment to maintaining at least a minimum degree of equity, common citizenship, and social cohesion. Private substitute schools, despite their relatively moderate fees of up to €130 monthly, are more attractive—and more feasible financially—for middle-class than for low-income and immigrant parents.[54] In Germany, therefore, a school's shortcomings are less about value and content than about social cohesion; this fact is reflected in the international school data results from 2001 on reading skills and the socioeconomic index for students at private dependent schools.[55] Whether an extension of private schooling would change the de facto limited accessibility of private schools remains an open question.[56]

Whether the way in which private schools have been regulated is a success depends a great deal on one's viewpoint. The objectives and conditions laid down in article 7, section 4, of the Basic Law are mostly achieved; social segregation in private schools is widely avoided, except in the case of private boarding schools, which cost up to €3,000 a month for tuition, room, and board and consequently are accessible only to students from wealthy families and the lucky few who receive school scholarships. They can be regarded as constitutional only if one separates school from boarding facility and applies the conditions for approval only to the former. But one should not overlook the fact that social cohesion is not primarily a problem of private schooling. Social segregation is much more a structural problem of the tripartite, *public* school system and the way public schools deal with heterogeneity, and that is the system in which private schools must operate. As a consequence of tracking and ability streaming, low-achievement pupils and immigrant students are enrolled in the lowest level of public secondary schools.

The regulatory system of public-private schooling is a compromise, particularly of the state and the churches or other religious communities. It protects the state interest in sociocultural and political cohesion; it allows religious instruction in public schools and requires ethics lessons for students who opt out, underlining the status of religious instruction as an "ordinary subject." Religious communities are free to operate their own schools and, in some *Länder*, receive even more funding than secular substitute school owners. With the exception of tiny fundamentalist groups such as Adventists, which fight for home schooling, religious communities typically do not complain about the requirement for equivalence with the general educational aims of public schools.[57] Finally, substitute schools are under continuous supervision with respect to the conditions of approval and funding; therefore there is no doubt that pupils of compulsory school age at substitute schools receive an education that includes all elements essential to teaching good citizenship. But compared with policies in other countries, the German regulatory framework for private dependent schools can be labeled excessive, since constitutional law requires that they meet basic standards that limit the scope of private schooling.

Notes

1. Basic Law (*Grundgesetz*), article 20, section 1.

2. Recently confirmed by *Oberverwaltungsgericht* Lüneburg (Lower Saxony Administrative Court) in *Adventists* v. *State of Lower Saxony*, 13 LB 407 5/01.

3. *Proceedings of the Federal Constitutional Court* (BVerfGE), vol. 34 (1973), p. 165, at p. 185.

4. Federal Administrative Court (BVerwG), *Die Öffentliche Verwaltung (DOV)* , vol. 52 (1998), p. 1058.

5. See Beauftragte der Bundesregierung für Ausländerfragen, *Bericht der Beauftragten der Bundesregierung für Ausländerfragen über die Lage der Ausländer in der Bundesrepublik Deutschland* (Berlin, Bonn: Foreigners' Representative, 2000), pp. 233–34.

6. See Lutz R. Reuter, "Schulrecht für Schüler nichtdeutscher Erstsprache," *Zeitschrift für Ausländerrecht und Ausländerpolitik,* vol. 21 (2001), pp. 115–19; Lutz R. Reuter, "Gesetzesvorbehalt und Migration: Anforderungen an schulrechtliche Standards für zugewanderte Kinder und Jugendliche," *Recht der Jugend und des Bildungswesens*, vol. 51 (2003), pp. 23–26.

7. Public confessional schools were reestablished in predominantly Catholic Länder; despite their decline in numbers, they still exist in North Rhine–Westphalia and Rhineland-Palatinate; in Bavaria, denominational classes may be established in public primary schools.

8. Deutsches PISA-Konsortium, *PISA 2000: Die Länder der Bundesrepublik Deutschland im Vergleich* (Opladen: Leske and Budrich, 2002), p. 190.

9. Its constitutionality was confirmed by the Federal Constitutional Court in three major rulings: BVerfGE, vol. 41 (1976), p. 29.

10. *Proceedings of the Federal Constitutional Court* (BVerfGE), vol. 34 (1973), p. 165, at p. 183; Hermann Avenarius and Hans Heckel, *Schulrechtskunde* (Neuwied: Luchterhand, 2000), p. 84; Constitution of Bavaria, article 131, section 1.

11. See *Catholic Church and Protestant Church* v. *State of Brandenburg, Proceedings of the Federal Constitutional Court* (BVerfGE), vol. 104 (2002), pp. 305–10; Hermann Avenarius, "Value Orientation in German Schools," *Education and the Law*, vol. 14 (2002), pp. 86–87.

12. On the constitutionality of this "educational goal," see Bavarian Constitutional Court, Vf. 18-VII-86 (May 2, 1988).

13. See Michael Bothe and others, "Erziehungsauftrag und Erziehungsmaßstab der Schule im freiheitlichen Rechtsstaat," *Veröffentlichungen der Vereinigung der Deutschen Staatsrechtslehrer*, vol. 54 (1995), pp. 7–164; Charles Glenn, "Germany," in Charles Glenn and Jan Groof, eds., *Finding the Right Balance*, vol. 1, *Freedom, Autonomy and Accountability in* Education (Utrecht: Lemma, 2000); Lutz R. Reuter, "Erziehungs- und Bildungsziele aus rechtlicher Sicht," *Zeitschrift für Pädagogik*, supplement 47 (2003), pp. 28–48.

14. Ständige Konferenz der Kultusminister der Länder in der Bundesrepublik Deutschland [KMK], *Sammlung der Beschlüsse der Ständigen Konferenz der Kultusminister der Länder in der Bundesrepublik Deutschland*, vol. 3, no. 824 (Neuwied: Luchterhand, 2004).

15. See Reuter, "Erziehungs-und Bildungsziele," pp. 28–48; Avenarius and Heckel, *Schulrechtskunde*, p. 526.

16. See KMK agreements of 25 October 1996 (print) and 28 February 1997, in KMK, *Sammlung*, vol. 3, no. 571 (2004).

17. See Achim Leschinsky, "Der institutionelle Rahmen des Bildungswesens," in Kai S. Cortina and others, *Das Bildungswesen der Bundesrepublik Deutschland* (Reinbek: Rowohlt, 2004).

18. See Hamburg Agreement of 1964 (1971, 1999), in KMK, *Sammlung*, vol. 1, no. 101 (2004).

19. Calculated on the basis of data from Bundesministerium für Bildung und Forschung (BMBF), *Grund- und Strukturdaten 2000/2001* (Bonn, 2002), pp. 56–57.

20. See Martin Baethge, "Das berufliche Bildungswesen in Deutschland," in Cortina and others, *Das Bildungswesen*, pp. 342–90; Hans-Werner Fuchs and Lutz R. Reuter, *Bildungspolitik in Deutschland: Entwicklungen, Probleme, Reformbedarf* (Opladen: Leske and Budrich, 2000).

21. For details, see Avenarius and Heckel, *Schulrechtskunde*, pp. 84–85, 480–82.

22. Deutsches PISA-Konsortium, *PISA 2000: Basiskompetenzen von Schülerinnen und Schülern im internationalen Vergleich* (Opladen: Leske and Budrich, 2001), p. 355.

23. See Helmut Fend, *Gesamtschule im Vergleich* (Weinheim: Beltz, 1982).

24. See Deutsches PISA-Konsortium, *PISA 2000: Die Länder*.

25. *Proceedings of the Federal Constitutional Court* (BVerfGE), vol. 34 (1973), p. 165, at p. 187.

26. *Proceedings of the Federal Constitutional Court* (BVerfGE), vol. 45 (1978), p. 400, at p. 416; BVerfGE, vol. 96 (1998), p. 288, at p. 306.

27. Avenarius, "Value Orientation in German Schools," pp. 438–40.

28. Arbeitsgemeinschaft Freier Schulen, *Handbuch Freie Schulen: Pädagogische Positionen, Träger, Schulformen und Schulen im Überblick* (Reinbek: Rowohlt, 1999), pp. 29–62.

29. KMK, *Sammlung*, vol. 2, no. 484 (2004); Christoph Führ, *The German Education System since 1945: Outlines and Problems* (Bonn: Inter Nationes, 1997), p. 169; Johann P. Vogel, *Das Recht der Schulen und Heime in freier Trägerschaft* (Luchterhand, 1997), pp. 1–14.

30. BMBF, *Grund- und Strukturdaten*, pp. 18–19, 56–59, 70–71.

31. Ibid., pp. 24, 70–71.

32. Ibid., pp. 70–71; Eurydice, *Formen und Status des privaten und nichtstaatlichen Bildungswesens in den Mitgliedstaaten der Europäischen Gemeinschaft* (Brussels: Education Information Network of the European Community, 1992).

33. *Proceedings of the Federal Constitutional Court* (BVerfGE) vol. 6 (1957), p. 309, at p. 355; BVerfGE, vol. 27 (1970), p. 195, at p. 200ff.; BVerfGE, vol. 90 (1994), p. 107, at p. 114.

34. The term applies to the traditional combined primary and basic lower-level secondary school, *Grund- und Hauptschule* or *Volksschule*.

35. KMK, *Sammlung*, vol. 2, no. 484 (2004).

36. *Proceedings of the Federal Constitutional Court* (BVerfGE), vol. 75 (1988), p. 40, at p. 63.

37. *Proceedings of the Federal Constitutional Court* (BVerfGE), vol. 23 (1968), p. 347; argument modified in BVerfGE vol. 27 (1970), p. 360; BVerfGE, vol. 70, p. 290. Also, *Proceedings of the Federal Constitutional Court* (BVerfGE), vol. 75 (1988), p. 40, at p. 63; BVerfGE, vol. 90 (1994), p. 107, at p. 117.

38. Baden-Württemberg, Brandenburg, Bremen, Hamburg, Mecklenburg–Western Pomerania, North Rhine–Westphalia, Saarland, Saxony, Thuringia, and Schleswig-Holstein.

39. Bavaria, Berlin, Hesse, Lower Saxony, Rhineland-Palatinate, and Saxony-Anhalt.

40. For example, Bavaria.

41. Only Brandenburg, North Rhine–Westphalia, Mecklenburg–Western Pomerania, and Saarland do not have waiting period regulations; six-year (and longer) waiting periods exist in Bavaria and Berlin, where a school must include all the grade levels for its type and two successful graduations must be carried out.

42. Even if all costs for personnel are subsidized, the actual financial support that private substitute schools receive from the respective school authorities covers only about 60 to 70 percent of all expenses; for details, see Vogel, *Das Recht der Schulen*, pp. 146–78.

43. Johann P. Vogel, "Das herkömmliche Bild der Privatschule," *Recht der Jugend und des Bildungswesens*, vol. 46 (1998), pp. 206–15; Frank-Rüdiger Jach, "Die Rechtsstellung der Schulen in freier Trägerschaft vor dem Hintergrund der neueren Rechtsprechung zu Art. 7 Abs. 4 und 5 GG," *Die Öffentliche Verwaltung*, vol. 55 (2002), pp. 973–77.

44. *Proceedings of the Federal Constitutional Court* (BVerfGE), vol. 88 (1993), p. 40, at p. 53.

45. Ibid., at p. 59.

46. See Norbert Niehues, *Schul- und Prüfungsrecht*, vol. 1, *Schulrecht* (Munich: C. H. Beck, 2000), pp. 125–29; Vogel, *Das Recht der Schulen*, pp. 77–78.

47. See summary of precedents in Schulrecht (SPE), *Ergänzbare Sammlung schul- und prüfungsrechtlicher Entscheidungen*, new series, no. 238 (Neuwied: Luchterhand, 2001) no. 238, pp. 1–188.

48. See ibid., p. 103; Federal Administrative Court, 6 C 3.91 (February 19, 1992).

49. See, for example, Bertelsmann Stiftung, "Konsequenzen aus PISA: Wir brauchen eine andere Schule," Position Paper (Gütersloh, 2002); Kiel Institute of International Economics, "Bildungspolitik für Beschäftigung und Wachstum," Research Paper 271 (Frankfurt: Deutsche Bank, 2003).

50. Avenarius and Heckel, *Schulrechtskunde*, p. 219; Vogel, *Das Recht der Schulen*, pp. 146–78.

51. Lutz R. Reuter, "Privatization of Education: The Case of Germany," *Education and the Law*, vol. 14 (2002), pp. 91–98.

52. Frank-Rüdiger Jach, *Schulvielfalt als Verfassungsgebot* (Berlin: Duncker and Humblot, 1991).

53. Interestingly, in the realm of politics, only the Green Party opposes this position. See Heinrich-Böll-Stiftung Bildungskommission, "Autonomie von Schule in der Wissensgesellschaft: Verantwortung in der Zivilgesellschaft" (Berlin, 2002).

54. Niehues (*Schulrecht*, p. 124) argues that a monthly tuition fee of € 80 or more might have a segregating effect; the *Proceedings of the Federal Constitutional Court* (BVerfGE), vol. 90 (1994), p. 107, at p. 199, stated in 1994 that all parents could not pay 90 to 100 euros.

55. Organization for Economic Cooperation and Development (OECD), *Knowledge and Skills for Life: First Results from PISA 2000* (Paris: OECD/Centre for Educational Research and Innovation, 2001), paragraph 7 (table 7.11).

56. OECD, *School: A Matter of Choice* (Paris: OECD/CERI, 1994), pp. 49–52.

57. See, however, Ingo Richter, "Privatschulfreiheit für die Grundschulen von Sekten?" *Neue Zeitschrift für Verwaltungsrecht*, vol. 11 (1992), pp. 1162–64.

9

School Choice and Its Regulation in France

DENIS MEURET

The *Conseil Constitutionnel*, roughly speaking the French equivalent of the U.S. Supreme Court, wrote in a decision handed down in 1977 that "liberty of teaching" (*la liberté de l'enseignement*) is "one of the basic principles recognized by the laws of the Republic" and one on which the Constitution of 1958 has conferred constitutional status.[1] Moreover, according to the Constitution of 1946, to provide "free, public" education is "a duty of the state."

Currently, about 65 percent of students in France's primary and secondary schools (that is, K–12 schools) attend the public school to which they are assigned by local educational authorities according to the catchment area in which they reside, which is defined by the *carte scolaire* (school district map). Fifteen percent attend a public school other than the one assigned, usually because they or their parents requested a "better" school, and 20 percent attend private, predominantly Catholic schools, which receive public funds for more than 80 percent of their costs.

This chapter explains the current situation, which resulted from violent and chaotic episodes in France's political history. It then discusses the status and regulation of private schools and the issue of choice among public schools. The focus in both instances is how regulation seeks to preserve social cohesion and promote the public interest. The conclusion considers what other school systems, particularly those of the United States, might learn from France's experience with publicly funded and regulated school choice.

State, Religion, and School Choice in France

The current guidelines for school choice in France—which make it easy to choose between private and public schools and hamper one's ability to choose among public schools—are somewhat unusual. How today's options came into being can be better understood after examining the historical and philosophical background of the French educational system.

Historical background

Throughout most of the nineteenth century, the public-private split within the French educational system was financial, not religious: private schools were those paid for by parents, and public schools were those subsidized by the state. Public schools were to be found only among primary schools. In both private and public schools, many teachers were members of religious orders.[2] The Ferry Law (1882), the first to make schooling obligatory (from ages six to thirteen), did not change this situation.

In 1886, however, a new law stipulated that public school teachers could no longer be members of a religious order. This abrupt shift occurred because the educational system was viewed as a crucial battleground in the long struggle between the French state and the Catholic Church. To understand why this law came into being, one must recall that at this time demand for education did not come from individuals or families, but from the state and the Catholic Church, both of which saw education as necessary for the sake of public life and public order. The leaders of both camps regarded education as having a decisive influence on the mind and spirit of students: whoever ran the schools would form the spirit of the nation.

Meanwhile, many regarded the Catholic Church of this period not only as one of the most powerful enemies of the republic, but also as an enemy of "modern civilization, progress, industrialism, capitalism, urbanization and almost every new phenomenon, which were denounced as a sources of temptations, degradation, and immorality."[3] Prost, an education historian, writes that private schools "owe their existence to the rejection by nineteenth-century Catholics of the philosophical principles of free inquiry and open criticism, which are at the roots of the public school."[4] Their conflict with the republicans, for whom the school was an instrument of reason and progress, could not have been stronger.

As a result of the 1886 law, the former religious teachers began to open private, fee-based schools. At the beginning of the twentieth century, more children attended Catholic schools than public schools. In reaction to this trend, the French government under the presidency of Emiles Combes passed laws between 1901 and 1904 that closed all schools operated by religious congregations. For the republicans, these laws seemed necessary to protect the republic. For the supporters of the Catholic Church, of course, they meant state dictatorship and ruin. This situation did not last long, however, because during World War I members of both camps had to fight and suffer together. After the war, it was impossible to keep these restrictive education laws in place.

By the start of World War II, private (mostly Catholic, fee-based) schools enrolled about 15 percent of primary and 45 percent of middle-school pupils. (The latter figure is high because, at the time, public middle schools also required parents to pay for their child's education.) At the high school level, public schools, which were not free but had a better reputation than most private ones, held sway, their dominance challenged only by a small number of very famous Catholic schools. By this time the Church had dropped the pretense that it was the only institution entitled to educate children. The Church's revised position was that *Catholic* children had to be educated in Catholic schools. This idea was the doctrine of Rome, expressed in the encyclical letter *Divini Illius Magistri*, and according to Prost, it has never been formally abandoned, even if it has been in abeyance.[5]

The Vichy regime had strong links with the Catholic Church, and so education policy shifted once again in 1940. Both public and private schools were required to teach children of their "duties toward God." The regime reauthorized the monastic orders to open schools, allowed localities to create private schools, and allowed private school students to receive public grants to help pay their school fees. Interestingly, the bishops proposed a voucher plan long before Milton Friedman.[6] But both the public and some parts of the regime itself were reluctant to finance private schools, and the financial help the schools received remained partial.

After the liberation, even that partial help was eliminated, and the situation of the Catholic schools became more precarious than ever because public secondary schooling had been made free. The Catholic Church responded by launching a strong public opinion campaign, arguing that Catholic children should not be educated anywhere other than in a Catholic school, which was, as mentioned, the Vatican's doctrine.[7] This was a challenge to the French conception of *laïcité*, or secularism—an ideal not unlike that of common schooling in the United States—which holds that children from all religions should be educated together in a religiously neutral space. Still, the Catholic

Church's campaign was successful. A pro-Catholic government was elected, and in 1951 two laws were passed, the *Loi Marie* and the *Loi Barangé*, which allowed for some public subsidies for private schools. The former allowed for public grants to private school students, the latter to associations that were themselves authorized to add to the pay of private school teachers.

The decades since World War II have been marked by continuous attempts by private schools to obtain more subsidies from the state and at the same time more protection for their religious identity (*caractère propre*). In 1959, with the *Loi Debré*, they gained the most important concession, full funding for teachers' salaries; in 1971, funding of some parts of their operating expenses; and in 1977 (*Loi Guermeur*), full funding of the retirement pensions of their teachers.

When the left came into power in 1981, Education Minister Alain Savary tried to combine private and public schools in a proposed General Public Service of Education, in which the distinction between public and private schools would have been weakened and the autonomy of public schools enhanced. He almost succeeded in finding a compromise with representatives of the Catholic schools, but the law that finally came up for discussion contained, under the influence of the more extreme leaders of the secular camp, some elements that the Catholics did not accept. As a result, the Catholic Church organized massive street demonstrations, and the project was shelved in 1984.

Philosophical background

In spite of their long rivalry, public and private schools in France share some important features. Their similarities derive from the philosophical roots of the French state, which grew out of the ideas of Jean Jacques Rousseau rather than John Locke, meaning that society is viewed first and foremost as a political community. For Rousseau, the "normal" state of affairs is one of domination, envy, and fear, not of individual freedom, free association, and exchange based on mutual interest: "Man is born free; and everywhere he is in chains."[8] Individual freedom therefore can proceed only from a political act, the *contrat social*, "a form of association that will defend and protect with the whole common force the person and goods of each associate and in which each, while uniting himself with the others, may still obey himself alone, and remain as free as before." In this view, other people represent a threat more than an opportunity and can be turned into the latter only by the political act of the *contrat*. The body created by this act is the Republic.

It would be unfair, both to France and to Rousseau, to consider the French state as a pure application of Rousseau's ideas. However, it is likely that Rousseau's legacy explains in part the fact that in France state action is conceived in a framework in which society is supposed to proceed from the state—without the state, society would end in barbarism and chaos immediately—while in the Anglo-Saxon world the state is supposed to proceed from and to be subordinate to society.

The idea that other people are a threat is common to Hobbes and Rousseau, and legitimates both Rousseau's Republic and Hobbes's absolutism. That in turn may help in understanding Tocqueville's observation that the French Revolution perpetuated absolutism as well as it destroyed it, resulting in "enhancing the might and rights of Public authority."[9]

As a consequence, in France, individuals have to show that they are worthy of their institutions more than institutions have to show that they serve individuals. Donzelot gives an example of this inclination in a comparison of U.S. and French urban policies: while in the United States ethnic communities generally are considered to be helpful in integrating their members into the wider society, in France they are considered the worst obstacles to integration.[10] While U.S. urban nonprofits like community development corporations aim at the empowerment of people who live in deprived areas, policies like the *Développement Social Urbain* in France aim at allowing institutions (schools, police, justice, employment institutions, and so forth) to reclaim their place and due respect in deprived areas. While in the United States the citizens associations in these areas are built from the bottom up, in France they come from the top down—that is, they are used by national institutions to reach and educate underprivileged populations.

These differing orientations toward institutions and individual interests have had powerful consequences for the educational system. One consequence is that the French educational system is strongly oriented toward achieving civic aims and preparing children for the role of citizen. It is a way of "providing to each child the symbolic framework for his belonging to the national community."[11] This may be related to Montesquieu's conception of republican government, which is grounded on *virtu*—that is, the subordination of one's personal interest to the public good—and "which has the greatest need for education."[12] This also explains, perhaps, the authoritarian aspects of the traditional concept of schooling in France, through which children would be pulled out of the traditional world of the "provinces," out of the ancient languages and superstitions, and enlightened by reason.

Of course, American education also has concerns about preparing children to become citizens, but they are somewhat different. First, despite the recent revival of Montesquieu's idea of republican government in American thought and politics, the liberal tradition still has a stronger influence on education. In this tradition, there is no place for subordination of the individual to an externally defined public good: "Only by being true to the full growth of all the individuals who make it up can a society by any chance be true to itself."[13] Civic education itself therefore aims for the full growth of the individual. To some extent as a consequence of this position, civic education is designed to fight selfishness and extreme individualism more than superstition.[14] In the United States, education is linked to the notion of development of the child's innate abilities. In France, the child's mind traditionally is considered either a repository of superstition and false ideas that must be eradicated or as shapeless clay that must be given form.

A second consequence of these different orientations is that, in the most traditional form of the French system, the idea that education has to meet children's needs, to say nothing of parents' demands, is considered nonsense. One of the current opponents of this parental-rights model, R. Debray, has written that "a teacher owes himself only to the logic of the subject he teaches."[15] Insofar as public education is oriented toward collective civic ends rather than individual interests, it is not so far from the most traditional Catholic conception of teaching, wherein "schools for the mass of the people are created *mainly* for giving religious instruction to the people, to lead them to a true Christian morality and piety."[16] The educational elite of the public system, those who go to *Normale Sup* or *Polytechnique*, could be seen as kinds of secular saints: like saints, they contend that it is possible to live here on earth according to the Principles of the Superior Order, which give the ordinary world its true significance and meaning.[17]

A third consequence, a decisive one for the relations of state and church regarding education, is that to a certain extent, in the traditional French conception of the state, church and state have a similar mission. Each party thinks it has a calling, reason on one side, faith on the other: for the state, that calling is to move society away from chaos; for the church, it is to move society away from evil. Their historic rivalry also is explained by their similarity: state and church are all the more rivals because they assign themselves a similar mission, a mission that presupposes a certain weakness of human beings. To put it simply: in the French mind, individuals are weak, so for the state (or the church), the church (or the state) is a threat; education, therefore, is all the more important.

This explains why the principle of "*liberté de l'enseignement*" has to be understood as "liberty to provide schooling" rather than as "liberty of schooling." That is, it is the right of the Catholic Church to teach its values in its (publicly supported) schools, rather than the right of parents to choose a school that accords with their values. Of course, as discussed later, both rights are identical for about 6 percent of families: the traditional Catholics who enroll all their children in Catholic schools. But these families are a minority (about 20 percent) among private school users. School choice in France is not a matter of satisfying parents' educational preferences, but rather a matter of two great institutional forces allocating the power—and the market—to themselves.

Against this idea, it might be argued that parents have a choice not only between private and public schools but also among private schools, as if the church, unlike the state, were in favor of parents' freedom to choose the form of schooling that their children receive. But in fact, the aim of Catholic schools is to provide an education inspired by the Catholic religion; to provide a choice among different versions of a Catholic education would mean a choice of different versions of Catholicism, which would contradict Catholic doctrine. The diversity provided by Catholic schools derives from the differences between them and public schools far more than from any differences among Catholic schools. The differences among private schools, like those among public schools, come primarily from the socioeconomic background of their students or from their degree of academic rigor far more than from their pedagogical or educational options.

The current political situation

The sharing of influence by church and state in fact explains why Catholic schools easily accept the obligation to admit children whatever their religion or absence of it: it is a way to transmit and increase the influence of Christian values. It also explains why, among modern Catholics, a majority have their children in public schools: they share with more traditional Catholics the aim of increasing the influence of Christian values, but they think that religious convictions should come from the personal decisions of individuals—a result that they believe is better guaranteed by enrolling their children in public schools than in Catholic schools. Moreover, they are eager to introduce their children to the wider society.

In addition, it explains why almost all French political parties accept that parents can choose between public and private schools, but not among schools inside the public sector. If the basic concern were to provide for parental choice or to allow families to find schools that suit the personality and interests of individual children, then these two forms of choice—to choose a private school or to choose among public school—would be equally valuable, but only the first form of choice is needed if the interest at stake is that of the Church as an institution. As a result, while most parents and even most teachers declare in polls that they are in favor of school choice, no one among the large political parties proposed extending choice during the 2002 presidential election campaign. Only two "parties" propose wider school choice in France. One is the small and politically marginal libertarian party of Alain Madelin. The other is Jean Marie Le Pen's National Front, which seems to have the support of some white people living in economically depressed areas who want to avoid sending their children to school with the children of some immigrants. In addition, some of Le Pen's supporters are moved by a kind of populist rejection of the state altogether.[18] Note also that the current government, although pro-market in its general orientation, does not promote choice or accountability among its education policies. Rather, it promotes the devolution of the management of nonteaching staff to regional authorities (there are about twenty-eight regions in France), which would have no consequences for students. This is another example that what is at stake in French politics is less the best way to serve people than the relative weight of institutional bodies—this time, not the state and the church, but national and regional bodies.

So far, we have presented two approaches to the question of choice in France, one historical, the other political. The historical vantage point shows the opposition between state and church, while political analysis displays their similarity. Both the opposition and the similarity help explain why a centralized educational system emerged: only the state was strong enough to challenge the power of the Catholic Church. This differs from the situation in the United States, where a mosaic of different religious denominations coexist relatively peacefully within a democratic state and where nearly all of the Protestant denominations historically have supported the idea of common schooling—as indeed they have done in France, but without great consequence since Protestants represent only 1 percent of the population.

It has to be said, of course, that today Catholic bishops no longer challenge the political primacy of the republic, and the public school camp does not ask for the suppression of Catholic schools. However, the church-state conflict remains fundamental to education policy in France, and that explains why, when the title of a book is *La Question Scolaire*, the French reader understands that it deals exclusively with the Catholic/public school question.[19] And only the continuation of this conflict can explain why the main street demonstrations in France for twenty years have been on that question—to prevent what was perceived as the integration of private schools in the public system in 1984, and to prevent what was perceived as an open door for a large increase of the Catholic share of the pie in 1993. The first of these two demonstrations led to the resignation not only of the minister of education, Savary, but of the whole Mauroy government, which was the first left-oriented government in France in the Fifth Republic. The conflict still burns under the ashes. The current situation is a standoff, stabilized by overt regulation, the aim of which is to guarantee the adherence of the Catholic schools to the values of the republic—and a more covert but widely felt resolve to keep the two systems' respective shares of the pie in their current proportions.

The idea of choice among public schools is of recent vintage, and it also is contrary to some fundamental features of the French educational system. Various features of French educational policy aim at limiting public school choice.

Public Regulation of Subsidized Private Schools

The regulation of private schooling in France is considered first, then its prevalence and what is known about its social effects.

Regulation

Currently, the cost to parents of private schooling is about three times the cost of public schooling, which is to say about three times nothing. The only available figures indicate that, in school year 1991–92, the entire annual education-related cost to parents per child in primary or secondary school was approximately 1,900 FF (about $300) for those who go to a public school in their catchment area, 2,800 FF for those who go to another public school, and 5,500 FF for those who go to a private school.[20] This has to be compared with the total educational cost (including public contributions), which at the time was about 26,000 FF per child.[21]

Private schools currently are funded as follows: the Ministry of Education pays the wages of the teachers and provides a grant (*le forfait d'externat*) that entirely covers the wages of nonteaching staff. Elected regional bodies (*conseils régionaux, conseils généraux*) provide a grant to pay operating expenses (heating, furniture, and so forth); this grant has to have the same value per student as the one given to public schools. Family fees and also some private grants pay for capital expenses (building construction and repair). Under a 1850 law that was never abrogated (*Loi Falloux*), regional bodies can pay up to 10 percent of the amount provided by family and private grants for the capital expenses of a school each year. *Conseils* that are ideologically in favor of private schools give 10 percent of that amount every year, whatever a school's true capital expenses. Other *conseils* subsidize the cost of the school's true capital expenses within the 10 percent limit.

Moreover, under the *Loi Debré*, private schools can be publicly subsidized only if they provide for a "true educational need" ("*un besoin scolaire reconnu*").

Therefore only private schools that have been in operation for at least five years are eligible for any kind of public subsidy; however, in areas where the population is increasing, the waiting period has been reduced to one year. Moreover, private schools sometimes request special concessions, which are granted if the local political climate is favorable to private or Catholic schools: for instance, a new school may be presented as an annex of an existing school rather than as a new one, thereby avoiding the waiting period.

Under the current public-private compromise, then, existing private schools are almost fully financed through public money, while it is somewhat difficult but not impossible to create new ones. This situation can be interpreted as follows: people do appreciate having private schools as an alternative to the public system; therefore they support public subsidies to private schools. However, they are not sure that they would like Catholic schools to become too powerful; therefore they are satisfied with a rule that guarantees their existence and their relative autonomy but hinders their growth. Proponents of private schools are aware of all this, and they accept the fact that their share of the market will not increase.[22] This is also why Catholic schools may be seen as a brake on the extension of private schooling across the country: they are seen as providing a sufficient safety valve.

As this makes clear, financing restrictions and general sentiments that prevent the expansion of private schooling constitute an implicit form of regulation. Public subsidies bring in their wake a variety of other forms of public regulation, which are strikingly extensive:

—There is one national curriculum for all schools. The content of academic schooling (not only the core curriculum) is the same in private as in public schools, but private schools may add religious courses, provided that they remain elective.

—Publicly subsidized schools cannot exclude any student on the ground of his or her religion, lack of religion, or ethnic origin. This is why religious education in subsidized schools cannot be compulsory.

—Private school teachers undergo, according to the *Loi Debré*, the same review by the same inspectors as public teachers. However, according to a personal communication to the author from a specialist in the field, they are reviewed only once, at the end of their probation period, while a public teacher undergoes review about ten times in his or her professional life.

—Similarly, private schools are in principle subject, like public schools, to administrative inspections by *inspecteurs généraux de l'administration*. However, according to a personal communication from the specialist mentioned above, only about twenty-five secondary private schools have been inspected since the *Loi Debré* was passed in 1959.

—More important, there is one set of national examinations for all schools. The true constraint on the curricula of private schools is that they must prepare students for the same examinations as do the public schools. These examinations, especially those for the *baccalauréat*, which allows a secondary school student to enter an institution of higher education, can take place only in public schools.

—When a public school decides that a pupil has to repeat a year of school, the decision applies to private schools as well, so private schools cannot be used to avoid repeating a grade.

—Private school teachers are recruited among persons who, in brief, pass the same kind of examinations, in front of the same juries, as do public school teachers. Salaries also are prescribed, and they are the same for public and publicly subsidized private schools. However, public and private teachers generally are not trained in the same institutions and do not belong to the same trade unions because of the strong anticlerical orientation of public staff trade unions.

At this point, in light of this extensive array of regulations, the reader may ask to what extent subsidized private schools differ from public schools. They do so in the following ways:

—Heads of private schools are chosen by the Catholic organization for private schooling, provided the *recteur* (the representative of the minister of education at the regional level) agrees.

—Private schools used to hire their teachers from among those who met the official qualifications, while public schools have no influence on who, in particular, comes to teach in them. Recently, however, the Catholic regional body has begun to hire private teachers, so the difference between the school systems is less striking.

—Private schools claim to make a difference through extracurricular activities, an academically oriented school climate, stronger discipline, and a distinctive ethos oriented toward certain moral values. Students report a more "familial" climate in private schools.

There are not many studies of the educational differences between public and private schools in France. Most of the existing studies deal only with how many and which children enroll in private schools, as discussed below.

How Many Students Attend Private Schools and Who Are They?

As can be seen in table 9-1, the proportion of students enrolled in the private sector has not increased since 1980. During this time enrollment in secondary schools grew rapidly, and the intake of private schools grew in the same proportion as that of public schools. As noted, this is not the result of a

Table 9-1. *Proportion of Students Enrolled in the Private Sector*

	1980–81 (percent)	2001–2002 (percent)
Primary school (6–10 years)	15	15
Middle schools (11–14 years)	19	20
High schools (15–17 years)	23	20

Source: Ministère de l'Education Nationale, *Repères et Références Statistiques* (2002).

deliberate, detailed policy, but of the difficulties involved in funding and creating new private schools and also of the fact that few people are dissatisfied with the public system.

About 95 percent of private schools are Catholic. The Protestants, whose schools were closed by the Edict of Fontainebleau in 1685 and reauthorized after the Revolution, gave almost all their schools to the state at the beginning of the twentieth century, with the idea that their best protection was state schooling and the policy of *laïcité*. About ten Protestant schools do exist, and there are a few Jewish schools. Only two Muslim schools, a middle school and a primary school, exist. A Muslim high school with only thirty students in a single ninth-grade classroom opened in September 2003 in Lille, in the north of the country, inside a mosque. Its promoters, who are said to be fundamentalist, protest that "courses will follow the national curriculum and will be open to all" and that "girls will be accepted with or without hijab." Such compliance is, as noted, among the conditions for receiving public subsidies.

It is important to note that a lot of students are "zapping" between private and public schools. While, as shown in the table, the share of students enrolled in private schools is about 20 percent, only 9 percent attend private schools for their entire primary and secondary school career, whereas 67 percent attend only public schools and 24 percent change from one to the other. This zapping means that about one-third of the French student population receive at least some private schooling during their school years. Moreover, only in 60 percent of families is every child enrolled only in public schools, while only in 6 percent of families is every child enrolled in private schools.[23]

The explanation for this is that often children enroll in private schools when they meet some difficulty in the public sector and may come back a few years later, which means that most parents, rather than being strong proponents of either private or public schools, have a more utilitarian relation to the school system.

Some authors, especially sociologists, argue therefore that enrollment in Catholic school is mainly a way for people of higher socioeconomic status to find "better" schooling, not a religious matter.[24] However, Héran (1996), using more sophisticated regressions, showed that the desire to feel a sense of belonging to the Catholic Church as a community was one of the strongest predictors of private enrollment. It may be observed that a lot of French declare themselves to be Catholic without really practicing the Catholic faith: according to a March 2003 poll conducted by the CSA Institute, 62 percent of French adults declare themselves to be Catholic, 6 percent Muslim, 2 percent Protestant, and 1 percent Jewish, while 26 percent declare no religion. At the same time, only 24 percent of the sample are certain that God exists, while 34 percent believe that it is likely.[25]

What are the other characteristics of private school users? Children from more affluent families are more likely to enroll in private schools, although this bias has decreased.[26] Other predictors of enrollment are a mother who received a post-secondary education, high income, and—especially—not being a foreigner. The proportion of foreign students is 9 percent in the public sector and only 2 percent in the private sector.[27] High socioeconomic status is also a strong predictor of "zapping" between the two sectors.[28]

When techniques similar to Héran's were brought to bear on a more recent year (1998), using a slightly different set of variables, predictors of enrollment in private middle schools included having a level of achievement that was neither very low nor very high; living in a town with a population of 20,000 to 100,000; being a child of farmers, shopkeepers, entrepreneurs, or service-class parents; and having a mother with a college degree.[29] This over-representation of entrepreneurs and the service class is still more pronounced in high schools. In addition, Tournier observed in a local survey of 1,400 students in five private and five public high schools that right-wing as well as practicing Catholic students were overrepresented in private high schools in the *département* of Isère.[30]

From a geographic point of view, two features are salient: private schooling is stronger in Catholic regions of France (Bretagne, Pays de Loire), and the higher the social status of a place the higher the proportion of private enrollment.[31] In the most exclusive districts of Paris (*VXIéme and VIIéme arrondissements*), the proportion of private enrollment may reach as high 60 percent, and the proportion of janitors' children is very high in public schools. So the opportunity to choose private schools is not evenly distributed across the French public.

The Impact of Private Schooling on Students and Society

Liensol and Meuret (1987), using value-added indicators, observed private high schools to be slightly less effective in preparing students for the baccalauréat than public schools in one eastern region of France.[32] However, Langoet and Léger (1994, 1997), using data on student school careers during the 1970s, found that after controlling for the social status of the parents, private school students had better school careers than public school students and that the finding was especially pronounced for children from more economically disadvantaged families (workers and clerks) who attended private schools (they attained the baccalauréat degree in higher proportions when enrolled in private schools). Some researchers have pointed out that this did not necessarily mean that private schooling was more effective for these groups, for two reasons. First, there is the familiar problem of selection bias: parents whose child attends private school are probably more interested in their child's achievement and more active in helping the child succeed. In addition, pupils who remain in private schools during all the middle-school years are the highest achieving of those who enroll in them.[33]

These researchers seem to be partly right. Chloe Tavan observed that during the 1990s, after controlling for the social status of the father, education of the mother, enrollment in preschool and kindergarten, family educational expectations and involvement, and time spent on homework,

—public and private school students' level of achievement at the end of primary school was the same, but obtained with less frequent grade repetitions in private schools

—both groups' level of attainment (that is, the probability of a successful school career) was the same in middle schools, but obtained with less frequent grade repetitions in public schools.[34]

So the effectiveness of public and private schools appears to have been about the same. However, in regard to social equity, Tavan's more sophisticated analysis confirms the results of Langoet and Léger: there was less academic inequality between children from high- and low-status social backgrounds in private than in public schools. However, there are no comparisons of private and public schools based on true measures of achievement in secondary schools. One reason for the absence of such studies is probably that both sides, content with the status quo, prefer not to know.

Whatever the effectiveness of the two sectors, it is clear that parents in the private sector are more satisfied. Several studies have made this observation for primary as well as secondary education.[35] Teachers are deemed competent by 85 percent of families that have all their children in the private sector but only by 69 percent of those whose children are in the public sector. Teachers are deemed receptive by 68 percent in the private and by 54 percent in the public sector.[36]

The same is true for students themselves. In a study that controlled for a large number of variables, private middle-school students more often saw their school as a "big family" and less often as a "court," a "factory," or a "circus" than did students in the public sector.[37] As a consequence, the reputation of private schools tends to be better than that of public schools, including on measures of effectiveness. In a 1984 campaign to influence public opinion, the private school camp, for the first time, used the ineffectiveness of the public sector as an argument against what it perceived as a threat to Catholic schools.

That parent and student satisfaction is stronger is the only thing known about the impact of private schooling. There are no studies on the long-term impact of type of school on students in term of their social values (tolerance, sense of solidarity, sense of belonging, adherence to democratic values, feelings of responsibility, absence of arrogance, commitment to equity), personal attributes (ability to take initiative, imagination), or religious beliefs (Do Catholic children who enroll in private schools remain Catholic more often when they grow up?). Therefore there are no data on the impact of school type on social cohesion. Likewise, the impacts of type of school on students' professional careers cannot be compared (For a given diploma and a given social origin, do former private school students find a job more easily? Do they find a better-paying job?). It has to be recalled that the answers to some of these questions are presupposed in the criticisms that each camp makes of the other. For instance, opponents of Catholic schools charge them with teaching charity rather than solidarity or equity and with organizing a subsociety based on a network of Catholic groups and organizations. Catholic school proponents, meanwhile, argue that public schools teach knowledge but not moral or social values. No systematic research has yet addressed these important topics.

An important exception, however, to the general lack of knowledge is that Tournier (1997) observed that not only were right-wing students and families overrepresented in private schools, but also that children in private schools were more apt to become right-wing irrespective of whether their fathers were right- or left-wing. In Catholic schools, some influence—peers or the school environment more generally—seems to be able to reorient, mostly to the right, the political ideas of children. Having tested and rejected alternative explanations, he concluded that the role of private schools in political socialization has probably been underestimated. So the attitude of right-wing local authorities, who tend to favor Catholic schools, appears to be rational.

In addition, private schools have effects on the public schools that compete with them. Here again, there are no systematic data. In two regions, more than 35 percent of primary students attend private schools, while this proportion is about 10 percent in the other regions. These two regions (Bretagne and Pays de Loire) are among those where the performance of pupils at the end of primary schooling is the highest, but other regions with far less or even very little private enrollment (Midi-Pyrénées, Rhône-Alpes, and Aquitaine) are similarly high-performing. The same applies to the rate of attainment of the *baccalauréat* and to the dropout rate.[38] So competition does, perhaps, have a positive effect, but a true comparison should hold constant features like socioeconomic status and language spoken at home. To my knowledge, no rigorous comparisons of this sort exist.

Discussion

The situation of the private school system in France is quite paradoxical. It is generally welcomed as a safety valve for the rather rigid provision of public schooling, as the high percentage of "zappers" demonstrates. (If a child does not succeed in a public school, the parents cannot try another public school, or, at least, they will find it very hard to do. Therefore the opportunity to send the child to a private school is welcome, even if the private and the public school curriculums are the same.) Nobody asks openly for its suppression, and most people—even among those who vote for the left—accept the fact that it is publicly financed. At the same time, the private-versus-public school issue remains highly contested in French political life: the right is, as shown, more favorable than the left to private schools. This is likely to be because the right has closer ties to the Catholic Church and because it is more skeptical about state institutions. The public-private issue is contested, but it also is commonly acknowledged to be a highly sensitive political topic: the general sense is that the less it is talked about—or researched—the better it is for everybody.

My interpretation of this situation is that the Catholic Church profits greatly from its position as the only entity allowed to provide an alternative to those who fail in the public system or who cannot abide it for whatever reason. The Church profits especially through its position as educator of the social elite. Indeed, I would guess that the narrower the definition of the elite, the higher the proportion of enrollment in private schools. Catholic schools therefore allow the Church to exercise an influence on society and government that is far greater than it would be otherwise, given diminished religious observance among a nominally Catholic population.

Let us say that acting as safety valve is the first social function of private schooling. Of course, the benefits of this function are ambiguous: while it is clearly desirable in the current public system, it also can immobilize criticism and prevent improvement within the system. Private schooling is accepted by those in the public system itself, perhaps because it makes the public system's rigidity more tolerable. If there were no private schools, for instance, it is likely that parents or students would more readily protest the worst schools and teachers, and indeed they might insist on more diversity inside the public sector, according to the "exit or voice" mechanism that Hirschman described.[39]

A second major function of the private school system is that it provides some families a more "familial" environment and perhaps also better teaching conditions. Since this appears to be especially beneficial to children of low socioeconomic status who attend private schools, it favors equality of opportunity. But this issue probably is more complex. It also may be seen as negative in the same way that Dobb and others found charter schools negative: choice schools may skim the best students among the disadvantaged—or those with more involved parents—and therefore, because of peer effects, be detrimental to the other schools and students in deprived areas.[40] It also is clear that private schools in France reinforce ethnic segregation, since they enroll so few immigrant children.

Another function of private schools is that they allow social groups that distrust the state, either for political reasons (*les personnes à leur compte*—farmers, self-employed craftspeople, shopkeepers, and professionals, who are prone to think that the state coddles people who do not pull their weight) or religious reasons (the 6 percent of traditional Catholics whose children attend only Catholic schools), to escape state schools.

Perhaps the public system is stimulated through competition, given the evidence of its good performance in areas where private schooling is strong. In any case, if it is true that the prevalence of the private sector is maintained at a constant level for political reasons, it is clear that its role as a competitor is limited accordingly, and the geographical distribution of any benefit of competition is quite uneven.

Choice among Public Schools

For primary schools in the public sector, a 1882 law makes the local authorities (*communes*) responsible for the organization of the *carte scolaire*—the map that defines the catchment area for a school. This law explicitly allows local authorities to opt for parental choice of school, but only one or two local authorities, among the more than 10,000 in the country, have done so.

For public middle and high schools, the *carte scolaire* was not implemented until 1963, during the Gaullist period, for the simple reason that only then did the growing number of students in secondary schools make it the easiest way to regulate enrollment. School catchment areas are defined by the regional offices of the National Education Administration (*les rectorats*) in agreement with the authorities of the *régions* or of the *départements* (*les conseils régionaux ou généraux*), which are elected bodies with general authority for the governance of their jurisdiction.[41] These areas are periodically redefined to take into account the evolution of the population in the various educational sectors. Sometimes, but not always, they are defined to enhance social mixing, to the extent that it is possible considering the pervasive difficulties created by urban social segregation. The idea that some exceptions to this rule could be tolerated—that is, that parents could ask that their children attend a public school other than the one in their catchment area—was first expressed in a 1980 decree.

However, Alain Savary, the Socialist education minister, was the first to make the *carte scolaire* more flexible, a change that resulted from his attempt in 1984 to integrate the Catholic schools into a General Public Service of Education. It was unthinkable either to suppress any choice in the proposed general service or to restrict it to some schools (the former private schools), so choice had to be extended to the entire public sector.[42]

However popular the idea of choice was among parents, Savary proceeded very cautiously—the proposal was presented as an experiment in only four areas of the country. More surprisingly, perhaps, right-wing prime minister Jacques Chirac, even in his quasi-Thatcherian period (1986–88), did not give up the experiment but cautiously extended the pilot programs.

Linked with this experimental feature of public-public choice is the fact that no legal text fixes any rule for making exceptions to mandatory assignment rules. The precise procedures are decided at the regional level, and they are not published. It is difficult for anyone to know what the criteria for obtaining an exemption really are.[43] One thing that skilled choosers know, however, is that it is generally preferable not to say, even if it is the truth, that they want to avoid a school because of the poor quality of its climate or its students' performance.

So, the first question to address is why the idea of choosing has come so late, so cautiously, and so stealthily, especially since most parents polled say that they prefer having a choice. The explanation is twofold. First, education is considered—especially by those teachers, intellectuals, and newspapers that decide what is acceptable discourse on education—not as a service that students receive in order to enhance their social or natural abilities (education as empowerment), but as a privilege to be given to those who show that they are worthy of it, offering them access to skills and knowledge that, while not necessary for life in society, are required to realize a superior conception of life (education as sorting). As shown, this is common to Catholic and state schools. Since education is not a service, the burden of proof rests on the student's shoulders, not on the schools, and there is no presumption favoring individual choice. In fact, the *carte scolaire* is so well suited to the principles of the educational system that most people think that it is as ancient as the system itself. Those who administer the *carte scolaire* operate with the conviction that parents who try to avoid a given school are pursuing their own interest at the expense of the common good. There is, indeed, some evidence that the overall effectiveness of the system is better guaranteed by mixing pupils of different levels of academic ability, at least at the beginning of middle school.[44] This is also the conviction of some parents, who therefore feel torn between the common interest and what they think to be the interest of their children.

Second, in the last twenty years, schools—which in France, unlike in the United States, receive equal funding throughout the nation—have been given somewhat more autonomy precisely in order to be able to adapt to meet the needs of every child, so there is no reason to think that one school will suit a child better than another. To adapt to every child means to allow each child to learn how he or she learns best. This has occurred because parents see choice far more as the opportunity to enroll in a "better" school than in a school that promotes other values or cultures—and also because the concept of *laïcité* (secularism) does not make much room for the idea that parents with different cultural or religious backgrounds should be provided with a school attuned to their preferred culture or religion (in sharp contrast with the case in the Netherlands, as other chapters in this volume make clear). The idea is not, of course, that parents have no right to educate and socialize their children according to their religion or culture. But for this kind of socialization parents have a whole host of other options outside the schools: newspapers and magazines, youth associations, summer camps, radio and TV stations, media events, catechism courses, and religious retreats, processions, and pilgrimages. The idea is that the role of the school is precisely to gather and mix these children, who are educated from different points of view at home, and teach them to live together—because, as adults, they will have to share the same country.

I am myself a good example of this role of the public school. The son of a minister, I was educated in a strong Protestant environment (family, friends, Sunday school, scouts, summer camp, and so forth) and was all the more glad to meet, in the public schools, friends who were Catholic or Jewish or who belonged to families with no religious affiliation. French Protestants generally believe that only "men of little faith" fear the consequences of their children associating with young people of other religions or with agnostics. I learned concretely at school that other faiths and cultures did and do exist. One might argue with John Rawls that faith-based or communitarian schools should be welcomed provided that they teach their students that they are free to think as they wish and to prepare them to be independent members of society.[45] But I regard this as not very realistic. Certainly the concrete experience of diversity is the best way to learn that other cultures and faiths exist and have value. This experience is nowhere provided better than in public common schools.

That is why schools that want to receive public subsidies in France must first be open to all.[46] And that is why the question of the *foulard islamique* (hijab) has been so difficult. Most teachers in France feel it is wrong to accept in their classrooms such a symbol of the domination and humiliation of women under fundamentalist Islam (as opposed to Islam as such, which does not require the hijab); they see it as contradicting the essential meaning of what they teach—freedom through reason and critical thinking. However, the *Conseil d'Etat* ruled that girls wearing the hijab had to be accepted in school, provided they attended all courses and that they did not use their hijab as a means of proselytizing. But most school directors found it very difficult to decide when proselytism began and asked for a law forbidding the hijab in school. Supporters of the hijab argued that *laïcité* means also that schools should accept girls who wear the hijab, provided that they wear it of their own free will.[47] Another argument was that if these girls were not accepted in public schools, it would favor the development of Islamic schools, which would be far worse for them than wearing the hijab.

However, a majority of policymakers were persuaded after numerous hearings of the Stasi Commission that the girls' wearing of the hijab had less to do with their free will than with the will of the fundamentalists who systematically proselytize through these young girls. They consequently passed a law stating that "in public primary and secondary schools, the wearing of emblems or clothing that conspicuously demonstrates a student's religious affiliation is forbidden."[48]

Regulation of Choice

In the first areas where choice was authorized, students had to choose three schools, in order of preference. Their choices were then examined by a commission representing the parents' association, the head of the school, and the district administration. The rules were, first, that families that asked for the school in their sector had absolute priority, and second, that the number of staff assigned to a school would be calculated according to the number of pupils it should enroll according to the *carte scolaire*. As mentioned, it is not clear whether these rules are the same today.

Families could choose among all "ordinary" schools. With the exception of a half-dozen "experimental schools," in France there are no public schools such as charter or magnet schools. Parents may prefer a school that is different from the one assigned, not because the curriculum is different—it is not—but because it is more convenient, because the interaction among students or between students and teachers is better, or because the schooling is more demanding.

The first reports of researchers on these experiments estimated that "all effects were negative."[49] Competition, they stressed, did not result in emulation but in ignoring weak pupils, which had negative effects on the global effectiveness of the system. Competition was harmful for equality of opportunity because of its segregating effects (for example, through implementation of tracking in order to attract or retain good students). Schools became inclined to use resources for objectives other than improving the teaching of weak pupils: these included maintaining "elite" courses (like Greek or German) at high cost, again to attract or retain good students; offering extracurricular activities such as special field trips and in-service training programs in companies; and so forth. The authors recommended better regulation, especially so that parents would not be obligated to choose—that is to say, parents would be given a place in their sector school, although they could ask for an exception. These recommendations were embraced by the educational administration, in spite of a significant potential drawback: making choice optional rather than requiring all parents to choose runs the risk that choice will tend to be exercised mainly by an elite of "skilled choosers" rather than parents as a whole. In addition, some mayors in small, rural areas who feared that some small middle schools in their locality would have to close forced the experiment to end.[50] The current regulation, issued in 1998, is clearer on principles and objectives than on procedures and criteria. Its two main aims are said to be to preserve some mixing of social classes in the schools and to protect schools from the "often unfair effects of cursory judgments [of schools by parents]."[51]

Because the *carte scolaire* may in fact be designed either to compensate for or to accentuate existing segregation, its obligation to limit social segregation is clearly expressed. Exceptions have to be used to encourage schools to cooperate and collaborate to offer students the school that suits their needs best, rather than to make schools compete to attract the best students; indeed, such "competition among schools is forbidden." The regulation states that the "objective is to preserve or institute social mixing as much as possible" and that "private schools have to cooperate in this attempt." Exceptions are authorized only to take certain uncommon courses or courses that are infrequently offered.

Of course, parents are apt to use this opportunity to ask for a place at certain renowned schools, but the regulations warn schools not to use parental choice to attract better students. As there are no studies on this topic, I can give only an account of my personal experience in Paris: at the middle-school level, sectors are designed to enhance the school mix to the (small) extent that urban segregation allows it, and exceptions are very rare. However, at the high-school level, students rank their preferences for three high schools, and the high schools with the best reputation choose the better students.

Prevalence of Choice

In 1990, 50 percent of middle schools and 27 percent of high schools were located in areas where the *carte scolaire* was softened by the possibility of obtaining an exemption from a mandatory local assignment. Until then, the names of these schools were published, but that is no longer the case. Therefore, how many schools are now involved or how the regions interpret the idea of exemption is not really known.

In 1992 a national survey asked 5,300 households about their experience with public school choice. Answers indicate that of primary school pupils— who, as noted, should almost never attend a public school other than the one in their sector—15 percent attended schools other than the one assigned. The corresponding figures were 12 percent for middle school and 20 percent for high school students.[52] These figures have to be considered approximate: for middle schools, Ministry of Education surveys indicated that 10 percent were choosers in 1991 and that 9 percent were choosers in 1998.[53] These figures at least suggest that public sector choice does not seem to be increasing.

These percentages were a surprise for the Ballion-Oeuvrard study, which deemed choosers in the experimental area to constitute only 10 percent of the total. So the prevalence of choice was about the same, for middle schools at least, in areas where the *carte scolaire* was and was not weakened. This was confirmed by studies in the Parisian suburbs, where in principle the *carte scolaire* is not at all weakened but which nevertheless a lot of students leave for Parisian city schools in order to avoid the schools closest to their homes, which have reputations for violence, poor schooling, and large immigrant populations.[54] In brief, it is most likely that the same percentage of students choose among public schools, irrespective of whether the administrative procedures formally accommodate choice or not.

Impact of Choice

Has the weakening of the *carte scolaire* increased student segregation? In 2000, 5 percent of students in French middle schools were foreign, and the dissimilarity index—the proportion of foreign students who would have to be displaced to obtain an even distribution—was 50 percent. Forty-three percent of middle school students were of low socioeconomic status, and their dissimilarity index was 28 percent.[55] So there is some segregation in the middle schools, but it is difficult to know how much the weakening of the *carte scolaire* is responsible.

Two different kinds of middle schools seem to be requested by choosers: renowned schools and ordinary ones. The latter are requested by parents who want to avoid schools with a very bad reputation. This represents on one hand a positive strategy—seeking excellence—and on the other hand a defensive move to avoid supposedly bad schools.[56] This is in line with research on the stability of school effects on student learning. This research (for example, Thomas and others 1997) has shown that school effects are strong and stable only for very ineffective or very effective schools.[57] So, regarding equity, two criteria are important: the equality of opportunity to attend quite effective schools and the equality of opportunity to avoid quite ineffective ones. To what extent poor students use choice to enroll in very effective schools is not known; what is known is that middle-class students most often avoid quite ineffective schools, whether by formal or informal means, and that bright students benefit from access to better schools.

There are two other indications of the impact of choice on segregation:

—Primary and secondary teachers are the most frequent users of public-public choice: 15 percent of the children of primary teachers and 19 percent of the children of secondary teachers attend a middle school that is not in their sector, while only 9 percent of the population as a whole does.

—Segregation of working-class children has not grown in French middle schools since 1984, while segregation of foreign children and of weak students has increased.[58] But it is not known to what extent these effects may be attributed to the weakening of the *carte scolaire*. Most likely its effect is quite small. If one supposes that teachers' children tend to be high achievers and that the high percentage of teachers' children outside of their school sector is a result of that policy—which may not in fact be the case—the weakening of the *carte scolaire* process has perhaps had some small responsibility for *academic* segregation.

It is interesting to note that in the United Kingdom during the same period, social and academic segregation decreased slightly (see Gorard, chapter 5 in this volume).[59] Choice was easier, but perhaps also more regulated, than in France.

Discussion

As with public-private school choice, the main aim of government regulation is to restrict choice within the public sector rather than to control its undesirable consequences. As a result, the opportunity to truly choose is highly dependent on the academic achievement of the student, which may result in increased academic and social segregation overall.

In the United Kingdom, for instance, choice is considered a means to enhance the effectiveness of the schools and therefore is associated with procedures that pursue this objective ("fresh start," inspections, and so forth). In France, it is considered a concession to pressure from parents, and most often in practice it becomes a matter of schools choosing students by their academic performance. This choice of students by schools, while theoretically excluded by administrative regulations, is in fact consistent with the meritocratic conception of justice that pervades the French system. An effect of this could well be an increase not so much in inequality among social groups as in the gap between the performance and careers of the least and the most able students.

In general, segregation, whether socioeconomic or academic, seems to be more acceptable in France when it is caused by academic tracking—for instance, by the distinction between vocational and general tracks—than when it is caused by choice. That is because the right to distinguish students is claimed in the first instance by the institution, and an institutional claim is generally regarded as more legitimate than a claim of parents or students. This is consistent with the assertion that choice's main effects lie in tracking, as previously stated. Finally, I would add that the idea that "some parents" cheat with the *carte scolaire*—an idea that is generally accepted—probably has a negative impact on public confidence in these institutions.

Concluding Remarks on Both Types of Choice

One feature is common to choice in both publicly funded private schools and public schools in France: embarrassment. These are things about which it is preferable not to talk, hence the absence of research on the impact of private schools and on the consequences of the weakening of the *carte scolaire*. Hence also the preference for a de facto "hidden choice," which cannot be regulated in order to promote social and academic equality of choice.

This embarrassment is caused mainly by what I have called the nature of the French educational system and the nature of the acceptable "discourse" that surrounds its governance, including conceptions of what is considered possible. According to this discourse, choice is judged to be intrinsically perverse. However, it has to be tolerated because of the necessity of having a "safety valve" and because of the strength of the groups that ask for it: the Catholic Church and the middle class.

Of course, discourse is not reality: I am not sure that the proportion of students who choose their schools is less in France than in the United States or perhaps even in England. However, the reigning discourse influences what can be overtly admitted, studied, praised, and regulated by principles on which everybody claims to agree. Some parents choose schools through their choice of housing, others by cheating on the *carte scolaire*, others, when possible, through official procedures. This situation seems to result in a system that favors high-income people, independent workers, teachers, right-wing people, and bright students. As such, it probably undermines the optimal functioning of political society by fostering some resentment toward those who figure out a way to choose or those who cheat.

One lesson to take from France is the importance of discussing the question of choice openly (which seems to be the case in the United States in any event), although, of course, open discussion will not eliminate the difficulties of implementing an effective and equitable form of choice.

Another lesson could be to develop choices among public schools as well as publicly funded private schools. If not, a clear advantage is given to private schools. This advantage may be reduced, as in France, by regulations that hinder the development of private schools, but such regulations in turn limit the positive effects of emulation between the two sectors. One kind of choice, particularly, has to be regulated: parents and students should know whether a school does or does not offer a minimum quality of education. If this is not done, the French example shows that it is quite impossible to prevent those who have adequate resources from escaping schools that they deem to be bad, which reinforces the existing social hierarchy if they are right and unfairly undermines the morale of teachers and other students—and the effectiveness and equity of the system—if they are wrong.

A final lesson would be that the most effective regulation of private schooling is provided by the baccalauréat, which ensures that the same curriculum is taught in all types of schools. That inspections provide a very weak control, if any control at all, already has been documented by an American observer, Frances Fowler.[60]

More generally, of course, the question of *laïcité* is not the same in a country where many denominations peacefully coexist and where religious communities are considered part of the political body and not as a threat to it.

However, as I see it, the French and U.S. cases are perhaps not so far apart. First, no natural law protects the United States from the hegemony of a given religion or at least from particular religious sensibilities, and it may be thought that the stronger a religion is—or the stronger religions, taken together, are—the more hegemonic it is or they are. So the relations between church and state in France are perhaps not so exotic as they appear at first glance. The tremendous growth of the influence of the religious right in the United States during the last twenty years argues for this thesis. Second, communities in the United States are part of its civil society insofar as they are a bridge between individuals and the whole society. If they split their members from the whole community or if they do not consider themselves part of wider society, there is no reason why they should peacefully coexist. So private schools deserve public subsidies only to the extent that they act as intermediaries, and some preference has to be given, for civic reasons, to those schools, private or public, where several communities meet.

A last possible lesson is that the government should, as in France, be obliged to offer schools of equivalent quality to people, no matter where they live, who do not want to go to a religious school. No one should be pressured into attending such a school by the absence of a good public school option.

Notes

1. Conseil Constitutionnel, Décision du Conseil 77–87 (November 23, 1977):

"Le Conseil Constitutionnel . . . ,

1. Considérant qu'aux termes de la loi . . . , les maîtres auxquels est confiée la mission d'enseigner dans un établissement privé lié à l'Etat par contrat sont tenus de respecter le caractère propre de cet établissement

2. Considérant, d'une part, que la sauvegarde du caractère propre d'un établissement lié à l'Etat par contrat . . . n'est que la mise en œuvre du principe de la liberté de l'enseignement

3. Considérant que ce principe, qui a notamment été rappelé à l'article 91 de la loi de finances du 31 mars 1931, constitue l'un des principes fondamentaux reconnus par les lois de la République, réaffirmés par le principe Préambule de la Constitution de 1946 et auxquels la Constitution de 1958 a conféré valeur constitutionnelle."

2. For the discussion in this chapter, I have used primarily A. Prost, *Education, société, et politiques* (Paris: Seuil, 1997); A. Prost, "Les écoles libres changent de fonction," in *Histoire générale de l'enseignement et de l'éducation en France* (Paris: Labat, 1982), pp. 413–43; T. Zeldin, *France 1848–1945: Ambition, Love, and Politics* (Oxford University Press, 1973); and T. Zeldin, *France 1848–1945: Intellect, Taste, and Anxiety* (Oxford University Press, 1977).

3. Zeldin, "Religion and Anticlericalism," in *France 1848–1945: Intellect, Taste, and Anxiety.*

4. Prost, "Les écoles libres changent de fonction."

5. Pope Pius XI, *Divini Illius Magistri*, encyclical letter (Vatican, December 31, 1929); Prost, "Les écoles libres changent de fonction," p. 413.

6. In fact, another voucher plan was proposed by a parliamentary commission as early as 1872, but it was finally rejected. W. Van Vliet and J. A. Smyth, "A Nineteenth-Century French Proposal to Use School Vouchers," *Comparative Education Review* (February 1982).

7. "Il n'y a pour le Chrétien d'école pleinement satisfaisante que l'école chrétienne. Le devoir que fait l'Eglise aux parents catholiques de lui confier leurs enfants apparaît ainsi dans la logique même de la foi." Déclaration de l'assemblée plénière de l'Episcopat, 1951, quoted in Prost, "Les écoles libres changent de fonction," p. 427.

8. Jean Jacques Rousseau, "Du Contrat Social ou Principes du Droit Politique (1762)," in *Oeuvres Complètes*, vol. 3 (Paris: Gallimard, 1964).

9. Alexis de Tocqueville, *L'ancien régime et la revolution* (1856) (Paris: Gallimard, 1967), p. 79.

10. Jacques Donzelot, *Faire Société* (Paris: Seuil, 2003). Donzelot supports his thesis with field research in Boston and in Marseille and also cites P. Grogan and T. Proscio, *Comeback Cities* (Boulder, Col.: Westview Press, 2000) in support of his arguments.

11. M. Fumaroli, "Non, Claude Allègre, l'Amérique n'est pas le modèle idéal," *Le Monde,* December 17, 1998.

12. Montesquieu, *De l'esprit des lois* (Paris: Gallimard, Idées, 1970), p. 80: *"C'est dans le gouvernement républicain que l'on a besoin de toute la puissance de l'éducation . . . . [en effet] la vertu politique est un renoncement à soi-même, qui est toujours une chose très pénible."*

13. John Dewey, "The School and Society" (1899), in D. A. Archambault, ed., *John Dewey on Education* (Chicago University Press, 1964), pp. 295–310.

14. Eamonn Callan, *Creating Citizens* (Oxford University Press, 1997).

15. R. Debray, "A M. le ministre de l'education," *Le Monde*, March 3, 1998.

16. *Syllabus*, encyclical letter (Vatican, 1864) quoted in Zeldin, *France 1848–1945: Ambition, Love, and Politics* .

17. D. Meuret, "Intérêt, Justice, Laïcité," *Le Télémaque*, vol. 14 (1998), pp. 53–65.

18. The libertarian rejection of the state is grounded on an opposition between the state and the individual, while the "populist" rejection of the state is grounded on an idealization of the people as a collective body, a more "holistic" position. One could not equate Le Pen with Madelin (or Nozick).

19. J. P. Visse, *La question scolaire* (Lille: Presses Universitaires du Septentrion, 1995).

20. F. Héran, "Ecole publique, école privée: qui peut choisir?" *Economie et statistiques*, vol. 293 (1996), pp. 17–40.

21. These expenses include fees, insurance, meals taken at school, school buses, books and other school supplies, and private lessons. Most of these expenses are likely to be higher in families whose children enroll in private schools. So, the difference is not only in the amount of the private school fees.

22. "There is no rush toward private schools. The number of students has remained the same for twenty years, and we still lost some students this year. We are not here to pluck the public chicken." Eric de Labarre, chairman of the private school parent association, 2002, quoted in *Nouvel Observateur*, October 2, 2003, p. 27 (translation by the author).

23. G. Langoet and A. Léger, *Le choix des familles: école publique ou école privée?* (Paris: Editions Fabert, 1997).

24. R. Ballion, "L'enseignement privé, une école sur mesure?" *Revue française de sociologie*, vol. 21, no. 2 (1980); G. Langoet and A. Léger, *Ecole publique ou ecole privée? Trajectoires et réussites scolaires* (Paris: Editions Fabert, 1994).

25. X. Ternisien, "En une décennie, les croyances ont reculé en France" ("In a decade, religious beliefs lost ground in France"), *Le Monde*, April 17, 2003.

26. Langoet and Léger, *Le choix des familles.*

27. J. L. Auduc, *Le système éducatif* (Paris: Hachette Education, 2001), p. 287.

28. Héran, "Ecole publique, école privée."

29. C. Chausseron, "Le choix de l'établissement au début des études secondaires," Note d'information 01-42 (Ministère de l'Education Nationale–DPD, 2001).

30. V. Tournier, "Ecole publique, école privée: Le clivage oublié" ("Public school, private school: The forgotten divide"), *Revue française des sciences politiques,* vol. 47, no. 5 (1997), pp. 560–88.

31. J. B. Champion and N. Tabard, "Les territoires de l'école privée et de l'école publique," *Economie et statistiques*, vol. 293 (1996), pp. 41–53.

32. B. Liensol and D. Meuret, "Les performances des lycées privés et publics pour la préparation au baccalauréat: Etude sur l'académie de Nancy-Metz," *Education et formations*, vol. 12 (1987), pp. 31–42.

33. C. Ben Ayed, "Familles populaires de l'enseignement public et privé," *Education et sociétés* 5 (2001).

34. Chloe Tavan, "Ecole publique, école privée: Comparaison de trajectoires et de la réussite scolaire," *Revue française de sociologie*, vol. 45, no. 1 (2004), pp. 133–65.

35. Chausseron, "Le choix de l'établissement au début des études secondaires"; Héran, "Ecole publique, école privée"; Langoet and Léger, *Le choix des familles.*

36. Langoet and Léger, *Le choix des familles.*

37. C. Choquet and F. Héran, "Quand les élèves jugent les collèges et les lycées," *Economie et statistiques*, vol. 293 (1996), pp. 107–25.

38. Ministère de l'Education Nationale, *Géographie de l'école* (1998).

39. A. O. Hirschman, *Exit, Voice, Loyalty* (Harvard University Press, 1970).

40. C. Dobb, G. Glass, and C. Crockett, "The U.S. Charter School Movement and Ethnic Segregation," paper prepared for a meeting of the American Educational Research Association, New Orleans, 2000.

41. What follows is partly inspired by D. Meuret, S. Broccolochi, and M. Duru-Bellat, "Autonomie et choix des établissments scolaires," *Cahiers de l'IREDU*, vol. 62 (2001).

42. A. Prost, "La loi Savary: les raisons d'un échec," in *Alain Savary: Politique et honneur* (Paris: Presses de Sciences Po, 2002); J. P. Obin, "Le projet d'établissement en France: mythe et réalité," *Politiques d'éducation et de formation*, vol. 1 (2001), pp. 9–28.

43. The author and colleagues asked in 2000 for appointments with six rectorats to ask questions on that topic. Four refused. Of the two that agreed, one agreed because of personal acquaintance with one of us. Some interviews showed the agents in charge to be strongly devoted to the *carte scolaire* as an expression of the common good, but we have no idea of how representative they were.

44. M. Duru-Bellat and A. Mingat, "La gestion de l'hétérogénéité des publics d'élèves au collège," *Cahiers de l'IREDU*, vol. 59 (1997).

45. J. Rawls, *Political Liberalism* (New York: Columbia University Press, 1993).

46. This condition is not without problems. It can be respected by a church that wants to exert a general influence more than convert the souls of the children. This is the case, in France, of the Catholic Church. But how is one to think that an Islamic school following Islamic principles, in which 80 percent of girls wear the *foulard*, is "open to all," even if it formally accepts anybody who wants to enroll? Clearly this principle means also that the environment and teaching in the school should be acceptable by all. This problem has not yet been fully seen in France because of the small number of "hard" religious schools.

47. T. Ramadan, "Pas de loi contre le foulard," *Libération*, May 7, 2003.

48. Loi 2004-228 du 15 mars 2004 encadrant, en application du principe de laïcité, le port de signes ou de tenues manifestant une appurtenance religieuse dans les écoles, colleges et lycées publics, Journal official du 17 mars 2004, p. 5190.

49. Robert Ballion and Françoise Oeuvrard, *Le choix du lycée* (Ministère de l' éducation nationale, 1989).

50. Auduc, *Le système éducatif*, p. 287.

51. Ministère de l'Education Nationale, Circulaire 98-263 du 29-12-1998, Bulletin Officiel de l'Education Nationale 99-1 du 07-01-1999, p. 9.

52. C. Gissot, F. Héran, and N. Mannon, *Les efforts éducatifs des familles*, Consommation et modes de vie 331–32 (Institut National de la Statistique et des Etudes Economiques-Résultats, 1994), p. 253.

53. Chausseron, "Le choix de l'établissement au début des études secondaires."

54. S. Broccolichi and A. Van Zanten, "School Competition and Pupil Flight in the Urban Periphery," *Journal of Education Policy*, vol. 15, no. 1 (2000), pp. 51–60.

55. D. Trancart, *Evolution de la ségrégation sociale dans les collèges publics* (Université de Rouen, 2001).

56. R. Ballion, *La bonne école* (Paris: Hatier, 1991), p. 258.

57. S. Thomas and others, "Stability and Consistency in Secondary Schools' Effects on Students' GCSE Outcomes over Three Years," *School Effectiveness and School Improvement*, vol. 8, no. 2 (1997).

58. Trancart, *Evolution de la ségrégation sociale dans les collèges publics.*

59. For primary schools, see H. Glennerster, "United Kingdom Education 1997–2001," *Oxford Review of Economic Policy,* vol. 18, no. 2 (2002).

60. Frances C. Fowler, "School Choice Policy in France: Success and Limitations," *Educational Policy,* vol. 6, no. 4 (1992), pp. 429–43.

10

Italy: The Impossible Choice

LUISA RIBOLZI

Questions about the public regulation of nonpublic schools and the role that such regulation should play in U.S. education policy cannot be immediately and obviously answered by examining Italy's experience, for two basic reasons. First of all, school choice was not considered an educational issue in Italy until the 1990s. Because there has not been much public debate on the topic, none of the various government administrations, whether left- or right-oriented, have ever developed a real strategy to promote school choice. Rather, the political debate has focused on the role of private institutions in the development of public values. Second, Italy's history is extremely peculiar, and it differs in particular from that of the United States. It would therefore be ill-advised to study local Italian processes with the idea that easily transferable lessons could be learned.

At the moment, public opinion in Italy regarding private schools is changing. In my view, this is no small thing. A real cultural turning point is approaching, and political decisions in the near future could either support cultural openness toward school choice or doom it.

This chapter begins with a description of the history of the Italian school system, considering in particular the position of nonstate private education as opposed to state-supported public education. It is important to make clear at the outset the peculiar terminology regarding the status of schools in Italy. Until recently, only schools run by the Italian nation-state were identified as *public* schools. Even schools run by municipal public authorities were considered private, as were schools run by religious or other private organizations.

The Italian School as a Device to Promote National Unity

In order to understand how school choice evolved in Italy, it is necessary first to recognize that the question of family choice of schools has nationwide ideological associations. The majority of Italians assume that the term pertains specifically to Catholic schools, and a distinction between them and private schools in general has emerged only recently. To this day, religious non-Catholic schools are scarce in Italy, and for the most part the schools that do exist are Jewish.

But despite the long and continued presence of the Catholic Church in Italy, the Italian school system developed as a strictly secular institution. Schools played a strong role in the political construction of the Italian nation. However, Catholic authorities did not participate in that process, because it involved the conquest of Rome and the confinement of the Pope to Vatican City. For this reason, *public* schools were equivalent to *state* schools in Italy, and Catholic schools were not considered part of the national school system but as segregating institutions, at odds with the very idea of Italian citizenship. The state has therefore focused primarily on controlling Catholic schools rather than on helping society to become more engaged in education.

This attitude, though prevalent, is not formally recognized by law, and the present debate is based on different interpretations of the Italian constitution. In fact, article 33 of the postwar constitution, adopted in 1947, states that "public and private bodies shall be entitled to establish schools and educational institutions, *with no financial costs for the State.*" That phrase sparked a seemingly endless series of political confrontations: supporters of school choice insist that it simply means that the state is not *obliged* to provide funding but could choose to do so. They also understand the provision to mean that the government should not allocate any funds to *start* a private school but could fund its operations. Opponents of school choice maintain that the phrase implies an absolute prohibition against state support for private schools.

Of course, had this been the real issue, the problem could have been solved fifty years ago by revising the Constitution. In reality, the centralized and monopolistic educational system in Italy rejects the notion that the right to educate children belongs primarily to parents and family, with schools in a subsidiary role. Until recently, the predominant ideological influences have not allowed the debate to concern family school choice. Public discussion has been confined to defining the distinction between public and private, wherein *public* refers exclusively to state schools and *private* to schools organized by institutions other than the state, although they also provide a public service.

I do not intend in this chapter to retrace the history of Italian schooling in detail, but I would like to outline the relationship that has existed between state and nonstate schools during three historical phases:[1]

—From the founding of the kingdom of Italy in 1861 until the rise of fascism in 1922, the basic state concern was how to build national unity. Although political unification had been achieved, cultural unity had yet to follow. In addition, most Italian citizens had only a very modest education.

—Under fascism (1922–45), schools were chiefly concerned with consolidating political consensus by educating the future leadership class on one hand and indoctrinating the young on the other.

—After World War II, a national educational system slowly began to emerge. The system consists of state schools (*scuole statali*) and recognized schools (*scuole paritarie*), which are private schools that conform to certain rules determined by the central education authority. This system was enshrined in the Constitution and, in 2000, in Law 62.

The nonstate school has had quite a marginal place in the Italian school system up to now, although for centuries the schools established by religious orders had been not only boarding schools for the aristocracy but also schools for the poor. According to Chiosso, "[t]he ancient and glorious tradition of nonstate schools certainly merits respect (as well as the acknowledgment of their merits within the history of the Italian schooling system), but it is undeniable that from the unity of Italy onward, schooling has been identified with the state school in the 'collective imagination.'"[2]

The Period of Consolidation of National Unity

As noted above, since 1861, when the nation of Italy was established, the Italian school system has been monopolistic. The government, aiming to create a common culture and provide modern education, adopted an interventionist educational policy. However, the Education Act of 1859 (*legge organica dell'istruzione* of November 13, 1859)—also called the Casati law, after the man who was minister for public instruction at the time—gave any private citizen meeting the required standards the opportunity to open a school. The liberal-oriented minister considered private schools, even if they were controlled by the government, to be a "statement of freedom." It was, however, a restricted form of freedom: the diplomas issued by private schools

Figure 10-1. *Illiteracy in Italy, 1861–1991*

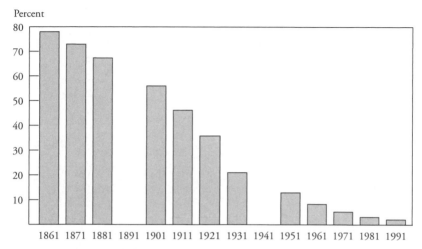

Percent

Source: ISTAT, *Statistiche dell'istruzione* (Rome), various years.

were not recognized by the state, a fact that prevented any real competition between the public and private school sectors. When Casati introduced this law, he mentioned Germany as a model for Italy, writing that there, although "the state provides education by means of its own institutions, it also controls the private education sector and allows private and official schools to compete in the educational arena."[3] The idea that competition could increase the quality of education is no recent notion in Italy.

Meanwhile, the young nation had to cope with several severe problems. Italy was a puzzle made up of a great number of pieces, previously independent states with different histories, cultures, languages, and levels of social development. But though they were quite different from each other in those fundamental respects, they shared one strong element: the Catholic religion. The new national government therefore considered the Church a threat to the effective unification and modernization of the country. The process of unification involved the elites and the middle class, a small minority of the population. Barely 10 percent of the citizens in the southern region could even speak Italian, and 78 percent were illiterate (see figure 10-1).[4] The Casati law was extended to the whole kingdom of Italy in July 1877. In spite of the fact that it was unfavorably criticized in the year it appeared, it has remained the foundation of Italian school law. According to some, the lasting power of this law is due not only to its internal cohesion—it is based on a strong though questionable model—but also to the fact that it fully represented the ideas and the expectations of the originally small middle class, which had wanted a unified Italy and continued to grow over the years.

Following the example of the French government, which also had centralized its school system, the Italian government identified nationwide homogeneity as a crucial standard for schooling. Homogeneity within the nation was considered necessary for building consensus, if not so much for developing a sense of citizenship. Italy pursued homogeneity in this sense through administrative interventions—for instance, by strengthening the school bureaucratic and inspection machinery.

The attempts at homogeneity were not uniformly embraced. The state-controlled school was seen by some as a form of "state ideological apparatus" rather than as the expression of an independent civil society.[5] The new Italian state, aiming to create a military and administrative elite, imposed a centralized bureaucratic model of schooling across the country, with no consideration of the diverse traditions of the regions—traditions that were appreciated by the Catholic Church. In this period, the extension of public schooling reduced the role of all nonstate schools but particularly of Catholic schools, because the Church supported the right of families to supervise the education of their children, in contrast with the state, which attempted to direct, control, and limit their right to do so.

Under Prime Minister Giovanni Giolitti's leadership, the Daneo Credaro law (1911) extended state control over the local elementary schools, which were run by the municipalities. The reason for this action was not only to extend political control but also to improve national development by centralizing educational policy. In a way, Giolitti's educational policy represented, for the first time, an attempt to fight illiteracy and to reduce inequalities among locally funded schools. The quality of public schools was probably low at this point. In 1919, Ernesto Codignola, an education scholar, called the school system a "diploma mill" because teachers were not specifically trained and qualified and were appointed without formal selection procedures.[6] He demanded that the monopoly of the state be abolished and school autonomy be introduced.[7]

In the election of 1913, Giolitti reached a formal agreement with the Catholic Church, recognizing that private schooling was "an important factor in the diffusion and elevation of national culture."[8] From this moment on, freedom in the educational sector grew: for instance, the Peoples' Party (*Partito popolare*), founded by Luigi Sturzo in 1919, and a group of intellectuals including Giovanni Gentile claimed that schools should not be subject to either the state or the Catholic Church.

From the very beginning of the formal school system, families were not really considered actors within the school. The elites either agreed with the pedagogical ideas of the public schools or their sons (seldom their daughters!) would enter private religious schools. The working class, having little political power, was served by local state schools, sometimes in a paternalistic way.[9] Most emigrants from Italy were unable to read and write; they did not speak standard Italian but regional dialects, and the various Little Italy neighborhoods that sprang up in their countries of destination were, in fact, regional enclaves. The concept of political and social participation was not yet familiar in Italian pedagogy.

The School System in the Fascist Period: Gentile's Educational Act

The Casati law was fully reformed by the Gentile law in 1923. Giovanni Gentile was a philosopher who had long asked for more autonomy in the school system, and he became minister for public instruction, a position that was renamed minister of national education in 1922. The main feature of Gentile's reform was its firm distinction between *education* for the elites and *training* for the lower classes. As for private schools, he wrote that public education "should be regulated so as to allow private schools to develop quality alongside public schools."[10]

Gentile worked to regulate the size and the organization of schools in order to improve the low quality of existing schooling. Through his reform, he tried to counterbalance the principles of classic education, which was "meant to educate the students' spirits," and the needs of the modern age by creating a new scientific secondary school (*liceo scientifico*). However, as the law noted, the classic secondary school (*liceo classico*) continued to be "the chief breeding ground for . . . the future upper class of the nation."

Gentile was inspired by fascist ideology, but it was too new to be explicit in his reforms, even if he claimed that reform was necessary to replace "neutral" schooling with a form of national education based on the idea of *patria* (fatherland) and the memory of Italy's past glory. The prevailing attitude was represented by the goal of maintaining continuity with classical Roman culture. The idea of the state being the sole educating agency excluded the possibility of families enjoying freedom of choice and of local traditions surviving, and in 1930 Mussolini identified the "totalitarian principle of education" as the way to strengthen the fascist revolution. In spite of a state policy designed to increase the population, the family itself played a marginal role both in choosing children's schools and in their use of leisure time, which was taken care of by Fascist Party organizations.

In February 1939, Minister Giuseppe Bottai promulgated his "school chart," though it was never put into effect. The center of the reform was the idea that the school system could and should be used to create political consensus to respond to the political needs of the fascist government. But at the same time, Bottai was aware that it was necessary for Italy to respond to the economic hardships of the 1930s, and he decided to extend and increase compulsory education across the country in order to improve the culture and the socioeconomic status of the working class and perhaps to strengthen its political indoctrination at the same time. It can be said that in the first eighty years of the Italian school system, the family was not considered a participating partner; its only task was to agree with the teachers and to subscribe to the official ideology. "School choice" was a mere phrase, devoid of substance.

School Reforms after World War II

The postwar constitution, adopted in 1947, reacted against fascist ideology in two different ways, in part by restoring prefascist values, in part by introducing new ideas that had been elaborated abroad during the fascist period. As for education, the Constitution recognized the primacy of the family's role (articles 29 and 30), although the school system continues to be centralized and monopolistic. Families cannot choose a school because children must enter the public school belonging to their catchment area. They can, of course, choose a private school, but private schools are not free. This has had two social consequences: first, the users of private schools have become increasingly upper middle class, and second, the total number of private institutions has decreased (see figure 10-2). The drop in the national birth rate, which reduced the number of students by 23.4 percent—from 11,437,679 in 1981–82 to 8,760,633 in 2001–02—disproportionately affected the private school sector, which suffered a 29.5 percent decrease in numbers. State schools underwent a 25.1 percent reduction in student population. The decrease has affected mainly private upper secondary schools, whereas private primary and middle schools have been less affected than corresponding state schools. From 2001 through 2003, the situation remained unchanged, but the number of private schools decreased from 5,229 to 5,020 (2,351 primary schools, 875 middle schools, and 1,794 upper secondary schools).

There were two main ideas behind the development of a single centralized state school system in the postfascist era. These ideas were taken for granted at the time, but, in my opinion, they are no longer valid.[11] The first assumption was that all schools should be alike in order to promote equality and protect the poor. It was taken for granted that pluralism would be ensured

Figure 10-2. *Percentage of All Italian Schools That Are Private, by Level*

Percent

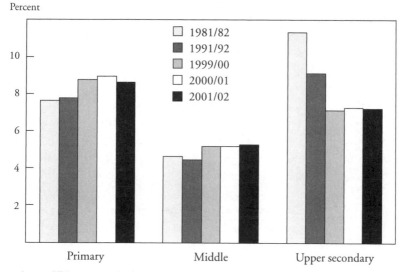

Source: ISTAT, *Statistiche dell'istruzione* (Rome), various years.

within a school by parents' participation, and the idea of school choice therefore was finally rejected, the notion being that all state schools were formally the same. In reality, conformity within the school system conflicts with the increasing diversity of students' educational needs, which may differ in school A from those in school B. The idea of a larger community whose inhabitants share common experiences, opportunities, and values is no longer a valid reference for schools, especially in increasingly fragmented and segregated urban areas consisting of neighborhoods that are homogeneous within themselves but quite different from one another. If no allowances are made to compensate for the socioeconomic and cultural differences among neighborhoods, schools reflect the environment in which they are located. Consequently, the single-model school system led to second-rate schools in the poor suburbs while those in the affluent residential quarters of the city turned out to be high-quality.

The second assumption was that the school should be neutral and restrain from shaping students' values. But, as Bernstein says, "often people in schools and in classrooms make a distinction between what they call the transmission of skills and the transmission of values. These are always kept apart as if there were a conspiracy to disguise the fact that there is only one discourse. . . . Most researchers are continually studying the two, or thinking as if there are two: as if education is about values on the one hand, and about competence on the other. In my view, there are not two discourses, there is only one."[12] In reality, every school and every teacher has a specific "model of adult and society" in mind, and they direct the pupil's socialization process accordingly. For instance, when Alexis de Tocqueville visited the United States in the 1830s, he observed that all schools "preach the same moral law in the name of God" and that teaching in common schools was based on the moral law inspired by Protestantism.[13]

The reasons for the orientation toward state monopoly of schools are diverse and complex. The most important are probably due to the interrelated problems facing the school system:

—Extensive illiteracy and the low quality of schooling implied that the "priority concerned primarily the education of pupils aged eleven to fourteen."[14] Decisionmakers thought that in a period of social and economic breakdown, only the direct intervention of the state could radically change the curricula and improve the population's level of education.

—The administrative bureaucracy was important, and it intended to maintain its privileges by renewing the status quo.

—Neutrality was not considered a real issue by the strong Catholic teachers' organizations, since they were confident that they would be able to diffuse their religious values across the entire "neutral" school system.

—Intellectuals and politicians had a persistent lack of confidence in private schools, as they considered Catholic schools especially to be ideologically oriented preserves for the rich.

—The political majority, although inspired by Catholic democratic ideas, did not apply the Church's principles of subsidiarity and social participation to the school sector. They agreed with the centralized welfare state model and with the goal of furthering equality and equal distribution of social goods, including education, by means of public intervention.

—The government was wary of the population's still deeply rooted regional affiliations. In order to avoid the proliferation of a "move to the particular," the state forced every student and every family to adapt to a common model.

Acknowledgment of the Value of School Choice

The nation's goals implied that the school system was to be one, standardized and centralized. If one wanted to attend a different kind of school, one had to pay for it. This model undoubtedly has had some historic merits. For instance, illiteracy has almost fully disappeared, and the percentage of students graduating or earning diplomas is much higher than in the past and close to the European average. But such a model seems to work well mostly from a quantitative, not a qualitative, standpoint: when the myriad demands of society require flexibility, a rigid structure is unsuitable. In particular, it was impossible for the bureaucratic approach to meet the growing demands of families, which were beginning to ask to take part in the education of their children through attentive involvement in their daily school life. In 1977, the so-called educational framework law (*decreti delegati*) allowed parents to participate on a number of school boards, but they had no decisionmaking power; ironically enough, they could have only an advisory role. Sociologists say that the first schools originated from an act of delegation of power by the family, but the Italian school system has seen itself as "allowing" the family to participate in school life. Parents are not considered active citizens but private people, so the concept of participation becomes quite ambiguous. Parents participate in educational affairs not on their own initiative but solely on terms established by the state. The fact that the state dictates the terms and limits the scope of parental participation has decreased the participation of parents in school life, as in public life generally. In a short time, participation in school became an activity only for parents already involved in some other form of political or social participation (for example, unions, political parties, local government), increasing the likelihood that less advantaged students would obtain less positive educational outcomes.

A Value Change in the Concept of Citizenship

"Educating for citizenship" is a process that is tightly linked to developing the feeling of belonging. It also is tied to building a common awareness of the real meaning of being a citizen of a given society—of its underlying values and the associated constraints. It is linked also to the acquisition of values, attitudes, and skills appropriate to a specific society.[15] Yet postwar Italy was still radically pluralistic from the point of view of language and traditions—it was television more than the schools that succeeded in generalizing the knowledge and use of the Italian language across the country—and the country still was torn by the ideological divisions that had existed during World War II.

This is why political decisions concerning school choice confirmed the former school model, which was founded on such values as neutrality, conformity, and centrality rather than on the family's right to choose the school. The latter was considered too risky a measure. It is certain that until the mid-1980s, the need for apparent uniformity within the school system, the perception of school choice as an issue peculiar to Catholics, and the general idea that "private schools are attended disproportionately by less capable students from richer families"[16] brought about stagnation in the debate about school choice. As mentioned, the debate focused on the intended meaning of the expression "*senza oneri per lo Stato*" ("without costs for the state"), the phrase prominent in school finance legislation. The prevailing view was that this rule proscribed the possibility of state financing of private schools either directly or indirectly, through, for example, vouchers.

The discussion about school vouchers evoked no action in Italy until 1986, when the vice secretary of the Socialist Party, Claudio Martelli, proposed the measure again. The debate that followed did not lead to action but brought about an important cultural result: the voucher proposal was no longer identified as exclusively a Catholic cause.[17] The issue would have been dropped once more, however, if it had not been related to the growing demand for civic and social participation that has characterized contemporary society, in Italy and elsewhere. This tendency is emphasized by two different phenomena:

—the *growth of local communities*, both from the economic point of view—through the development of "horizontal" districts (with an organized network of small enterprises belonging to the same line of business) and "vertical" districts (with enterprises that are leaders in different lines of business)—and from the social point of view, through the rediscovery of a more localized cultural identity

—the *growth of people's desire for social interaction and solidarity*, expressed not only through their membership in associations, but also through voluntary service and activity in the third sector, in philanthropic and nonprofit community and civic organizations.

Given the fact that society is more differentiated, social solidarity is no longer founded, as in the past, on the sharing of religious or ideological creeds learned within the family, but on common behavioral rules that are learned mainly in one's secondary socialization process—that is, in school. Italians have begun to consider cultural diversity a value, no longer merely a risk, and they believe that schooling should pursue not only shared values and academic competence but also positive exposure to different values.

In the child development process, the cognitive dimension and the ethics dimension are not separable; the school's task is to facilitate the acquisition of academic knowledge but also the development of social competence and emotional maturity and to promote character building, a positive approach to life, and a confident relation to one's own community. Civic education develops along four interlinked levels, which together constitute the behavioral model of the individual as citizen:

—the level of *personal identity*, which is a fundamental requirement for each individual if one is to develop an understanding of the value of one's rights and duties

—the level of *community and ethnic identity*, which is necessary in order to define the role of one's ethnic group or community vis-à-vis the individual and the state or the supranational community

—the level of the *nation*, which, though the most emphasized so far, currently is facing difficulties as it is "compressed" between the local and the global level

—the *global* or *supranational* level, which now is gaining ground and defining the role of the individual as a citizen in the global community.

In any case, neither cultural indoctrination nor the consensus building that characterized the entire history of Italy's educational policy is at the center of civic education in Italy. What is central is the development of a critical capacity to be used by the individual in managing his or her relation to society, through the mediation of the community. The development of citizens' awareness in a time of global reorganization has to take into account the growing uncertainty about the structure of the social order and the characteristics of the social contract that ties the state to its citizens. That aim cannot be attained by a "neutral," undifferentiated education system, but by one that has the social resources to develop *school connectedness*, which works to counter "social pathologies."[18] Pathologies are fostered when society ignores the fact that the state is a product of its citizens, not vice versa, and that the citizen has given up his or her own freedom in exchange for a security that the state can no longer ensure. Moreover, the relationship between the citizen and state is not absolutely fixed at a given point in time but is subject to renegotiation based on emerging political consensus. The Italian social contract is now seen as leaning more toward Locke and less toward Hobbes.

Like other sectors (the national health service, for instance), the school sector also has recently begun to assert the principle of subsidiarity, which encourages the direct intervention of citizens in government initiatives and considers excessive centralization of services as risky because it coincides with the centralization of power.[19] As Tocqueville noted, "[a] free society is above all a self-government project, in which autonomous and wise citizens associate in order to give rise to a government based on their own consensus so as to guarantee the rights of freedom and to promote the common good." The citizen is different from the subject: "He is sovereign, the depository of power, the voter of political leaders, who are supposed to serve him: therefore the citizen is ultimately liable for the political order." Public policies that reduce the citizen's responsibilities are oppressive and stifle the capacity of individuals to govern themselves.

It is necessary, on the other hand, that the school system develop *social competence* among students. Social competence involves positive attitudes toward membership in associations, cooperation, and other such indications of sociability. However, the school system can do that only if the centralized power of bureaucracies is tempered, as such authorities tend to defend their survival by promulgating complicating norms and regulations. The phrase *school autonomy* is entering the debate on school reform, and it brings about the need to sustain in actual fact, not only in words, the family's right to choose its child's school both in the state and in the private sector.

Autonomy and Choice: a Winning Combination

If one assumes that Italy has been a relatively uniform country as far as race, religion, language, and culture are concerned, school choice seems to emerge as an attractive solution to Italy's current social and educational challenges. In reality, however, Italy's linguistic unity is relatively recent and its cultural unity is still doubtful, apart from the population's general adherence to common values and acquisition of a few common cultural characteristics. Religious uniformity has diminished in the face of increasing secularization and the growth of minority groups from non-Catholic countries, although the discourse about the "Muslim challenge" to civic values and national identity, proclaimed by the *Lega* party in northern Italy, has not been relevant in the political arena until very recently. Italy has only a recent history of immigration: it was an emigrants' country until the 1970s. For instance, between 1901 and 1913 more than 3 million Italians emigrated to the United States. In forty years, that became 15 million total. The percentage of foreign-born students in Italian schools, which was 0.06 percent in 1983–84, grew to 2.31 percent in 2001–02, with 55.6 percent (101,145 pupils) coming from non–European Union countries.[20]

In the field of education, and as stated in the Law *Guermeur*, "hitherto private schooling meant a small number of nondenominational schools that were mainly inspired by a particular educational philosophy and by a greater number of denominational Catholic or Protestant schools. This distinction is actually no longer applicable, given the fact that Muslim schools are being established almost everywhere in increasing numbers, along with the spreading wave of immigration from North Africa and from the Middle East. These schools have already been granted legal status and public financing has been allocated to them in France and in Germany."[21]

Nevertheless, in 1994, when the *Polo delle Libertà*, the new political movement led by Silvio Berlusconi, proposed introducing school vouchers to facilitate private school choice, the reaction was basically ideological, and the proposed measure was thought to be ultimately promoted by the Catholics. The
real debate started when President Oscar Luigi Scalfaro declared:

> This concept is rooted in democracy, pluralism, monopoly-free culture.
> In a state that had reached—permit me to say—a degree of quasi-per-
> fection, of right harmonization between state school and independent
> school, families, whose duty it is by natural right to educate their chil-
> dren, would be able to choose freely among different, equally available,
> unrestricted options costing the same amount of money.[22]

The reactions in the press and among leftist intellectuals and politicians
were very violent. The hypothesis circulated that the intervention by the president, who is a practicing Catholic, might have been made in agreement with
the Vatican. *Repubblica*, a daily newspaper, claimed that "the Pope's lobby is
leading its crusade," disseminating propaganda in an obvious effort to gain
support for the Catholic Popular Party before elections. It would take too
long to report all the examples of political statements by leftist politicians.
Still, there was a new twist to the debate: before, the opposition to private
school financing was ideological, not rational; since then, there has been general awareness of the fact that the issue today involves a different conception
of the role of the state.[23] The center-right government had to resign before
any decision was made on the schooling question, but since the mid-1980s
the debate has tended to be ideology free. Finally, the program of the center-
left government elected in April 1996 (in which the Catholic Popular Party,
whose position always has been inclined to favor the acknowledgment of the
public role of private schools, was represented) includes the explicit acknowledgment of the principle of equality in both state and nonstate schools.

One year later, on March 15, 1997, Law 59 (the so-called Bassanini Law),
which instituted reforms in public administration, was passed. Article 21 of
the law grants autonomy to state schools. The fact that autonomy did not
result from a law concerning school reform but from a law concerning the
reform of public administration reveals that there was still strong opposition
to breaking the state's central monopoly on subsidized education. Law 59
asserts the right to school choice, since it introduces the principle that
schools are validated not so much by their belonging to the state as by their
educational plan (which has come to be known as the educational offer plan,

or POF), for which the state has only to establish essential guidelines for school performance and achievement. The stated principle of accountability has a logical consequence for private schools: the nonpublic status of non-state schools is no longer tenable when they have to meet the same requirements as state schools.

Nevertheless, the ideological debate became inflamed and only three years later, in spite of the rising conflicts within the center-leftist majority in power, Law 62 passed on March 10, 2000. Law 62 contains "regulations for school equality and measures concerning the right to schooling and education and training." Article 1 states, "The national educational system, according to article 23, paragraph 2, of the Constitution, consists of state schools and *paritarie* (acknowledged) schools, whether private or established by the local authorities."

The law introduced the concept of "equality," which is granted to schools that comply with eight specific conditions, ranging from "an educational plan conforming to the Constitution's principles" to "suitable premises, furniture, and educational equipment." For the moment, financing is to be allocated only to private primary schools and to private sector interventions on behalf of handicapped children. It also contemplates a progressive allocation of funds dependent on state budget priorities. At the end of the third year of experimentation, the minister for education was to submit a report to Parliament and at the same time collect all the administrative regulations on this subject in a single Consolidation Act.

This law represents a real step forward, both from the cultural point of view and in terms of education policy, because for the first time public and private schools are no longer opposed. The autonomous state schools and the acknowledged private schools are considered equally worthy, and the country's educational system is identified as a *comprehensive national* system, not just a *state* system (in Italian, the "state" refers strictly to the political representation of the population; it excludes "civic society," that is, social actors acting independently in families and in the third sector—in church, charities, cultural associations, and so on).[24] Nevertheless, the law still suffers from certain limitations:

—The reference to article 33 of the Italian constitution does not resolve the question of "with no costs for the state."

—The financing of private schools is bound to state budget conditions; if funds are lacking, it would run short, because state education would come first.

—The acknowledgment of equality is validated by the regional directors for education, whose evaluation criteria sometimes are different.

At present the reform process is following two basic trends:

—From the normative point of view, the different regulations still in force are being consolidated in a single act in order to avoid all possible complications and contradictions.

—From the financial point of view, the guidelines allocate available financial resources to both state and private schools on an equal basis, so if funds are allotted for teachers' education and training, for development of new educational technologies, or for support of handicapped children, then all schools, not only state schools, will now be able to apply for monetary support.

Recurring ordinary financing cannot yet fund extensive solutions: in 1999 a primary school pupil cost $5,354 to educate, a middle-school student $6,206, and an upper secondary school pupil $6,741.[25] In acknowledged schools, the pupils' families have to cover education expenses themselves. To overcome that social inequality, a number of proposals are being advanced both in the field of school financing (agreements with the schools, repayment of expenses for teachers' salaries, and so forth) and of family financing (school vouchers, tax deductions, and so forth). Conventions (pacts between government and school that exclude the family's direct involvement) were and still are refused by school choice supporters, because "it would immediately tie all free schools to state and regional decisionmakers—that is, to parties and bureaucrats."[26]

Some regions under center-right governments have introduced school vouchers by following different criteria (only for private schools or also for state schools; the same amount for all schools or different amounts according to family income, child's age, and so forth). On the other hand, local authorities already cover part of the educational costs in government-run schools, with an average amount of $940 (2001) for each pupil.[27]

Conclusions

Two recent policy developments may give rise to the government funding of private schools in Italy. First, under current law, local education authorities can, at their discretion, subsidize acknowledged public schools up to the per-pupil amount that they contribute to government-run schools. To date, it is unclear to what extent such subsidization is actually occurring. Second, based on a September 2, 2003, administrative act of the Ministry of Education and the Ministry of the Economy and Finance, a lump sum of €30 million will be made available to reimburse Italian families for a portion of the costs of sending their children to private schools. To qualify, the student must be subject to Italy's compulsory education requirement (six to fifteen years of age) and must be attending a private school that is "acknowledged" as acceptable by education authorities. The reimbursements are promised for school years 2003 through 2005. If all eligible families request reimbursement, then the amount will be about €300 each, or approximately 10 percent of the average annual tuition at acknowledged private schools.

This analysis introduces one more key issue that might change the Italian school system. On October 18, 2001, the Reform Law, which concerns a number of articles of the Italian constitution, was published. Article 117 grants the state exclusive authority regarding the "general measures for education," although "education is subject to concurrent legislation, apart from the areas of school autonomy and of vocational education and training," which already are under the regions' authority. This means that regions, provinces, and municipalities could modify any norm, so long as the general measures for education—measures that actually need further definition—are not contradicted.

In addition, article 114 states that "the republic is organized into municipalities, provinces, metropolises, regions, and state." A number of regions support the principle of "no costs for the state," but because the state is only one subject of the republic, the other subjects could be entitled to finance private schools. It is evident how complex the situation is and how rapidly it is developing after decades of inaction. The problem seems now to be whether families really want to be liable for their children's education and how ready teachers are to cooperate with them. Nonstate schools need resources to perform their educational functions, not just to survive, and they will be able to use them properly only if they convey meaningful values and make their students aware of how important it is to prepare themselves to become active citizens in their democracy. As Stefano Versari notes,

> In order to be truly democratic and to improve the quality of life, any society needs the cooperation of all of its members. That is why education has such a key role to play today—because central to the calling of schools is their duty to prepare all children to participate in the life of the community and to assume their mutual responsibility for it.[28]

Notes

1. For an excellent summary, see the section on Italy in Charles L. Glenn, "Schools between State and Civil Society" (Boston College, 2003).

2. Giorgio Chiosso, "Scuola dell'autonomia e nuova cittadinanza," in Alessandro Pajno, Giorgio Chiosso, and Giuseppe Bertagna, *L'autonomia delle scuole* (Brescia: La Scuola, 1997), p. 118.

3. Quoted in Chiosso, "Scuola dell'autonomia," p. 131.

4. The literacy rate in Italy reflected vastly different regional situations. Whereas in Southern Italy less than 10 percent of the population could read, in Lazio and Tuscany the figure lay somewhere between 20 and 25 percent, and in Piedmont and Lombardia the percentage was a relatively whopping 55 percent.

5. The Marxist concept of "state ideological apparatus" has been formulated by Louis Althusser, "Idéologie et appareils idéologiques d'état," *La Pensée* 151 (June 1970), pp. 6–49.

6. Ernesto Codignola, "Il problema della nostra scuola media," a speech quoted in Chiosso, *Scuola dell'autonomia*, p. 147.

7. The autonomy of state schools was introduced by Law 59 in 1997, a full eighty years later, and the state monopoly over education was finally abolished by Law 62 in 2000!

8. Luigi Ambrosoli, *Libertà e religione nella riforma Gentile* (Florence: Vallecchi, 1980), p. 10.

9. The percentage of citizens entitled to vote was 2 percent until 1882; it increased to 6.9 percent in 1887 and to 9.7 percent in 1892.

10. Giovanni Gentile, *Scritti pedagogici. La riforma della scuola in Italia* (Milan: Treves, 1932), p. 13.

11. Luisa Ribolzi, *Il sistema ingessato. Autonomia, scelta, e qualità nella scuola italiana*, 2nd ed. (Brescia: La Scuola, 2000), pp. 17–22.

12. Basil Bernstein, *Pedagogy, Symbolic Control, and Identity* (London: Taylor and Francis, 1966), p. 46.

13. Alexis de Tocqueville, *De la démocratie en Amérique* [1837], in *Oeuvres complètes d'Alexis de Tocqueville* (Paris: Gallimard, 1951).

14. Mario Reguzzoni, *La riforma della scuola in Italia* (Milan: Franco Angeli, 2000), p. 13.

15. Judith Tuorney-Purta, ed., *Democratic Teacher Education: Programs, Processes, Problems and Perspectives* (State University of New York Press, 1975).

16. Daniele Checchi and Tullio Jappelli, "School Choice and Quality," Working Paper 91 (Salerno: Centro Interuniversitario di Studi di Economia e Finanza, February 2002), p. 9 (www.dise.unisa.it/books).

17. See my remarks in Luisa Ribolzi, ed., *Il falso dilemma pubblico-privato* (Turin: Edizioni della Fondazione, 1987).

18. James J. Coleman, ed., *Educational and Political Development* (Princeton University Press, 1965).

19. Ingemar Fagerlind and Lawrence I. Saha, *Education and National Development*, 2nd ed. (Oxford: Pergamon Press, 1989). See also David Hursh, "Civic Education," in Torsten Husén and T. Neville Postlethwaite, eds., *The International Encyclopedia of Education* (Oxford: Pergamon Press, 1994).

20. The percentage of foreign-born students in state schools was 2.36 percent and in private schools (mainly nursery schools) 1.56 percent. It is not easy to say how many of them are Muslim: students coming from Muslim countries, such as Morocco, Egypt, Tunisia, and Pakistan, represented probably half of the non-E.U. students.

21. Gianfranco Rescalli, ed., *La scuola privata nell'Unione Europea* (Florence: La Nuova Italia, 1999), p. 31.

22. Speech of President Oscar Luigi Scalfaro, delivered at the Fourteenth Congress of the Office Internationale de l'Einseignement Catolique, Rome, March 1994.

23. In *Unità* (March 1, 1994), the daily of the PDS (the former Communist Party), Mr. Berlinguer—who later, in his capacity as minister for education, would present Law 62—stated that "the distinction is not between Catholics and non Catholics, supporters of public or private schooling, but between supporters of autonomy and supporters of bureaucracy."

24. At the end of the experimental phase, in school year 2003–04, the existing variety of nonstate schools should come to an end in Italy: schools will then be either state or acknowledged or strictly private (that is, not recognized by the state).

25. Organization for Economic Cooperation and Development, *Education at a Glance* (Paris, 2001). U.S. dollar equivalents based on purchasing power parity.

26. Dario Antiseri, "Introduzione," in Luigi Binante, ed., *Scuola pubblica e privata nel mondo: Sistemi scolastici tra competizione e intervento dello Stato* (Rome: Armando, 2001), p. 11. On educational financing in Italy, see also Eugenio Somaini, *Scuola e mercato. Problemi e prospettive dell'istruzione in Italia* (Rome: Donzelli, 1997).

27. The average value is much lower in the southern regions. That is why delegating more responsibility for financing to the regions might cause further inequalities among schools.

28. Stefano Versari, ed., *La scuola della società civile fra Stato e mercato* (Soveria Mannelli: Rubbettino, 2002), p. 171.

11

Do Public and Religious Schools Really Differ? Assessing the European Evidence

JAAP DRONKERS

As the preceding chapters in this volume demonstrate, parental choice in education—parents' freedom to choose their children's school—is a major topic in educational policy in many European nations.[1] In Europe as in the United States, parental choice in educational systems often is advocated as a means to introduce competition for pupils between schools and to decrease the level of bureaucracy in and related to schools, thereby improving the quality of teaching and perhaps reducing the cost of education.[2]

One common assumption of advocates of publicly funded parental choice in the United States is that private schools—especially religious schools—are more effective than public schools. It is increasingly argued that religious, especially Catholic, schools not only provide more effective learning environments but also offer a more effective civic education. This chapter tests those assumptions by reviewing the available empirical evidence with respect to the relative effectiveness of religious schools in a number of European societies, including some already discussed, in order to make some systematic comparisons and generalizations. Several additional examples are introduced and key points in some previous chapters are briefly recapitulated in an attempt to determine what can be said—and the limits of what can be said—on the basis of the available evidence.

An earlier version of this chapter was presented at the annual meeting of the American Educational Research Association, Seattle, April 11, 2001.

This review of European evidence should be of interest to a non-European audience because continental European educational systems present a better opportunity than the educational systems of the United States and England to test the relative performance of religious and of public schools. Unlike their counterparts in the United States and England, parents in a number of European societies have long had the opportunity to make a real choice between comparable schools—mostly between public and religious schools—without paying very high fees to the latter. These religious schools are most often Catholic or Protestant schools that operate within a national educational system and receive state grants.

The coexistence of public and religious schools within one national educational system is the unintended result of three processes in these European societies: the struggle between the state and the established churches in Europe; the fight between the eighteenth-century *anciens régimes* (most of which had one state church and suppressed religious minorities) and nineteenth-century liberal governments (which claimed to be neutral toward all churches); and the emergence of new socioeconomic classes in the nineteenth century (skilled workers, craftsmen, laborers) that rejected the dominant classes, whether liberal or conservative. In a number of places (Austria-Hungary, Belgium, France, German *Länder* (states), the Netherlands, Scotland) these processes had more or less comparable results, with the establishment of public and subsidized religious school sectors that offer parents a choice of schools with the same curriculum and usually similar financial costs. However, the size of the public and religious school sectors varies greatly between and within these places for specific historical reasons, and religious schools disappeared in some of them under communist regimes.[3] Understanding the specific historical experiences of different societies is very important to understanding their current educational systems, although I cannot explore those experiences in depth here. But the long and varied experience with publicly funded religious and public schools in Europe explains why the available evidence is of interest to the United States and England, with their distinct educational systems.

Despite the increasing irrelevance of church and religion in the everyday life of most Europeans, religious schools have not dwindled away. Eurydice (an information network on education in Europe maintained by the European Commission) illustrates this fact for the member states of the European Union during the 1990s.[4] On the contrary, the religious school sector in societies with relatively religiously inactive populations is growing or is strongly overrepresented. This is true not only for societies that traditionally have had such schools, but also for those in which religious schools were abolished under communist regimes (Hungary, the new German *Länder*). One possible explanation is that the teaching in religious schools is generally more effective than that of public schools because religious schools, although they no longer strive for the religious socialization of students, still try to attain other noncognitive goals—such as tolerance, social cooperation, and discipline—that are valued by irreligious parents. There also are other explanations for the rise of religious schools in the former communist societies: the distrust of the state as provider of collective goods like education; the lower effectiveness of public schools as a consequence of malfunctioning state bureaucracies; and a lower level of community building by parents and teachers around public schools than around religious schools.[5]

This chapter summarizes all the available empirical research, systematically comparing the cognitive and noncognitive outcomes of primary and secondary public and religious schools in several European countries. We do not discuss here comparisons with schools outside the state-funded private sector (for instance, Waldorf schools in Germany; anthroposophic schools in the Netherlands; exclusive private schools in France, Italy, and England[6]), because such comparisons have the same drawbacks as comparisons between public and religious schools in the United States: the high cost of genuinely private schools might lead to the selection of students with a greater likelihood of finishing school successfully; in addition, educational outcomes might not be easily compared insofar as the schools operate outside a system with a national curriculum and final examinations. Research comparing cognitive and noncognitive outcomes of public and religious schools in Hungary, Scotland, Flemish Belgium, France, Germany, the Netherlands, and England/Wales was found.[7] More information is provided on the status of public and private schools in Hungary and Scotland given that the others are covered elsewhere in this book. For the others, research evidence presented earlier in this book and some additional studies are summarized.

Hungary

The Catholic Church dominated religious education in Hungary until Protestant schools were introduced in the sixteenth century.[8] Religious secondary schools had an important role under the nineteenth-century Austro-Hungarian monarchy, and they maintained their position until the imposition of a communist government in 1948. Surviving statistics indicate that students at Jewish and Lutheran schools were more extensively educated than students at other religious schools and that their grades were higher. Karády explains these differences with reference to the marginal role of the small

Lutheran church in Hungary as well as to the assimilation efforts of the Jews, which made a good education more important to them.[9] Historically, ethnic, national, and religious differentiation was a crucial aspect of the Hungarian educational system, but religious education was all but abolished in Hungary after 1948. The Catholic Church—70 percent of the Hungarian population is Catholic—was permitted to keep eight secondary schools, and one Calvinist and one Jewish school were permitted. No Lutheran schools were allowed. The annual intake of students was limited to forty, the curriculum and textbooks were controlled, and the schools were required to celebrate state rather than religious holidays.

The collapse of communism has restored the legal basis for the reemergence of religious education in Hungary, although the process has been slow. As early as 1985, a new law declared "free choice of education," but the number of religious secondary schools did not immediately increase. Religious schools of the old regime generally had been nationalized under communism, and many of their buildings had been used as public schools for five decades. Only in 1991, when a law was passed dealing with former church properties and compensation for past confiscations, did churches begin to reclaim their old schools, including the original buildings. The process has been a slow: the 2001 deadline for completing the process has been extended to 2011.

In Hungary, most religious secondary gymnasiums reappeared after the fall of communism in 1989. (Hungarian gymnasiums are the most prestigious type of secondary school, as in Austria, Germany, and the Netherlands. They are more or less comparable to the old British grammar schools.) Although their number in Hungary is still small, the increase is significant.[10] In fact, the expansion of enrollment in religious gymnasiums was larger than in public gymnasiums. Religious gymnasiums have to teach the same basic curriculum as public gymnasiums, and students from both have to pass a comparable final examination in their final year of school, at age eighteen; they also have to pass the same entrance examination in order to continue their studies at a college or university. In addition to the previously mentioned explanations for the increase in religious schools in the former communist countries, in Hungary the standard of religious education historically was high.

In the school year 1998–99, 8 percent of secondary schools and 20 percent of gymnasiums were religious institutions.[11] Nearly two-thirds of the religious schools were Catholic, about one-fourth were Calvinist, and about one-tenth were Lutheran. Only a few institutions existed for other denominations (for example, Jewish gymnasiums). By number of students, Protestant schools are larger than Catholic schools and Jewish schools are smallest. Because theology faculties and church-run teacher training colleges also have only recently begun to operate, religious schools have to deal with a shortage of teaching staff; therefore the student-teacher ratio in religious gymnasiums is higher than in public ones (the situation is worst in Catholic and Calvinist schools). Not all students in religious schools belong to the church to which their school belongs, but there is an 80 percent correspondence.

The law requires religious schools to provide students with the same scholastic product as public schools. This means that they have to teach the national curriculum, but there is some flexibility, and they are free to add religion courses. To obtain state financial support, each school must function as a "public provider of the national curriculum" in addition to its specific religious curriculum. The local municipalities administer an annual payment of state support, drawn from the state budget, that is based on student enrollment; a student from a state school and a student from a religious school have the same "value." In addition, religious schools must make a formal declaration that their activities meet state and local requirements, and local municipalities decide whether a school does in fact comply with state regulations.

The state has provided some special support directly to religious schools to assist with their reorganization. In addition, churches support their schools financially from various other sources, with money obtained from the state budget, from abroad from related churches, or from taxpayers in Hungary, who have a right to direct 1 percent of the tax they pay to a specific beneficiary, such as a charity or a religious school.

Dronkers and Robert is the only study that has tested whether the pupils of religious grammar schools in Hungary have higher grades and a better opportunity to enter vocational colleges or universities than comparable pupils of public grammar schools.[12] Their results, based on data from a self-administered survey of fourth-grade secondary school students, show clearly that pupils at religious grammar schools in Hungary do attain higher grades and more success at entering universities and vocational colleges. This is especially true for pupils at Catholic grammar schools, but there are clear indications that Calvinist and Lutheran grammar schools may catch up with Catholic grammar schools in the near future.

The superior results of pupils in religious grammar schools cannot be explained by their more selective social composition. On the contrary, controlling for pupils' and parents' characteristics tends to increase the differences in results between pupils from public and religious grammar schools. Dronkers and Robert do not exclude the possibility that the differences are caused by the higher academic ambition of pupils in religious schools, because they do not have a direct indicator of academic ambition at the end of secondary school. However, because they do control for grades, which are a good indicator of academic ambition, the greater success of Catholic school students with respect to entering higher education is most likely not due to differences in academic ambition between pupils from public and religious grammar schools. The results of their analyses support the claim that religious schools in Hungary are, on average, more effective than public schools.

Scotland

Scotland had, as an independent kingdom until the Union of 1702, a history of institutions that were distinct from those of England and Wales and other parts of the United Kingdom, and one of those distinct institutions is the education system.[13] The secretary of state of Scotland is responsible for Scottish education. The Scottish educational system has a strong reputation for providing effective education based on long-established key values. The fundamental idea is to provide free, compulsory education for all children within a specified age group that is based on a broad curriculum tailored to the age, aptitude, ability, and the individual needs of the child. Parents are legally responsible for ensuring that their children of school age receive an effective education.[14] Therefore parents can provide education by other means: children can be enrolled in an independent school or parents can educate their children at home. Education, not schooling, is compulsory when a child is of school age (currently five to sixteen years of age).

Religion has been a complicating factor in the Scottish educational system. The preindustrial system was run by the established Church of Scotland. From the mid-nineteenth century, there was substantial Catholic Irish immigration into the rapidly industrializing and urbanizing Clydeside in the west of Scotland, but poverty and discrimination combined to block the social mobility of many Irish immigrants.[15] As long as Catholic schools were controlled by the Catholic Church, the provision of education was severely constrained by the financial condition of the Scottish Catholic Church and the unavailability of state subsidies. By 1918 or thereabouts, virtually all Catholic schools were taken over by the state, including the eleven secondary schools.[16] Catholic schools subsequently retained their religious identity within the state sector, and in the late 1970s, they taught 19 percent of Scottish pupils. Scottish Catholics continue to experience social disadvantages, however, although probably not to the same degree as Catholics in Northern Ireland.

The state system of secondary education at the end of the 1970s incorporated three distinct phases of historical development of the Scottish educational system. There is the first generation, sixty-six schools that constituted the national secondary school system in the nineteenth century, none of which are Catholic. Second are the 126 second-generation schools founded or designated between 1902 and 1918, ten of which are Catholic. Then there is the third generation, 278 state schools, seventy-one of which are Catholic.

There is only one systematic study of the differences in effectiveness between Catholic and public Scottish schools. Using data from the 1981 Scottish School Leavers Survey, McPherson and Willms found that after controlling for the socioeconomic composition of schools, pupils in Catholic schools in Scotland performed better on the final examinations, especially in English and in arithmetic.[17] These higher scores were worth one or two passing grades on final examinations, and they add considerably to the young person's chances of finding a job after leaving school or of gaining admission to favored postsecondary institutions. The authors note that their findings controvert casual pessimistic public judgments of the performance of Catholic schools, which are sometimes based on Catholic schools' unadjusted examination results. These results are inaccurate because of the greater representation of Catholic than non-Catholic school pupils in the lower socioeconomic groups.

Belgium

As Jan de Groof describes in chapter 6, the Belgian constitution guarantees the rights and freedoms of ideological and philosophical minorities, and they have been carefully protected since the independence of Belgium in 1830.[18] These rights and freedoms became the battleground of two "School Wars," in 1870 and 1958, which led to the establishment of a School Pact among all parties. The original compromise implied that the state had the right and even the duty to establish religiously neutral schools at all educational levels. In exchange for acceptance of this principle, the private schools (almost all Catholic) received state financing. These rights and compromises ensure that all parents will at least be able to decide whether they want a Catholic or a secular school, while in the larger cities other options also are available.

Education in Belgium can be organized with tax support by a variety of sponsors ("networks"). Three networks now exist: *community schools*, which are directly controlled by the central government; *official schools*, which are directly controlled by provincial or local authorities; and *free schools*, which are directly controlled by individuals and associations. Community and official schools are similar to the public schools elsewhere in continental Europe. The Belgian educational system is further differentiated by language, with completely separate systems for Dutch (Flemish), French, and the small number of German schools. The "free" schools, which are not under the direct control of national, provincial, or local authorities, are nearly all Catholic: in 1984 they accommodated somewhat fewer than half the students in the French- and German-speaking areas, but two-thirds of those in the Dutch-speaking areas.[19] Private schools receive the same 100 percent funding on a per-pupil basis as provincial and locally controlled schools, provided that they conform to program requirements and agree to inspection by the Ministry of Education. Inspections focus on subjects taught (number of hours, global curriculum, but not textbooks) and the language used, and they may also concern pedagogical methods and the religious or philosophical bases of instruction.

The effects of Belgian public and Catholic schools on the cognitive and noncognitive achievements of the pupils have only barely been studied. One of the reasons is the politically sensitive character of the School Pact, which discourages scientific research on its effects. Belgian society during the last quarter of the twentieth century was marked by another cleavage that discourages comparative research on school types, namely, the conflict about the federal structure of Belgium between the Dutch-speaking north (Flanders) and the French-speaking south (Walloon).[20] Research on parental choice of public and religious schools in Flanders began in the 1970s with the study of Billiet on the motives of parents for choosing schools.[21] The reasons parents gave for selecting a public or a Catholic school concerned the educational program of the school and practical matters such as distance from home. Parental social class did not affect whether students attended public or Catholic schools. However, the fact that parents did not explicitly mention religion does not mean, according to Billiet, that the religious identity of the school was unimportant. To the contrary, religious considerations appear to have been extremely important and simply taken for granted in the selection process. The chance that children from Catholic families would chose a Catholic school was 50 percent if their parents were not integrated into a Catholic community but 97 percent if they were. Students ended up in Catholic schools because they and their families lived in a social milieu in which the decision was almost automatic. Freethinking liberals (nonreligious conservatives and liberals, Social Democrats), distinguished by a common aversion to organized religion, displayed an equally distinctive pattern, and their children were very likely to end up in public schools. Thus differences in lifestyle and in religious convictions and behavior distinguished those who chose Catholic schools from those who chose public secular schools in 1970s Flemish Belgium.

Studies of the cognitive and noncognitive effectiveness of Flemish schools were not undertaken until the 1990s. Brutsaert built on the conclusions of Billiet by studying whether differences in Catholic and public schools, including differences in discipline and academic expectations, affected the well-being of their students.[22] Brutsaert defined well-being in terms of adjustment to school life as reflected in such affective outcomes as self-esteem, sense of mastery, stress, fear of failure, sense of belonging in school, and educational commitment. In 1989–90 he sampled 1,882 sixth-grade pupils in forty comparable elementary schools in Flanders representing a wide range of institutions with regard to size, organizing authority, degree of urbanization of the school location, and gender composition of the teaching staff. Brusaert compared the well-being indicators separately for girls and boys. Catholic school boys scored significantly better on all but one indicator of well-being (commitment to study). Girls in Catholic schools also tended to score better, but the differences were not significant. Interestingly, the better results for boys disappeared after adjusting for parent socioeconomic status and school characteristics like number of pupils and gender of teachers. Therefore any difference in well-being for boys in public and Catholic schools can be attributed to selective enrollment (based on socioeconomic status) and the increasing feminization of the state schools' teaching staff. In contrast, after controlling for the same factors, it appears that girls do indeed seem to benefit from Catholic schools, demonstrating statistically significant gains in terms of self-esteem and sense of control.

Brutsaert also has studied differences in learning outcomes in public and Catholic elementary schools, using the same Flemish schools that he used in the study of well-being.[23] To measure learning, he used the students' grade-point average, as reported by the sixth-graders themselves.[24] Children attending public schools were disadvantaged with respect to their socioeconomic and family backgrounds.[25] After controlling for background factors, Brustaert found that children's grade-point average tended to be higher in Catholic schools than in public schools. Moreover, children from lower socioeconomic backgrounds in particular did better in Catholic schools than comparable children in public schools. This result flies in the face of the Flemish public schools' explicit commitment to equalizing achievement among students. Brustaert offers some possible explanations for the higher cognitive outcome of Catholic schools: the schools' more strenuous demands; the "Pygmalion effect," caused by greater expectations of higher achievement; and more extracurricular activities.

Other Belgian sociologists have recently studied differences between Flemish public and Catholic secondary school pupils with respect to three politically charged attitudes: *ethnocentrism, authoritarianism,* and *sexual and bioethical liberalism.*[26] *Ethnocentrism* is a blanket term indicating a form of cultural closeness among members of the same ethnic group ("in-group") and the degree of hostility toward members of "out-groups," in this case ethnic minorities such as Turks and Moroccans.[27] *Authoritarianism* refers to Adorno's original indices of antidemocratic tendencies in the authoritarian personality.[28] The measure focuses on the subject's preference for a repressive, violent reaction toward wrongdoers in Belgian society. *Sexual and bioethical liberalism* gauges attitudes regarding sexuality, sexual orientation, prostitution, abortion, euthanasia, suicide, and killing in self-defense.[29] There at first appear to be differences between the attitudes of pupils in public and Catholic schools. Pupils in official schools (schools directly controlled by provincial or local authorities) score higher on ethnocentrism, on authoritarianism, and on sexual and bioethical liberalism than pupils in the Flemish community schools (directly controlled by the Flemish community government) and in the Catholic schools. However, these generalizations ignore differences in the types of secondary schools across these sectors. Community schools and official schools are more likely to provide technical and vocational education, and students who attend these schools have lower academic abilities. If one controls for that, there is no difference in pupils' attitudes in public or Catholic schools. Elchardus and Kavadias make clear that Catholic schools in Flanders recruit from the higher social strata.[30] The old single-sex Catholic schools that offer only general education recruit more students from the upper middle and the upper class. Single-sex Catholic schools tend to recruit students on a higher academic track, and that explains the differences in attitudes between pupils of public and religious schools.

Therefore, and perhaps surprisingly given the history of the Belgian educational system, these studies indicate that Flemish Catholic schools have a far smaller impact than one would expect on religious socialization. Pupils from Catholic schools have more or less the same attitudes towards abortion, euthanasia, and homosexuality as their counterparts. The major difference in pupils' attitudes is a consequence of their different secondary education tracks or school types. This suggests that the division of Belgian society in terms of values is no longer fostered along religious lines but according to a combination of achievement and secondary school type. The continued success of Flemish Catholic schools can likewise be explained best not by successful socialization in religious values, but rather by their success in offering the most valued school type in secondary education to more or less religious pupils.

France

Denis Meuret provides a good summary of the violent history of private schooling in France, of the political nature of the conflict between advocates of public and private schools there, and of the compromise reached in which partial funding of private schools is provided in exchange for regulations that severely reduce these schools' autonomy. The French overview is important to the topic of this book, because the French political debates on the position of private and public education have strongly influenced the debates in other continental European societies. For example, the French constitutional term "freedom of teaching" can also be found in the German and Dutch constitutions, although its interpretation has become very different. The same holds for the current French compromise of partial funding of regulated private schools: plans for similar arrangements are found in Italy and Spain.

Given the importance of the French example, one would expect many empirical analyses of the effectiveness of French public and private schools. However, there is only one comprehensive study of differences in the effectiveness of public and Catholic schools in France.[31] Langouët and Léger found that the dropout rate between the first and third years for students in state secondary schools was significantly higher than that of comparable students in the Catholic sector (34 percent versus 24 percent).[32] Pupils who were children of employees (the term "employee" is commonly used in Europe to indicate a social class that is higher than "skilled worker" but lower than "management") or manual laborers benefited more strongly from this positive effect of Catholic schools. The same held for the dropout rate between the first and fifth year of secondary school: it was 61.5 percent in state schools and 51.3 percent in Catholic schools. Children of parents from the middle management and employee strata benefited most from this effect. In the end, the graduation rate was lower in the state schools (21.7 percent) than in the Catholic schools (28 percent). The great beneficiaries of the French Catholic schools are children of employees, because their graduation rate in Catholic schools is practically equal to the rate of children of middle managers in both state and Catholic schools.

Langouët and Léger discuss seven misconceptions about French religious schools. Meuret mentions some of these points, but they are worth summarizing:[33]

—Underestimating the percentage of pupils who have attended religious schools by focusing only on the percentage in a certain year: a large proportion of all French pupils (35 percent of the cohort of 1972–74; 37 percent of the cohort of 1980) attended religious schools on a temporary basis.

—Misunderstanding the real motives of those attending religious schools by confusing educational motives with religious motives: only a small minority chose religious schools for religious reasons.

—Assuming that the existence of public and religious sectors provides families with a free choice and that this choice necessarily decreases social inequity within education and opens the doors of private schools to the lower classes. Langouët and Léger make clear that many families do not have any choice, first because of geographical inequalities—Catholic schools are more available in some regions; in other regions there are hardly any—but also because of social inequalities.[34] Given the lower density of Catholic schools in France, they are simply too far away for many lower-class families to be a real option.

—Idealizing the positive effects of school autonomy and the competition between public and religious schools on the quality of teaching and the level of achievement. After controlling for the social background and initial scholastic ability of pupils entering different schools, the differences between Catholic and public schools were much smaller, although they were still significant and different for pupils from different social groups.

—Underestimating the differences in the scholastic success of pupils from different social classes in public and religious schools. Farmers' children achieved better in public schools, while children of manual laborers and school employees achieved better in religious schools.

—Portraying the present public school as democratic and socially neutral and serving all children without making distinctions among them. If public schools are more democratic in their recruitment than religious schools, they are less democratic than religious schools in that they create larger differences in scholastic success among pupils from different social classes and they lead to the massive and early dropout of pupils from the working classes.

—Assuming that the relation between the public and religious schools is stable and unchangeable. The social composition of the two sectors changed between 1973–80 and 1980–87, in that the social class distribution of parents of pupils in religious schools became less different from the national distribution. The effects of both sectors likewise changed during that period: the religious sector continued to do much more to reduce social inequalities in scholastic success than the public sector. In addition, the strategies of the different social classes also changed: children of professionals and higher-level officials increased their participation in public education, while children from other classes increased their participation in religious schools.

Germany

Lutz Reuter provides an extensive overview of the complex school choice situation in Germany.[35] One part of this complexity is a consequence of the broad freedom of the separate *Länder* (regions) in education within the federal framework. Another part is the distinction within the German nonpublic school sector of private independent schools (complementary schools) and the private dependent schools (substitute or alternative schools). Despite the large variety of public, private independent, and private dependent schools, there has been hardly any systematic comparison of the effectiveness of these school types in Germany. As Reuter remarks, the current system of public and private schooling seems to be accepted and there is no significant public pressure or even discourse about changing it. The same holds for the academic debate: in his overview of quality within the educational system, Fend, a distinguished scholar, does not discuss possible quality differences between public and private schools.[36] Reuter expresses surprise that private schools were not able to reap the benefits of the public frustration over evidence of the below-average quality of German secondary schools.[37] But there are only three studies on the effectiveness of public and private, government-dependent schools in Germany (both in the old and new *Länder*), and all were initiated by non-Germans. The private dependent schools analyzed in these three studies are either Catholic or Protestant schools, which receive a major part of their budget from their state.

Grammar Schools in North Rhine–Westphalia

Dronkers and Hemsing analyzed the educational attainment of 3,240 grammar school pupils of the tenth grade in North Rhine–Westphalia in 121 school classes at sixty-eight grammar schools (*Gymnasien*).[38] They were interviewed for the first time in 1970 at the age of approximately sixteen years. All pupils were asked about their social background, their attitudes toward school, and their educational plans. In addition, intelligence tests were given, and the students' parents, teachers, and principals also were interviewed.[39] In 1985, 61 percent (1,989) of the former pupils—then approximately thirty years old—were interviewed again, and they were identified by the school that they attended. This interview provided information on the social background, the achievements, and future life plans of the students. Dronkers and Hemsing reported that pupils in Protestant and Catholic secondary schools in North Rhine–Westphalia had higher educational outcomes than those in public schools, after controlling for other characteristics. This cannot be explained by a greater selection of intelligent pupils in Protestant or Catholic schools or by their parents' social class. Pupils in Catholic schools obtained higher grades at the end of grammar school, while pupils at Protestant schools attained higher educational levels in secondary education and were more successful in their further studies. Interestingly, pupils of nonreligious private schools do not have higher outcomes than pupils of public schools, after controlling for characteristics of parents and pupils. This difference can be explained by the distinction between a value community, which reinforces common religious and pedagogical values (private dependent schools), and a functional community, which may serve to maintain social class distinctions (private independent schools).

Dronkers and Hemsing also found that the success in university and occupational levels of pupils of Protestant and Catholic schools in North Rhine–Westphalia were equal to those of pupils at public schools, after controlling for unequal educational outcomes and other characteristics. There was one exception: pupils of Catholic schools had lower-level occupations in their first jobs. A possible explanation is that Catholic grammar schools also function as seminaries for the training of priests, who attach less value to high status on their first job. Do pupils who attend religious schools become more religious as a consequence? Adults who were pupils in Catholic schools did attend church services more often than pupils from private or public schools. But that was not true for adults who were pupils in Protestant schools, which suggest there is no general religious school effect on later religiousness. A possible explanation for this is that there were more future priests among Catholic school students than future Protestant ministers among Protestant school students, and of course these future priests wind up attending church quite regularly.

Mathematics and Natural Sciences in Three Old Länder

Dronkers, Baumert, and Schwippert analyzed the Third International Mathematics and Science Study (TIMSS).[40] The main survey was carried out in 1995–96 with a cross-section of students in grades 7 and 8 (mostly thirteen- and fourteen-year-olds). A representative sample of classes stratified according to state and school type was taken, covering 150 schools with one seventh and eighth grade each. TIMSS-Germany is designed longitudinally, with two measurement points at the end of the seventh and the eighth grades. Unlike the main international study, TIMSS-Germany also includes information on parents' socioeconomic background and measures on basic dimensions of mental ability.[41] The German TIMSS data contained five private government-dependent schools, scattered throughout three west German states:

Bavaria, North Rhine–Westphalia, and Rhineland-Palatinate. There were also nine public *Realschulen* and thirteen public *Gymnasien* (grammar schools) in the same states. The pupils were still at the beginning of their secondary school careers, so the possible effects of attending public and private dependent schools might have been underestimated. Dronkers, Baumert, and Schwippert rejected their hypothesis that pupils at private dependent schools in Germany have higher learning results in mathematics and natural sciences than pupils from public schools. This was clearly not the case, whether one controls for parental characteristics, intelligence, or earlier performance in mathematics and natural sciences. But pupils in German public and private dependent schools differ clearly in their average intelligence levels. The higher intelligence level of private dependent school pupils cannot be explained by a stronger selection in these schools, because the parental backgrounds of pupils at public and private dependent schools do not differ significantly. The most likely explanation seems to be that private dependent schools offer a learning environment that stimulates the intelligence. Nevertheless, the higher intelligence scores at private dependent schools do not lead to greater achievement in mathematics and natural sciences. A possible explanation of this contradiction is the difference in the "hidden curriculum" of public and of private dependent schools, explained in the following discussion.

Cognitive and Noncognitive Outcomes in Old and New Länder

Dronkers, Baumert, and Schwippert analyzed a database provided by a longitudinal study entitled Learning Processes, Educational Careers, and Psychosocial Development in Adolescence (BIJU).[42] This study began with the investigation of the main cohort during the school year 1991–92. Data collection started with pupils in the seventh grade (the beginning of secondary school in Germany). The sample of school classes comprised some 8,000 students from 212 schools of all secondary school types in three states of west and east Germany (Mecklenburg-Western Pomerania, North Rhine–Westphalia, and Saxony-Anhalt). In order to separate the effects of school and grade, two classes per school were included in the sample.[43] The authors used two waves of the BIJU data; pupils were tested in the seventh grade and retested in the tenth grade (halfway through secondary school). There were five private dependent schools (four *Gymnasien*, one *Gesamtschule*) in the first wave and four private dependent schools in the second wave (only *Gymnasien*) with enough valid data in the BIJU, scattered throughout the three German states. The authors included all public schools of the same type in the same state with enough valid data for the core variables. Because the pupils were only halfway through their secondary school careers (tenth grade), the possible effects of attending public and private dependent schools might have been underestimated. Dronkers, Baumert, and Schwippert accepted their hypothesis that pupils of private dependent schools in Germany have higher cognitive and noncognitive scores on some tests than pupils from public schools, after controlling for other characteristics of schools and of parents. For the cognitive tests this was true only for English in the seventh grade and for biology in the tenth grade. But pupils attending private dependent schools did worse on mathematics in the tenth grade. For the noncognitive tests, seventh-grade students in private dependent schools also differed from pupils in public schools in their self-assessment of academic ability (lower) and willingness to help others (higher). Pupils of public and private dependent schools scored equally on the other cognitive and noncognitive tests.

A difference in the hidden curriculum of public and private dependent schools can explain the difference in effectiveness in natural sciences and mathematics and foreign languages. Within each German state, public and private dependent schools have the same curriculum and therefore do not officially deviate in what they offer their students. But on average teachers in private dependent schools might focus less on the highest results in mathematics and natural sciences and concentrate more on foreign languages, general knowledge, and noncognitive aspects of education (motivation, social competence, and so forth). That is precisely what was found in these analyses: pupils of private dependent schools did better on English tests but had the same results in mathematics and natural sciences; were more modest about their own academic ability but had higher intelligence scores; and claimed less often to help people because others, like their parents, expected them to help. A preference for foreign languages, general knowledge, and noncognitive aspects of education might be a result of the religious traditions in these private dependent schools (the majority being Catholic). But this preference might also reflect the wishes of parents who believe that these aspects of education are more important for upward social mobility or maintaining a high social position than the highest scores in mathematics and natural sciences. As long as private dependent schools are more successful in *homogenizing* (equalizing) the learning results in mathematics and natural sciences, parents might believe that less focus on these subjects by private dependent schools is not harmful to the life course of their children.[44]

The Netherlands

The Netherlands often is wrongly regarded as having a "unique" educational system with respect to parental choice of schools. Central to the Dutch arrangement are the constitutional principle of freedom of education and the constitutional right of public and grant-aided private institutions to financial equality. But in other European countries (for example, Germany) religious schools also have a constitutional right to state financial support. More unusual is the large size of the Dutch private school sector, although Belgium has a private school sector of nearly the same size.

A summary of the Dutch research on the differences in effectiveness of public and religious schools is provided by Dijkstra, Dronkers, and Karsten in chapter 3. I mention only some highlights here; there are too many studies of the differences between public and religious schools in the Netherlands, unlike other European countries, to present them in any detail. It is worth noting that in the Netherlands the major part of this research is done by university institutes without financial support from Dutch educational authorities, who deny differences in effectiveness because they are politically unacceptable.

Dutch research contains significant evidence of the positive effects of Catholic and Protestant schooling on academic achievement. These differences, all adjusted for differences in the student intake of public and private schools, are reported in terms of drop-out rates, test scores, degrees, attainment, and so forth, both for primary and secondary schools. However, a number of apparent exceptions to the general religious school advantage complicate the picture.

The first deviation is that public schools in regions with a majority of Catholic or Protestant schools have greater effectiveness than public schools in regions with a majority of public schools. Second, schools that are both nonreligious and private have on average lower effectiveness than public schools, after controlling for the social composition and characteristics of the student body. Third, orthodox Protestant schools do not have greater effectiveness than public schools or less strict Protestant schools.

The fourth deviation is that the higher effectiveness of religious schools seems to be restricted to a certain historical period, the end of the 1960s to the 1990s. A possible explanation for this is the predominance of religious considerations in choosing a school before the 1960s and the disappearance of the small-scale advantages of religious schools during the 1990s due to the fact that individual Catholic and Protestant schools have become large schools directed by large-scale organizations supervising more and more schools.

Because of these four deviations and the denial by Dutch educational authorities of differences in the cognitive effectiveness of public and religious schools, the debate over the extent to which these differences are really important and lasting is still unsettled. But most studies show differences in school effectiveness that vary with denomination, after taking into account the differences in pupil characteristics and school population. Insofar as these differences follow a regular pattern, the average effects are mainly negative for public schools and positive for private religious schools, with the nonreligious private school and the orthodox Protestant school being exceptions. It seems that Catholic schools in particular and to a lesser degree Protestant schools provide better learning environments.[45] These results seem slightly more pronounced in primary education than in secondary education. Dutch private religious schools have a reputation for offering educational quality, which, as research shows, is an important factor in parents' favoring religious schools in the Netherlands.

Most of the studies on school effectiveness are limited to the effects of sector on the cognitive domain of learning. Much less research has been undertaken to investigate possible differences between sectors in other domains—which is at least as interesting, particularly in the light of the "pillarized" history of the current Dutch school system, which links schools to distinct religious communities with distinct socialization processes and value systems.[46] The picture of the noncognitive effects of religious schools is far less clear than that of their cognitive effects. Sometimes denomination-specific differences are reported, but mostly they are not, especially after controlling for the individual characteristics of pupils and their parents. On the whole one cannot find large differences among public and religious schools in the noncognitive domain, despite the special claims made on behalf of religious schools.

Dykstra, Dronkers, and Karsten point out in chapter 3 that the equal funding of private and public schools has promoted the diminution of prestigious elite schools outside the state-subsidized sector. Religious and public schools' right to equal financing has prevented the skimming off of the most able students by either public or religious schools. Before the 1970s, the choice of a religious or public school was made not on educational but on religious grounds. As a result, the long experience with parental choice has not increased educational inequality in Dutch society. The differences between the effectiveness of religious and of public schools are quite recent, coming only after the pronounced secularization of Dutch society, and these differences could become the basis for new forms of inequality. Differences between parents in their knowledge of school effectiveness, which correlate with their own educational level, could certainly contribute to new inequalities. Free school choice provides possible means of ethnic and social segregation of schools, not necessarily only by catchment area and public or private sector, but more often within the same catchment area and sector. The existence of free school choice thus can deepen the social and ethnic inequality among schools and thereby in society at large. But this possible deepening of social and ethnic segregation of schools in the Netherlands does not necessarily deepen the social and ethnic segregation between the public and religious school sectors, because public schools also benefit from—and are part of the system of—free school choice.

The United Kingdom

In chapter 4, Neville Harris shows that the position of religious state-funded schools in England and Wales is quite different from that of those in continental Europe and the other parts of the United Kingdom. Archer has described quite convincingly the causes (the struggle between church and modernizing state) and consequences of this difference (nation versus market orientation).[47] This is not the place even to summarize her argument, but it is important for the American reader to keep in mind the deep rift between the English and the other European educational systems. In 1939, about half of all schools in England were run by the Church of England and the Roman Catholic Church, although they provided for less than one-third of the total school population. Under the 1944 Education Act, all Roman Catholic schools and a minority of the Church of England schools opted for "aided" status, which offered greater autonomy in staff appointments and the content of religious education, combined with aid for all operating costs and some capital costs. The other Church of England schools opted for "controlled" status: they were entirely funded by the educational authorities with hardly any autonomy or freedom of staff appointment, but they maintained their own religious character. In addition to these Catholic and Anglican schools, other Protestant, Jewish, Muslim, and Sikh aided schools have more recently been established.

The main debate on school choice in England and Wales is not about these religious schools (aided or controlled) but on the devolution of decisionmaking power to schools at the expense of local education authorities. Harris's chapter ably explores the struggles surrounding devolution. Perhaps because of this recent focus on devolution and earlier struggles over comprehensive secondary schools, it is hard to find empirical studies of the differences between public and religious schools in England and Wales.

Although useful information on the academic performance of all English schools is provided by the Office for Standards in Education (Ofsted), it does not help to determine whether religious schools do better or worse than nonreligious schools. The main problem is the unwillingness of the English educational inspectorate and the academic community to publish school performance indicators controlled for input differences in schools, as is done in France and the Netherlands. The only scientifically sound data on differences in cognitive effectiveness of public and religious schools that I found are those of Morris on cognitive performance in English Catholic secondary schools.[48] His analyses suggest that students at those schools did better academically than comparable students in public schools. Those analyses are, however, descriptive rather than systematic.

The devolution of power to schools and the educational reforms of the 1990s have made "choice" schools of all publicly funded schools in England and Wales, as Stephen Gorard describes in chapter 5. One of the major debates is over whether this strong increase in the opportunity for school choice in England and Wales has increased the social segregation of schools. Gorard shows that there was hardly any important change in the level of segregation from 1989 to 2001. Student integration seemed to have improved during the mid 1990s, but by the start of the twenty-first century it returned to the level that existed before free school choice.

Conclusion

This review of systematic evidence concerning the differences in the effectiveness of public and religious state-funded schools in seven different European societies highlights several important general points. First, differences in school success and cognitive outcomes clearly exist between public and religious schools in Belgium, France, Hungary, the Netherlands, and Scotland, and these differences cannot be explained by the different social compositions of the student populations or by other obvious social characteristics of pupils, parents, schools, or neighborhoods. These differences in effectiveness are less clear in Germany, although there are some indications of the higher effectiveness of German religious schools, especially if schools are analyzed within the context of a single *Land* (region). However, differences in noncognitive achievements, which often are the main argument for the existence of state-funded religious schools, are not found in Flemish Belgium, hardly at all in the Netherlands, and only partly in Germany. There also exist a number of indications in various societies (France, Germany, Hungary, and Netherlands) that children attending religious schools often do so for academic or social—not religious—reasons. The two last points contradict the raison d'être of state-funded religious schools, because the right of parents to determine the moral and religious education of their children always has been more or less explicitly the basis of state recognition and funding of religious schools. But the higher cognitive effectiveness of state-funded religious schools also contradicts this raison d'être of religious schools, which maintain throughout that they do not want to compete with state schools for better academic outcomes. As a consequence, most state-funded religious schools and their organizations in various European societies tend to deny any higher cognitive effectiveness and try to avoid any research in that direction. Also, state schools and their organizations tend to avoid research on their lower cognitive effectiveness in order to avoid embarrassment and political defeat by religious organizations, with which they have struggled so long for hegemony. This avoidance of political difficulties and embarrassment around a politically sensitive topic can explain why the research on effectiveness of public and state-funded private schools in Europe is not as extensive as one might expect given the disproportionate size of and the current increase in the state-funded school sector in various European countries.

Second, it appears that given the high level of state support for religious schools in these European societies and the relatively low school fees, differences in school effectiveness of religious and nonreligious public schools cannot be explained by large financial contributions from parents whose children attend religious schools. In various continental European countries the law forbids large financial contributions from parents as a condition for obtaining state grants. The spending levels are mostly equal across the public and the state-funded private school sectors, because in most cases that is an essential element of the compromise between the state and the churches. If there exists a supplement for children with special needs, both sectors will profit from it in a more or less comparable way. If financial inequality does exist in these countries, in most cases schools in the state-funded private sector tend to be poorer.

Third, there is no evidence that more school choice in itself promotes the degree of social segregation of school sectors (the Netherlands) or even of same-sector schools (England). Neither is it true that public schools serve students from the lower classes best, while religious schools are more geared to serving the interests of the higher classes (for example, France, Germany, Netherlands, and Scotland). The results do not justify any easy correlation between social class and public or private schools. Free school choice can lower the degree of social segregation of neighborhoods, but at the same time increase the degree of social segregation of schools: the ultimate results of such contradictory movements are impossible to determine for certain.

This review allows only preliminary conclusions about the higher effectiveness of religious schools in European societies, but the direction of the results is clear. Religious schools are generally more effective in the cognitive domain than public schools, while they no longer differ in the effectiveness of religious socialization because the majority of the religious schools no longer engage in religious socialization.[49] This makes religious schools attractive for nonreligious parents who wish to maximize the educational outcomes of their children. The increase in the percentage of pupils attending religious schools in various European countries since the 1970s may illustrate their attractiveness. The importance of the differences in the cognitive domains indicates that educational systems with public and state-funded religious schools give parents a real choice among schools of different quality.

While systematic evidence is spotty at best, based on the evidence that is available, it does not seem to be the case that the much greater availability of publicly subsidized parental choice in Europe than in the United States has increased educational inequality or segregation or undermined either student learning or civic socialization. Public and religious schools in European societies exhibit higher levels of general achievement and smaller differences in average achievement among schools than those in the United States. [50] In principle, therefore, European educational systems with public and religious subsidized school sectors are indeed a better place to test the basic assumption of the parental choice debate—that private and religious schools are more effective. However, because of the political sensitivity of the question of the effectiveness of public and state-funded religious schools, the evidentiary base for drawing conclusions is thin. Not enough is known about the effects of school choice in Europe, but what is known is generally comforting.[51]

Notes

1. Organization for Economic Cooperation and Development (OECD), *School: A Matter of Choice* (Paris: OECD/CERI, 1994).

2. J. E. Chubb and T. M. Moe, *Politics, Markets, and America's Schools* (Brookings, 1990).

3. OECD, *Education at a Glance: Indicators 1998* (Paris, 1998), p. 139.

4. Eurydice, "Private Education in the European Union: Organisation, Administration, and the Public Authorities' Role" (Brussels: Education Information Network of the European Community, 2000), graph 2.

5. With perhaps the exception of Poland, these former communist societies have not become very religious since the fall of communism.

6. Also, for England we use the term public school in the usual international meaning of the word (schools organized and paid for by the local public authorities) instead of the misleading English meaning (selective private schools organized by educational entrepreneurs).

7. There is also some research on this topic in Spain, but these studies are not yet accessible.

8. In this section I use information from J. Dronkers and P. Robert, "Are the Newly Established Religious 'Gymnasiums' in Hungary More Effective?" EUI Working Paper SPS 2003/6 (San Domenico di Fiesole: European University Institute, 2003); also published in *European Societies*, vol. 6 (2004) pp. 205–36.

9. V. Karády, "Juifs et luthériens dans le systéme scolaire hongrois," *Actes de la recherche en sciences sociales*, vol. 69 (1987), pp. 67–85.

10. About 12 percent of all pupils in secondary education attended Catholic, Calvinist, Lutheran, or Jewish gymnasiums in 1998.

11. Religious education is more widespread at the secondary level. Church-run schools represent only 5 percent of primary schools in Hungary; G. Halász and J. Lannert, eds., *Jelentés a magyar közoktatásról 2000* (Budapest: OKI, 2000).

12. Dronkers and Robert, "Are the Newly Established Religious 'Gymnasiums' in Hungary More Effective?" No comparable study of school effectiveness of Hungarian primary schools and their religious affiliation exists.

13. In this section on the Scottish educational system, I use C. Teelken, "Market Mechanisms in Education. A Comparative Study of School Choice in the Netherlands, England, and Scotland," Ph.D. dissertation, University of Amsterdam, 1998; and A. McPherson and J. D. Willms, "Certification, Class Conflict, Religion, and Community: A Socio-Historical Explanation of the Effectiveness of Contemporary Schools," in A. C. Kerckhoff, ed., *Research in Sociology of Education and Socialization. A Research Annual. International Perspectives on Education* (Greenwich, Conn. and London: JAI Press, 1986).

14. Education Act, part 2, section 30.

15. Social and political conflict between Catholic Irish and Protestant Scots is not unique to Scotland. The current troubles in Northern Ireland can be seen in part as a conflict between Protestant immigrants from Scotland and local Irish Catholics.

16. Also, the Protestant schools run by the Church of Scotland were taken over by the state in 1918. The Church of Scotland still has the right to be represented on the education committee of every regional authority.

17. McPherson and Willms, "Certification, Class Conflict, Religion, and Community."

18. For the description of the Belgian system, I draw on C. L. Glenn, *Choice of Schools in Six Nations* (U.S. Department of Education, 1989); and M. Elchardus and D. Kavadias, *The Socializing Effects of Educational Networks: The Relevance of the Distinction between Public and Private Schools with Relation to Noncognitive Outcomes of Last Year Pupils in Flanders (Belgium)* (Vrije Universiteit Brussel, Department of Sociology, 2000).

19. A negligible minority of these "free" schools are Protestant, Jewish or based on a specific educational method.

20. One explanation for the absence of research on cognitive achievements of pupils in public and Catholic schools might be the absence of a national final exami-

nation at the end of secondary school in Belgium, in contrast to France, the Netherlands, and some German *Länder*.

21. J. Billiet, *Secularisering en verzuiling in het onderwijs; een sociologisch onderzoek naar de vrije schoolkeuze als legitimatieschema en als sociaal proces* (Universitaire Pers Leuven, 1977). I am not aware of comparable studies in French- or German-speaking Belgium and doubt their existence.

22. H. Brutsaert, "State and Catholic Elementary Schools in Belgium: Differences in Affective Outcomes," *Research in Education*, vol. 54 (1995), pp. 32–41.

23. H. Brutsaert, "Home and School Influences on Academic Performance: State and Catholic Elementary Schools in Belgium Compared," *Educational Review*, vol. 50 (1998), pp. 37–43.

24. Students also were asked to rank themselves academically vis-à-vis their peers, and the answers to this question closely correlated with the self-reported grade point averages.

25. Such students tend to have lower socioeconomic status, mothers who are more often unemployed, less parental involvement in children's education, and more family disruption.

26. M. Elchardus, D. Kavadias, and J. Siongers, "De invloed van scholen en andere socialisatievelden op de houdingen van leerlingen," *Mens en Maatschappij*, vol. 74 (1999), pp. 250–68; Elchardus and Kavadias, *The Socializing Effects of Educational Networks*.

27. Turks and Moroccans are the largest groups of non-European immigrant workers who have come to Europe since the 1960s.

28. T. W. Adorno and others, *The Authoritarian Personality* (Harper, 1950).

29. An adapted form of the index used in the European Values Study.

30. Elchardus and Kavadias, *The Socializing Effects of Educational Networks*.

31. A possible reason is the political nature of any debate on the effectiveness of public and private education in France, and the tendency of social scientists to shy away from politically incorrect topics.

32. G. Langouët and A. Léger, *École publique ou école privée? Trajectoires et réussites scolaires* (Paris: Editions Fabert, 1994).

33. Ibid., pp. 140–44.

34. This regional difference in availability of Catholic schools has deep historical roots, dating back to the sixteenth-century religious wars and the French Revolution in the late eighteenth century.

35. See chapter 8 in this volume.

36. H. Fend, *Qualität im Bildungswesen. Schulforschung zu Systembedingungen, Schulprofilen und Lehrerleistung* (Weinheim/München: Juventa, 1998).

37. Publications of the Third International Mathematics and Science Study (TIMSS) and Programme for International Student Assessment (PISA).

38. J. Dronkers and W. Hemsing, "Effektivität öffentlichen, kirchlichen, und privaten Gymnasialunterrichts. Bildungs-, Berufs- und Sozialisationeffekte in nord-

rhein-westfälischen Gymnasien (Differences in educational attainment and religious socialization of ex-pupils from grammar schools with public, Catholic, Protestant and private background in the German state of Nordrhein-Westfalen during the 1970s and 1980s)," *Zeitschrift für Erziehungswissenschaft*, vol. 2 (1999), pp. 247–61 (available in English at www.iue.it/Personal/Dronkers).

39. Amthauer's intelligence test.

40. J. Dronkers, J. Baumert, and K. Schwippert, "Are German Non-Public Secondary Schools More Effective at Teaching Mathematics and Natural Sciences?" (European University Institute, 2002), available at www.iue.it/Personal/ Dronkers.

41. For further information on the German TIMSS data and measurement of mental ability, see J. Baumert and others, *TIMSS Mathematisch-naturwissenschaftlicher Unterricht im internationalen Vergleich. Deskriptive Befunde* (Opladen: Leske and Buderich, 1997).

42. J. Dronkers, J. Baumert, and K. Schwippert, "Erzielen deutsche, weiterführende Privatschulen bessere kognitive und nicht-kognitive Resultate?" in L. Deben and J. van de Van, eds., *Berlin und Amsterdam. Globalisierung und Segregation* (Amsterdam: Spinhuis, 2001).

43. For further information, see K. Schnabel, *Prüfungsangst und Lernen* (Berlin: Waxmann, 1998); and O. Köller, *Zielorientierungen und schulisches Lernen* (Berlin: Waxmann, 1998).

44. An indication of the greater potential of private independent schools to homogenize learning outcomes in mathematics and natural sciences is their smaller standard deviations on these outcome tests.

45. It is still too early to draw conclusions on the cognitive effectiveness of Dutch Islamic schools, but it already is clear that they do not deviate negatively from non-Islamic schools with comparable characteristics.

46 "Pillarized" refers to the segmentation of Dutch society in separate networks of organizations and institutions (unions, hospitals, journals, schools, clubs, libraries, and so forth) on the basis of religion and ideology (Catholic, Protestant, social-democrat, neutral).

47. M. S. Archer, *Social Origins of Educational Systems* (London/Beverly Hills: Sage, 1984).

48. A. B. Morris, "The Catholic School Ethos: Its Effect on Post-16 Student Academic Achievement," *Educational Studies*, vol. 21 (1995), pp. 67–84; A. B. Morris, "So Far, So Good: Levels of Academic Achievement in Catholic Schools," *Educational Studies*, vol. 24 (1998), pp. 83–95.

49. These preliminary conclusions also underline the necessity of a systematic and sophisticated Europe-wide study of differences in the effectiveness of public and religious schools, such as that recently carried out in J. Dronkers and P. Robert, "The Effectiveness of Public and Private Schools from a Comparative Perspective," EUI Working Paper SPS 2003/13 (European University Institute, 2003).

50. J. Scheerens and R. J. Bosker, *The Foundations of Educational Effectiveness* (Oxford: Pergamon, 1997), pp. 76-78.

51. A first example of such a more sophisticated and systematic comparison of effectiveness in reading and mathematics in public schools, private dependent schools, and private independent schools in eighteen OECD countries is the analysis of the OECD's PISA data in Dronkers and Robert, "The Effectiveness of Public and Private Schools from a Comparative Perspective." But again, this analysis has been carried out by two independent academics.

PART 2

Analysis and Commentary

12

Civic Republicanism, Political Pluralism, and the Regulation of Private Schools

WILLIAM GALSTON

I n reviewing the various chapters in this volume, one is struck by the difficulties inherent in the formulation of the question raised in the title of the
conference that gave rise to the volume: "Regulating School Choice to Promote Civic Values: What Can the U.S. Learn from the Experience of Other
Nations?" For example, the anodyne phrase "regulating school choice" covers, and to some extent conceals, the diversity of national stances toward the
idea of choice itself. Denis Meuret shows that in France, the official stance is
ideologically negative. The idea there is that if parents do reject a school, it is
for bad reasons, such as to avoid mixing with other populations; "choice,"
therefore, "is judged to be intrinsically perverse. However, it has to be tolerated because of the necessity of having a 'safety valve' and because of the
strength of the groups that ask for it." Until recently, Luisa Ribolzi indicates,
the Italian stance was similar to and influenced by the French example. By
contrast, in the United States choice is a central value (increasingly, the central value) of public culture. To defend a proposal on the grounds that it
enhances choice is to put one's adversaries on the defensive.

These divergent stances toward choice reflect, in part, differing assessments of the market. While Americans recognize that markets can spin out of
control, they are disposed to believe that suitably regulated markets promote
efficiency and quality. If Meuret is right, the French reject this proposition

outright. Adam Smith's idea that individuals pursuing their own interests are unintentionally promoting the interest of all is, he says flatly, absent.

But the clash over choice points to even deeper differences. Since the Revolution, the dominant political ideals in France have been civic republican ideals. In this outlook, Meuret explains, "society is supposed to proceed from the state." One thing he means by this, I take it, is that the liberties of intermediate associations and social groupings are seen as delegations of state power, revocable whenever the state comes to regard them as threatening the unity of the "national community." One may recall that Tocqueville's *Democracy in America* was in part an effort to persuade French republicans that their ingrained hostility to intermediate associations, while historically understandable, was in fact at odds with the long-term vitality of self-government. One is not surprised to learn that during the Third Republic, under the presidency of arch-republican Emile Combes, laws were passed banning religious schools outright.

There are parallels to this in the American experience. For example, nativism and anti-Catholicism surged after World War I. In the early 1920s, acting through a ballot initiative, the people of the state of Oregon adopted a law requiring parents and legal guardians to send all children between the ages of eight and sixteen to public schools. In intention and practice, this amounted to outlawing nonpublic schools. The Society of Sisters, an Oregon corporation that maintained a system of Catholic schools, sued to overturn the law on the grounds that it was inconsistent with the Fourteenth Amendment to the Constitution. In the case of *Pierce* v. *Society of Sisters*, decided in 1925, the U.S. Supreme Court emphatically and unanimously agreed:

> We think it entirely plain that the Act . . . unreasonably interferes with the liberty of parents and guardians to direct the upbringing and education of children under their control. . . . The fundamental theory of liberty upon which all governments in this Union repose excludes any general power of the State to standardize its children by forcing them to accept instruction from public teachers only. The child is not the mere creature of the State; those who nurture him and direct his destiny have the right, coupled with the high duty, to recognize and prepare him for additional obligations.[1]

This case explicitly advanced a conception of free government at odds with that of civic republicanism. Remarkably, it stands unchallenged to this day as an authoritative declaration of U.S. policy and public philosophy.

That said, it is not entirely clear how this public philosophy is to be understood. The standard reading of the "fundamental theory of liberty" that the Court invokes links it to, or translates it into, the language of inalienable rights, a move with deep roots in American history and legal practice. In my view, which I have defended elsewhere, this theory of liberty—and of the rights flowing from it—is rooted in a distinctive social ontology: social life is divided into a number of distinct spheres of activity and relations, each of which enjoys a distinctive authority.[2] These spheres are not arranged vertically, with the sphere of politics at the top. Rather, families, voluntary associations, and churches (among others) coexist with state institutions and enjoy a (limited) range of self-determination outside the legitimate control of the state. This social ontology bears a family resemblance to the theory of "subsidiarity" central to Catholic social thought and also to the position defended by the British pluralists; it is perhaps most closely related to the idea of "sphere sovereignty" developed by nineteenth-century Reformed Calvinists, which is influential in the Netherlands to this day.

In Vermeulen's chapter, for example, we learn that the Dutch constitution guarantees the right not only to establish private schools but to give them a "distinctive religious or philosophical character," which, he says, may be regarded as the "core of the freedom of education." He continues:

> Guarantees of the educational freedom of private organizations can be regarded as safeguarding pluralism and thereby parental choice, ensuring that parents can send their children to a school based on their preferred religious or pedagogical principles. The parental right of choice *as such* is not guaranteed explicitly in the Constitution's provisions. Nevertheless, in my view this right, being one of the main reasons for respecting the freedom of education of private schools, has the status of an unwritten constitutional principle.

This powerful if inexplicit principle, then, denies any comprehensive primacy of the state over families. "Civic values" (whatever they may be) do not always trump "family values," as they do for civic republicans. In my judgment, this contrast between pluralist and civic republican conceptions of state power constitutes one of the principal theoretical underpinnings of the current debate over educational choice.

I do not wish to suggest, however, that pluralism and civic republicanism represent anything like a binary choice. It would be more accurate to place them at opposing ends of a theoretical (and policy) continuum, a fact that becomes apparent when one compares the regulatory strategies that different nations employ. Public oversight of private schooling in France is so strict and comprehensive that after sketching its requirements, Meuret pauses to observe that the reader may wonder whether these allegedly private institutions can really be all that different from state schools. While somewhat more flexible than the French, the German regulatory system described by Lutz Reuter is still significantly prescriptive. To be approved as the legal "substitute" for a public school, a private school must comply with four rigorous "equivalence" norms and structure its finances to prevent the socioeconomic segregation of students. In addition, the basic moral values and political principles of the German national constitution represent "fundamental educational aims" that are to be taught in all schools, whether public or private. Underlying these requirements, Reuter stresses, is the most fundamental objective of all— namely, the imperative of social integration, a process in which education plays a central role. And, as Glenn and De Groof make clear, numerous other European countries—Greece, Portugal, and Switzerland, among others— employ national curricula and pedagogies that limit private schools' opportunity for variation. (In this respect, they are more restrictive that Germany, which does not require a uniform curriculum.) By contrast, regulatory systems in Finland, Sweden, and Spain are considerably more permissive.[3]

As one might expect, regulation in the Netherlands lies at the pluralist end of the continuum. While there are broad national norms addressing teacher qualifications, student admissions, and curricular content and quality, their application to private schools is limited by constitutional protections of the right to educational freedom. According to Vermeulen, regulation is further limited by the state's reluctance to prescribe moral standards. There is a "general dislike of the state as teacher or inculcator of virute," which is reflected also in the absence of explicit education for citizenship. There is, he remarks, nothing in the Dutch curriculum like the French *éducation civique* or even the more modest citizenship education recently incorporated into the national curricular norms of England and Wales. One possible explanation is that given the Dutch embrace of social and political pluralism, the degree of civic unity needed to sustain public institutions and civility is lower than in more homogeneous systems. Another possibility is that while the requisites of civic unity are not less demanding in the Netherlands than elsewhere, the ordinary processes of Dutch social life somehow produce what is needed, without the direct involvement of the schools. Whatever the truth may be, the Dutch model appears to be working.

The United States stands between the civic republican and pluralist poles. On one hand, the *Pierce* decision lays the constitutional foundation not only for educational liberty, but also for extensive regulation of private schools. As the Court observed in its decision,

No question is raised concerning the power of the State reasonably to regulate all schools, to inspect, supervise, and examine them, their teachers and pupils; to require that all children of proper age attend some school, that teachers shall be of good moral character and patriotic disposition, that certain studies plainly essential to good citizenship must be taught, and that nothing be taught which is manifestly inimical to the public welfare.[4]

But how far may such regulation go? What does it mean to regulate "reasonably" and within constitutional limits? In two other important cases, also brought in the 1920s, the Supreme Court's decisions helped define the parameters within which legitimate regulation of private schools has subsequently functioned. The first is *Meyer v. Nebraska*, decided in 1923.[5] Seized by the same nativist passions that swept other states, including Oregon, Nebraska passed a law forbidding instruction, in any school, in any modern language other than English. Under this statute, a trial court convicted a teacher in a Lutheran parochial school of the crime of teaching a Bible class in German. The Supreme Court then struck down this law.

The majority decision noted that "it is the natural duty of the parent to give his children education suitable to their station in life; and nearly all the States, including Nebraska, enforce this obligation by compulsory laws." This kind of legislation is not in itself constitutionally suspect: "The power of the State to compel attendance at some school and to make reasonable regulations for all schools . . . is not questioned." The issue is whether Nebraska's law was reasonable; the Court concluded that it was not:

> That the State may do much, go very far indeed, in order to improve the quality of its citizens, physically, mentally, and morally, is clear; but the individual has certain fundamental rights which must be respected. A desirable end cannot be promoted by prohibited means.

Nebraska's law employed such means, because it violated both the teacher's right to conduct instruction in German and the parents' right to engage him to do so:

> The desire of the legislature to foster a homogeneous people with American ideals prepared readily to understand current discussions of civic matters is easy to appreciate. But the means adopted, we think, exceed the limitations upon the power of the State.

In a remarkable passage, the Court went beyond even the Constitution, to philosophy. The majority's decision identified the underlying theory of

Nebraska's law with the civic practices of Sparta and the pedagogical principles of Plato's *Republic*. But "their ideas touching the relation between individual and State were wholly different from those upon which our institutions rest" and could not be implemented "without doing violence to both letter and spirit of the Constitution." Here again, the Court seems to suggest that civic republicanism is incompatible with the most fundamental moral and philosophical commitments undergirding the American regime.

The second key case defining the limits of permissible regulation is *Farrington* v. *Tokushige*, decided in 1927.[6] Faced with a proliferation of schools teaching the Japanese language to students of Japanese ancestry, Hawaii, then a U.S. territory, enacted a law strictly regulating all foreign language schools. Among its other provisions, the law imposed a per capita tax on these schools and gave the territorial government the right to determine their hours, courses of study, entrance requirements, textbooks, and teacher qualifications. The Supreme Court found that this law and the administrative measures adopted pursuant to it "go far beyond mere regulation of privately supported schools. . . . They give affirmative direction concerning the intimate and essential details of such schools." Enforcement of the act, the Court concluded, would destroy most of the regulated schools and would deprive parents of a fair chance to obtain the instruction, not obviously harmful, that they desire for their children: "The Japanese parent has the right to direct the education of his own child without unreasonable restrictions," but the law in question represents "a deliberate plan to bring foreign language schools under a strict governmental control for which the record discloses no adequate reason." Because the law was inconsistent with constitutional guarantees of equal liberty, it could not stand.

I said earlier that the United States stands somewhere between pluralism and civic republicanism. I can now be more precise. Like France, the United States believes that civic unity can be sustained only through explicit efforts, in which schools have an important role. The state may therefore reasonably regulate all schools, public and private, to promote civic unity, and these regulations may include civic education requirements as well as mandates concerning schedule, physical plant, and teacher qualifications. But like the Netherlands, the United States believes that it is essential to safeguard citizens' liberty to shape and choose distinctive forms of schooling that express their deepest commitments. This commitment to protecting expressive liberty and to the political pluralism that helps frame and support it circumscribes the rightful authority of the state to regulate private schools. Some regulatory issues fall squarely on one side of this line, while others create boundary disputes.

Two things are clear, however. First, the state's power to regulate does not ordinarily extend so far as to impair those features of a school that provide its distinctive character. The power to regulate cannot be a backdoor strategy for obliterating all meaningful differences between public and private schools. Second, there are some things that the government may not rightly require all schools to do, even in the name of forming good citizens. The appeal to the requirement of civic education is powerful, but only in civic republican regimes is it dispositive. In polities that embrace a measure of political pluralism, as does the United States, claims based on religious liberty may from time to time override the state's interest in education for civic unity.

Regardless of one's views on these theoretical issues, anyone who compares systems of education must be struck by the intimate connection between education and the broad features of what I call public culture, which differs from country to country. Public culture—the characteristic outlook that suffuses people's attitudes to politics, morals, and social life—does not drop from heaven fully formed, but develops through time in response to key stimuli. It is both historical and path-dependent.

These features of public culture make it very difficult for policies and institutions that are embedded in one public culture to cross national boundaries, or even for one country to learn from the experiences of another. The contexts are too different to permit a reliable assessment of any one variable in isolation. Moreover, differences in public cultures shape corresponding differences in civic values. So when a conference convenes to investigate the relation among regulation, choice, and civic values, one must immediately ask, *which* civic values? Here, too, history matters. It is impossible to read the narratives of the French and Italian educational systems outside the context of a centuries-long struggle between republican institutions and the Catholic Church, which shaped (some would say disfigured) the civic cultures of these countries. It is just as difficult to encounter the central moral principles and political institutions of the German national constitution without reflecting on the horrors of World War II and Germany's sincere efforts to uproot the social and cultural bases of Nazism. The complex tension between Catholicism, Protestantism, and rationalism shaped the distinctive "pillarized" Dutch political culture. And so forth.

In comparison to European countries, the United States is larger, more ethnically and religiously diverse, and more devout. In the U.S. context, nothing like Dutch "pillarization" is possible, or even conceivable. To give constitutional protection to private and religious education is to open the door to pedagogies that depart significantly from the cultural mainstream. In the eyes of critics, taking the next step—offering public support for such schooling—threatens to cross the line between toleration and endorsement and to trigger deep conflict. To advocates, powerful norms of equal treatment render this step permissible, perhaps even mandatory. However this may be, it seems safe to say that the characteristic American blend of cultural diversity, individual liberty, and freedom of association makes it far less likely than in Europe that shared informal norms can be relied on to police the perimeter of educational acceptability.

It would be too pessimistic to conclude that the comparative study of educational systems can yield no useful cross-national lessons. Certain effects of school choice may be similar, regardless of political culture. For example, there are some remarkable resemblances between the consequences of school choice in France and the United States. In both countries, parents availing themselves of choice are more satisfied, students experience schooling as communitarian rather than bureaucratic, and the educational attainment of students with low socioeconomic status (SES) in schools of choice tends to rise far more than it does for higher-SES students in these schools. In the same vein, the experience of a number of different countries points toward the generalization that choice tends to tug against attaining the goal of social integration. Parents generally seek out schools with higher median SES and lower concentrations of students they perceive as different from themselves and undesirable, on either ethnic or socioeconomic grounds. Given standard assumptions about preferences, choice systems tend to increase social sorting into discernibly different subpopulations. To the extent that a society pursues social integration and believes that attaining that goal requires integration of schools, it will be compelled to restrict school choice.

In this connection, it is important to keep in mind what the chapters in this volume so clearly illustrate—that "choice" is a rubric covering a wide range of policies. There are not only distinctions between permitting choice, encouraging it through public funding, and institutionalizing it through public structures such as pillarization but also decisions about the kinds of families and institutions that are eligible for public support. All of these considerations shape the aggregate consequences arising from individual choices. For example, it is one thing to offer funded choice to low-income families whose children are trapped in failing schools, quite another to offer funded choice to everyone. The former is unlikely to increase ethnic and class segregation and may even work to counteract it; the latter almost certainly would exacerbate the tendency toward ethnic and class homogeneity within schools. It would be a serious mistake to impute the negative social consequences of comprehensive choice to the more targeted policies that many U.S. advocates are urging. (This is not to preclude the possibility that such policies may give rise to other fundamental objections.)

There may be some policy instruments that can be detached from one nation's particular institutional history and public culture and successfully transplanted elsewhere. A good example is the system of civic education employed by the Canadian province of Alberta, described by David Campbell. The goal is to combine the often competing objectives of accountability and autonomy; the means is an examination in which the civic education of every student in every school, public or private, is "gauged according to the same standard." In such a system, obtrusive government oversight can be minimized and different schools may pursue civic education in distinctive ways, subject only to the requirement that at the end of the day, graduating students demonstrate the required competence in the subject. And in such a system, it would soon become apparent whether certain kinds of schools are less effective than others in promoting civic values. For example, accumulating evidence refutes the long-standing belief that U.S. Catholic schools are less pro-civic than public schools.[7]

In principle, any state, province, or nation that can reach agreement about the core content of civic education can use some version of the Alberta model. The United States has reached a workable consensus on the matter (witness the wide acceptance of the National Assessment of Educational Progress exam), as have many other nations. Here, at least, is one example of a strategy for bringing together individual choice, educational freedom, state regulation, and the promotion of civic values and for doing so in a manner that may well be workable across boundaries.

Notes

1. *Pierce* v. *Society of Sisters,* 268 U.S. 534–35 (1925).

2. See William Galston, *Liberal Pluralism: The Implications of Value Pluralism for Political Theory and Practice* (Cambridge University Press, 2002), chap. 3.

3. Charles Glenn and Jan De Groof, *Finding the Right Balance: Freedom, Autonomy and Accountability in Education* (Utrecht: Lemma, 2002).

4. *Pierce* v. *Society of Sisters,* p. 534.

5. For the following citations to *Meyer* v. *Nebraska,* see 262 U.S. 400–02 (1923).

6. For the citations to *Farrington* v. *Tokushige,* see 273 U.S. 298–99 (1927).

7. See Patrick J. Wolf, "School Choice and Civic Values in the U.S.: A Review of the Evidence," in Paul Hill and Tom Loveless, eds., *Choice in Education: Getting the Benefits, Managing the Risks* (Brookings, forthcoming); David E. Campbell, "Making Democratic Education Work," in Paul E. Peterson and David E. Campbell, eds., *Charters, Vouchers, and Public Schooling* (Brookings, 2001).

13

Regulatory Strings and Religious Freedom: Requiring Private Schools to Promote Public Values

RICHARD W. GARNETT

I n *Zelman* v. *Simmons-Harris*, the U.S. Supreme Court ruled that governments may, consistent with the First Amendment, allow religious schools to participate in school choice programs.[1] That the Constitution *permits* us to experiment with programs that include religious schools, however, does not mean that we *should*. Nor does the *Zelman* decision answer the many difficult questions about how such experiments and programs should be designed, implemented, and regulated.

Accordingly, the aim of this volume is to enrich our conversations and illuminate the regulatory options that we face by canvassing other countries' experiences with school choice. As more and more American jurisdictions move forward with voucher programs and other choice-based reforms, how ought these experiments be structured to realize their promise while guarding against unintended harms? In particular, as public money flows to private and religious schools, what regulatory strings and conditions ought to accompany those funds in order to ensure that the schools serve the public purposes and deliver the public goods for which they are being paid? How do we hold nonstate schools accountable while respecting and protecting educational diversity, religious freedom, parents' rights, and church autonomy? Questions like these invite number crunching on the nuts and bolts of education policy and program design, but they also prompt deeper reflection on the purpose of education, the authority of the state, the demands of liberal pluralism, and the dignity of the human person.

This volume has as its focus a particular question: What can we in the United States learn from other countries' experiences with school choice about regulating private schools to promote public values? In my view, this book's account of other nations' practices and experiences should serve as a cautionary tale for those who value the distinctiveness of religious schools and the authentic freedom of religious believers. Yes, public funding of private education is widespread abroad, but so are regulation, oversight, and homogenization. And so, we can agree with the Supreme Court that our Constitution permits governments to include religious schools in publicly funded voucher programs yet still worry about what James Burtchaell has called "the dying of the light" and the possibility that these schools might be ideologically commandeered by government or merely tempted irresistibly to fade into the background sameness of state schooling.[2]

John Coons once observed that "the case for choice in education goes much deeper than . . . efficiency" and that the "larger reasons for believing in choice" are "equal in dignity to those that underlie our great constitutional freedoms." As he put it, "[s]hifting educational authority from government to parents is a policy that rests upon basic beliefs about the dignity of the person, the rights of children, and the sanctity of the family; it is a shift that also promises a harvest of social trust as the experience of responsibility is extended to all."[3] I would go even further: Choice in education is not only consonant with but also constitutive of the common good; it also can be seen as a crucial aspect of parents' responsibility and vocation—of what Stephen Macedo has called, in another context, "their great office"[4]—to "participate in God's creative activity" through the formation of their children.[5]

Still, many thoughtful and reasonable people worry that increased parental choice could undermine the purported mission of public education in the United States, namely, to create a well-educated and tolerant citizenry that is united by its shared values and loyalties and, at the same time, by appreciation for its ethnic, cultural, and religious diversity. Forty years ago, Justice Brennan captured eloquently this heart of the common-school faith, proclaiming that "the public schools serve a uniquely public function: the training of American citizens in an atmosphere free of parochial, divisive, or separatist influences of any sort—an atmosphere in which children may assimilate a heritage common to all American groups and religions."[6] The concern about choice, then, is not just that private schools—like, say, private airlines, sanitation companies, or mail carriers—will win out in a competitive market, but that such a victory would balkanize U.S. communities and hamstring the civic development of the nation's children, saddling them with an unhealthy, sectarian narrowness. David Campbell relates, for example, that some critics in Canada argue that public support for private schools "will only splinter Ontario's increasingly diverse population—an outcome antithetical to Canadians' collective vision of their nation as a harmonious blend of different cultures" and that one prominent official has warned that choice could "result in racial, ethnic and religious apartheid in our educational system, as well as intolerance and ignorance."

These concerns, even if overblown, cannot be dismissed out of hand. As I write, in the late summer of 2003, the world is reeling from the news of the bombing by an al Qaeda–affiliated terrorist group of a hotel in Jakarta. Reporting the attack, the *Wall Street Journal* noted that Indonesian terrorists recruit from among the alumni of religious schools funded by adherents of a particular form of Islam, prevalent in Saudi Arabia, known as Wahabism. According to the *Journal,* the parents of many poor Indonesian children seize the opportunity offered by these schools, which "represent their [children's] only chance to learn to read and write. Once there youths are steered down a dead-end street of violence and hatred." The *Journal* went on to praise the efforts of Pakistan's President Musharraf to bring the local religious schools under a central licensing scheme, create a new standard curriculum, and monitor their activities.[7]

Nevertheless, Charles Glenn is probably right to object that "the idea that schools that undermine societal norms would flourish unchecked under a well-designed voucher program is a sort of ghost story to frighten the gullible." In fact, students whose parents are permitted to choose their schools—public or private, religious or secular—are no less tolerant, respectful, decent, and public minded than children educated in public schools (and they are likely better educated); private and religious schools are no less likely, in Luisa Ribolzi's words, to "convey meaningful values and make their students aware of how important it is to prepare themselves to become active citizens in their democracy." David Campbell's research strengthens this impression,[8] as does B. P. Vermeulen's contribution, which closes with the observation that "fears that a system like that of the Netherlands, which is based on freedom of education and school choice, is detrimental to social cohesion and integration are unjustified."

Still, one need not be a crusading secularist, a Jacobin statist, or even a civic republican to agree that the health of civil society depends crucially on the formation, development, and training of capable, decent, other-regarding persons who are concerned with and motivated by the common good.[9] People care about education not just because they think that facts and figures matter but also because they think that values, beliefs, and aspirations matter. After all, a democratic political community can no more perpetuate itself without attending carefully to the dispositions of its citizens than a religious community that does not evangelize each new generation can hope to thrive and survive. We can agree, then, with William Galston that "liberal democratic citizens are made, not born"; with Macedo that "we should not take for granted a shared civic life robust enough to master the many centrifugal forces to which modern life gives rise"; and with Michael McConnell that "a liberal society is always at risk" and "vulnerable at its foundations."[10] The question remains: does the perceived fragility of democratic values require, or even justify, restrictions on school choice or intrusive regulation of private and religious schools?

This difficult question points to a real tension in our constitutional tradition. On one hand, Americans celebrate dissent, disagreement, and iconoclasm. With Justice Douglas, they honor "the right to be nonconformists and the right to defy submissiveness" and to celebrate "lives of high spirits rather than hushed, suffocating silence."[11] They invariably are moved both by Justice Robert Jackson's eloquent warning that "compulsory unification of opinion achieves only the unanimity of the graveyard" and his ringing proclamation that "if there is any fixed star in our constitutional constellation, it is that no official, high or petty, can prescribe what shall be orthodox in politics, nationalism, religion, or other matters of opinion."[12]

At the same time, we recognize that Justice Jackson's stirring rhetoric cannot, in the end, be taken seriously as a description of how our government does, or even should, act. We realize that *of course* governments—even liberal, constitutional governments—prescribe orthodoxy. As Steven Smith has written, Jackson's words "committed [us] to a course of massive collective delusion," one that "requires us to pretend [that] government cannot and therefore does not prescribe—does not officially stand for—any 'right opinions.'"[13] Thomas Jefferson's quip about polytheistic pick-pockets notwithstanding, even liberal, constitutional governments cannot be indifferent to "matters of opinion." Quite the contrary: As Edmund Burke once observed, "it is [precisely] the interest, and it is the duty, . . . of government to attend much to opinions."[14] The right question, then, is not whether there should be a public orthodoxy, but rather what our public values are and what steps our government may take to promote and inculcate them

And so we return to the question presented: what can we in the United States learn from other countries' experiences with school choice about regulating private schools to promote public values? There is, of course, a great deal we might learn. In particular, though, the essays gathered here sound three themes that are especially instructive for us in the United States.

—*First:* Private and religiously affiliated schools, no less than public schools, can and do equip children for meaningful participation in the public life of contemporary democratic societies. They provide a crucial public good, and, generally speaking, they do it well. There is, therefore, no "first principles" reason why such schools and those who attend them should categorically be denied public funding. In an overwrought moment, Justice Hugo Black once asserted, as a truism of political morality, that "state aid to . . . religious schools generates discord, disharmony, hatred, and strife among our people, and . . . any government that supplies such aid is to that extent a tyranny."[15] These essays confirm that Justice Black overstated his case: more than half of all Dutch students attend religiously affiliated schools that are fully funded by the government; 30 percent of students in Canada's Ontario province attend publicly funded Catholic schools; in England and Wales, many religious schools are "aided" and many Anglican schools are "controlled" by the state; and even France—where doubts about Catholicism's civic bona fides still run deep—pays the lion's share of the cost for the 20 percent of French students who attend private, primarily Catholic, schools. These nations are not tyrannies.

Thus the mere fact that public funds are used to pay for education in non-state schools should not be viewed as a recipe for division, disengagement, or theocracy. Philip Hamburger, Steven Smith, and others have demonstrated that strict "no aid" separatism was never really the command of the First Amendment's establishment clause, properly understood.[16] Similarly, this volume reminds us that Justice Black's no-funding principle might be prudent, but it is not an indispensable linchpin of a free society. There are good reasons to worry about government funding of education in religious schools, but the survival of democratic government is probably not one of them.

—*Second:* The pervasive public funding of religious schools abroad has resulted in what Charles Glenn calls an "ambiguous embrace." The studies collected here should give us pause and prompt us to ask whether public funds—and, more specifically, the oversight, regulation, and intrusion that inevitably accompany them—pose a danger not only to private schools' distinctiveness and independence, but also and more particularly to the mission and freedom of authentically religious schools. In my view, a healthy civil society can safely tolerate—indeed, it should welcome and likely depends on—meaningfully religious schools. If the price of school choice were the loss of such schools, it would not be worth even the substantial benefits it promises. In fact, it is precisely the concern that school choice programs might require or induce religious schools to water down their religious character that leads many devout religious believers to oppose vouchers. Similarly, some have contended that vouchers should be supported precisely in order to enable increased secularizing regulation of religious schools.[17]

And so, while the various contributors to this volume provide us with many helpful models, guideposts, and templates, they sound a warning as well. Even a cursory examination of European and British practices reveals both that the flow of public funds to private and religious schools is nearly universal and that government oversight of such schools, their practices, and their curricula is far more pervasive and homogenizing than in the United States. Indeed, in many of the countries studied in this volume, it is far from obvious that any meaningful distinctions remain between state and church schools or that "religious" schools retain any kind of distinctly religious identity or mission. For example, Vermeulen emphasizes that in the Netherlands "a majority of Catholic and Protestant schools do not, in fact, have a strongly distinctive religious character anymore"; many of these "are in fact religiously neutral." Dykstra, Karsten, and Dronkers agree: in particular, "the religious identity of Catholic schools has become very weak. There are few traces left of specifically Catholic elements." If the essays collected here establish anything, then, it is that the practices of private and religious schools—for example, the hiring and firing of teachers, the selection of students, curricular content, religious instruction, worship requirements, and so on—are closely regulated by governments in continental Europe and Great Britain, notwithstanding the fact that most of these countries acknowledge educational freedom as a basic human right and purport to value diversity in schooling.

What is the lesson for us? Although this volume shows that private and religious schools in the United States are anomalously independent, it is still widely (and reasonably) assumed that public rules and values can and should follow public funds and that education that is funded by the government may, at least to some extent, be regulated to protect the government's interests. And why not? After all, it is "black letter" constitutional law that Congress may and does enthusiastically promote policy goals that might exceed its enumerated powers simply by attaching conditions to the money it spends.[18] Particularly in the realm of education, we are reminded over and again that government policies, priorities, and paperwork are tied inextricably to government funds. We might conclude, then, that with respect to the matter of requiring private schools to honor and teach public values, reasonable regulatory conditions attached to school vouchers "are entirely a matter of political discretion. The Constitution does not require them, and it does not forbid them."[19] Cautioned by the state of religious education in other countries, we might also conclude that the "embrace" of public funding is too "ambiguous," and the danger to educational diversity and religious schools' distinctiveness too great, to justify the risk of school voucher experiments.

There is, however, more to the matter of regulating religious schools to privilege and produce public values than just political discretion. We can learn much from other countries' experiences with school choice, but there is also for us the matter of what our Constitution and traditions permit. It turns out that our Constitution meaningfully constrains the ability of government to engage in the ideological commandeering of these schools directly through regulation or indirectly through conditions attached to financial support or tuition vouchers. Put differently, efforts to require private and religious schools to compromise their distinct ethos, or religious mission, as a condition of participating in an otherwise neutral school choice program would likely be unconstitutional.[20]

For starters, it is a bedrock principle of American constitutional law that private and religious schools have a right to exist and operate (subject, of course, to reasonable regulation) and that parents have a right to select such schools.[21] From this it would seem to follow that government could not require that such schools' curricula, hiring criteria, and admissions standards mirror precisely, in every respect, those of the public schools. In addition, although the First Amendment's doctrinal niceties often are difficult to unravel, it is clear that government could not, even in the name of civic education, regulate the content of education in a way that "established" or "endorsed" (or condemned) religion. It could not impose curricular or other requirements that excessively "entangle" state actors in the internal affairs of a church, second-guess the interpretation or enforcement of religious doctrine, or unduly infringe on the autonomy of a religious community by, for example, regulating the hiring of school leaders or religious education teachers. Nor could the state single out, for special penalties or official disapproval, specifically religious practices, beliefs, or activities. And so on.

It is also likely, at least under current law, that if conditions related to civic education were attached to school vouchers they would be challenged and evaluated in light of recent developments involving the First Amendment's free speech clause.[22] It is well established that the outflow of government cash for the purchase of items or services with an expressive component may in some cases be regarded for First Amendment purposes as "government speech." In such cases, the government may "say" pretty much whatever it wants, even if it favors some viewpoints and values over others.[23] On the other hand, government spending programs sometimes create not vehicles for the government's own "speech" but "forums" for private expression. And a growing number of free speech cases teach that government may not create, operate, or manage a "public forum"—including public programs that fund expressive and educational activities—using "viewpoint discriminatory" rules.[24]

The point here, of course, is not to unravel the Supreme Court's efforts to draw a line in these and similar cases. It is enough to say that there are plausible arguments that vouchers should, for doctrinal purposes, be framed as a way of facilitating the private "speech"—that is, the expression of a preference for a particular school, with a particular message or ethos—of parents and nonstate schools. To be sure, analogies between "speech" on one hand and education funding, curricular content, or parents' choice on the other are not perfect and should not be forced. The argument here is *not* that public education *is* private speech, nor is it that the provision by government of public services always and necessarily triggers application of the free speech clause. Instead, the claim is merely that parents' choices about education can plausibly be framed, for constitutional purposes, as protected expression. Parents are "speakers," the argument goes, when they make "decisions about whether, when, and through which such intermediaries they prefer to communicate with their children."[25] On this view, monies disbursed through a school voucher program are fairly regarded as creating a "public forum" rather than a vehicle for "government speech."

Does this mean that governments could not attach curricular and other conditions to school vouchers or, more generally, that the state could not regulate private schools to promote public values? Not at all. It simply means that the rules governing publicly funded voucher programs may not discriminate against particular viewpoints, including religious ones. The Constitution's "viewpoint neutrality" requirement—even assuming that it would apply to regulatory strings attached to vouchers—leaves room for reasonable oversight and even for meaningful "civic education" requirements. Nothing about this free speech clause/"public forum" line of argument undermines the basic point that the government is entitled to make sure that it is getting the "education" it is paying for.

In addition to the several protections afforded religious schools by the Constitution, there is another reason why those of us who value religious schools should not be too quick to conclude, in light of other countries' experiences, that vouchers are unacceptably risky, and it is provided by David Campbell's chapter, in which he describes the practice in Canada. To be sure, certain features of Canada's regulatory practice—for example, the fact that even the content of religious education in Ontario is subject to the provincial education ministry's approval—are troubling. In Alberta, however, it appears that authorities have elected to attend to concerns about civic education and good citizenship not through intrusive oversight of private and religious schools' internal practices or through micromanagement of their curricula, but instead through meaningful, generally applicable examinations.

Alberta's school system, as described by Campbell, includes state schools and publicly funded Catholic schools, as well as subsidized private and religious schools, charter schools, and home schooling. Complementing this diversity, however, is the province's curriculum-based external exit examination system, which evaluates not only students' skills and knowledge of facts but also their progress toward "responsible citizenship." Students in public and, for example, Catholic schools take the same tests and proceed toward the same goals, which are viewed as entirely consonant with the aims of Catholic education. Again, an advantage of Alberta's examination system is that it makes it possible for the government to verify that it is getting what it is paying for without imposing a complex, intrusive, and possibly hostile battery of regulations on distinctive private and religious schools. A testing regime like Alberta's would seem not only to reduce the likelihood that authentically religious schools would be required or tempted to compromise their mission, ethos, or faith but also, as Campbell points out, to offer these schools the opportunity to prove that engaged and committed religious believers can be good, liberal citizens and that the norms of nonstate schools and associations are not necessarily at odds with the common good.

—*Third:* A final, instructive theme that winds through many of these essays—one that admittedly is a bit more abstract—concerns the role of nonstate associations in the task of education. Reviewing the practices and premises of many European countries, one sees a striking willingness to employ state power and processes in the production of civic virtues through education, rather than rely on the norm-generating capacities of families, associations, and civil society. Indeed, it could be that one of this volume's more provocative lessons is that the funding and regulation of private education is often closely tied to the state's efforts to protect itself from potentially destabilizing moral and ideological competition from nonstate institutions generally, and—in several countries—from the Roman Catholic Church in particular.

In France, for example, as Denis Meuret describes, schooling is and has long been arranged and regulated in a way explicitly intended to limit the Church's perceived power. According to Meuret, public regulation of private schooling "has to make sure that the Catholic church will not use its influence through education in order to undermine the republic." In Italy, too, education was until fairly recently employed by the relatively new and vulnerable Italian state as what Luisa Ribolzi calls a "national unity device." As she relates, the rise of the Italian school system was strictly connected to the political construction of the nation, which took place without the Church's participation; "the state has therefore focused primarily on controlling Catholic schools rather than on helping society to become more engaged in education." Even in Germany—which is, as Lutz Reuter explains, constitutionally committed to permitting pluralism in education—the regulatory regime of contemporary schooling consciously aims toward societal integration and reflects a post-Nazi realization that a democratic state cannot afford to be neutral or laissez-faire when it comes to values in education.

These conflicts and struggles are instructive for us, in at least two ways: as in France and Italy, though perhaps not to the same extent, the debate in the United States over the extent to which private schools, and education generally, may and should be regulated to promote public values cannot be separated from the anti-Catholicism that has shaped American law and life in deep and abiding ways.[26] This is a difficult matter to discuss, particularly in light of the overly casual manner in which the "anti-Catholicism" charge is leveled in contemporary American politics. Still, we cannot avoid the reality that, for at least a century, the education debate, the defense of government schools, and the case for civic education were inseparable from the respectable anti-Catholicism of America's judicial and intellectual elites.

To be sure, neither American nor Italian and French anti-Catholicism is reducible to prejudice, bias, or bigotry. In the United States, there was more to the matter than knee-jerk dislike of Irish immigrants, Pope Pius IX, or Al Smith. As Michael McConnell has reminded us, "the establishmentarians of this earlier era were not merely narrow-minded bigots. They had genuine reasons for fearing that the moral and cultural underpinnings of Americanism were endangered by the influx of strangers to these shores."[27] Certainly, the experiences of the Church in Europe with radical individualism and revolutionary anticlericalism prompted more than a few intemperate, anti-liberal, nuance-free papal pronouncements concerning democracy and religious freedom: Pope Pius IX, for example, writing in 1864, dismissed as "insanity" and "injurious babbling" certain liberal claims regarding liberty of conscience and the freedom of speech.[28] As a result, what Meuret says of nineteenth-century France was true for the United States as well: the "leaders of both camps"— the French state and the Catholic Church—"regarded education as having a decisive influence on the mind and spirit of students: whoever ran the schools would form the spirit of the nation."

In today's conversations on civic education, liberalism is seen by many as being at risk from the rival values being promoted by religious "fundamentalists" and other allegedly intolerant subgroups, just as, perhaps, republican virtue and national cohesion were once perceived as threatened by European immigrants and authoritarian, pre–Vatican II Catholicism. It seems appropriate, then, that we situate today's conversations in the context of our long-running public debate about Catholicism's compatibility with American democracy and about the fitness of Roman Catholics for American citizenship. My own hope for these conversations would be for a wider appreciation of Catholic social teaching on human freedom, solidarity, and the common good and for increased openness to the possibility that these teachings are a help, not a hindrance, in the formation of good citizens. Here again, Campbell's description of the civic education regime in Alberta—where the Catholic schools have explicitly embraced, in their own idiom and for religious reasons, the province's civic aims—is encouraging.

Moving away from the issue of anti-Catholicism, though, we should also note that European concerns about competition from mediating associations in the formation of citizens owe more to civic republican premises than to the pluralist values reflected in the structure and text of our own Constitution. For us, the freedom of association—and of associations—is "crucial in preventing the majority from imposing its views on groups that would rather express other, perhaps unpopular ideas."[29] The Rehnquist Court, in particular, has in recent years "been pursuing a coherent jurisprudence that invigorates decentralization and the spontaneous ordering of social norms that Alexis de Tocqueville celebrated in *Democracy in America* as being the essence of the social order generated by our Constitution."[30] In our tradition, mediating associations play an important structural role in safeguarding political liberty.[31] At their best, they serve as seedbeds of civic virtue and social capital but also as the hedgerows of civil society; they serve both as "laboratories of innovation" that clear out the civic space needed to "sustain the expression of the rich pluralism of American life"[32] and as "critical buffers between the individual and the power of the State."[33]

William Galston notes, in chapter 12 of this volume, that civic republican political ideals are often linked with the notion that "society proceeds from the state"; "liberal pluralists," on the other hand, regard the state as proceeding from or existing alongside the institutions of civil society. In the lively discussions at the conference from which these essays proceed, it was similarly and several times observed that these two theoretical models—the pluralist and the civic republican (or, perhaps, the "statist")—lead to distinct conceptions of educational choice. In the more statist model—in France, perhaps—

the education of children and the administration of schooling are seen, ultimately, as the tasks and prerogatives of the state. School choice is accepted, if at all, as a way for the state to achieve its own goals more efficiently; private schools are, like public schools, merely delegated carriers of the government's own educational messages. Or, as Reuter says with respect to Germany, "private schools serve to complete and enhance the state system."

As I mentioned above, this suggested distinction between educational funding as government speech and school vouchers as the facilitation of individual expression—or, as Ribolzi puts it, between the school as "state ideological apparatus" and education as "the expression of an independent civil society"—is important in American free-speech law. It also brings us back to my claim that other countries' experiences should serve as a cautionary tale for those who attach both civic and religious importance to the survival of distinctive, authentically religious schools. Education is a public good, but it is not simply the business of the state; it is much more than that. Henry Adams once wrote—or, more precisely, he complained—that education is "a sort of dynamo machine for polarizing the popular mind; for turning and holding its lines of force in the direction supposed to be the most effective for State purposes."[34] In my view, however, the chief end of education is, as Jacques Maritain put it, "above all to shape man, or to guide the evolving dynamism through which man forms himself as man."[35] And so, as we consider the extent to which private schools should be regulated to promote public values, we should not accept, as the French model appears to do, the premise that parents, religious schools, and nonstate associations act merely as the subcontractors of the state when they educate.

The Supreme Court's decision in *Zelman* is not and does not purport to be the end of our public conversations about education, government funds, civic values, and religious freedom. Indeed, one of the virtues of Chief Justice Rehnquist's majority opinion in the case is precisely that it invites further developments, dialogue, and deliberation, in the chambers of our legislatures and in the courts of public opinion. This volume confirms and illustrates that the worthy and important conversations anticipated by the Supreme Court in *Zelman* are now under way.

Many believe that the case for school choice sounds not only in the register of efficiency, competition, and outputs but also in terms of authentic pluralism, religious freedom, and social justice. As Neville Harris puts it, "individual choice is increasingly seen in terms of the right to respect of personal integrity and beliefs rather than merely a facet of consumerism." Others fear, however, that voucher programs could harm the low-income and at-risk students they are intended to help by diverting funds from government schools or that private and religious education, if not regulated carefully, could undermine shared liberal values, impair the inculcation of civic virtue, and threaten social cohesion. *Zelman* does not purport to co-opt or pretermit such discussions high-handedly; rather—as the chief justice once put it, speaking about the assisted-suicide debate—it "permits this debate to continue, as it should in a democratic society."[36]

Notes

1. *Zelman* v. *Simmons-Harris,* 536 U.S. 639 (2002). In my judgment, *Zelman* was rightly decided and defensibly reasoned. See Richard W. Garnett, "The Right Questions about School Choice: Education, Religious Freedom, and the Common Good," *Cardozo Law Review,* vol. 23 (2002), pp. 1281–313; Richard W. Garnett, "The Story of Henry Adams's Soul: Education and the Expression of Associations," *Minnesota Law Review,* vol. 85 (2001), pp. 1841–83; Nicole Stelle Garnett and Richard W. Garnett, "School Choice, the First Amendment, and Social Justice," *Texas Review of Law and Politics,* vol. 4 (2000), pp. 301–63.

2. James T. Burtchaell, *The Dying of the Light: The Disengagement of Colleges and Universities from their Christian Churches* (Grand Rapids, Mich.: Eerdmans, 1998).

3. John E. Coons, "School Choice as Simple Justice," *First Things* (April 1992), p. 15.

4. Stephen Macedo, *Diversity and Distrust: Civic Education in a Multicultural Democracy* (Harvard University Press, 2000), p. 275. Macedo refers to the "great office" of liberal citizenship.

5. Pope John Paul II, *Familiaris consortio* (Apostolic Exhortation, The Role of the Christian Family in the Modern World) (Boston: St. Paul Editions, 1981), para. 36.

6. *School District of Abington Township* v. *Schempp,* 374 U.S. 203, at 241–42 (1963) (Brennan, J., concurring).

7. "Carnage in Jakarta," editorial, *Wall Street Journal,* August 6, 2003, p. A12.

8. See David E. Campbell, "The Civic Side of School Reform: How Do School Vouchers Affect Civic Education?" Working paper 4 (University of Notre Dame, Program in American Democracy, May 2002).

9. There is a rich and growing scholarly literature on "civic education" and on the challenges posed by religious faith, teachings, and communities to certain conceptions of political liberalism. See S. Macedo and Y. Tamir, *Nomos XLIII: Moral and Political Education* (New York University Press, 2002); Diane Ravitch and Joseph Viteritti, eds., *Making Good Citizens: Education and Civil Society* (Yale University Press, 2001); Macedo, *Diversity and Distrust*; Meira Levinson, *The Demands of Liberal Education* (Oxford University Press, 1999); Stephen L. Carter, *The Dissent of the Governed: A Meditation on Law, Religion, and Loyalty* (Harvard University Press, 1998); Stephen G. Gilles, "On Educating Children: A Parentalist Manifesto," *University of Chicago Law Review,* vol. 63 (1996), pp. 952–1034; Michael W.

McConnell, "Multiculturalism, Majoritarianism, and Educational Choice: What Does Our Constitutional Tradition Have to Say?" *Legal Forum*, vol. 1991, pp. 123–151 (University of Chicago Law School); William A. Galston, "Civic Education in the Liberal State," in Nancy Rosenblum, ed., *Liberalism and the Moral Life* (Harvard University Press, 1989); Amy Gutmann, *Democratic Education* (Princeton University Press, 1987); Bruce A. Ackerman, *Social Justice and the Liberal State* (Yale University Press, 1980).

10. William A. Galston, "Expressive Liberty, Moral Pluralism, Political Pluralism: Three Sources of Liberal Theory," *William and Mary Law Review*, vol. 40 (1999), p. 870; Macedo, *Diversity and Distrust*, pp. 278–79; Michael W. McConnell, "The New Establishmentarianism," *Chicago-Kent Law Review*, vol. 75 (2000), pp. 457–58.

11. *Papachristou, et al.* v. *City of Jacksonville*, 405 U.S. 156, at 163 (1972).

12. *West Virginia State Board of Education* v. *Barnette*, 319 U.S. 624, at 641–42 (1943).

13. Steven D. Smith, "*Barnette*'s Big Blunder," *Chicago-Kent Law Review*, vol. 78 (2003), pp. 625–26.

14. Edmund Burke, "Speech on the Petition of the Unitarians," in *The Works of the Right Hon. Edmund Burke*, vol. 7, 9th ed. (Boston: Little Brown, 1889), pp. 39, 44.

15. *Board of Education* v. *Allen*, 392 U.S. 236, at 254 (1968) (Black, J., dissenting).

16. Philip Hamburger, *Separation of Church and State* (Harvard University Press, 2002); Steven D. Smith, *Foreordained Failure: The Quest for a Constitutional Principle of Religious Freedom* (Oxford University Press, 1999).

17. See James G. Dwyer, *Vouchers within Reason: A Child-Centered Approach to Education Reform* (Cornell University Press, 2001).

18. See *South Dakota* v. *Dole*, 483 U.S. 203 (1987).

19. Ira C. Lupu and Robert W. Tuttle, "*Zelman*'s Future: Vouchers, Sectarian Providers, and the Next Round of Constitutional Battles," *Notre Dame Law Review*, vol. 78 (2003), p. 972. Lupu and Tuttle go on to note, however, that the Constitution probably *does* require that regulatory conditions be "religion neutral," that is, that they apply to religious and secular private schools alike.

20. "The desire of the legislature to foster a homogeneous people with American ideals prepared readily to understand current discussions of civic matters is easy to appreciate. But the means adopted, we think, exceed the limitations upon the power of the State." *Meyer* v. *Nebraska*, 262 U.S. 390, at 400 (1923).

21. See *Pierce* v. *Society of Sisters*, 268 U.S. 510 (1925).

22. See Lupu and Tuttle, "*Zelman*'s Future," p. 979. The authors note that recent free speech cases, "while not a model of clarity and consistency," can "be fruitfully applied to schools participating in voucher programs."

23. See *Rust* v. *Sullivan*, 500 U.S. 173 (1991).

24. See *Rosenberger* v. *Rector and Visitors of the University of Virginia*, 515 U.S. 819 (1995).

25. Gilles, "On Educating Children," pp. 937, 1016, 1018. Also, see Coons, "School Choice as Simple Justice," p. 17: "Schools that are freely chosen are the prox-

ies for parental ideas that seek entry into the public dialogue" and are "loudspeaker[s] for those who freely support it with their presence and wish to cooperate in its message" (ibid).

26. For more detailed discussions of education and anti-Catholicism in America, see John T. McGreevy, *Catholicism and American Freedom* (W. W. Norton, 2003); Hamburger, *Separation of Church and State*; Charles Leslie Glenn, *The Myth of the Common School* (University of Massachusetts Press, 1988).

27. McConnell, "The New Establishmentarianism," p. 459.

28. Pope Pius IX, *Quanta Cura* (A Number of Concerns), encyclical letter (Vatican City, 1864), paragraph 3.

29. *Boy Scouts of America* v. *Dale*, 530 U.S. 640, at 647 (2000).

30. John O. McGinnis, "Continuity and Coherence in the Rehnquist Court," *Saint Louis University Law Journal*, vol. 47 (2003), pp. 875–87, 885.

31. See Garnett, "The Story of Henry Adams's Soul."

32. Peter L. Berger and Richard John Neuhaus, "Peter L. Berger and Richard John Neuhaus Respond," in Michael Novak, ed., *To Empower People: From State to Civil Society*, 2nd ed. (Washington: American Enterprise Institute, 1996), pp. 45–48; Peter L. Berger and Richard John Neuhaus, *To Empower People: The Role of Mediating Structures in Public Policy* (Washington: American Enterprise Institute, 1977), p. 36.

33. *Roberts* v. *U.S. Jaycees*, 468 U.S. 609, at 618–19 (1984).

34. Henry Adams, *The Education of Henry Adams: An Autobiography* (New York: Modern Library, 1996), p. 78.

35. Jacques Maritain, *Education at the Crossroads* (Yale University Press, 1943), p. 1.

36. *Washington* v. *Glucksberg*, 531 U.S. 702, at 735 (1997).

14

School Choice as a Question of Design

CHARLES L. GLENN

W e suddenly find citizens and legislatures making all kinds of demands upon the school system," wrote a Teachers College professor more than eighty years ago. "Since many of the proposals that are being made among us have been exemplified in the school systems of other nations, it might be well for us, before undertaking any radical reorganization of the spirit and method of American public education, to find out what has resulted from the application of similar policies in other countries. Furthermore, a study of the administrative systems which those other nations have built up will aid in guiding our heightened desire for greater educational efficiency."[1]

Of course, many Americans hold stubbornly to the notion that we have nothing to learn from the experience of other countries, that our country is so much larger, our people so much more diverse, that our situation is unique. As a former state education official, I would reply that the differences of scale between, say, Belgium or the Netherlands and Massachusetts are unimportant, and that Brussels or Rotterdam is dealing with a higher proportion of immigrant children than is Boston. There is much that we can learn from democracies with which we share so many values and habits of democracy, so many stubborn problems of equal opportunity and integration.

This volume of essays is a notable—and in American policy discussions, all too rare—attempt to learn from the experience of other countries. While the announced focus was on the relationship between school choice and civic values, the actual result is a good deal broader.

My colleague Jan De Groof and I led off the conference that generated this book with a synopsis of the massive study of the mechanisms of school autonomy and accountability in twenty-six countries that we published in two volumes in 2002, but the papers and subsequent discussion have turned in a useful way to the outcomes of educational policy decisions.[2]

It has proved very difficult in the United States for policy analysts to reach any sort of consensus about the relative effectiveness of public and private schools and the impact of such public policies as magnet schools and vouchers for private schools. Coleman and Hoffer; Chubb and Moe; Bryk, Lee, and Holland; and many others have argued that there is a "Catholic school advantage," especially for African American pupils. The more recent research by Jay Greene, Paul Peterson, and others on the effects of both public and private voucher programs have seemed to show that they produce modest but solid improvements. Each of these studies, however, has come under heavy criticism on a variety of technical and (perhaps more relevant) ideological grounds, and De Groof and I decided, in our book, to avoid attempting to make judgments about the effectiveness, in terms of measurable outcomes, of the different ways of organizing schooling. Such judgments would be especially difficult to make and to support in a multination study, given all the factors that affect both organization and outcomes. Five primary claims are made on behalf of school choice:

—It is a fundamental right of families.
—It improves the quality of schools through competition.
—It can promote diversity among schools.
—It can promote civic virtue by engaging youth in their schools.
—It can counter residential segregation and promote stable integration.

Each of these claims comes well equipped with critics prepared to argue that the actual effects are just the opposite of those intended. In fact, the critics are partly right; that is, the effects can be negative, when school choice operates within a legal and policy framework that is not designed with the necessary care. On the other hand, they are wrong in claiming that such negative consequences are unavoidable. Much depends on the social and historical context within which educational choice functions, and much depends on good policy design, incorporated into laws, regulations, and incentive systems.

This is why, for example, the Dutch have been tinkering with their system of educational choice for more than eighty years, constantly making adjustments as circumstances change and new problems or demands arise. The chapter by Ben Vermeulen—at present a key figure in this process—reflects the always-changing nature of this dynamic system and reminds us that there is no Platonic ideal of the management of school choice that can be valid for all times and all countries. We can learn a great deal, in the United States, from the more extensive European experience with choice, but we still have to figure out how to apply that experience, and we have to do so state by state.

This chapter discusses briefly each of the claims made for the advantages of school choice and the criticisms of those claims, with a few words about the design requirements in each case based on what Jan De Groof and I have learned about the successes and shortcomings of different systems among western democracies.

School Choice as a Fundamental Right

This claim, which is rarely mentioned in U.S. policy discussions, has been central for Europeans, to such an extent that the other claims we consider here have received relatively little attention. As Jaap Dronkers shows in his masterful overview, there is actually rather little research comparing academic and other outcomes of public and private schools, and the Dutch government even discourages such research. If choice on the basis of freedom of conscience is a constitutionally guaranteed right, it is politically inconvenient to point out that certain choices may produce better academic results than others.

Neville Harris gives a good illustration of how school choice functions to reduce the sort of conflict over schools that has been so debilitating to U.S. education. In the *Kjeldsen* case, the European Court of Human Rights upheld the right of the Danish government to require sex education in schools, while pointing out that Danish parents had a right to send their children to schools that corresponded with their own convictions about how it should be provided. The court recognized that it was impossible to teach about such sensitive matters without adopting at least an implicit view of the world: "In fact, it seems very difficult for many subjects taught at school not to have, to a greater or lesser extent, some philosophical complexion or implications."[3]

Many Europeans would, of course, agree with Stephen Gorard's off-handed remark that faith-based schools are *"anachronistic,"* but it is remarkable that, even in the face of a high degree of secularization, a substantial proportion of parents in the countries discussed in this book express a preference for schools with a religious character. Of course, for some parents this may simply reflect a perception that these schools are more academically effective, but my own reading of the Dutch, Belgian, Scottish, French, and other research on school choice motivation suggests that there is something more at stake, something like a residual sense that children benefit from exposure to a coherent religious perspective even if their parents have grown largely indifferent to religion.[4] Think of how many children in the United States are dropped off at Sunday school by parents who then go out for coffee!

Does a desire to have the education of one's children occur in a setting marked by a religious worldview rise to the level of a protected right of conscience? Most European countries have concluded that it does and that government has an obligation to make exercising that right possible for families of modest means by removing any financial barriers that impede them.

Perhaps the most common criticism of educational choice by its opponents in the United States is that it will allow all sorts of weird and harmful alternatives to flourish: the "David Koresh schools" imagined in the television ads with which the California Teachers Association defeated the state voucher initiative or the Islamic school in Tampa, Florida, which, in July 2003, lost its eligibility for a state program that provides scholarships for low-income children through private donations because of its connection with two men accused of supporting terrorist attacks against Israel. A few years ago, a legal scholar argued that religious schools are inherently harmful to children and that society has a duty to prevent that harm, even if that involves violating the free exercise clause of the First Amendment.[5] How can we justify, critics ask, the exercise of the right of conscience for a school based on an alternative worldview when that may prove harmful to children and to society at large?

As we will see again and again, this is a design issue: for the protection of both children and society, government has every right to ensure—through general supervision and through intervention when necessary—that schools do not teach in ways that harm either. Thus in *Pierce* v. *Society of Sisters* (1925), the U.S. Supreme Court noted that the right to operate nonstate schools does not contradict "the power of the state reasonably to regulate all schools, to inspect, supervise, and examine them, their teachers and pupils; to require that all children of proper age attend some school, that teachers shall be of good moral character and patriotic disposition, that certain studies plainly essential to good citizenship must be taught, and that nothing be taught which is manifestly inimical to the public welfare."[6]

Every one of the countries that De Groof and I studied has found a way to address the same issue. To take an example at random, the Spanish constitution of 1978 requires that nonpublic schools, most of which are publicly funded, provide instruction that is based on respect for the principles of human and civil rights. As David Campbell discusses in his chapter, in Alberta, Canada, denominational schools are subsidized by the government and the public schools may include religiously based alternative programs that, for example, reflect a Jewish or a Reformed Protestant (Calvinist) approach. In language that applies to all schools, the school law there states that

> 2.01(1) All education programs offered and instructional materials used must reflect the diverse nature and heritage of society in Alberta, promote understanding and respect for others and honour and respect the common values and beliefs of Albertans.
>
> 2.01 (2) For greater certainty, education programs and instructional materials referred to in subsection (1) must not promote or foster doctrines of racial or ethnic superiority or persecution, religious intolerance or persecution, social change through violent action or disobedience of laws.[7]

Although the Alberta Committee on Tolerance and Understanding has expressed concern about the potentially divisive effect of publicly funded denominational schools, it has been forced to concede that the dual system in several Canadian provinces had not had that effect. "In fact," Thiessen comments, "it can be argued that such structural pluralism has served to enhance the cause of unity and religious tolerance in Canada."[8] In contrast, there is the monopolistic public system in the United States and the ongoing conflicts over it.

The idea that schools that undermine societal norms would flourish unchecked under a well-designed school voucher program is a sort of ghost story to frighten the gullible. Vermeulen's excellent chapter on how the Dutch system has accommodated and regulated some forty Islamic (and several Hindu) schools shows how such issues can readily be addressed through sound policies and oversight.

School Choice as a Way to Improve Schools through Competition

The claim that competition improves schools is heard mostly in English-speaking countries; on the Continent it has taken a very distant second place behind the argument for freedom of conscience. The argument is that "market" pressures make schools focus more on satisfying parents and thereby more effective and also that such pressures tend over time to eliminate ineffective schools that do not improve.

It is difficult, under ordinary circumstances, to prove or disprove that claim. Most schools that operate under deliberate choice programs, such as magnet schools, charter schools, and private schools receiving vouchers, are educationally distinctive and are chosen at least in part for that reason, so it is difficult to determine whether their greater effectiveness is the result of market competition or simply of their educational distinctiveness. For example, Peter Mortimore and his colleagues, though no friends of denominational schooling, found in their careful study of schooling in London that Church of England and Catholic "voluntary aided" schools had a definite advantage in producing good educational outcomes. There was "a consistent pattern of associations between voluntary status and schools' effects upon a number of the cognitive and non-cognitive outcomes. . . . It is likely that schools which were chosen for very specific reasons may have had the advantages of greater parental support for their educational aims and, because of such support, were helped to be more effective." And, again, "voluntary schools, based on denominational membership, may also elicit a greater commitment from both parents and pupils, which may act as a strong cohesive force."[9]

We could say that these positive effects are byproducts of market forces but do not provide a direct demonstration that competition improves schools. It is, so far as I know (and Jaap Dronkers' chapter seems to confirm this), only in the United States that a certain amount of ingeniously designed recent research—that of Caroline Minter Hoxby and of Jay Greene, in particular—seems to confirm a competition effect independent of school distinctiveness.

Critics of school choice invariably point out that there are losers as well as winners in any competition and that therefore education will get worse for some students even as it gets better for others. That can happen, of course, and it happened on a massive scale over the last half-century as millions of American families moved to the suburbs, drawn in part by the prospect of better schools for their children. Affluent parents who live in cities—like the Clintons and the Gores a few years ago—often put their children in selective and expensive private schools, leaving other children to receive an inferior education in the public schools. Both are examples of school choice, though there are no vouchers involved . . . and no mechanisms to provide preferential access for children from low-income families.

Parental choice guided by public policy is in fact less likely to result in social class and racial segregation than is the "invisible" operation of choice by parents without such policies. In New Zealand, whose choice program has been criticized as inequitable, the norm for school attendance was, as in most Western democracies, that most children attended the state school serving a geographically defined residential area. As in other countries, that led to a very substantial degree of social class and sometimes of racial sorting out within the educational system. In New Zealand, "the zones reinforced any differences in residential segregation due to housing prices or areas with large amounts of state housing," thus fostering inequities.[10] Poor and minority families had no choice in many cases but to attend failing schools.

The effect of the school choice policies adopted in New Zealand has been that "equity has received more discussion than has ever been the case before. Many teachers and parents have become more aware of the need for equality of educational opportunity and the difficulties faced by people from disadvantaged groups than was the case earlier."[11] The Education Act of 1989 entitled any person to free enrollment and free education at any state school, unless demand exceeds capacity. The 1989 law retained individual school attendance zones based on residence but specified that students had a right to select a school outside the zone. Oversubscribed schools were to admit students through a random lottery. When the National Party took power in 1991, attendance zones were abolished, the requirement of a lottery was dropped, and oversubscribed schools were allowed to develop "enrollment schemes" specifying how applicants would be selected. These could not discriminate in violation of the Race Relations Act of 1971 or the Human Rights Commission Act of 1977 but otherwise their administration was at the discretion of the school's trustees. To a considerable extent, enrollment schemes incorporate residential criteria; 83 percent of the schools with such policies in 1997 defined home zones, in addition to other criteria for admission. In that year, 22 percent of secondary and 16 percent of elementary schools had enrollment schemes.[12] Much of the criticism of the operation of parental choice in New Zealand has been directed at the way that enrollment schemes may allow oversubscribed schools to give preference to more "desirable" pupils.[13] Surveys indicate, however, that parental satisfaction with this system of choice is high; 85 percent of parents surveyed said their child was attending their first choice of school. The choices of the remaining 15 percent of parents have been limited by transportation, the school's enrollment, and cost. A large majority of parents are now actively involved in deciding the course of their children's schooling. Two-thirds of New Zealand parents whose children are in school already had decided which school they would like their child to attend next and the majority (63 percent) of those parents could envisage no obstacle to prevent their child from going on to that school.[14]

In New Zealand, as in Scotland, the United States, and elsewhere, studies have found a strong trend toward parents seeking to move their children to schools with a higher social-class enrollment. Lower-status parents are just as likely as higher-status parents to indicate a preference for a high-status school, and they are more likely to seek to send their children to a school other than their neighborhood school.[15] As "consumers" of education, parents often believe (correctly, research suggests) that their children will benefit from having classmates from high-achieving families. It would be morally obtuse to fault parents who seek a better educational environment for their children, but the result may be to widen the social-class gap between high-performing and low-performing schools.

After all, as Denis Meuret points out in his chapter, "the French example shows that it is quite impossible to prevent those who have adequate resources from escaping schools that they deem to be bad." The issue comes down, again, to the design of policies and incentives that level the playing field, so that (as in few other areas of life) the poor and those who are liable to experience various forms of discrimination are able to make the same sorts of choices that those of us who are more fortunate make for our children as a matter of course.[16]

School Choice as a Way to Promote Diversity among Schools

A third argument for school choice is that it makes it possible for schools to differentiate themselve in a broader variety of ways and thus to respond more adequately to the varied demands of families and the varied abilities and interests of students. After all, a school that is required to serve the whole population of a geographically defined catchment area has to offer a sort of lowest-common-denominator education that, while it may not satisfy any parent completely, is sufficiently inoffensive to minimize controversy. Allowing parents to exercise choice among schools opens the door to educational distinctiveness and thus to a more effective and satisfying system overall.[17]

As Stephen Gorard's chapter points out, the current Labour government in Britain has placed a strong emphasis on promoting diversity, with the minister for education arguing that "the model of comprehensive schooling that grew up in the 1960s and 1970s is simply inadequate for today's needs . . . the keys are *diversity*, not uniformity."

Critics of school choice point out that diversity of schooling can easily lead to a return of academic selection, which can in turn produce negative effects for those who are not selected for the higher-level schools. To deal adequately with this charge would require consideration of the arguments for comprehensive secondary education and "heterogeneous grouping," taking us well beyond the scope of these comments. It is worth pointing out, however, that chapter 8 by Lutz Reuter reports that the results on the international PISA testing for Bavaria, whose schools follow the traditional selective German model, were much better than those for Bremen, whose schools are organized on a comprehensive basis.

Diversity of schooling takes many forms other than religious; in Sweden, for example, most of the new schools set up since passage of the 1991 legislation providing vouchers have been pedagogically rather than religiously distinctive.[18] It is evident, as Vermeulen points out, that educational systems increasingly will be under pressure to respond to what parents want, whether it is a religious or philosophical world view, some pedagogical theme, or some other aspect of a particular school that convinces them that the school will be good for their children. Opponents will, as Meuret notes, find it easier to accept "segregation" when it is caused by housing patterns or by academic selection than when it is the result of choices made by parents. The last, they will insist, makes the public educational system subject to private considerations and benefits. Of course, it is almost the definition of a free society—affirmed by the various international covenants defining universal human rights—that parents be able to make such decisions on behalf of their children. That assertion, however, will not satisfy neo-Jacobins who believe that the child belongs to the state rather than to his or her family.

The discussion of these issues in the Netherlands over many decades has been especially interesting, since it has been based on a way of thinking about society that stands in diametrical opposition to that in which the state stands at the apex of the social order and assigns roles and responsibilities to the institutions of civil society. In what is referred to as sphere sovereignty—or, sometimes, as horizontal subsidiarity—Abraham Kuyper and other Dutch thinkers have insisted that "the family, the business, science, art and so forth are all social spheres, which do not owe their existence to the state, and which do not derive the law of their life from the superiority of the State, but obey a high authority within their own bosom; an authority which rules by the grace of God, just as the sovereignty of the State does." Education is one of those spheres, and among the most important, because it touches on the deep things of life and on the relationship between children and parents and between children and their own future. Unfortunately, Kuyper pointed out, "the government is always inclined, with its mechanical authority, to invade social life, to subject it and mechanically to arrange it. But on the other hand social life always endeavors to shake off the authority of the government."[19] It is because so much is at stake in the question of the control of education that the conflicts that arise in this sphere are particularly bitter, both in the United States and, for example, in France. The resolution of these conflicts, in the Netherlands and elsewhere, has been through a strong government role in ensuring the adequacy of all schools, and a strong parental role in choosing among schools found to be adequate.

Diversity of schooling is also criticized from another angle—that it will weaken efforts to make all schools accountable for providing an adequate education and thus to ensure that all children have equal educational opportunities, whatever choices their parents may make. There is much to be said in favor of more explicit educational standards than have been provided in the United States, at least until recent developments in a number of states, and the jury is still out on how the proliferation of charter schools, for example, can be reconciled with a state curriculum framework or such a framework reconciled with school distinctiveness, whether of a pedagogical or religious form. That is the central theme of a recent book that De Groof and I wrote, and that is why we called it *Finding the Right Balance: Freedom, Autonomy, and Accountability in Education.* As we considered various countries, we were especially intrigued by those that required all schools to meet common standards but allowed schools to propose alternative standards that were equivalent but different. Vermeulen mentions this option in the Netherlands, and we found it also in Finland, Hungary, and elsewhere. It makes good sense, and it is similar to the conditions under which charter schools are approved in some states.

School Choice as a Way to Engage Youth and Promote Civic Virtue

A fourth claim is that school choice makes it more possible than in the current monopolistic U.S. public education system to engage youth and their families in the life of the school and, in so doing, to help create in them those virtuous dispositions necessary to a free and just society and a republican form of government. Even such opponents of educational vouchers as Amy Gutmann may concede that "private schools may on average do better than public schools in bringing all their students up to a relatively high level of learning, in teaching American history and civics in an intellectually challenging manner, and even in racially integrating classrooms," while still insisting that "public, not private, schooling is an essential welfare good for children as well as the primary means by which citizens can morally educate future citizens."[20]

But, of course, it is not "citizens" who educate children—except in neo-Jacobin fantasies—but parents and teachers, and the crucial policy issue in civic education is how parents and teachers can be motivated and empowered to behave in ways that serve as examples of civic virtue to the children and youth under their care.

My 1995 study, for the U.S. Department of Education, of the changes occurring in the educational systems of central and eastern Europe as they emerged from communist rule convinced me that, just as civil society was reviving in Poland and other countries in part through the cooperation of parents and teachers in creating new schools that corresponded to their convictions about good education, so we could seek such a revival in America's inner cities by making such cooperation possible. Under this strategy, government—that is, society as a whole—would articulate clear expectations and create procedural safeguards; in addition, it would direct its efforts to encouraging a vigorous civil society by making "space [for] uncoerced human association and also [for] the set of relational networks—formed for the sake of family, faith, interest, and ideology—that fill this space."[21] This is the sphere of life that has largely been squeezed out of inner-city residential areas, and only a radical breaking-up of the smothering asphalt of government provision of education could, I argued, make space for a garden of vigorous new life. I wrote:

> Inner-city schools do not generally play a positive role in this garden-making. On the one hand, they are perceived (not always fairly) as places of disorder, unable to bring their weeds under control, while on the other they offer a harsh and sterile soil for the growth of cooperation and mutual trust. Schools typically function in a bureaucratic fashion which increases the alienation of poor parents and children.

> Public schools, however, do not belong to the communities that they serve; families are members of inner-city churches, but they are clients of inner-city public schools—all the difference in the world. Schools that truly belong to the parents who send their children provide settings of unparalleled capacity for developing habits of responsible activity on the part of adults and children alike. Accepting the promotion of such schools as an appropriate goal of public policy would be consistent with other "reinventing government" measures such as tenant management and ownership of housing developments. It would by no means be a magic remedy for the ills caused by social disorder and weakened families, but it would create the framework within which healing could begin.[22]

Critics, on the other hand, fear that parental choice of schools will divide communities and reduce commitment to the common project of civic life, in effect, as noted above, privatizing the public good of education. They misunderstand the nature of community in contemporary American (or western European) life: for most of us, it is no longer defined by a residential area but rather by voluntary association around shared interests. One of the most powerful of these interests is that of parents for the education of their children, which commonly brings them into association with other adults who have a similar concern—even (or perhaps especially) in the case of families that are home schooling. Within these associations, civic virtues are nourished and practiced.

Does that describe most American schools? Unfortunately, no. In fact, at least for many Americans, it is their churches that give them the opportunity to develop the capacity to be active participants in civic life, as Sidney Verba and his associates have shown. "The churches that African-Americans attend," they write, "have special potential for stimulating political participation . . . they belong to churches whose internal structure nurtures opportunities to exercise politically relevant skills. . . . . Running a rummage sale to benefit the church day care center or editing a church newsletter provides opportunities for the development of skills relevant to politics even though the enterprise in question is expressly nonpolitical."[23] The institutionalized public schools in our cities are not able to function in this way, but many independent community and religious schools do—indeed they must or they could not survive.[24] Surely it is wise public policy to create conditions that would permit more parents to become involved in the schools their children attend, not as passive participants in periodic open houses but as creators, sustainers, and participants in important decisions, just as many of them are in their churches. "Markets in educational services" alone will not automatically provide such opportunities to learn and to practice the civic virtues, but a well-designed program of support for parental choice and institution building can.

That this is not simply wishful thinking is suggested by recent studies in which Steven Vryhof, David Campbell, and others have shown that, in fact, students in private religious schools compare very well on various measures of civic virtue with those in public schools, which allegedly are more committed to the democratic project. A typical study found that "students in Catholic schools perform better than students in assigned public schools on all three objectives of a civic education—capacity for civic engagement, political knowledge, and political tolerance."[25] Similarly, Alan Peshkin, a self-proclaimed unsympathetic observer of the fundamentalist Protestant school that he studied, found that "seldom . . . has any American school been as professedly, unabashedly, unremittingly absorbed by normative considerations as the Christian school" and that "the public school's material advantages are overshadowed by their comparatively poor discipline, social problems, undedicated teachers, and indifferent parents, and also by their inability to develop character and to teach the truth." Peshkin reported that "75 percent of the public high school students responded that school should emphasize character development, but only 39 percent reported that in fact it did so. . . . 93 percent of the Bethany students compared with 80 percent of the public high school students responded that they would approve of a black family moving next door."[26]

No research has proved, or could prove, that school choice will inevitably have positive effects on the civic virtue of students; there are too many other intervening factors. One can say with considerable confidence, however, that what I have called "the myth of the common school" as the sole legitimate and effective "maker of citizens" will not stand up under scrutiny.

School Choice as a Way to Counter Residential Segregation and Promote Stable Integration

The final claim about school choice that we will consider is that it can provide a means of achieving stable racial integration on the basis of the willing participation of parents, in contrast with what has proved to be the inherently unstable desegregation achieved temporarily by mandatory reassignment of students based on their place of residence.

In Massachusetts, where from 1970 to 1991 I headed what was recognized as the most active state program for promoting school desegregation, we found that using mandatory assignments was rarely successful: few of the white pupils assigned to racially balanced schools actually went or remained. When we began using magnet schools and then universal choice-based assignments in more than a dozen cities, however, the results were much more stable and they provided an impetus for improving schools in order to attract and retain pupils with other options. Reflecting on this experience later, I expressed regret that we had not shown more respect for the concerns of parents from the beginning and thereby perhaps have avoided the turmoil that wracked Boston for several years.[27]

The approach we used had its limitations: the choices offered to parents did not extend beyond the available public schools, and one of my last acts as a state official was to call for charter schools and for vouchers in order to create a more dynamic system that would become a more powerful driver of school improvement.[28]

Critics of school choice like Gary Orfield contend that it tends to increase segregation. As with other criticisms, we should acknowledge that it can have that effect, but the weight of the evidence is that even unregulated school choice, as it now exists between public and private schools and between charter schools and public schools with attendance districts, has the net effect of increasing integration. Jay Greene found in his nationwide study that "more than half (55 percent) of public school students were in classrooms that were almost entirely white or almost entirely minority in their racial composition, while 41 percent of private school students were similarly segregated.[29] Good design, such as offering financial incentives for integrated schools, can have an even more positive effect.

In chapter 5 of this volume, Stephen Gorard points out that "since the introduction of extended choice in the United Kingdom in 1988, the overall level of segregation in the school system has declined," since most segregation is caused by geographical factors and choice permits parents to choose schools outside of the residential areas to which they may be confined by their income. Scottish researchers had already noted a similar phenomenon following enactment of the Education (Scotland) Act of 1981, pointing out that "for those who cannot choose [a] school through house purchase or private schooling the legislation does seem to have provided an attainable mode of choice," employed disproportionately by upwardly mobile working-class families.[30]

Concluding Remarks

Our international conference and the papers prepared by the participants have given us all a chance, as Reisner wrote after World War I, "to find out what has resulted from the application of similar policies in other countries" and, we could add, from different ones as well. The emphasis on outcomes was especially valuable, and it should remind us that school choice, like other reforms, should not be expected to suddenly transform a system of schooling that has evolved over many decades and includes millions of employees concerned about protecting their position.

School choice has not been a disaster in any of the countries examined, nor has it been a magic solution to problems that are deeply embedded in the nature of the educational system. The measurable effects of recent school choice policies on academic achievement, on civic virtue, and on integration and educational equity have been modest, but they have been in almost every case positive.

In the last analysis, Americans need to be reminded by our European colleagues that the argument for school choice is based on the fundamental right of parents to make decisions about the education of their children, within a framework of public accountability for the quality and the civic effects of the various schooling options. And this brings us back, one last time, to the need for laws, policies, procedures, and interventions that have been thought through carefully—and therefore to the central importance of good design.

Notes

1. Edward H. Reisner, *Nationalism and Education since 1789* (Macmillan, 1922), p. vii.

2. Charles L. Glenn and Jan De Groof, *Finding the Right Balance: Freedom, Autonomy, and Accountability in Education*, 2 vols. (Utrecht: Lemma, 2002).

3. Ibid., vol. 2, p. 114.

4. Charles L. Glenn, *Why Parents in Five Nations Choose Schools* (Quincy: Massachusetts Department of Education, 1988).

5. James G. Dwyer, *Religious Schools v. Children's Rights* (Cornell University Press, 1998).

6. *Pierce* v. *Society of Sisters,* 268 U.S. 510 (1925).

7. Alberta School Act, section 2.01, Alberta Statutes and Regulations, 1999, c28 s3.

8. Elmer John Thiessen, *In Defense of Religious Schools and Colleges* (McGill-Queen's University Press, 2001), p. 39.

9. Peter Mortimore and others, *School Matters* (University of California Press, 1988), p. 221, 273.

10. Cathy Wylie, *Can Vouchers Deliver Better Education?* (Wellington: New Zealand Council for Educational Research, 1998), p. 80.

11. Peter D. K. Ramsay, "Picot-Vision and Reality in New Zealand's Schools: An Insider's View," in Bob Lingard, John Knight, and Paige Porter, eds., *Schooling Reform in Hard Times* (London: Falmer Press, 1993), p. 274.

12. Wylie, *Can Vouchers Deliver Better Education?* p. 80.

13. Edward B. Fiske and Helen F. Ladd, *When Schools Compete* (Brookings, 1999).

14. Wylie, *Can Vouchers Deliver Better Education?* p. 158.

15. The Smithfield Project, 1993, cited in Fiske and Ladd, *When Schools Compete,* p. 196.

16. Charles L. Glenn, "Letting Poor Parents Act Responsibly," *Journal of Family and Culture,* vol. 2, no. 3 (1987), pp. 48–52.

17. Charles L. Glenn, "School Distinctiveness," *Journal of Education,* vol. 176, no. 2 (1994), pp. 73–103.

18. Frank-Rüdiger Jach, *Schulverfassung und Bürgergesellschaft in Europa* (Berlin: Duncker und Humblot, 1999), p. 248.

19. Abraham Kuyper, *Lectures on Calvinism* (Grand Rapids, Mich.: Eerdmans, 1931), pp. 90, 91.

20. Amy Gutmann, *Democratic Education* (Princeton University Press, 1987), p. 65.

21. Michael Walzer, "The Idea of Civil Society," *Dissent,* vol. 38 (Spring 1991), p. 293.

22. Charles L. Glenn, "Free Schools and the Revival of Urban Communities," in Stanley W. Carlson-Thies and James W. Skillen, eds., *Welfare in America* (Grand Rapids, Mich.: Eerdmans, 1996), p. 425.

23. Sidney Verba, Kay Lehman Schlozman, and Henry E. Brady, *Voice and Equality: Civic Voluntarism in American Politics* (Harvard University Press, 1995), p. 383.

24. Joan D. Ratteray, "Independent Neighborhood Schools: A Framework for the Education of African Americans," *Journal of Negro Education,* vol. 61, no. 2 (1992), pp. 143–46.

25. David E. Campbell, "Making Democratic Education Work," in Paul E. Peterson and David E. Campbell, eds., *Charters, Vouchers and Public Education* (Brookings, 2001), p. 258.

26. Alan Peshkin, *God's Choice: The Total World of a Fundamentalist Christian School* (University of Chicago Press, 1986), pp. 61, 84, 325, 332.

27. Charles L. Glenn, "'Bussing' in Boston: What We Could Have Done Better," in Kofi Lomotey and Charles Teddlie, eds., *Forty Years after the* Brown *Decision: Implications of School Desegregation for U.S. Education* (New York: AMS Press, 1996).

28. Charles L. Glenn, "Controlled Choice in Massachusetts Public Schools," *Public Interest,* vol. 103 (April 1991).

29. Jay P. Greene, "The Hidden Research Consensus for School Choice," in Peterson and Campbell, *Charters, Vouchers and Public Education*, p. 95.

30. Alastair Macbeth, David Strachan, and Caithlin Macauley, *Parental Choice of School in Scotland* (University of Glasgow Press, 1986), p. 334.

15

Regulation in Public and Private Schools in the United States

JOHN F. WITTE

There is a legendary television commercial in the folklore of American school choice battles. It appeared in conjunction with a referendum to create private school tuition tax credits in the state of Oregon in 1992. The commercial begins with a tight, close-up shot of a teacher writing in chalk on a blackboard. One can hear voices, but not clearly. The camera moves back, revealing a teacher wearing a Ku Klux Klan hood and robe. As the camera pans further, the backs of a class of small children, also dressed as Klansmen, appear. The advertisement was designed to highlight the claim that if educational choice came to Oregon, the result would be extremist schools of the worst form. After one or two days, the commercial was pulled as too offensive even for U.S. debates over educational choice.

But the commercial was designed to emphasize two points: that school choice would lead to extremism in education and that it would lead to an extremism that was vehemently discriminatory and antidemocratic. In the parlance of this volume, such schools would not promote and could undermine public values. These problems linger in choice debates, and they have entered the European debates as Muslim families have sought Muslim schools in the Netherlands, England, and France. I suspect that there, as in the United States, these are not really important, long-term concerns.

What to make of such claims for extremist schools? The press in the United States would absolutely love to find the Ku Klux Klan school depicted in the fictitious television commercial. What an exposé! But these schools simply are not there, or if they appear they do not last. Parents would have to support such schools if they were totally private; if public or publicly supported, they would be subject to regulation, political pressure, and media coverage. And if a small number did survive, who would care? Charles Glenn, in chapter 14 in this volume, nails this correctly: "The idea that schools that undermine societal norms would flourish unchecked under a well-designed voucher program is a sort of ghost story to frighten the gullible."

Apart from extremist schools, however, there is concern that private schools might imperil public or community values. I suspect that the idea that private schools and educational choice might undermine or fail to promote democratic community values or civic education adequately is also a red herring, like the Oregon commercial for Ku Klux Klan schools. But it must be taken more seriously. The problem of democratic/public values and choice involving private schools, especially publicly financed private schools, raises several issues. The matter can be divided into two subissues: educating students for citizenship in a democratic country; and the treatment of religious education, which is crucial to most private schools in America.

Resolving the first problem requires more empirical evidence than is presented in the essays in this volume or than is available elsewhere. This volume offers considerable evidence on how other countries teach about civic values and democratic processes, and there is a flurry of interest in the subject in the United States.[1] Until recently, there was little direct evidence on how that education varies from public to private or independent schools or on its effects on civic values. Yet that is the crucial issue for understanding the effects of expanding choice on civic education in this country. According to a meta-analysis of eighteen empirical studies, all but one completed after 1997, Patrick Wolf finds that on average private school students appear to adhere to an array of civic values at least as much as, and perhaps more than, their public school counterparts. Those values range from political tolerance to patriotism, with self-reports of voluntarism and political participation measuring civic behaviors.[2]

There is considerably less work on the actual teaching of civic education, especially in private schools. However, we have no reason to believe that private schools would seriously adopt antidemocratic curricula. My extensive work with private schools in the United States over fifteen years has never found a case where these schools promote antidemocratic or by any definition anticivic values that would lead their small charges into the streets to bring down the local gendarme, to trash the local market, or to attack people beyond their personal reference groups. Why would private schools do such things? Again, there may be fringe schools out there, but they certainly are not an immediate threat to the American republic.

Currently a number of studies of civic education in public schools are under way.[3] I have no doubt that the results will be depressing, finding that we have collectively relinquished that obligation. Stephen Macedo's study convincingly argues that there is even a reluctance to take civic education seriously enough to warrant its rigorous evaluation.[4] There may be historical reasons for this that are no longer valid, such as the way civics used to be taught. I am old enough to have suffered through high school "civics" in a small town in the 1960s. I remember the class being cynically classified by students as intellectually slightly above driver's education, but pragmatically legions below it. I recall a monotonously repetitive directive: VOTE. It sank in. To this day I vote in all elections—even for county scribe and jailer. I believe that in Fort Atkinson, Wisconsin (where I attended high school), for better or worse, they have eliminated required civics.

Religious education is a critical issue for private schools. First, 85 to 90 percent of those attending private schools in the United States attend religious schools. In 1965, 90 percent of the religious students attended Catholic schools. Since then, that percentage has declined to approximately 50 percent, but other religious denominations, especially evangelical Christians, have expanded to keep the religious percentage more or less constant.[5] Any serious threat to religious instruction and practice will evoke vehement opposition from those schools. So religion in private schools matters.

It also matters in the Constitution and in the history of education in the United States. The "strict wall of separation," in a phrase coined by Jefferson, was inaugurated into constitutional doctrine much later and was essentially inoperative in education for the first 140 years of the republic. Indeed, the major movement toward private schools, the growth in Catholic schools from 1890 to 1960, was inspired by the Protestants and by the use of the Protestant Bible in public schools.

As of this writing—and the world is changing rapidly—private schools are essentially unregulated in the United States because of crucial opinions and the "reading" of the First Amendment to the U.S. Constitution. The amendment as applied to religious freedom reads: "Congress shall make no law respecting the establishment of religion, or prohibiting the free exercise thereof." The current precedent defining what that means is the *Lemon* v. *Kurzman* case in which the court specified a tripartite test to determine the constitutionality of a potentially religious program or policy in public schools. To pass constitutional muster, it must be demonstrated first that the action promoted a secular legislative purpose; second that its primary effect must neither advance nor inhibit religion; and third that there must be no excessive entanglement between the state and religion.[6]

The recent *Zelman* v. *Simmons-Harris* decision, which by a 5-4 margin validated the Cleveland, Ohio, voucher program that sent students almost exclusively to private religious schools, determined that public provision of monies to private school parents did not abrogate the First Amendment.[7] The decisions generally followed the Lemon tests. But what remains—and will be the grounds for the next major First Amendment war—is what will happen in the future to the "entanglement" issue. That is because legislative and court actions will undoubtedly be brought against voucher programs on the basis of the argument that when considerable public money is involved, private schools can no longer avoid some degree of regulation. Voucher supporters will vigorously oppose such an action.

The object of the chapters in this volume is to suggest ways in which U.S. policymakers can learn from other countries about regulating private schools to promote public values. In the remainder of my comments, I am going to present a broader set of issues concerning regulation of education. The real concern in the United States is how we regulate schools, both public and private. And I wish to extend this topic to consider the general issue of regulation as opposed to the narrower issue of how to regulate schools to promote public values. In what follows, I hope to convince the reader of the following:

—The other comparable countries in this volume surpass the United States in dealing with the provision of civic education and religious instruction in all forms of schools.

—The United States overregulates public schools, as do other comparable countries, but underregulates private schools.

—There is a common set of regulatory guidelines that should guide regulation of both private and public schools in the United States.

The Status of Civic and Religious Education

The chapters in this volume often discuss "civics" and "religious" education as similar at least in the pedagogical or regulatory sense. In the American case, they cannot be confused. The former refers to the knowledge, skills, and values necessary to function in a specific community, defined here as a democratic community. In common practice the translation of these capacities into educational standards or topics might be expected to vary considerably from one community to another.[8] These chapters give us a view of how at least the topics covered in such education are defined in Europe and Canada. As stated above, ongoing research in the United States will provide a description of what is being done here in public education and what should be done in the future.

I doubt that there are any reliable data on what is being done in private schools or other schools of choice in the United States. At least I know of no systematic evidence, and I see none in the literature referenced here. Again, we must fall back on the speculations of the American contributors to this volume regarding if and why private schools would be less able or willing to provide such instruction.

Religious education can refer to two different things: education regarding beliefs and practices in a particular faith; or education about religion, stressing comparison of religions and their tenets. It is clear from the chapters on England and Wales, France, and Germany that religious education of the second form is a required and accepted part of the curriculum in all schools in these countries. Also, as in the United States, private schools seem free to provide religious instruction and conduct the ceremonies of the specific religion that defines their schools. In fact, in England and Wales, state-run schools are *required* to provide religious instruction and conduct the ceremonies of the Church of England.

What we know less about from these chapters is what is taught of religion in American public schools. The sense is that we are tentative, certainly ecumenical, and probably avoid the subject entirely most of the time.

Religious education and practices in schools (for example, Mass and confession in Catholic schools) are undoubtedly a lightening rod for American educational choice. When the public supports such schools, should the common taxpayer pay for Catholics to attend morning Mass, for Jews to attend synagogue, or for Muslims to pray on school time? Again, the European experience is compelling. In a number of countries, although they are characterized as increasingly secular, such practices are allowed, often with parents having the right to withhold their children. And it appears, with the possible exceptions of France and Italy, there is little controversy over these practices.

Red Herrings and Stalking Horses

I find it difficult to believe that on the basis of existing experiences with private or charter schools in the United States that either extremist schools or curriculums that fail to promote public values and democracy are serious potential problems for school choice programs and policies. My quandary with these issues is actually more conspiratorial. It seems possible that the prospect of regulating private schools on religious grounds could be used as a general defense against all forms of regulation of private schools, including those receiving considerable public monies. Thus the red herring of regulating private schools to prevent antidemocratic instruction or religious indoctrination becomes a stalking horse for choice supporters to resist sensible regulation of all kinds. In his chapter in this volume, Richard Garnett alludes to, but does not support, this possibility. He writes:

> The studies collected here should give us pause and prompt us to ask whether public funds—and, more specifically, the oversight, regulation, and intrusion that inevitably accompany them—pose a danger not only to private schools' distinctiveness and independence, but also and more particularly to the mission and freedom of authentically religious schools.

However, the Milwaukee Parental Choice Program, the first and largest voucher program in America, more than suggests this possibility. Since its expansion to include parochial schools in 1995, there has been essentially nothing systematic known about the students, teachers, curriculum, or student or school performance—nothing other than school expenditures—for a program affecting more than 12,000 students and costing $60 million a year. There have been suggestions and legislative proposals by voucher advocates to evaluate the program but not to submit private schools to the routine forms of reporting and regulation that exist for public or charter schools in the state. There also have been clear pronouncements by lawyers and legal institutes supporting the voucher program that any such regulatory efforts will be met with determined legal challenges.

A Sensible Information and Regulatory Framework for Public and Private Schools

In the United States, we have almost no regulation of religious schools because, under current case law, it would entangle government with religion and violate the free exercise clause of the First Amendment (see above). This remains despite the recent exception of voucher programs from the establishment clause in the *Zelman* decision. On the other hand, we have, by American (not European or Canadian) standards, considerable regulation of public schools, including a new level of requirements established by the No Child Left Behind legislation. Although there remains state-level latitude in implementation, the law requires specification of state standards, testing, accountability, and the designation of failing schools. This is a quantum leap for American schools, and because federal monies are tied to compliance, it is having an enormous impact. Although careful reading of this volume suggests that American schools are still considerably less regulated than European or Canadian schools, we are clearly moving in their general direction.

I believe both European and American regulatory regimes are wrong. Private schools in America are woefully underregulated and public schools are woefully overregulated. And since in many European countries most regulations apply to both public and private schools, all schools there may be overregulated. But this is not a volume about what other countries should do, only about what we can learn from them.

American education is all about variance. Our education systems—at the district level and school level and even within schools—differ dramatically on the basis of geography, size, and space; demographics of families, students, and teachers; educational performance; community values applied to education; and resources and expenditures at all levels. This diversity is reflected in a number of interesting ways. First, within the United States in 2002–03, there were 13,942 legal school districts. However, many of them are configured very differently. One state (Hawaii) and the District of Columbia had a single district, while Texas had 1,039 districts. The sizes of districts vary from an average of 35,860 pupils per district in Maryland (excluding the 184,000 in Hawaii) to 341 in Montana. Perhaps the wildest indicator of geographic diversity is the coverage of an individual school in terms of square miles. It ranges from 1,100 square miles in Alaska to 3.5 in Rhode Island—which may make a difference in terms of busing policy.

Families and students also vary dramatically. The percentage of white students varies from 35 percent in California (excluding the 4.6 percent in Washington, D.C.) to 96 percent in Vermont. Free lunch eligibility varies from 24.7 percent in Vermont to 65.3 percent in Mississippi. And, as is well known, spending per pupil also varies by more than 100 percent, from a low of $5,190 per pupil in Utah to $10,829 in New York.[9]

This diversity in most instances is much greater than in other countries discussed in this volume and other developed countries. For example, the Organization for Economic Cooperation and Development (OECD) has recently published a wide range of education statistics, some of which include measures of the variance within countries. For example, on an international index of occupational status of parents with primary and secondary school children, the United States has an index score of 52.4, which ranks above the OECD average of 48.9. However, perhaps more telling, the standard deviation in the U.S. index is .8, which is eight times higher than the OECD standard deviation of .1 and higher than that of any other country including Mexico, with only .7.[10] In addition, the United States ranks fourth in the percentage of students whose language spoken at home is different from the test assessment language. The others are the multilingual countries of Luxembourg and Switzerland, and Australia.[11]

This diversity also carries over to performance on standardized tests in the United States compared with that in other OECD countries. On international tests of reading literacy among fifteen-year-olds, the United States ranks slightly above the OECD average (504 to 499), but has a 350 percent greater standard error (7.1) than the OECD average (2.0). The next closest country is Japan, with 5.2.[12] And the differences are even larger for math literacy (standard error of 7.5 for the United States and 2.1 for the OECD average) and science literacy (7.3 for the United States and 2.0 for the OECD). In each of these areas the United States is 5 and 3 points below the OECD mean scores.[13] Finally, while the United States does quite well on civics knowledge and interpretative skills of fourteen-year-olds, ranking fourth, again the variance within the United States is second only to that in Poland.[14]

One could argue that this diversity actually requires considerable regulation. However, unless the goal is the radical removal of such diversity—a goal that I would argue is of questionable value and impossible to achieve—it is difficult for me to visualize an effective, centrally driven, and extensive regulatory regime, a one-size-fits-all model.[15]

Given such diversity and a very long tradition of local control of education, regulatory regimes should be humble and devolved. The first critical step should be a "baby step"—to provide the information essential for allowing taxpayers to evaluate their investments and parents and families to choose schools. The second level of regulation would be to permit suitable political units (states, districts, schools) to use the information, if they so choose, to regulate curriculum, pedagogical approaches, and student performance. Therefore it is necessary and normatively appropriate to give information to two relevant groups: parents and families of potential students; and taxpayers and the public authorities that represent them.

As U.S. public authorities move toward providing more public monies for private schools, the schools need to anticipate receiving a very simple set of queries from families and taxpayers. Curiously, when one views state and school district websites, similar sets of information seem to be provided. The basic idea is that education regulation should primarily be about *information*. Why? Because taxpayers and their agents need to have some assurance that their money is being well spent or spent in a way that is consistent with their values. And families need the information to make informed choices for their children.

There are four essential areas in which we should provide information and perhaps subsequent regulation of schools, both public and private: admission of students; curriculum and pedagogy; student achievement; and expenditures and financial information. The rationales for providing this information and its uses vary for families and public entities.

—*Admission of students.* The central questions in this area are straightforward: who is admitted to which school, on the basis of what criteria? For public schools this may seem to be a non-issue, inasmuch as students who show up in a particular geographic area are admitted to the appropriate school in that area. In reality, for many years there have been very complex assignment systems in many school districts, including magnet schools, intra- and interdistrict choice, and, more recently, charter schools. The matter of admission to private schools under voucher programs has been a critical issue from the beginning of that debate.[16]

The regulatory interests of families and the public vary considerably on the issue of student admissions. Parents focus on options for their children, and they need information on potential schools, which may include the mission, curriculum, and pedagogy of the school. It may also include information on teachers and student peers for their child. Parents also will be very interested in the application process.

The orientation of taxpayers and their public representatives differs from that of parents and families. The public concern will be more centered on opportunities for all students; the equity of the assignment and admission procedures; and the level of diversity within schools or other educational units.

Curriculum and pedagogy. Again, the basic questions are straightforward: what is being taught, and how? But, as before, families and taxpayers may have quite different information requirements. Parents and students are looking for a curriculum and pedagogical approach that teach what they believe the student should learn and provide the best environment for learning. That may mean that they are interested in detailed, specialized curricula such as language instructions, advanced placement courses, classical education, or perhaps Montessori or Marva Collins methods of instruction. They also may be interested in extracurricular offerings and other nonacademic opportunities. Religious instruction and practice in the school also is of interest to some parents, especially those currently choosing private schools for religious reasons.

Taxpayers and public authorities share some of these interests, but again they may focus more systematically on the basic academic offerings, the links between curricula at different levels, and the overall district or even state coverage in such areas as special education for disabled students. They also may be interested in how well the curriculum achieves established subject standards. Finally, they may have a state interest in how civics education is conducted. If religious instruction and practices are being offered, the public may have an interest in knowing how that is done, especially in whether it allows for the right to opt out of such instruction.

—*Student achievement.* The general issue concerns the educational outcomes for students. Embedded within that statement, however, are innumerable lists of possible outcomes. They will undoubtedly cover basic "academic" knowledge and skills but also could include employment prospects, social skills, personal identity, health concerns, and, of course, mastery of civic and public values.

Families may again have more interest in outcomes as they relate specifically to their children. How do they do on standardized tests relative to others? How likely are they to be able to move to the next grade level or to graduate from high school? Is the student achieving at an appropriate level, so that there is a reasonable expectation that postsecondary goals can be met? Are specialized goals, such as acquiring necessary credits for college admission, being met?

Much of the same information needed by families is also of interest to the public, but obviously at a different level of aggregation. Are schools and districts improving or sliding in their performance? How does their performance compare with that of other similar schools or districts? What is the range and variance of achievement across all groups and between relevant racial, gender, and socioeconomic groups? Is the information system adequate to assess performance relative to established subject standards? How does that performance measure up?

—*Expenditure and financial information.* Finally, something must be known about the costs of education. Parents again have narrower concerns, such as how much tuition they might have to pay and what additional fees are charged for books and extracurricular activities. But they may also be interested in overall expenditures per pupil, teacher salaries, and so forth.

The public has additional concerns. The overall level of expenditures and their rate of growth relative to that of various tax bases is one. For elected and appointed officials, the response of the public to these costs will be critical; therefore they may want considerable detail in terms of expenditures so that they can be controlled and used more efficiently. There also is an ongoing concern with equity in spending across districts and schools.

Conclusions

These lists of information needs are only suggestive. In the United States, they probably would best be compiled at the state level for inclusion in a uniform state information system. What is interesting is that in some states existing reporting and information systems or those being constructed for public schools probably satisfy most of these requirements. For example, Wisconsin now has a website that includes most of the information listed above for all districts and all schools in those districts; it goes back three years. Individual student level data are aggregated at the school level. The basic system includes student demographic data and detailed breakdowns of test data by grade, gender, race, free-lunch eligibility, and disability status. Graduation rates and attendance are included for each school. The system also includes information on the race, gender, educational attainment, and attendance of teachers and detailed information on programs, curricular options, and extracurricular activities. Financial data also are available, some on the website, some not. The system covers every public school in the state, with fairly sophisticated search software.

In conclusion, I urge two things. First, the information required on all schools should not be built into the colossal systems that I suspect characterize many of the European states covered in this volume and elsewhere. In this regard, the European Union should not be our model. Unfortunately, that already has occurred in some American states, and it may become a national practice, introduced by the No Child Left Behind legislation. States, with considerable local input, should determine the minimal information that is essential and how that information is used to monitor and regulate districts and schools.

Second, these reporting requirements should be extended to private schools receiving public vouchers. Charter schools in Wisconsin and almost all states with charter school laws (forty) are already covered by such requirements. Private schools not receiving public monies probably cannot be compelled to report under existing constitutional interpretations (and of course some staunch voucher supporters would say that that applies to voucher schools as well). However, they might be wise to adhere voluntarily to these requirements. Why? First, as families begin to make more use of this information in their search for schools, private schools simply will not be in their search sets. Second, private schools may do comparatively quite well.

This call for inclusion of private voucher schools in an information-based regulatory system should not be read either as a call for excessive regulation or for states to have the unrestrained right to regulate whatever they want. Certainly in the case of private religious schools, Richard Garnett's well-argued case for limiting the regulation of religious instruction as protected speech makes a great deal of sense. I would hope that the same would be true for public schools, but I fear that political correctness and fears of legal or other entanglements are limiting teaching and speech in our public schools more than we would like to admit.

But most important, my theme is that when significant public money is involved, there is a compelling public interest in knowing how that money is being spent and with what results. This means that private schools receiving vouchers or some other form of substantial public aid should no longer be able to hide all activities behind the free exercise clause of the First Amendment. If they take the money, they have to accept public responsibility for its use, and that means accepting a minimal level of accountability.

Notes

1. Much of this interest has been stimulated by Robert Putnam's famous book *Bowling Alone: The Collapse and Revival of American Community* (Simon and Schuster, 2000). More directly on the topic of the problems inherent in modern civic education is Stephen Macedo, *Diversity and Distrust: Civic Education in a Multicultural Democracy* (Harvard University Press, 2000).

2. Patrick J. Wolf , "School Choice and Civic Values: A Review of the Evidence," paper presented at the annual meeting of the American Political Science Association, Boston, August 29–September 2, 2002.

3. In addition to Macedo's study cited above, William Galston has under way at the University of Maryland a major empirical and theoretical project on civic education; see his website at www.puaf.umd.edu/faculty/. There is also a Center for the Study of Participation and Citizenship at Indiana University that was started in 1999 and held a major conference in November 2003; see www.indiana.edu/~civiced/.

4. Macedo, *Diversity and Distrust.*

5. John F. Witte, *The Market Approach to Education in America: An Analysis of America's First Voucher Program* (Princeton University Press, 2000).

6. *Lemon* v. *Kurzman*, 403 U.S. 602 (1971).

7. *Zelman* v. *Simmons-Harris*, 536 U.S. 639 (2002).

8. For example, approximately one month after September 11, 2001, the school board in Madison, Wisconsin, on the objection of several parents, banned the recitation of the Pledge of Allegiance (with its reference to God) and the singing of the national anthem (as a "battle hymn"). Following a national outcry and a "listening session" the next week that lasted until 2:30 A.M., a recall petition was circulated but failed. And in the spring election, the school board members who supported the ban

were re-elected. Such might not be the case in other American communities, and the civic education lesson implied might be quite different.

9. All of these data come from the U.S. Department of Education, Common Core of Data database for 2002–03, available on the Internet (http://nces.ed.gov/ccd/ [June 22, 2004]).

10. Organization for Economic Cooperation and Development (OECD), *Education at a Glance: OECD Indicators 2002* (Paris, 2002), table A9.1, p. 101.

11. Ibid., table A10.1, p. 103.

12. Ibid., table A5.2, p. 72.

13. Ibid., tables A6.1 and A6.2, pp. 80, 81.

14. Ibid., table A8.1, p. 91.

15. That is undoubtedly part of the reason for the increasing uproar over the No Child Left Behind legislation enacted several years ago.

16. Witte, *The Market Approach to Education in America;* and William G. Howell and Paul E. Peterson, with Patrick J. Wolf and David E. Campbell, *The Education Gap: Vouchers and Urban Schools* (Brookings, 2002).

16

A Regulated Market Model: Considering School Choice in the Netherlands as a Model for the United States

CHARLES VENEGONI AND DAVID J. FERRERO

The Dutch example demonstrates that open educational choice that includes the public subsidy of religious schools can exist without weakening civic cohesion. Indeed, there is much to suggest that choice can be part of a system that strengthens it. Evidence from parental preferences and student attitudes, for example, indicates that religious schools can do at least as well as public schools in promoting strong civic values, perhaps even better. And the reasons that Dutch parents give for preferring religious schools over state-run schools are more likely to assuage liberal-democratic anxieties about public support for public religious schools than they are to encourage proponents of sectarian religious education. There seem to be many reasons for the success of the Dutch system from a civic perspective, including an already strong civic identity among its citizens and a regulatory scheme that includes needs-based funding and nationwide access to a common core curriculum. However, very recent developments in the Netherlands in the wake of a large influx of Muslim immigrants should serve as an admonition to observers who are too sanguine about the benign effects of publicly supported religious schooling on liberal-democratic political culture. Both the sources of the Netherlands's successful system of choice and the nature of the recent challenges to it hold important lessons for policymakers.

Special thanks to Keely Merrigan, research associate at the Bill and Melinda Gates Foundation, for research support on this chapter.

Parents' motivations for choosing religious schools in themselves help explain the success of the Dutch system from a civic perspective. In the Netherlands, where nearly two-thirds of students attend publicly supported private schools, the majority of which are religious schools, only a minority (about 30 percent, depending on the local situation) of parents give religious reasons for choosing religious schools.[1] Instead, as Anne Bert Dijkstra, Jaap Dronkers, and Sjoerd Karsten note in their chapter in this volume, parents choose religious schools because "the values-oriented character of religious schools leads them to stress secular, nonreligious values (for instance, tolerance of homosexuality) as a significant aspect of schooling in the broader sense."[2] The authors cite studies revealing that Dutch parents are interested in having their children learn about differing world views in the course of providing them with a strong ethical orientation that reflects Dutch public values—that is, they choose religious schools for largely secular ethical reasons that reinforce critical elements of the political culture, such as tolerance and fairness. Broadly construed ethical values and not religion per se attract the Dutch to religious schools.

Given the large number of citizens who are educated in religious schools and the toleration and civic mindedness of the Dutch, it is hard to believe that the educational system has proven an impediment to civic values. Even as Islamic populations demand their own schools and resist assimilation into Dutch public culture and values, they continue to prefer religious schools to state-run public schools because of the greater sensitivity of Catholic and Protestant schools for Islamic beliefs and values. At worst, inquiry into the relationship between civic values and education suggests that "noncognitive behavior" related to civic values is not greatly influenced by a school's religious affiliation, although Catholic schools appear to excel in affective categories that are less directly related to civic concerns.[3]

Indeed, the Dutch experience gives the United States even more reasons to consider opening the door to school choice, and some of them are corroborated by the American experience with religious schools, specifically, Catholic schools. American studies routinely find Catholic schools to be superior academically to their public counterparts. This is especially and less controversially true in urban areas, where less affluent students are in the majority.[4] Dijkstra, Dronkers, and Karsten's analysis of studies of "cognitive effectiveness" in Dutch schools, after adjusting for socioeconomic and other externalities, finds that Catholic schools are the most effective in producing cognitive outcomes. Nonorthodox Protestant schools rank next, followed by public schools. The lowest cognitive outcomes are associated with the smallest but fastest-growing of the sectors: orthodox Protestant and (nonreligious) private schools, whose comparatively wealthier students perform below expectations raised by their socioeconomic status.

The success of Catholic and non-orthodox Protestant schools in the Netherlands is associated with other factors that have parallels in the American educational experience. As in the United States, progressive education reigned in Dutch education circles in the 1960s and 1970s. In the Netherlands, this was accompanied by society's accelerated move to secularism. It is within this environment that religious schools in the Netherlands consolidated their advantage in terms of numbers of students enrolled. Using "freedom of education" as their defense against the progressive educational policies that dominated public schools, Catholic and nonorthodox Protestant schools maintained a "mild educational conservatism" that appealed to parents regardless of their religious affiliation. This traditionalism, combined with cognitively oriented values instruction, is seen by Dutch parents as contributing to the superior academic performance of Catholic and nonorthodox Protestant schools.[5] These circumstances have parallels in the American experience, in which Catholic schools maintained more traditional, common core curricula than did public schools, which were far more subject to progressive educational theory and practice. At the same time, the emphasis on social and economic justice brought by Vatican II (the mid-1960s reform of the Catholic Church) and the continued Catholic attention to these issues no doubt had a profound effect on Catholic schools, which throughout the late twentieth and early twenty-first centuries have been more apt than other schools to impart strong civic values.

But in the United States, educational policy currently forbids students free access to Catholic schools. In American cities, where the Catholic approach has been so relatively successful, assimilating such schools into the public system would provide students with immediate options that they could not otherwise afford. With so many parallels between Catholic (and nonorthodox Protestant) schools in the Netherlands and Catholic schools in the United States, it is hard to ignore the Dutch model. A choice policy that allowed the constitutionally sanctioned assimilation of Catholic and similar religious schools, one that would be income dependent, would provide immediate access to quality education for at least some of the neediest students. Urban Catholic schools in the United States already enroll large numbers of non-Catholic students.[6] And the Catholic orientation toward social and economic justice potentially makes for a situation similar to that found in Dutch Catholic schools, where broader and more secular moral values become the bases for religious education. Regardless of Catholic education's association with positive civic values, the issue involving funding religious schools in the

United States is far more encumbered by legal and political considerations than it is in the Netherlands. Nonetheless, Americans should at least be intrigued by the correlations found linking Catholic schools and (secular) civic values in both the Netherlands and the United States.

Not all religious schools discussed by Dijkstra and her colleagues evince such a positive correlation with promoting common civic values, however. They cite a 2001 study by Braster that reveals that only students educated in orthodox Protestant schools show effects in their social and political value orientation that can be related to their religious education.[7] Here it is crucial to note that religious schools in the Netherlands overwhelmingly are represented by Catholic and nonorthodox Protestant schools. Outside of these two major categories, there are two others that are associated with religious identity: the orthodox Protestant (read fundamentalist Christian) and the fundamentalist Islamic—two groups of Dutch citizens who do not share the polity's public values and whose growth threatens the tranquility the Dutch have enjoyed in their educational institutions. These two groups recently have attempted to resist the assimilationist policies and practices of the Dutch system with respect to curriculum, certification, and other features of schooling.[8] They have accordingly proliferated legal challenges to the schools by asserting their rights to separate practices. Orthodox Christian schools deny employment to homosexuals based on "mission," and Islamic parents protest requirements imposed on students, especially girls, as in the case cited by Vermeulen in which Muslim parents objected to girls wearing bathing suits for swim class.[9] Clearly two principles are at odds—tolerance of cultural differences and inculcation of liberal-democratic values—and the Dutch are hard pressed to accommodate both. Dutch courts and policymakers, once relatively free of the sorts of lawsuit that have hamstrung public schooling in the United States, are finding themselves subject to increasing sectarian legal pressures. In this emerging political climate, the Dutch are finding the religiosity of religious schools to be a barrier to rather than a medium for the transmission of civic values.

Religious schools in the Netherlands support and advance civic values and cohesion in inverse proportion to the degree that they foreground their religious missions. More precisely, fundamentalist religious schools, whether Christian or Islamic, pose problems for the more secularized Dutch culture when they assert their religious beliefs beyond social, juridical, and institutional norms. We see evidence of the same pattern in the United States. A meta-analysis of American studies on the relationship between civic values and religious and private schools conducted by Patrick Wolf for the Brookings National Working Commission on Choice in K–12 Education reveals parallels to the Dutch scene. Taken together, the studies he reviews suggest that in the aggregate religious and secular private schools may do slightly better than public schools with respect to students' civic values and behaviors. [10] Wolf acknowledges that Catholic schools are overrepresented in these studies. What he does not recognize is that when Catholic schools are removed from his tables, the remaining schools are slightly *less* effective in educating for civic values and social cohesion than public schools. And his review reveals a negative correlation between students' level of tolerance and being educated in American fundamentalist Christian schools. Christian academies (fundamentalist schools common in the South) have been associated with "white flight" from public schools,[11] and their doctrinal emphases (open intolerance of homosexuals, teaching creationism, and so forth) might serve as a further caution for Americans considering the funding of religious schools. With the likely proliferation by proportion that such fundamentalist schools might realize under an expanded choice model (including Christian, Muslim, Judaic, and ethnonationalist groups), Americans should not assume that the positive civic orientation now associated with schools of choice would endure—at least not without strong safeguards.[12]

In fact, John Witte's and Charles Glenn's confidence aside, the expansion of public funding to religious schools should be a matter of concern to those worried about social cohesion. Richard Garnett, who argues for light regulation in the funding of religious schools, is more prudent in his frequent use of the conditional and in his recognition that this is a matter that in many circles is far from settled. Whether a school's mission should trump prevailing legal and professional standards is far from decided, in theory or in practice. Constitutional questions abound, and even the *Zelman* decision, as Garnett rightly acknowledges, is not decisive. At the very best, whether to fund religious schools at all will be subject to myriad constitutional determinations. Then, if funding is deemed legal, there will be a host of regulatory issues to consider. The debates surrounding the legal and regulatory issues will themselves be divisive. But they will be nowhere near as polarizing as what will follow if religious schools are funded and left free of regulations limiting the degree to which they can invoke "mission" in matters such as hiring, admissions, and curriculum. Fundamentalist religious practices by definition are derived from interpretations of religious sources (for example, the Bible or the Koran) that often are inconsistent with prevailing constitutional law and scientific standards of inquiry. Should schools funded by public dollars be permitted to discriminate (for example, not hire homosexuals because of putative biblical proscriptions) or teach religious belief as science (for example, teach biblical accounts of creation in biology classes instead of evolution-ary theory) because of their ostensible mission? The protracted and bitter civil litigation over such questions might itself be reason for the political and legal system to avoid attempting to pass legislation on them. This would be a mistake. The Dutch experience reveals that containing mission is accomplished through regulation (as Glenn, Garnett, and Witte fear will be the case in the United States). It also reveals that when such regulations cannot contain mission, social cohesion can be threatened.

Americans can learn two seemingly contradictory lessons from the Dutch. On one hand, funding all religious schools without restraint on their right to use their mission to inform their practices could threaten civic cohesion. In addition, the Dutch case also shows that there is little educational motivation for doing so, since the orthodox Protestants schools perform less effectively in achievement studies than their Catholic or nonorthodox counterparts. On the other hand, some religious schools, notably Catholic, offer better environments for high achievement and cultivation of strong common civic values than do most public schools. The Dutch experience suggests that religious schools in the United States could be regulated so as to forbid separatist practices and the catechetical teaching of religious values and at the same time maintain their moral tone and orientation within a secular framework. While there are many reasons to believe that school choice that did not regulate religious practice would be dangerous and would lack viability in the United States, it is hard to deny that some American religious schools offer potential educational advantages similar to those seen in the Netherlands.

Enhancing Competition and Social Equity through a Regulated Market

Americans might also take note of the broader institutional context in which the Dutch religious schools have realized their success, a context that balances the needs of the market and of society's civic health. Dutch policies governing student funding and a national curriculum stand out here, both for their contrasts with U.S. policies and their apparent role in providing families of all backgrounds with fair access to high-quality educational opportunities. In the Netherlands, schools are funded out of the national coffer. Funds are distributed with some attention to student need. The education of a poor, non-Dutch-speaking immigrant child can be funded at a level of up to 1.9 times the amount allocated for the education of an affluent native-born Dutch student.[13] This system attempts to compensate schools for the relative difficulty and greater cost of educating students from impoverished and non-native backgrounds. This system turns the U.S. funding system on its head. While the U.S. federal government funds a host of compensatory programs aimed at mitigating inequalities in American society, its contribution to overall per-pupil funding is around 7 percent.[14] The remainder in most states is funded by a combination of state and local revenues.[15] As a result, affluent communities spend more money per pupil than working or lower-class ones, an inversion of the resource distribution that obtains in the Netherlands. These differences no doubt reflect broader social and political differences between the two countries that bear on social integration and political socialization across ethnic and class lines. The Dutch enjoy lower levels of poverty, narrower disparities of wealth, near-universal access to health care, and other benefits that are associated with civic comity and high levels of school achievement.[16]

Likewise, the national curriculum and assessment system employed in the Netherlands contributes much to the fairness of educational opportunity and the overall academic success of Dutch schools and to the success of religious schools in particular.[17] In comparative international studies of education, Dutch students usually rank among the top performers among industrialized nations.[18] Furthermore, studies routinely reveal that national systems that have highly centralized curriculum and assessment requirements perform better than systems that do not.[19] But while the Dutch emphasize commonality, they do not require uniformity, nor are they inflexible in allowing local and individual school differences.

After a compulsory eight years of common primary education, the Dutch secondary system branches out into four overlapping systems: VWO (pre-university education), HAVO (senior general secondary education), MAVO (junior general secondary education), and VBO (pre-vocational education). Each of these systems is separate, but they share some achievement targets and curricular and assessment requirements. Each leads to a specific postsecondary experience, but even the least academic allows for a path back to the postsecondary (university) education intended for the most academic of the four programs. Contrary to American misconceptions, these systems are not rigid "tracks," but a means by which individuality is attended to, while commonality, quality, and equity are ensured. This system reveals an openness to difference that many Americans believe to be absent in national curriculum-based models. And while all schools are required to follow the national curriculum and assessment system appropriate to their type of school, the systems vary in their broad purposes and allow up to 50 percent of examinations to be written at the school site, facilitating the further individualization of school mission.[20] It would appear that the Dutch have the best of both worlds here: accountability and freedom. And the quality and number of schools that across the board enjoy relative success verify the efficacy of the Dutch model.

Americans who believe that publicly funded schools should be held accountable for the achievement of students from all socioeconomic and ethnic backgrounds should be encouraged by the Dutch assessment system, which is underwritten by common curricula. Those who fear that innovation and experimentation will be stifled should be reassured by the number of curricular and assessment options available and the degree of freedom at the local school level. Accountability constraints do not seem to have deterred the Dutch from opening schools with diverse pedagogical approaches, not only between but also within the four secondary systems. As in the United States, progressive educational practices coexist with more traditional ones. At present, educational debates over pedagogy in the Netherlands center on the Study House movement, a progressive pedagogical approach that emphasizes less traditional rote and academic forms of learning in favor of more unconventional, collaborative, and active forms. In addition, the Dutch system includes schools based on different pedagogical philosophies, such as Montessori and Waldorf. Any concerns about monolithic uniformity should be dispelled by the realities of the Dutch educational scene. There is no reason to believe that if choice in the United States is governed by a central curriculum and assessment system such as the Netherlands's that options could not be kept open to all potential providers. In theory, the Dutch combination of choice regulated by several broad curriculum and assessment options offers ample opportunities for innovation and experimentation. Accountability is demanded, but not to such a degree that the recent history of Dutch pedagogical debate differs greatly from that found in the United States. But in the Dutch system, with the close eye it keeps on accountability through curriculum and assessment, educational achievement is generally far higher and more evenly distributed than it is in the United States.[21]

Applications to establish schools could be bounded, as in the Dutch model, by fiscal and other regulatory constraints related to a school's potential for meeting accountability targets. Charters could be procured within these contexts by a provider that satisfies all legal requirements. While some curricular practices might be constrained (for example, teaching a biblical account of creation in a science class), in general the pedagogical purpose and approach of a school could vary broadly. At the same time, there would be no need to dismantle an effective public school system in an expanded choice regime. Even in the Netherlands, 30 percent of schools are "public." Given historical contrasts, one would expect, even with expanded choice, the percentage of public schools in the United States to be far higher for the foreseeable future.

National diploma exams and common curricula are associated in the research on Dutch schools with more than gains in achievement. They also have been correlated with factors leading to decreased segregation, and they can be related readily to a number of other salutary conditions found in Dutch schools.[22] Detailed public information is required in the Dutch model, and much of it is derived from examinations. The Dutch public makes good use of this information, and while it seems to be contributing to the consumerization of schooling, it no doubt enables parents to choose well on the basis of academic performance.[23] Moreover, it is worth noting that common curricular and assessment requirements are particularly effective in mitigating the negative effects associated with high rates of mobility. Poor students move more often than wealthier ones, and in the United States, where curriculum varies widely according to locality and even within districts, this high rate of mobility has baleful effects.[24] In the Netherlands, mobility rates are a far less significant factor, neutralized at least in part by the common curricula and assessment system.[25] Should the United States consider expanding choice in education more widely, it would have to recognize that such a system is in fact a central feature of the world's most extensive and successful system of choice. The history of and political reality in the United States are such that this kind of commonality would most likely remain a state rather than national concern and would rely more heavily on common performance standards and assessments—and less on required content of the curriculum—than one finds in the Netherlands. Nonetheless, the Dutch example clearly suggests that common accountability requirements for all schools, public and private, do not threaten freedom and choice, as American choice proponents often aver. Rather, they enable a system of choice that promotes accountability and enhances both quality and fairness.

However it may be adapted as a model for the United States, the Dutch system provides an outcomes-based means for regulating education that eliminates the need for the local school board model of governance that many choice advocates find so problematic. The Dutch system affords the public an alternative to the cacophony of competing interest groups and institutional incoherence that plagues American education. In the Netherlands, the Inspectorate of Education coordinates the various inspectorates, umbrella organizations, education unions, parents' organizations, educational support services, professional organizations, and higher education and research.[26] "The inspectorate has no official role in preparing education policy," but it consults with and advises the Ministry of Education and the Dutch parliament on the policies whose implementation the Inspectorate monitors and it provides support for the "network of specialist organizations and agencies" within the Dutch system.[27] Schools' practices are developed within the policies mandated by Parliament and implemented through the Ministry of Education, but as noted, such policies by no means preclude diversity and innovation in instructional approaches. Indeed, the Inspectorate's role is at least in part to cultivate such differences, containing them within the Dutch common system. And to ensure that the Dutch choice system is honored, the government maintains the highly influential Onderwijsrad (Educational Council) "as a 'watchdog' for freedom of schooling."[28] The Dutch system is intent on providing checks and balances on educational freedom through accountability-oriented quality control.

The Netherlands has redefined public education, offering nearly 70 percent of its students education in nonpublic schools—the highest percentage among the countries in the Organization for Economic Cooperation and Development—and using those schools to foster and transmit strong civic values and achieve academic excellence.[29] The Dutch model balances parents' rights with a strong normative, civic-oriented school curriculum. Pluralism is encouraged and protected, while there is a balancing commitment to liberal and social democratic principles. What is striking from an American perspective is the apparent ease with which the two priorities coexist. Even in the current strife precipitated by the Muslim influx, the Dutch endeavor to maintain a "balanced combination of market forces and the state."[30] Both pluralism and choice are required and are givens in the Dutch model. However, in the Netherlands, schools that offer alternative values and instruction methods exist within a larger social context informed by the nation's commitment to education as a civic and public good, one whose quality and availability are crucial to the country's democratic pluralism.

Conclusion

In the Netherlands, schools have freedom. Providers are diverse. Parents are supported in their right to choose. However, the positions of all stakeholders in the system are orchestrated and interdependent. School levels are aligned, and teacher education and broader postsecondary experiences that include employment are integrated into the system in a model of centralized organization. It appears that the Dutch have it both ways: freedom and coherence. Their professionally regulated market model seems to offer great potential as a model for choice in the United States, where advocates desire more market competition while opponents worry that choice would lead to greater social fragmentation and further decline in fairness and accountability.

The Dutch ability to have it both ways suggests hitherto unexplored possibilities for designing a system of choice in the United States. We close with the following recommendations for reframing deliberations about choice and policies that might govern it:

—*Reconsider the conventional dichotomy between market competition and regulation.* Critics of American public education are warranted in their criticism that the system is overregulated. However, it would behoove them to distinguish between regulations that unduly hamstring educators and those that can enable effective action on behalf of children and the broader society. The Dutch experience suggests that regulating certain desirable academic *outcomes* through a system of well-defined standards and assessments for which *all* schools, public and private, are held accountable benefits all parties to the social contract.

—*Reconsider the conventional dichotomy between the common curriculum and educators' freedom to educate.* The Dutch engage in the same sorts of debates between pedagogical "progressives" and "traditionalists" that Americans do, yet they have figured out how to accommodate Montessori, Waldorf, Study House, and other progressive models alongside more traditional models without sacrificing core commitments and common aims—which, after all, most educators share at some level.

—*Rethink the relationship between religious schools and civil society.* In the United States, we are accustomed to thinking of religious schools as institutions dedicated primarily to transmitting and extending particular religious world views. In the Netherlands, by contrast, religious schools serve as alternative providers of a secular ethical world view that is both cosmopolitan and allied with the secular liberal values on which Dutch democracy depends. The evidence suggests that it is the character of the school that matters most for Dutch success, rather than the existence of choice itself. Policies that ensure that schools of choice share certain common features lies as close as choice to the heart of the Dutch system.

—*As a corollary to the preceding point, beware of religious and other groups with separatist tendencies.* A century of Dutch success in drawing on its "pillars" to support a shared public culture is now threatened by the growth and self-assertion of religious-cultural groups that resist Dutch mechanisms of political socialization. This in a country where such institutions are strong and means of legal challenge comparatively weak. The United States is more vulnerable to such challenges, with its history of successful litigation by groups seeking exemption from academic and assimilationist public school requirements, and the strong religious and ethnonationalist streak in its political culture.

If policymakers in the United States are serious about student achievement, basic fairness, and civic cohesion as well as pluralism, educators' autonomy, and parents' freedom to direct their children's education, then the successful example of countries like the Netherlands can point the way to a host of policy innovations that could provide the United States with that hitherto elusive combination of freedom, cohesion, fairness, and excellence.

Notes

1. Geoffrey Walford, "Funding for Private Schools in England and the Netherlands: Can the Piper Call the Tune?" Occasional Paper 8 (New York: National Center for the Study of Privatization in Education, November 2000), p. 12 (www.ncspe.org/publications_files/209_OP08.pdf [February 2004]); and Anne Bert Dijkstra, Jaap Dronkers, and Sjoerd Karsten, "Private Schools as Public Provision for Education School Choice and Marketization in the Netherlands and Elsewhere in Europe," Occasional Paper 20 (New York: National Center for the Study of Privatization in Education, June 2001), p. 14 (www.ncspe.org/publications_files/209_OP08.pdf [February 2004]).

2. See Dijkstra, Dronkers, and Karsten, chapter 3 in this volume.

3. Ibid.

4. Nina H. Shokraii, "Why Catholic Schools Spell Success for America's Inner-City Children," *Backgrounder*, vol. 1128 (Heritage Foundation, June 30, 1997) (www.heritage.org/Research/UrbanIssues/BG1128.cfm [February 2, 2004]).

5. Dijkstra, Dronkers, and Karsten, chapter 3.

6. Dale McDonald, *United States Catholic Elementary and Secondary Schools 2002–2003* (Washington: National Catholic Educational Association, 2003), Executive Summary; and Gill Donovan, "Enrollment Down in Nation's Catholic Schools," *National Catholic Reporter*, vol. 39, no. 8 (April 18, 2003), p. 8.

7. J. Braster, "De effecten van verzuild basisonderwijs op de waardeoriëntaties van Nederlandse jongeren," *Sociale Wetenschappen,* vol. 44 (2001), pp. 49–69.

8. Dutch educational policy has a strong assimilationist thrust. All Dutch schools, irrespective of their orientation, are subject to the same system of national curriculum and assessment, though waivers are available on a case-by-case basis. Also, by law the language of instruction is Dutch, and all teachers in the Netherlands must be nationally certified in government-accredited schools.

9. Ben P. Vermeulen, "Hof Den Bosch 5 September 1989," *Rechtspraak Vreemdelingenrecht*, no. 96 (1989), p. 19.

10. Patrick J. Wolf, "School Choice and Civic Values in the U.S.: A Review of the Evidence," in Paul T. Hill and Tom Loveless, eds., *Choice in Education: Getting the Benefits, Managing the Risks* (Brookings, forthcoming).

11. For examples of recent studies suggesting that southern Christian academies have been associated with "white flight" from public school alternatives, see Sean F. Reardon and John T. Yun, *Private School Racial Enrollments and Segregation* (Harvard University, Civil Rights Project, June 26, 2002); and Shelia Hardwell Byrd, "Class Struggles: How Segregation Endures in South's Rural Schools," Associated Press, March 15, 2003.

12. Wolf, "School Choice and Civic Values in the U.S."

13. Dutch Ministry of Education, Culture, and Science, *Education, Culture, and Science in the Netherlands Facts and Figures, 2002* (Zoetermeer, January 2002), p. 135 (minocw.nl/english_oud/general/figures/index.html [February 3, 2004]).

14. Elise St. John and Frank Johnson, *Statistics in Brief: Revenues and Expenditures for Public Elementary and Secondary Education: School Year 2000-01* (U.S. Department of Education, National Center for Education Statistics, June 2003), pp. 1–2 (www.nces.ed.gov/pubs2003/2003362.pdf [February 3, 2004]).

15. Ibid.

16. United Nations Development Programme, *Human Development Report 2003. Millennium Development Goals: A Compact among Nations to End Human Poverty* (Oxford University Press, 2003), pp. 237–339 (www.undp.org/hdr2003/ [February 3, 2004]); and David G. Green and Ben Irvine, "Health Care in the Netherlands," Background Briefing 4 (London: Civitas, the Institute for the Study of Civil Society, January 2003) (www.civitas.org.uk/pubs/bb4Netherlands.php [February 3, 2004]).

17. Dijkstra, Dronkers, and Karsten, chapter 3.

18. Organization for Economic Cooperation and Development (OECD), *Education at a Glance: OECD Indicators 2001* (Paris, 2001) pp. 305–19; Sayuri Takahira and others, *Pursuing Excellence: A Study of U.S. Twelfth-Grade Mathematics and Science Achievement in International Context* (Government Printing Office, revised August 1998), pp. 30–36; and Laurence T. Ogle and others, *International Comparisons in Fourth-Grade Reading Literacy: Findings from the Progress in International Reading Literacy Study (PIRLS) of 2001* (GPO, 2003), pp. 4–7 (www.nces.ed.gov/pubs2003/2003073.pdf [February 3, 2004]).

19. John H. Bishop, "Privatizing Education: Lessons from Canada, Asia, and Europe," in C. Eugene Steuerle and others, eds., *Vouchers and the Provision of Public Services* (Brookings, 2000); and William H. Schmidt and others, *Why Schools Matter: A Cross-National Comparison of Curriculum and Learning* (John Wiley, 2001).

20. Inspectorate of Education of the Netherlands, *The Inspectorate of Education of the Netherlands: 2001* (Utrecht, 2001).

21. OECD, *Education at a Glance: 2001,* pp. 305-19; Takahira and others, *Pursuing Excellence*, pp. 30–36; and Ogle and others, *International Comparisons in Fourth-Grade Reading Literacy,* pp. 4–7.

22. Dijkstra, Dronkers, and Karsten, chapter 3.

23. Ibid.

24. Hanna Skandera and Richard Sousa, "Mobility and the Achievement Gap," *Hoover Digest: Research and Opinion on Public Policy* 3 (Hoover Institution, Stanford

University, 2002) (www-hoover.stanford.edu/publications/digest/023/skandera.html [February 3, 2004]).

25. Dijkstra, Dronkers, and Karsten, chapter 3.

26. For a list of organizations associated with the inspectorate, see Inspectorate of Education of the Netherlands, *The Inspectorate of Education*, pp. 50–52.

27. Ibid., p. 26.

28. Dijkstra, Dronkers, and Karsten, chapter 3.

29. OECD, *Education at a Glance: OECD Indicators 2003* (Paris, 2003), table C2.3.

30. Dijkstra, Dronkers, and Karsten, chapter 3.

Contributors

Patrick J. Wolf
Georgetown University

Stephen Macedo
Princeton University

David Campbell
University of Notre Dame

Jan De Groof
College of Europe
Belgium
University of Tilburg
The Netherlands

Jaap Dronkers
European University Institute
Italy

Anne Bert Dijkstra
University of Groningen
The Netherlands

David Ferrero
Bill and Melinda Gates Foundation

William Galston
University of Maryland

Richard W. Garnett
University of Notre Dame

Charles L. Glenn
Boston University

Stephen Gorard
University of York
United Kingdom

Neville Harris
University of Manchester
United Kingdom

Sjoerd Karsten
University of Amsterdam
The Netherlands

Denis Meuret
University of Burgundy
France

Lutz Reuter
Bundeswehr University of Hamburg
Germany

Luisa Ribolzi
University of Genova
Italy

John F. Witte
University of Wisconsin–Madison

Charles Venegoni
Civitas Schools
Chicago

Ben P. Vermeulen
Free University Amsterdam
Catholic University Nijmegen
The Netherlands

Index

Accountability: Belgium, 15, 175–77; effect of school choice on, 348; Italy, 282; Netherlands, 375; U.S. concern for, 375. *See also* Exit examinations; National curriculum and examinations; Quality standards

Adams, Henry, 335

Adler v. *Ontario* (Canada *1996*), 202

Admission policies: Belgium, 173–75; France, 244, 247; Netherlands, 44–46, 58, 74; United Kingdom, 98–99, 119, 134, 140, 142, 149, 150–51; United States, 363

Adorno, T. W., 296

Agostini v. *Felton* (U.S. *1997*), 191

Aguilar v. *Fenton* (U.S. *1985*), 191

Ali, Hirsi, 41

Anti-Catholicism, 332–34

Anti-discrimination policies and laws: Canada, 202; England, 98, 106; Netherlands, 43, 46, 49; New Zealand, 345. *See also* Segregation effects; *specific international treaties and countries for individual acts*

Assessment of differences between public and religious schools, 287–312; Belgium, 293–96; France, 297–98; Germany, 299–302; historical and social background, 287–89; Hungary, 289–92; Netherlands, 302–05; Scotland, 292–93; United Kingdom, 305–06

Attendance policies. *See* Compulsory schooling

Autonomy of schools: Belgium, 167, 169–71, 175–76; Canada, 190; Germany, 215, 225–26; Italy, 280–83; Netherlands, 10, 34–35, 38–51; United Kingdom, 95

Ballion, R., 259

Baumert, J., 300–02

Bayefsky, Ann, 205

Begum case (U.K. *2004*), 114–16, 117